MURDOCH

The Making of a Media Empire

William Shawcross

A TOUCHSTONE BOOK
Published by Simon & Schuster

禾

TOUCHSTONE
Rockefeller Center
1230 Avenue of the Americas
New York, NY 10020

Copyright © 1992, 1997 by William Shawcross
All rights reserved,
including the right of reproduction
in whole or in part in any form.

TOUCHSTONE and colophon are registered trademarks
of Simon & Schuster Inc.

Designed by Irving Perkins Associates

Photo research by Natalie Goldstein

Manufactured in the United States of America

1   3   5   7   9   10   8   6   4   2

The Library of Congress has cataloged the Simon & Schuster edition as follows:

Shawcross, William.
Murdoch / William Shawcross.
p.   cm.
Includes bibliographical references and index.
1. Murdoch, Rupert, 1931–   .   2. Mass media—Australia—Biography.   I. Title.
P92.5.M87S5   1992
070'.092—dc20
[B]   92-38399
CIP

ISBN 0-684-83015-9

CONTENTS

8 CONTENTS

Part Four:

THE VILLAGE 329

PROLOGUE

Today, information is the most powerful and lucrative commodity in the world. Its trade changes the face of the globe and delineates the future. Just as the railroad barons drove the communications revolution of the nineteenth century, so the media barons are driving and defining the end of our own.

A handful of companies dominate the market in information. Of the giants, only Rupert Murdoch's company News Corporation stretches around the earth, and only his was conceived and built by, and remains in the hands of, one man.

News Corporation is testimony to Murdoch's brilliant, intuitive and ruthless instincts. He built the company himself after inheriting a small Adelaide newspaper from his father. Since the 1950s, his life has been a series of unending assaults. One battle followed another—more newspapers, more television, more space, more power. His life appears as a series of psychic leaps, in perpetual acceleration and endless acquisition, with no step far enough, no property an adequate reward. "My past," he said, "consists of a series of interlocking wars," wars fought for victory in the information revolution and mastery of the communications industry which drives it. Communications is the ninth-largest industry in the United States, and growing at almost 10 percent a year, faster than any other sector except health and medicine. Communications is shrinking much of the world into a global village. In that village, Murdoch is one of the most powerful barons.

Just as railroads joined some points and not others in the nineteenth century, modern communications are unevenly spread. The information map of the world is like a weather map. It shows a dense mass of organized information over North America, Europe and Japan, very little over the former Soviet Union and almost nothing over Africa. The greater the activity, the greater the wealth. The industrial society is being replaced by the information society, which is transforming the world's economy, its political institutions, the nature of sovereignty and traditional relationships between governments and peoples, and between people and power.

One hundred years ago, less than 10 percent of the labor force was involved in information activities. The vast majority were employed in agriculture and industry. Today more than half the labor force of the United States works in the information area. Agriculture and industry together account for only about 30 percent, and are no longer the major engines of social development. They are being replaced by a force which is still undefined. It draws on human resource capital to transfer knowledge into many kinds of physical and social activity, to generate wealth in new ways, and in so doing to alter goals and values profoundly. We are moving toward a world in which information production and distribution will overshadow material production.

With the technological revolution has come a financial revolution. The growth of the world financial market in the last thirty years is so vast that it is almost impossible to conceive. In the 1960s the volume of foreign exchange transactions was about $3 trillion a year. In 1984 it was about $32 trillion.* The next year it *doubled* to $65 trillion. By 1987 it was about $87 trillion, which was more than twenty-three times the U.S. gross national product, several times the gross world product. Nowadays billions of dollars are traded daily on sparkling screens

---

* All dollar amounts in this book are American unless designated as "A$" (Australian dollars) or "HK$" (Hong Kong dollars). In a few cases, to avoid confusion with other currencies, "US$" is used to refer to American dollars.

in Tokyo, London and New York. The trade is constant, the profits vast.

Historically, nations issued currency and mandated its value; this was part of sovereignty. Now, the international market weighs and assesses currencies every minute of the day. Politicians were slow to realize what was happening, but the money traders swiftly drove their trading caravans across the new electronic routes, and created a new monetary system governed by the Information Standard.

Every minute of every day, detailed information about every major country's political, economic and fiscal policies is transmitted to hundreds of thousands of screens in trading rooms around the globe. There is no place to hide. The new world favors those who pursue policies of which the traders approve.

The questions and the problems raised by these revolutions are stupendous. The information overload, to use Alvin Toffler's phrase, is both back-breaking and mind-breaking. In the postindustrial information age, people begin to ask whether full access to all information is desirable even if it were feasible. There is a danger of a new kind of literacy gap stemming from unequal access to the resources of new communications and information technologies.

Democratic societies must consider such issues as unequal access to information. They have to weigh the implications of a literacy gap for concepts such as "the consent of the governed." And if it is true that we neither need nor can cope with it all, what responsibilities does that place upon the so-called gatekeepers, the journalists and publishers whose tasks are to sift, distill, interpret and disseminate information?

On the international scale there is another consequence, unacceptable to many. It is the ineluctable spread of the American Dream. The new communications networks are like a huge megaphone blaring American messages across the world.

Already by the end of the 1970s, "U.S. cultural imperialism" had stirred great resentment and contributed, for example, to the rise of Shia fundamentalism in the Middle East. It had also embroiled

UNESCO in a hopeless and costly debate about the Western domination of the flow of news.

But the amount of information flowing across the world from the United States in the 1970s was nothing to what is now being exported. Half a dozen companies now dominate a vast proportion of the world's media. Time Warner is the largest media organization in history, controlling an unprecedented number of periodicals, books, films and television programs—in all stages of creation, production and dissemination. Following close behind are Sony, Bertelsmann, Berlusconi, Disney—and Murdoch's News Corporation. Although only two of these companies are wholly American controlled, all are inspired and informed by American values and American products (even Sony has married itself to Hollywood).

Entertainment is a vast American growth industry. The volume of global communications traffic is growing at between 10 and 15 percent a year—which means that it is roughly doubling every six years. Much of this comes from the United States. Even as America's political and economic influence is declining, its cultural influence continues to grow. Euro Disney opened its gates in 1992 to complaints by French intellectuals that it was a "cultural Chernobyl" and the ultimate trap set by the mighty American mouse. Michael Jackson and Madonna or their successors will continue to be the greatest international stars and, as such, the worldwide prophets of the American Dream. It is a dream in which millions of people have believed for over a century, and in which Rupert Murdoch has much invested. He is an agent of influence.

This is an unauthorized biography, though Rupert Murdoch agreed to talk to me. It was first published in longer form in Britain and Australia in fall 1992. I have reedited this edition, cutting some of the stories and characters, particularly in Murdoch's early life, which are less relevant to American readers. I have brought the book up to date to include some of the latest campaigns which Murdoch has fought in his unending wars around the world.

Murdoch's battlefields and trajectory—from Adelaide through Sydney, London and New York and on to Hollywood—seems to me to provide an extraordinary narrative of capitalism at this time. He is using the leaps of technological progress to try to transform the world. The communications revolution is changing the world, and Murdoch and a few others are forcing the pace of that change. He is one of the most powerful men in the world. And there is every reason to suppose that his power and his reach will continue to grow.

WILLIAM SHAWCROSS
April 1997

Part I

THE EARLY
YEARS

1

CRUDEN

Of the many questions asked about Rupert Murdoch, one comes up again and again: Why? Why has he spent forty years, all his adult life, restlessly flying around the world to build an international empire? Why does he never pause? Is he driven by political ambition or the desire for personal vindication? What makes Rupert run? To borrow from the famous quest in *Citizen Kane,* what, who or where is his Rosebud?

This is not a psychohistory, but the passage of Murdoch's life and times and the changes through which he progressed will provide some of the answers to these questions. He contains within his character both an extraordinary gambling instinct and a certain dour puritanism. Perhaps that is not so surprising. One of his grandfathers, Rupert Greene, was a roistering, charming half-Irish gambler. The other, Patrick Murdoch, was a stern pillar of the Free Church of Scotland. Traces of each man are found in Rupert Murdoch's conflicting nature. From his Scots Free Church ancestors he seems to have inherited a deep and abiding distaste for the English establishment and its traditions.

Rupert was nine when the Very Reverend Patrick John Murdoch died in 1940. Patrick had been born in 1850, almost a century before and half a world away; he grew up in the herring fishing port of Pitsligo on the Moray Firth in Scotland. His father, James (Rupert's great-grandfather, born in 1817), was a clergyman, one of the 190 probationers and 470 ministers who broke with the established Church of Scotland in the great Disruption of May 1843.

James Murdoch and his son were part of the birth of the Free Church in the latter half of the nineteenth century. With contributions from Presbyterian supporters worldwide, the dissidents built hundreds of new churches and schools, creating an alternative Presbyterian establishment. They challenged the established Church of Scotland and the government in London, and won.

Patrick John Murdoch was raised in a culture which was Calvinist, fiercely democratic, socially enlightened, self-reliant, pragmatic and energetic. He became an assistant to an influential preacher in London, and in 1878 he was himself ordained as a minister at Cruden, a small fishing village in Aberdeenshire.

In 1882, after four years as a minister, Patrick married Annie Brown. Two years later, in 1884, he accepted "a call" to the Free Church in Melbourne, Australia, at a time when Scottish immigration to the southern continent was gathering pace. He and his family arrived in Melbourne in October 1884, almost exactly a century after the first convicts were transported from Britain to New South Wales.

MELBOURNE

As the nineteenth century closed, the world was just becoming used to telephone and radio. But Australia, newly settled, had only recently been linked by cable to the Northern Hemisphere. The telegraph, invented in 1837, had taken several decades to reach Australia. Until then, newspapers competed for foreign news by posting lookouts on South Head, the entrance to Sydney Harbor, to watch for ships. Each paper would launch a whaleboat, dash out to the ship and scoop up the mail packets and overseas newspapers. These were rushed back into the city on horseback, where they were rewritten and published as fast as possible.

Patrick Murdoch's bluestone church stood at the corner of William and Lonsdale streets, where the Australian Broadcasting Corporation later built radio studios. He was an enthusiastic preacher who disapproved of sermons over an hour long. Three years after his arrival, he moved to Trinity Church in Camberwell, a Melbourne suburb, remaining minister there until his retirement on December 31, 1928. He died twelve years later.

Patrick Murdoch was a worldly man who was involved in the politics of church and state. He loved golf and bowling and was tall, broad-shouldered, straight-backed and "full of Christian fun." A fellow clergyman said that "he with a few others moulded the mind and shaped the policy of the Presbyterian Church as it is today in Australia," and it was said that "young and old of both sexes felt the magnetic force of his personality."

Patrick was a convinced supporter of the freedom of the press; he called it "probably the strongest foe of tyranny," and he argued that "no autocrat can tolerate the widespread dissemination among his people of a free discussion of his conduct."

Patrick and Annie Murdoch had seven children. Keith, the second son and third child, was born on August 12, 1885. His childhood and youth were made wretched by the curse of an appalling stammer.

After school, he decided not to attend a university and told his father of his spiritual calling toward journalism. His father was unenthusiastic but spoke to David Syme, owner of the Melbourne *Age* and a prominent member of his congregation. Syme arranged for the boy to be given a job covering the middle-class suburb of Malvern.

Keith worked hard and found that his stammer aroused the sympathies of those he interviewed. He lived frugally, even austerely. He was saving every penny in order to go to London to study at the London School of Economics, and to find a cure for his stammer. By 1908 he had saved £500, enough for a steerage ticket to London and a year's board and lodging.

London was a terrible disappointment to Keith. He was homesick and his introductions were no help. He found it impossible either to break into Fleet Street or to find a cure for his stammer. He lived alone and made himself toast on his penknife over a gas ring. He missed his family more and more.

Still stammering, Keith returned to Melbourne in 1910. In 1912, he became Melbourne parliamentary correspondent for the Sydney *Sun*, a lively evening paper. His interest in politics was becoming a passion.

GALLIPOLI

On April 25, 1915, two divisions of Australian and New Zealand Army Corps (Anzac) soldiers landed on a bleakly rocky shore at Gallipoli in the Dardanelles. They were cut down by Turkish soldiers under the command of Mustafa Kemal, later known as Atatürk. About sixteen thousand of them were killed or wounded. Who was to blame? Many Australians hold the English responsible. That was the first part of the legend. The second part was that only Keith Murdoch was prepared to tell the truth.

In essence the story has it that the young Keith Murdoch, a courageous war correspondent, had made his way onto the beaches of Gallipoli and was appalled by the suffering and the incompetent command of the British. Defying British censorship, he wrote the truth, and as a result the British commander in chief was recalled, the war against Turkey was abandoned, and a royal commission was created to investigate the war. It was even sometimes said that Murdoch brought about the fall of the British government. The story needs to be examined, not only for its intrinsic merit, but because

Keith Murdoch's influence on his only son Rupert was immeasurable.

In 1915, Keith Murdoch was appointed London editor of the United Cable Service, a minor news agency. His father's old friend Andrew Fisher, then prime minister, assigned him to stop in Egypt en route to London in order to investigate complaints by Australian troops about delays in their mail. He was allowed by General Sir Ian Hamilton, commander of the Dardanelles Expeditionary Force, to visit Gallipoli after he explicitly accepted the censorship regulations. After a week in the area, he came away with an idealized vision of the Australian troops and an appalling impression of the British command. He decided that Australian boys were being sacrificed by British incompetence and broke his word to Hamilton. He wrote a bitter tirade to his prime minister, Andrew Fisher. It was tendentious and filled with errors, but it was powerfully written. When he reached London, Lord Northcliffe, proprietor of the *Times*, saw that it reached the British cabinet. Its precise effect is hard to evaluate, but within months Hamilton was replaced and the Australian force was withdrawn from the Dardanelles. Hamilton blamed Murdoch for his downfall, even though he established that the letter was inaccurate. Murdoch talked up his own role as best he could.

The episode established Murdoch in both London and Australia as an unusual man. He was lucky that the letter was not published until fifteen years after his death. Neither its tone nor its accuracy reflected well on him, and he later acknowledged he had made mistakes which he regretted.

When Rupert Murdoch was asked about his father's letter in 1989, he replied, "It depicted a very idealized sense of the Australian soldier being sent to slaughter by the gin-and-tonic-swilling Brits three miles off the shore. Very powerful letter."

"It's a great letter," agreed his interviewer, Gerard Henderson. "You can't really forget it. On the other hand there were a lot of Brits on Gallipoli, too, which these days many of us don't seem to remember."

"Oh, sure, it may not have been fair," replied Rupert Murdoch, "but it changed history, that letter."

FLEET STREET

Keith Murdoch spent the rest of the war in London enjoying his new-found notoriety. He fell completely under Lord Northcliffe's spell. From him he learned much about the newspaper business which he then went home to apply in Australia, and later taught his son, Rupert.

Before Alfred Harmsworth, Lord Northcliffe, went mad, he was a communications genius. The foundation of his empire had been a paper called *Answers,* a marvelous vehicle in which to display his love of trivia. The subjects tackled were diverse: "Strange Things That Happen in Tunnels," "Why Jews Don't Ride Bicycles," "Do Dogs Commit Murder?," "Can a Clergyman Marry Himself?," "Can Fish Speak?"

The paper really took off when Harmsworth (as he then was known) began to stage competitions such as one that asked readers to guess the number of people who crossed London Bridge every day. His most famous competition offered the winner "£1 a week for life," which a tramp had apparently told Harmsworth was his great dream of wealth. The prize was to go to the person who could guess the value of the gold in the Bank of England on a particular day. The circulation of *Answers* rose to 200,000. In 1896 Harmsworth founded the *Daily Mail,* which sold 400,000 on its first day. "We've struck a gold mine," he declared.

His philosophy was simple—and crucial. "A newspaper," he declared, "is to be made to pay. Let it deal with what interests the mass of people. Let it give the public what it wants."

At the end of 1900, he traveled to New York and, at the invitation of Joseph Pulitzer, designed the first issue of the *World.* It came out on January 1, 1901, a tabloid of twelve pages and four columns. It created a sensation. Harmsworth insisted that no article should be longer than 250 words, and the paper was described as "All the News in Sixty Seconds."

In 1908, now Lord Northcliffe, he acquired a newspaper to match his ego, the *Times*. The owners were reluctant to sell it to such a cad, but business was business, and it was losing money. No one was more horrified than the staff, who regarded themselves then (and later) as keepers of a Holy Grail and hated Northcliffe's attempts to make the paper more popular, to take it downmarket.

Keith Murdoch had been impressed by listening to a speech by Northcliffe on his first visit to London. Now Northcliffe became one of his great confidants, and the most important influence on his life. They were like father and son. By the end of 1920 Murdoch had caught the attention of the directors of the Melbourne Herald and Weekly Times company, who offered him the editorship of the *Herald*, an evening broadsheet, at £2,000 a year. Northcliffe urged his protégé to accept.

When Murdoch took over, the *Herald* had a circulation of about 100,000. The paper had no competition. Its layout was fusty, the reporting solid but boring, the news pages slack.

When he promoted himself to managing editor, he strengthened the *Herald*'s business side, and followed Northcliffe's advice to run serials, start a woman's page, set up stunts and introduce competitions. He made the editorials shorter and the paper crisper. To the horror of the Melbourne Establishment, he even staged a beauty contest.

In Murdoch's hands, the circulation of the *Herald* rose from 100,000 to around 140,000 within a year. Not everybody approved. "Indeed," wrote one critic, "some observers considered Murdoch's influence begot a somewhat callow approach to the important as well as the trivial affairs of the world." Others accused Murdoch of being a "yellow journalist."

In the late 1920s Murdoch began to expand the Herald group's empire. The *Sporting Globe*, the *Australian Home Builder*, the *Listener In*, *Aircraft*, *Australian Home Beautiful* and *Wild Life* were among the magazines that the group launched or acquired. It also bought the *Sun News Pictorial*, the *Herald*'s competitor.

In 1928, Murdoch was made managing director. In 1929, he had the Herald group acquire radio station 3DB, thus becoming the first Australian newspaper publisher to enter broadcasting. He introduced swift printing presses, pioneered wire photo services and published the first radio picture from overseas.

Murdoch watched as nationwide newspaper chains were established in the United States. He was determined to create such a chain in Australia. Under his leadership, a *Herald*-based syndicate took over the *West Australian*. Then he went to war in Adelaide. He bought the small *Register* and, by dint of fierce competition, induced the owners of the morning *Advertiser* and then the afternoon Adelaide *News,* which was only ten years old, to sell out to the Herald group. He became chairman of Advertiser Newspapers and put in a young man named Lloyd Dumas as managing editor. Advertiser Newspapers Ltd. and News Ltd. remained separate companies with their own stockholders and their own plants.

In 1931 Murdoch joined the board of the Adelaide *News*. In 1933 the two Brisbane morning dailies were added to the group and were merged to become the *Courier-Mail*. Murdoch also acquired huge tracts of forest in Tasmania and began to create the continent's newsprint industry.

Meanwhile his private life had also developed well. In 1928 he married Elisabeth Greene, a determined girl who became a devoted wife, a formidable mother and an eminent figure in Melbourne society.

"My side is pretty Australian," said Dame Elisabeth in interviews for this book. She enjoyed talking about her family, who came from Scotland, Ireland and England.

Her grandfather, William Henry Greene, was an Irish railway engineer who had moved to England and then emigrated to Australia in the 1860s.

Her father, Rupert, was born in 1870. As a boy Rupert Greene was a scalawag, and he learned little at school. He became the New Zealand Loan and Mercantile Agency's leading wool expert and was well liked by his colleagues. In his private life he was a dashing character, a gambler and a spendthrift, always verging on the edge of catastrophic debt.

Elisabeth was her father's favorite. She recalled, "He was great fun; very gifted, a great sport, and he had a great eye. He was always gambling on horses and cards. He was popular and amusing and had no idea of responsibility. We had a very checkered family life."

Rupert Greene's gambling debts were often so great that his wife had to rent out their home and move the family into an apartment. He was always improvident but he remained a wild, swashbuckling and delightful character. In every way, he was the antithesis of the righteous parson Patrick Murdoch, and of the ambitious, serious-minded Keith. But there is at least as much of Rupert Greene as of Patrick Murdoch in their grandson, Rupert.

Throughout the 1930s Keith Murdoch's power and influence grew as he extended the reach of the Herald group. He was knighted in 1933, the same year that heart problems laid him low for months. When he recovered, he was frequently away from home, expanding the Herald group's empire and thinking increasingly of how to nurture his own. By 1935 Murdoch and the Herald group had interests in eleven of the country's sixty-five radio stations. As the *Australian Dictionary of National Biography* put it, "Whatever the prime motive—profit, power, or pulpiteering—Murdoch had forged the first national media chain."

There was no love lost between Sir Keith and the Fairfax family, who were considered the aristocracy of the press, especially in Sydney, where their newspaper dynasty was established. On one occasion Murdoch wrote: "I am learning at last how contemptibly mean and selfish SMH [Sydney *Morning Herald*] people can become. We have to remain partners with them in many things but my feelings at present are strained."

The other great newspaper dynasty was that of the Packer family. In 1939, Frank Packer, the head of Consolidated Press, had slid into financial trouble. His *Daily Telegraph* was losing money and the *Australian Women's Weekly* was not yet making it. Packer started to negotiate with Murdoch to sell out to the Herald and Weekly Times group. The Fairfaxes were loath to have Murdoch expand into Sydney. They decided to subsidize Packer. What he needed was a twopence rise in the cover price of the *Telegraph*. The Sydney *Morning Herald* had no need for such an increase, but the Fairfaxes agreed to a simultaneous price rise in February 1940, purely to frustrate Murdoch. Rupert said later that one of the things his father taught him was "Never trust a Sydney newspaper proprietor."

In 1932 the Murdochs moved from their town house in South Yarra to a mansion in the neighboring suburb of Toorak. They also acquired a ninety-acre property about thirty miles south of Melbourne, near the seaside community of Frankston. Keith named it Cruden Farm, after the Aberdeenshire village of his grandparents. Gradually, Cruden Farm was transformed into a country house in the American colonial style, with Georgian porticoes and big open fireplaces. Outside there were sunken gardens, stables with English fittings, a tennis court, rock gardens and a driveway lined with eucalyptus. This was the country home of the four Murdoch children: Helen, born in 1929, Rupert (christened Keith Rupert) in 1931, then two more sisters, Anne in 1935 and Janet in 1939.

There are two views of the young Rupert Murdoch's relations with his parents. One, which subsequently became the conventional wisdom, was that they were remote and tough with him, preoccupied with their own lives, quick to find fault, slow to praise and even slower to demonstrate affection. Many associates have speculated that Murdoch's drive and restlessness owe much to the denial of his father's approval at an early age.

This theory is emphatically repudiated by his mother, by his elder sister, Helen, and by Murdoch himself. He insists that his father was a loving parent and a hero to him. He says that his mother was far sterner with the children: "Dad was the indulgent one. He was older and valued his time with us all the more. He indulged my sisters particularly, but me as well. My mother was the severe one."

From an early age, the young Rupert was aware of the power and the glory and the sheer fun which accrued to his father from newspapers. Keith used to take his son around the *Herald*'s office on Flinders Street, and Rupert often said later that the smell of the ink, the noise of the presses and the highly charged atmosphere were irresistible. "The life of a publisher is about the best life in the whole world. When kids are subjected to it there's not much doubt they'll be attracted to it." On weekends he loved lying on his father's bed, watching as he went through the papers, marking the good and bad bits.

Lady Murdoch imposed high standards upon her children. She wanted them to have good, Christian values and feelings of obligation and duty. She insisted they understand that money—and all other rewards—had to be earned. Nothing should be taken for granted. "Maybe they thought I was an old monster in those days," she said. "But I think they all really appreciate it now."

Rupert had contrasting memories of his two grandfathers. The Reverend Patrick Murdoch was a benign old man sitting in a wicker chair in his garden. Rupert Greene—"Pop Greene" to the children—was quite another matter. Despite, or perhaps because of, Keith's disapproval, he was always fooling around with the children, buying them ice cream, encouraging disobedience, helping them to get into scrapes. He allowed them to drive his car when they could hardly reach the pedals; Helen drove it right through a neighbor's fence. He was the sort of older relation every child dreams of. Elisabeth Murdoch said later of her son, "On Keith's side he is all Scottish. That's what makes him good. But he probably gets a bit of color and zest from my side of the family. Perhaps Rupert inherited his gambling instinct from my father." Rupert Murdoch himself said that his own father dreaded the influence of Rupert Greene. "My father thought he was a wild, drinking, gambling man. They all got on for the sake of family life, but it was one of my father's nightmares that I'd turn out like my grandfather, which I probably did, a bit."

It was a privileged and in many ways idyllic childhood, filled with nannies, tea parties, ponies, dogs and outings.

In 1938 Keith bought a sheep station on the Murrumbidgee River near Wagga Wagga. There were a couple thousand acres of river flats and behind that about fourteen thousand acres of rolling, rocky hills. It was a classic sheep station with a history to match.

Rupert and his elder sister, Helen, would ride all day, or catch rabbits and hares and water rats. Rupert sold the animals for their skins. Water rats were the most valuable catch, but they were hardest to get. Rupert recalled: "We would climb out on fallen trees across a river and attach an open rabbit trap on a wire, and put a bit of aniseed on some meat. The smell would attract the rats and the trap would break their necks." Then they had to be pulled out of the water and skinned. If catching them was the most difficult part of the operation, skinning was the most unpleasant, and Rupert made Helen do that. He sold the skins for sixpence each. Although Helen had to do the dirty work, and although she was older, he gave her only one penny per skin.

At Cruden, their home outside Melbourne, the young Rupert dealt in manure as well as rabbits. He collected it around the paddocks and down on the beach at Davies Bay, where there was a family boathouse. Again, Helen and his younger sisters were enlisted as peons; he would then take the bags around to all the old ladies, who doted on him. "I always say that Rupert got his start in life from rabbits, and manure. I never saw any of the money. Rupert did. He spent it on gambling at school," said Helen.

Apart from such business flair, Rupert's mother said that she considered Rupert "an ordinary little boy," amenable and thoughtful. He liked real things. He liked toys that actually worked. "He had no time for imaginary things, fairy tales and so on. He liked links with reality." Helen agreed: "He didn't like pretendy games." There was one other characteristic his mother noted: he could not bear dissension at home. "He was a very gentle little boy." To Helen, he was "a bit of a cat who walked alone."

In 1941, at the age of ten, Rupert was sent off to boarding school. Sir Keith was against it, but Lady Murdoch insisted.

The ethos of Geelong Grammar was not attractive to Rupert. He was not prepared for the dislike of his father that he encountered. He discovered that the power newspaper barons wield rarely makes them popular. "I felt a loner at school," he recalled, "probably because of my father's position. Bullied a lot. I'm sure my kids have had much the same. We've never talked about it."

Ostracism had a crucial effect on Rupert: "It made me realize that if you're going to do your job as a publisher or a principal in the media, you've got to be your own person and not have close friendships which can compromise you. That philosophy just evolved, I think. It made you realize you were not looked upon as just another successful businessman, farmer, et cetera."

On weekends, the Geelong Grammar boys could get a pass that allowed them to leave the confined school premises and head off into the nearby hills, with or without bicycles. Some boys used to row long distances; others visited a café in Geelong itself, a short bus ride away. Rupert, taking a leaf from his grandfather Greene's book, often used to slip off to the racetrack for a bet on the horses. He kept a motorcycle at a shop nearby.

OXFORD

After Geelong Grammar, it was off to Worcester College, Oxford. Sir Keith hoped that after Oxford Rupert would embark upon life as a newspaperman.

Sir Keith's own powers, political and physical, were waning. He was sixty-five, he had had a weak heart for almost twenty years and he had recently suffered another heart attack. He no longer exercised the influence he had once enjoyed over national politicians, and his authority even within the Herald group was diminished. The effects of his weak heart were compounded by a cancer operation. He had retired as managing director of the Herald group in 1949, though he remained chairman.

Conscious of time running out, Sir Keith concentrated on consolidating his own small newspaper group, which he hoped to leave to Rupert. Starting in the late 1920s, he had acquired control of Queensland Newspapers, whose principal property was the Brisbane *Courier-Mail*. In 1948 he proposed to the Herald group's board that they relinquish their monopoly of Adelaide newspapers. He wanted to buy those shares of the Adelaide *News* held by the Adelaide *Advertiser*, which itself was controlled by the Herald group. He promised in writing that if his family ever wanted to sell their shares in the Queensland Newspapers company, they would offer them back to the Herald group. His offer was refused.

When Rupert arrived in Britain, after a trip through Europe with his parents, he went first to Birmingham for a summer job on the *Gazette*, which his father had arranged. Britain five years after the end of the Second World War could seem a gloomy place to a brash young Australian. The wartime sense of solidarity had disappeared. Industrial relations were bitter. The country was still hemmed in by all sorts of rationing and restrictions as it attempted to rebuild and create a new welfare state. Newsprint was rationed, a restriction imposed in the interest of the balance of payments. As a result, papers were very thin, and many of them were not very good.

In Birmingham, Britain's second city, Rupert found himself a room and had a fine old time on the *Gazette*. "I even got the diary [gossip column]," he said. He went dog racing, the popular sport in Birmingham, and he noticed that the sports pages were the best-read pages in the tabloid papers.

Sir Keith wrote to him, saying, "I do hope, dear boy, that you are not doing too much but using your time usefully and are in good shape and heart. . . . You will, I am sure, make a proper exit from Birmingham and say grateful goodbyes to your colleagues, your bosses and your friends."

In fact, after his stint on the *Gazette*, Murdoch suggested to the *Gazette*'s proprietor that the editor, Charles Fenby, was incompetent and should be fired. They were astonished and did not take his advice.

In October 1950, Rupert went up to Worcester College. Most of the British undergraduates had either served in the war or already done two years' national service. They were mature and, to a young Australian, rather stuffy. Rod Carnegie, who followed Rupert Murdoch from Geelong Grammar to Oxford, also thought that most of them were pretty inhospitable to Australians far from home.

Murdoch's principal tutor at Oxford was Asa Briggs, who was on his way to becoming one of the most doughty members of the British intellectual, academic and broadcasting elite. At Sir Keith's request, Briggs spent a lot of time with Murdoch, and taught him to think logically. Murdoch called him "Isa," a term of endearment which Briggs enjoyed. A mutual friend was another young history tutor, Harry Pitt, who very much liked Murdoch. "He had no sense of class nuances," Pitt recalled. "He just had a good time at Oxford." Murdoch agrees.

Like his father on his own first visit, however, he did not thrill to Britain. "There were a lot of Australians who embraced everything that was English and rejected everything that was Australian," he recalled. He, by contrast, was idealistic about Australia. "I hugely resented Aussies there who said they'd never go back." He would come close to fisticuffs on the issue of patriotism. "I was very passionate about Australia. It was special, it was different." He also came away with a dislike bordering on contempt for what he saw as "English" characteristics. He found the country complacent and uncompetitive. As for the ruling class, it left him bursting with spleen ever after. "They distrust money," he has asserted. "They despise business. They create the social and psychological currents which have done so much damage to Britain and its willingness to change."

Murdoch had one of the best rooms in college—the De Quincey room. He had a car, which was an almost unheard-of luxury for an undergraduate, yet he also affected to be a socialist, if not a communist. He had a bust of Lenin in pride of place on his mantelpiece. This may have been nothing more than a sign of Rupert's cockiness. Perhaps he wanted only to provoke his father. But it was provocative in other ways. In the early 1950s, Stalinism was at its most aggressive. The Cold War was beginning. The countries of Eastern Europe were being subjected one by one to Marxist-Leninist terror. To be a Leninist at such a time was scarcely a joke.

His Geelong Grammar friend Richard Searby, who was now a tall, handsome and serious classicist at Corpus Christi College, has been quoted as saying that no one took Rupert's politics very seriously. Asa Briggs agreed. Still, the combination of money, Marxism and arrogance did not endear him to everyone.

Outside of Oxford, Rupert's best friend in England was probably the Melbourne *Herald*'s London correspondent, Rohan Rivett. Rohan, his wife and their young children lived less than an hour's drive from Oxford. Murdoch was a frequent visitor, and they became his Australian family in England. Years later Nan Rivett remembered him as very exuberant and untidy, his shirttails always hanging out. Her children adored him—he was like a big bouncy dog. Rohan and Nan were always concerned lest his parents find out about his gambling. Nan Rivett thought that Rupert was always trying to convince his mother that he was as good as his father, something Lady Murdoch clearly doubted.

Rivett saw as much of Rupert as he could, and at the end of 1950 he wrote to Sir Keith, "I am inclined to prophesy that he will make his first million with fantastic ease."

After Rupert made a trip to Paris in early 1951, Rivett wrote that "he delighted Nan and me with his exceedingly shrewd and money-saving junketings in Paris, which suggest to me he will probably prove the greatest income maker from an expense account in *Herald* history when he comes back on the payroll."

During the 1951 Easter vacation, the Rivetts took Rupert to Switzerland. Rivett wrote to Sir Keith that his development in the last year had been amazing: "His resources and ability to work things out and get things done are first rate. . . . Nancy and I found him a grand travelling companion in every way and from the first moment until the return he was picking up information, asking questions and absorbing new impressions with enthusiasm."

Sir Keith wrote constantly to Rupert, giving him news about the family newspapers, hoping to draw his firm interest. Sir Keith's overriding concern now was to settle his affairs so as to leave enough money for his wife and daughters and the beginnings of a newspaper empire for Rupert. Indeed, almost every business move he made in the last four years of his life was directed to this end. He was always worried that Rupert was not responding, and was frittering away his time in Oxford. At one stage Rupert was doing so badly in his studies that Sir Keith decided to bring him back to work on the newspapers in Australia. His mother's intervention saved him.

In the northern summer of 1951, Sir Keith, now quite unwell, made his last circumnavigation. He flew first to the United States, and in Washington he was given two minutes with President Truman. In London, he summoned Rivett to his suite at Claridges hotel and offered him a new job as the editor of one of the two papers he owned personally, the evening tabloid Adelaide *News.* Rivett was overjoyed.

Keith bought a new car, a Ford Zephyr, and told Rupert he could drive it through Europe and then ship it back to Melbourne from the Middle East. He would fly in for part of the trip himself. Thus began a fantastic journey.

From London they drove via Zurich, where Sir Keith joined them, to Yugoslavia. Despite the wretched appearance of people in Belgrade, Rupert thought that Tito was "certainly a very great man indeed, and the only man capable of doing half what he is doing now. Just to hold that country together is the work of a genius."

Yugoslavia, he wrote to the Rivetts, persuaded him that the Russians now had a terrible choice:

> Do they wait for the present arms effort of the West to culminate in busting the Western economies and walking in . . . or is the risk of this not taking place and the power of the US becoming so great that they are finally 1) either bullied into peaceful submission (almost impossible, I would say) or 2) exterminated by a war brought on by the Americans taking their present efforts to a logical and historical conclusion—namely war?

Sir Keith left him in Athens and flew back to Melbourne. "That was the last time I ever saw him. I don't remember any particular parting or anything."

After further adventures in Crete, Turkey and Egypt, Rupert returned to Oxford. He moved into digs on Headington Hill with another Australian from Geelong Grammar, John Piper. They had a little attic flat at the top of the house. Murdoch promptly took his landlord to court to get the rent reduced. "And I won. Something like four pounds a week reduced to one pound," he recalled later.

In 1952 Murdoch decided to run for secretary of the University Labour Club. In those days, and for a long time thereafter, a candidate was not permitted to canvass openly, but had to solicit votes in a quiet, British way, using his friends to recommend their man to potential voters. Murdoch despised such hypocrisies and ran an energetic campaign. "Rooting for Rupert" was its slogan.

In May 1952, the student paper *Cherwell* declared: "Australian ex-journalist, Rupert Murdoch . . . bombarded Club members with so many plaintive appeals that undergraduate canvassing and social-ist majorities hit new highs." The paper continued, "Turbulent, trav-elled and twenty-one, he is known . . . as a brilliant betting man with that individual Billingsgate touch. He manages *Cherwell* publicity in his spare time." A fortnight later, *Cherwell* announced: "Rupert Murdoch, cataclysmic chauffeur from the outback, prototype of Hol-lywood's peripatetic publicists, has plastered the town and papered the notice-boards."

Back home, Sir Keith was becoming iller and more worried. De-spite the empire he had built for the Herald group, he had not made enough money to be sure that he could leave his family as secure and comfortable as he wished. He and Elisabeth both felt that the group had failed to reward him adequately. Letters to his banks, his brokers, his accountant and to Rupert revealed his constant, nagging anxiety to leave the family financially liquid, and especially to clear an over-draft, which he had run up partly in order to leave the foundation of a newspaper empire to Rupert.

He was desperate to increase his share of Adelaide *News* stock. At the end of 1951 he sold more of his small parcel of Herald group shares. He wrote to Rupert to say that he was mortgaging what he could to buy more of the *News.* Rupert said later, "He was never trying to create a dynasty, but he knew there would never be a place for me at the *Herald,* on which he held a paltry number of shares. I guess he wanted me to have an opportunity in journalism."

In early 1952, Hugh Cudlipp of the *Mirror* came to Melbourne. Sir Keith told him he was concerned about Rupert's "alarming left-wing views." Cudlipp did not think he really need worry, but worry was part of Sir Keith's style.

Sir Keith wrote to Rivett, "I am very worried about Rupert in that he does not write home enough. When he gets going, he writes well, and wins marks; but he must learn that all human relationships, even those with his family, have always to be kept in repair; and are infi-nitely worth a lot of trouble and study. . . ." He also asked Rivett not to "inflate" Rupert. "You have talked once or twice in your letters of his 'brilliant prospects.' His prospects depend entirely on himself."

Rupert made another tour of Europe and wrote a long and typically ebullient description to the Rivetts—nine pages in magenta ink: "It's been striking me that perhaps you may be in need of some big stuff. Wouldn't that dish rag which you call your front page be vastly improved by some REALLY BIG WORLD SCOOP STORIES under big and startling new names in journalism." He proposed himself as special correspondent at the Labour Party's annual national conference, to counter "the ridiculous and damaging lies told by the morning warmongers. What about it? Herr Commissar for Truth, Peace and Women?"

His travels had ended in Deauville. At the casino, he lost all his francs the first night, and was left with only unchangeable Italian lire in an expensive French hotel.

So, waiting for the Bank to pull its finger out and send money I amassed a colossal bill and studied the wheels to perfect THE system—with one eye on the floor for dropped chips. Once an old lady did drop a 1,000-francs chip and went away without noticing it. I pounced! Soon there was 5,000 francs, which bought a pornographic novel, a shave, a cable to London, some drinks, and a few small 100 franc chips with which to really amass a fortune. But fate was against me. And finally back to Oxford only £50 worse off.

At the end of September Rupert wrote a long and enthusiastic letter to his parents. It arrived on Thursday, October 2. Sir Keith read it with the greatest pleasure. He was delighted and encouraged. "I think he's got it," he said to his wife. It was a judgment she always remembered with gratitude. That Saturday, Sir Keith wrote to one of his daughters, "My beautiful and good Anne . . . We had a splendid letter from Rupert and he is forgiven some of his misdemeanours. . . ." A few hours later, during the night of Saturday–Sunday, October 4–5, 1952, he died in his sleep. His funeral was held before Rupert managed to return from Oxford. It was a considerable Melbourne occasion.

In his will, written in 1948, Sir Keith had declared his intention:

> WHEREAS I desire that Queensland Newspapers Pty Ltd of Queen Street Brisbane and another Newspaper Company approved by my trustees should continue to express my ideals of newspaper and broadcasting activities in the service of others and these ideals should be pursued with deep interest AND WHEREAS I desire that my said son Keith Rupert Murdoch should have the great opportunity of spending a useful altruistic and full life in newspaper and broadcasting activities and of ultimately occupying a position of high responsibility in that field with the support of my trustees if they consider him worthy of that support. NOW I HEREBY BEQUEATH . . .

Over the last four years, as Sir Keith's business fortunes had waxed and waned, three codicils had been added to the will. Originally Rupert had been left a package of shares in Queensland Newspapers; eventually he inherited a major part of Cruden Investments, a family company that held both the Brisbane and Adelaide stock.

Rupert was anxious to keep both the Adelaide *News* and the Brisbane *Courier-Mail*, but his mother felt that the family could not afford to do so. Her daughter Helen says that Elisabeth's childhood memories of her father had given her a terror of debt. She was also heavily influenced by the trustees of Keith's estate, in particular by Harold Giddy, the chairman of the trustees. When Rupert had gone back to Oxford, Giddy persuaded her to sell the family's shares in the Brisbane *Courier-Mail* to the Melbourne *Herald.* Since Giddy was also chairman of the *Herald,* there were those who thought he had a conflict of interest, Rupert among them.

After he returned to Oxford, Rupert resumed his correspondence with Rivett—but overnight the tone and subject matter had changed astonishingly, and become far less frivolous. Suddenly he became interested in the minutest details of the Adelaide *News'* finances. His letters showed that he had an instinctive feel for money and power, and how to use them both. He was very frustrated. He was sure that if he had been in Australia, he could have persuaded his mother to keep the Brisbane *Courier-Mail* as well as the Adelaide *News*. But far away in Oxford, he wrote to Rivett, "I have the feeling I am fighting a one-man battle. Oh for the bloody sun! . . . If it weren't for good friends, I'd have shot myself in this bloody place long ago. Rain, wind, sleet, slush, shit, snow, and starch!"

He spent Christmas 1952 with Douglas Brass, a courteous reporter, and his wife, a friend of his mother, who were now in London for the *Herald*, and cheered up a little in the new year. In 1953, he wrote to Rivett, "Your letter of the 15th December is especially interesting. I take it that with the reduced price of newsprint beginning to show itself in the balance sheet, and after taxation, the total profit this year should be in the vicinity of £55,000. Is this not right?"

Rupert then turned to politics. Princess Elizabeth had recently succeeded her father, George VI. Rupert thought her first Christmas address both dull and arrogant, and wrote, "I personally entirely deprecate this thoroughly NEW theory that the Monarchy is above criticism. Don't misunderstand me, I'm not advocating a Republic—which I don't believe in, anyway. . . ."

He added an extraordinary postscript, written in magenta ink, reaffirming his loyalty to Lenin. "Yesterday was the 29th anniversary of the Great Teacher. We stood to attention for one minute in front of THE BUST on the mantelpiece and drank several toasts—and then settled down to some good reading of adulatory Russian poetry."

He was honing his political instincts in other ways. With an election imminent in South Australia, he wrote to Rivett, "I implore you not to speak out too loudly on either side." He never wanted to be identified with a loser. In February 1953 he recounted a dinner with one of the great Australian newspaper barons, Frank Packer, at the Chancellors' house: "Packer must be the biggest crook in Australian newspapers, but equally he is the cleverest and he may, in the not too distant future, be in a position to give us great help."

In a postscript he asked, "Just how much are we spending on: a) circulation PROMOTION b) advertising PROMOTION? NO paper can expect to make headway without VERY generous expenditure in these depts." It was already clear that whereas Sir Keith's letters to Rivett had been much concerned with editorial content, Rupert's dealt first with the bottom line.

Through March, April and early May 1953, Rupert continued to worry about the estate, and about how the Adelaide *News* could beat off the Adelaide *Advertiser*, which, as part of the Melbourne Herald group, had far greater resources. All the while, his final exams were rushing toward him, and he was terrified—with good reason, for he had done hardly any work. "What about coronation cover?" he wrote in April. The choice seemed to be between a syndicated article by Hannen Swaffer and one by Godfrey Winn. "I strongly suggest the former. A mad republican is always better than a pansy."

By this time, Asa Briggs was trying to cram him every day for his finals in June. In the end he obtained a third-class degree.

When the term ended, he did not return at once to Australia. He thought about making a tour of American newsrooms, but instead decided to do a stint on the London *Daily Express*, undoubtedly the best school for what its proprietor, Lord Beaverbrook, called "the Black Art of journalism."

Murdoch wrote to Rivett about "the Beaverbrook brothel," but he enjoyed it. "The Beaver" was a wicked and in some ways wickedly attractive man. He had fantastic style and an outrageous sense of mischief. The *Express* was nothing if not racy, with brilliant subediting and snappy headlines. His Lordship was a formidable role model, and undoubtedly proved to Murdoch that the best way to run a newspaper was to hold enough stock to make one independent. "If you work for me," Beaverbrook said, "you will never become a millionaire, but you will live like one." Murdoch intended to be one—by working for himself.

On the *Express* he was given a place at the subeditor's desk under the eye of Ted Pickering. No berth in Fleet Street could have been better. His months in Beaverbrook's "brothel" left Murdoch with an abiding admiration for the craft of the London subeditor. Later he called Pickering "my first great mentor."

All the time, he was thinking of how to increase the circulation of the Adelaide *News* and how to undermine the *Advertiser.* He told Rivett he was definitely coming to work on the *News.* He did not want a proper job or apprenticeship but "please don't get the impression that I will be walking in as a cocky bastard to tell you what's wrong with everything. . . . I will of course be treading softly for a considerable time. . . ."

In August 1953 the Kinsey report on American sexual mores was published. Rupert was still at the *Express* in London; the Patrick Murdoch in him reacted with horror, and his telegram to Rivett is worth quoting in full:

LONDON EXPRESS TODAY QUOTE KINSEY BALLYHOO BURSTS ON WORLD TODAY PROMOTE SALES HUMAN FEMALE SEX LIFE BOOK STOP SUMMARY HERE STOP PREPOSTEROUS DOCUMENT STOP SWEEPING FINDINGS BASED INTERVIEWS FIVE THOUSAND WOMEN EXHIBITIONISTS BOASTERS LEGPULLERS STOP FORTUNATELY AVERAGE AMERICAN WOMAN TOTALLY UNLIKE KINSEY CREATURES STOP EXPRESS DOES NOT INTEND PUBLISH SINGLE WORD OF THE STUFF UNQUOTE EYE TRUST WE DO NOT EITHER STOP FAMILY NEWSPAPERS LIKE OURSELVES GAIN GREAT CUDOS LEAVING THIS MUCK ALONE STOP FORNICATION MASTURBATION FRUSTRATION UNSUITABLE FOR ADELAIDE FAMILY FIRESIDE STOP HOPE YOU AGREE STOP EYE FELT EYE SHOULD EXPRESS THIS BEST REGARDS ALL MURDOCH.

In a handwritten note a few days later, Rupert related that he had been to Cornwall for the weekend—"Nearly got married off but I should get out of the country intact, I think! I trust my cable about Kinsey didn't offend you. I feel strongly about the subject. Cunt is not our line—especially when it's phoney—as this undoubtedly is. We might warn our readers of this without publishing the phoney figures. But that's all."

At the beginning of September 1953, he flew home via South Africa. At the age of twenty-two, Rupert Murdoch arrived in Adelaide, to take up his inheritance and to begin the first of what he himself called his lifelong series of battles with others and with the world.

ADELAIDE

When Rupert Murdoch traveled to Adelaide, it was, his mother said, "like going into the wilderness," far from Melbourne. At the time, the Australian press was still dominated by the Fairfax family, with their flagship, the Sydney *Morning Herald;* the Melbourne Herald group; and Frank Packer, who published the *Women's Weekly* and the tabloid Sydney *Telegraph.*

When Rupert Murdoch arrived at the *News'* small white offices opposite the railyard, he was greeted by Rohan Rivett. Editor now for almost two years, Rivett had had a difficult time holding the paper's circulation at some 75,000. Rupert's first priority was to confront the much bigger Adelaide *Advertiser,* behind which stood his father's old company, the Melbourne Herald group.

As Murdoch saw it, Sir Keith's body was hardly cold, and the eulogies were barely set in type, when the *Herald* tried to destroy what little remained of the small empire Sir Keith had hoped to leave Rupert. The older Rupert became, the more wrong he thought it that his mother had been pressured by the trustees into selling the Brisbane *Courier-Mail.* "It shouldn't have been too difficult to merge the

Queensland papers and the *News* in some way so that we had the majority," he said later.

The *Herald's* continuing threat was personified by Sir Lloyd Dumas, the chairman of the Adelaide *Advertiser*, which was 45 percent owned by the Herald group.

While Rupert was still at Oxford in early 1953, Sir Lloyd had gone to see Lady Murdoch. In Rupert's words, he said, "Hate to do this, but my board of directors insist. We have to start a Sunday newspaper against you"—against the *News*.

The threat was substantial. The *Advertiser* was a far bigger paper and had a larger organization than the *News* and its *Sunday Mail*. It already outsold the *News* by two to one during the week. Dumas' purpose was to make the Murdochs sell out. He offered Lady Murdoch £150,000 for the company.

Rupert's reaction was instant and predictable: "It made me angry. I thought they were trying to take advantage of my mother. They certainly wouldn't have dared do it in my father's time. I said, 'To hell with the idea. We'll fight 'em.' "

Murdoch and Rivett decided to publish Dumas' threat to Lady Murdoch, which he had put in a letter. "So we put out a poster: BID FOR PRESS, et cetera," Murdoch recalled. "Dumas was outraged."

Murdoch remembers the battle as his own David-against-the-established-Goliath story: "They produced a very handsome broadsheet, very newsworthy. They had every service in the world in it, color printing of comics, everything. We had this little paper with great loyalty, the Adelaide *Sunday Mail*."

The *Mail's* editor, Ron Boland, gave the *Advertiser* more than a run for its money, and Murdoch loved the contest. A nasty circulation war between the two Sunday papers continued for almost two years. It failed to destroy the *Mail*, but the struggle cost them both heavily. Murdoch says that various oblique approaches were made to him through the Adelaide Establishment suggesting compromise or merger; "I told them to go to hell."

Eventually, to Murdoch's great satisfaction, Sir Lloyd backed down. In 1955 he and Murdoch agreed to a scheme to merge the two Sunday papers. Each group took a 50 percent share in the new paper. This was an unusual compromise for Murdoch, but he rationalized it by saying that the *Sunday Advertiser* was not so much merging as being compelled to disappear. "That was the truth," he later insisted. "They'd go out of business and take a fifty percent interest in our paper, which we would control, run, print and get management fees for." The agreement enabled Murdoch to claim his first victory.

Murdoch startled the *News* staff with his energy. There was not one phase of the paper's production process that he did not see at first hand. "He was," said Ron Boland, "always up and going." He was a bustling, pudgy figure in those days, rushing around town, puppy fat bulging out of his dark suits, rolling up his sleeves in the newsroom, dirtying his hands with ink, studying typefaces and ad rates, learning all of the trade. The house magazine published a boyish picture of him with wavy hair and full lips and asserted, "With a terrific zest for work, and a breezy personality, he has readily fitted into the office picture."

He took a flat at Glenelg, a seaside resort close to Adelaide. He was always running, always forgetful, always coming over to the Bolands' or the Rivetts' house with shirts needing buttons sewn on. He loved parties and established a tradition of raucous New Year's Eve office parties which often ended in boisterous gambling games. He was known around town, and even out of state, as "the Boy Publisher."

At first Murdoch and his editor collaborated well. They had a family history in common. Rivett had called his third child Keith and asked Rupert to be godfather. All the while Murdoch applied himself to learning his trade and badgered everyone in every department for information—finance, production, advertising rates, distribution, newsprint costs, union problems. He wanted to know everything and to change everything. Criticisms and suggestions were constant.

Murdoch insisted on cutting costs. The entire editorial staff shrank to fewer than forty people. The political reporter, Frank Shaw, said later that he and another reporter, Ken May, might write up to twenty stories a day. "We produced three editions a day and in the last edition there might be as many as six page changes," recalled Shaw. The average paper had thirty-six pages; on Fridays, forty-eight pages. The circulation increased.

Australian politics at this time was still dominated by Robert Menzies, a close Churchill ally during World War II. Murdoch loathed him, and saw him as a British sycophant. Much later he acknowledged that many of his early political ideas were badly thought out, but, he said, "there was a respect for freedom, and a rather romantic acceptance of the Australian ideal of egalitarianism which, I think, was bred into us very early in the Murdoch family."

At this stage, Murdoch began a relationship which was to stand him in good stead for years to come—with the Commonwealth Bank. He understood that one of the great virtues, often overlooked, of the newspaper game is its cash-and-carry nature. Credit hardly exists; readers pay real money every day for the millions of papers they buy, and every day the publisher gets paid. The practice is not always as neat as the theory, but it is usually pretty straightforward nonetheless. Newspapers, therefore, are good bets.

When Murdoch arrived in Adelaide, the *News'* bank was the National Bank of Australia (later Australian National Bank), which was also banker to the Melbourne Herald group, including the *Advertiser.* After Murdoch's first attempt to take over the *Advertiser* was rebuffed, he established a relationship with the Commonwealth Bank in Sydney, a relatively small and conservative bank owned by the federal government. They liked him and gave him full support. Within a few years, News Ltd. had become the Commonwealth Bank's biggest client. As News grew, so did the bank.

Murdoch understood that bankers wanted repayment on schedule above all. Vern Christie, who became managing director of the bank, said later that his relationship with Murdoch was one of the easiest and most confident that he had with any client: "He would call me on a Friday and ask, 'Would you stand by me if I need another hundred fifty million dollars?' And the relationship was such that I would say yes. The reason for such confidence? He has never, ever not performed with his banks as he said he would. He always meets every payment."

In 1956 Rupert Murdoch married. His bride was Patricia Booker, a young woman who had worked as an air hostess and at the Myers department store in Adelaide. She was pretty and blond. His family was worried about the match, and attributed it to his loneliness in the "wilderness." Part of the couple's honeymoon was spent inspecting the properties he had acquired. Marriage did not in any way slow him down—nor did the birth of their daughter, Prudence, in 1959. The child was given full rein in the relaxed Murdoch household and went to bed more or less when she chose. They began as a happy family.

By the second half of the 1950s, the *News* was making enough for Murdoch to think of stretching out of Adelaide. When he looked at other newspaper families—Fairfax's, Beaverbrook's, Northcliffe's, Cecil King's—he saw empires, or at least chains. First he expanded a minor interest in Southdown Press, a Melbourne-based magazine publisher, into total ownership. Despite opposition from cautious board members, he bought *New Idea*, a weekly women's magazine published in Melbourne. Next came his second newspaper—the *Sunday Times* in Perth, the small, quiet, provincial capital of Western Australia, some fourteen hundred miles from Adelaide.

The *Sunday Times* was losing money, but Murdoch wanted it. "We had to buy the first thing that came along," he said. "Expand or die" was already his watchword.

The deal done, Murdoch began haring across the continent to Perth every Friday, bucketing around in a DC-3 or DC-4, tumbling off the flight and driving straight into the *Sunday Times* office to tear up the front page and many others besides. He personally licked and kicked the paper into the shape he wanted. He did so briskly and without sentimentality, firing all those whom he considered deadwood and importing subeditors and reporters from Adelaide. The paper at once became more sensational, and its sales increased.

After Perth, Murdoch marched forth to other properties: little papers in out-of-the-way towns — Darwin, in the Northern Territory; Alice Springs, in the desert heart of Australia; and Mount Isa, a mining center in Queensland, where he loved to play two-up, the working-class gambling game in which coins are spun in the air. "You'd get a couple of hundred people shouting and they could build up a terrific atmosphere," he recalled. "The real game is the gamble on knowing when to stop."

AMERICA

By now the shadow of America was beginning to loom over Murdoch, as it did over the world as never before, not only because of its military and economic might, but also because of television. Murdoch has always had a flair for spotting trends. Early on, he understood the potency of the combination of America and the box. "In the 1950s you had to be in TV," he said later. And to be in TV you had to be into America.

By the end of the 1950s he was visiting the States regularly, particularly after he decided that News Ltd. had to break into television. He immediately loved the country, especially New York. The America that Murdoch found, and began in his guts to understand, was the America that came over the next forty years to dominate the world.

The 1950s were the cradle of the American television revolution, which was to force fantastic social change throughout the industrialized world. Regular commercial color television started in the U.S. In 1950, the centenary of the first telegraph cable across the English

Channel, France and Britain were linked by TV for the first time. RCA developed the Vidicon, which was more adaptable, more sensitive and cheaper than traditional TV cameras. The first high-definition video recording on magnetic tape was made by Bing Crosby Enterprises in the U.S. Wide-screen movies were introduced by Cinerama. Twenty-one European countries agreed to share VHF waves, thus providing a real alternative to congested medium wavelengths. The first pocket-sized transistor radio was made in Japan by Sony.

Australia was several years behind America in the development of television. There was no television in Adelaide until 1957, though both Sydney and Melbourne already had three stations, two commercial and one run by the Australian Broadcasting Commission. The commercial companies were run by the two most powerful newspaper families: the Fairfaxes controlled Channel 7 and the Packers Channel 9 in Sydney. In Melbourne, the Herald and Weekly Times group ran Channel 7 and David Syme and Company, the publisher of the *Age*, was a partner in Channel 9. These four stations had already created two mini-networks. Now the government planned to grant licenses in both Adelaide and Brisbane. At first it seemed likely that each town would get only one license.

Murdoch presented himself as the champion of monopoly, arguing against competition in Adelaide television. He told the Australian Broadcasting Control Board that the losses caused by competition would be enormous. But his appeal was rejected, and the government awarded two licenses each in both Brisbane and Adelaide. In Adelaide, the group sponsored by the *Advertiser* was given Channel 7, and Murdoch's group, Southern Television Corporation, was granted Channel 9. Determined to get on the air first, Murdoch rushed off to America with Ron Boland, the editor of the *Sunday Mail* in Adelaide.

They started on the West Coast, and spent time at studios in Los Angeles, on the lookout for programs they could afford for the new station. In Las Vegas they sampled everything that the desert city had to offer. Murdoch plunged on to the tables. "I always used to try and get the money off him to stop him," Boland said later. Wherever they went, Murdoch had Boland collect things like magazine racks, for ideas to exploit back home. There was a lot to grab hold of. So much was changing in America.

Murdoch developed a number of contacts at the American television networks in Los Angeles and New York, the most important of whom was Leonard Goldenson of the American Broadcasting Corporation. Goldenson had come to television through Paramount Pictures. In 1951 he had bought the American Broadcasting Company for $24.5 million. For the next twenty-five years he struggled to bring ABC up to a par with the two other national networks, NBC and CBS.

Of Murdoch's first trip to New York, Goldenson said later, "Fortunately he happened to come to see ABC first. I was very impressed with him from the start." He invited the young Australian to lunch at Sardi's and was so taken by his drive that he asked to buy a share of News Ltd. Murdoch agreed to let ABC have 6 percent.

From the start Goldenson had felt that television could and would become a worldwide medium, so he set out to acquire foreign television stations as partners. This was before the development of satellite communications; he envisaged several international networks linked by cable.

Murdoch already had similar ambitions and wrote later that Goldenson was "in many ways a role-model, though we came from very different backgrounds." He thought Goldenson was twenty years ahead of his time. "Leonard's success was always an inspiration and encouragement. He proved you *can* buck the odds."

Murdoch wanted to start a weekly television magazine in Australia, and for that deemed it essential to visit the offices of the American model, *TV Guide*. He and Boland rented a car in New York and drove down to Philadelphia, where *TV Guide* had been published by Walter Annenberg since 1953. He found he was not the only visitor trying to understand and exploit the phenomenon of *TV Guide:* "They had all these boring foreigners coming to see how to copy them," he later recalled. Few of them were as well equipped as Murdoch to duplicate Annenberg's success. But in those days his ambitions were limited. "It never occurred to me then that I would ever be starting anything in America," he said later. "The thing was to get out of Adelaide. Into Sydney, Melbourne."

Back in Adelaide, he dashed around imparting what he had learned, bouncing ideas, barking orders. He started an Australian version of *TV Guide,* but his main energies went into getting Southern Television off the ground. The man he chose to set up the new station was Bill Davies, who had until then been running a commercial radio station, 5KA. Davies was a British émigré; he had been a police prosecutor for South Australia and then won a talent contest to be a radio announcer. He had a fine voice and a stentorian presence to match, and was known affectionately to some as "Bullshit Bill."

Murdoch gave Southern TV an office at the *News.* His instruction was simple: beat Channel 7 onto the air. They succeeded.

The station made a splash. Although Murdoch, typically, ran it as cheaply as possible, at one time it boasted a ballet and an orchestra. The emphasis, however, was on stunts and personalities. The station broadcast live breakfast television, live children's programs and a magazine called "Adelaide Tonight." Southern TV liked to think of itself as the little guy, battling the might of Channel 7 and its *Advertiser* backers, a self-image that Murdoch has always favored. The station began to make a great deal of money—enough to enable Murdoch to escape Adelaide.

SYDNEY

Sydney in the 1960s was thriving, expanding, pushing itself to become one of the great cities in the English-speaking world. It was here that the Rupert Murdoch whom the world came later to know was truly formed. In Sydney, he began to put together the foundations of a publishing company which would have been noticed far earlier had it been based in New York, a company that owned newspapers, books, printing, newsprint and television. He did it by competing harder and more fiercely than anyone else. It was at this time, too, that he honed his instinct for the mass market.

Sydney journalism has always been one of the fiercest of newspaper battlegrounds. When Murdoch entered it in the late 1950s, it was dominated, as it had been for most of the century, by three groups. The Fairfax and Packer families still ran the two largest. The third, much smaller, group was owned by Ezra Norton, the owner of the *Daily Mirror* and *Sunday Mirror.* Norton's father had given him astringent advice to pour "a bucket of shit" over people who showed signs of being uppity. His papers had faithfully done so. In 1958 Fairfax bought Norton's papers, the evening tabloid *Mirror* and its Sunday sibling, largely to keep them out of the hands of the Melbourne Herald group, which had become even more expansionist since the death of Keith Murdoch.

Knowing that the Sydney moguls were determined to defeat trespassers, Murdoch approached the city covertly. He had a Sydney businessman, John Glass, make an exceedingly good offer for a company called Cumberland Newspapers, which distributed some 400,000 suburban papers a week. Murdoch's identity as the real purchaser was revealed only after the deal was signed.

But that was small beer. What Murdoch wanted was a full-scale Sydney paper. In 1960 he got it when Rupert "Rags" Henderson, managing director of Fairfax, decided to sell him the Mirror papers.

The Fairfax group made a capital gain of some £500,000 from the sale of the *Mirror,* but Murdoch knew that he had a steal: "I was amazed they agreed," he recalled later. He paid only £600,000 down and another £1.3 million over six years. "They were pretty sure that I'd never make the payoffs, that I'd collapse," he said. He knew he would not. At a bargain price, he had acquired printing plants in Sydney, Brisbane and Melbourne. On top of that, he had a Sydney Sunday paper and a daily evening paper that he was determined to make the best-selling evening tabloid in Australia. It was reported that he danced a jig when the final documents had been signed and that he called his friends in triumph.

Soon after he moved to Sydney, Murdoch decided to fire Rohan Rivett from editorship of the Adelaide *News*. He sent him a curt letter ordering him to leave the office that very day. This came at the end of a long and exhausting trial in which the *News* had been accused of seditious libel by the South Australian government. Now that he was mostly in Sydney, Murdoch no longer wanted an independent-minded editor in Adelaide. He said later, "It became quite clear that what would be a reasonable partnership if I was there was not going to work in my absence." So I decided it was time we parted company. Some people wondered why I hadn't done it before. But I liked Rohan. He was strange and egocentric, but a good, well-intentioned man." Nan Rivett said that although the break was inevitable, Rivett was very upset, and disillusioned by Murdoch.

Murdoch replaced his old friend with Ron Boland, who had been editor of the *Sunday Mail* and who was much more of a nuts-and-bolts journalist. Under Boland, the *News* became less of a crusading newspaper. There were more cats up trees in Adelaide and fewer uprisings in Ankara. Murdoch had had enough of advocacy journalism. He was expanding his empire and was more interested in cash than in confrontation, in profits than in political positions. He wanted editors who were safe rather than scintillating, whom he could rely upon however far away he might be. From now on that would almost always be so.

❖ ❖ ❖

The *Mirror* building was a former chocolate factory on the corner of Holt and Kippax streets, in Surry Hills, an area of old residences and decaying small factories in inner Sydney. Murdoch knocked down walls and made a large office, which he hung with the Australian paintings he was collecting. Most of the journalists adored Murdoch and his contagious energy.

For a short time, he tried to take the *Sunday Mirror* slightly up-market, but the paper did not gain circulation. With losses mounting, Murdoch began to suggest to his editor that some "cheesecake" might not be amiss. The editor disagreed and left, and Murdoch brought the Sunday paper downmarket again.

One of the perks of owning the *Mirror* was that Murdoch now had an office and a man in New York, a base for his frequent visits. In 1960 he and his New York correspondent, Zell Rabin, whom he would hire to edit both the *Sunday* and the *Daily Mirror*, made a trip to Cuba. Murdoch was impressed with Fidel Castro. He wrote a rather starry-eyed article arguing that the United States must reverse its opposition to Cuba—the future of Latin America was at stake.

Back home, a camaraderie developed among the staff, who found Murdoch alternately (and unpredictably) genial and irritable. "You could never get close to him on editorial matters; he was only interested in circulation," said Betty Riddell, a distinguished journalist who had covered the Normandy landings and was now one of the paper's columnists. "But he was a lot of fun a lot of the time."

"All the young reporters thought it was terrific to have a young proprietor," said Doug Flaherty, another veteran of the *Mirror* newsroom. "He brushed aside the old public-service attitude of promotion by death, and moved up people he wanted. We all benefited from it."

Murdoch's personal prejudices were developing also; he ordered the subeditors not to wear colored shirts and especially not suede shoes. He thought only "homos" (as he called them) wore suede shoes. He also disapproved of adultery, dirty jokes and women in trousers.

The day started early, as the *Mirror* was an evening paper. Rabin often shaved in the office, which Murdoch thought rather disagreeable. After the first edition was printed, bundled and trucked over the city, there was time for the journalists to relax, call their bookmakers or brokers, and fiddle expense reports, which they called "swindle sheets." These infuriated Murdoch, who believed that the hacks were robbing him—as undoubtedly they were. One payday morning he grabbed a bundle of expense reports, stormed into the newsroom, climbed onto a desk and angrily tore them into confetti. This had a salutary effect—for a week or two. More often, when Murdoch was in a good mood, Friday evenings would end with the boss taking part in heated two-up games in the newsroom. He always needed to win.

The old "larrikin" (hoodlum) spirit of newspaper brawls which had prevailed at the end of the last century in Sydney returned to the city in the 1960s. The Fairfax papers offered a £5,000 guessing contest; Packer raised the ante to £10,000, and each of them promoted these games on their television stations. Murdoch doubled the odds and offered a game of £20,000, and then Packer and Fairfax joined forces and offered a joint game worth £50,000. The prizes were cars, then swimming pools, then tracts of land, then houses. The competition was probably the toughest in the world.

Murdoch was determined to see the *Mirror*'s circulation overtake the *Sun*'s. The *Sunday Mirror* became a byword for titillation, sensationalism and vulgarity. Even Sydney's hardened readers were surprised by the huge headlines, deep cleavages and wide smiles. The billboards of the time give the flavor: "WHIPPING FOR HUSBAND—Wife's Rage"; "TENNIS STAR SHOCKS PRIEST"; "GIRL 13 RAPED 100 YARDS FROM HOME"; "GANG RAPES GIRL 10"; "WHY MY SON IS A KILLER—Mother's Story"; "PROWLER STRIPS WOMAN NAKED"; "BANNED SEX BOOKS, Free for Some"; "LASH FOR 3 RAPISTS, Judge's Sentence"; NUDE TOP IN BUS. SYDNEY SHOCK. PICTURE"; "SEX OPERATION OR GAOL—Judge's Order"; "PROWLER STRIKES AGAIN—Woman Attacked." And much more besides.

Murdoch did not invent or impose this sort of journalism; it had always come naturally to Sydney. One of the greatest exponents of it, Steve Dunleavy, had been an ace reporter on the *Mirror* before Murdoch acquired it. Journalist clichés were made for Dunleavy, the epitome of the bad boy on the news desk, the assiduously smiling picture snatcher, the imaginative inventor of the quotable quote. Dunleavy was a good-looking, hard-drinking, womanizing, roustabout swashbuckler with an astounding gift for turning dross into lively cliché, drear facts into purpled prose. To some he personified the underside of Murdoch's operation, if not of Murdoch's own personality. "Mad Dog and Mogul," Dunleavy and Murdoch have been called.

"The Sydney competition was so fierce that reporters would do anything to get a story—literally anything," said Dunleavy later. "I lost count of the number of times I posed as a cop, a public servant or a funeral director."

The editors of the *Sun* and the *Mirror* did everything to "spoil" each other's stories in the next edition. They reveled in denouncing each other's credibility. They mocked each other's claims to have more readers. They scorned each other's posters and headlines. (There was much to scorn, for both were often misleading.)

There was also cruelty. There was one series on sexual antics in a Sydney school, which led to such headlines as "WE HAVE SCHOOLGIRL'S ORGY DIARY." The *Mirror* then reported that one schoolboy had been suspended. Soon afterward the boy was found hanging from a clothesline, but the *Mirror* did not report that. The girl who wrote the diary was found to be a virgin; her diary was all hallucination. It was the *Mirror* which had driven the boy to suicide. Years later, Richard Neville, a leading 1960s counterculture journalist, questioned Murdoch about the story. "Haven't you ever made a mistake?" asked Murdoch.

Some brakes were applied, sometimes. Murdoch had brought in his father's friend and employee Douglas Brass as editorial director of News Ltd. Brass, who had known Murdoch since he was a boy, was a former war correspondent and latterly chief of News' London bureau. Some said that Brass was the conscience of the outfit, but Murdoch was keener on competition than conscience. He both supported and frustrated Brass, a technique he has always employed with executives, making them happy one moment, despairing the next, bypassing them when disagreement was in the air.

"I saw and still see myself as a friend of Rupert's," said Douglas Brass. "He is warmhearted and generous, hyperactive and adventurous, and he has a superb mind. But of course he can be utterly ruthless and, I'm afraid, will tread people down when they get in his way."

Brass felt that Murdoch was not interested in money as such. "I'm not saying he didn't enjoy power. Who doesn't! But his father wielded it in a much more gentlemanly fashion."

Murdoch was always searching for promotions to boost sales. One idea was to serialize new books which were getting a lot of publicity anyway. Morris West's *The Devil's Advocate* was a complicated work, and Betty Riddell's task was to pare it without loss of plot or characters. "I reported to Murdoch I had solved the problem by cutting out the religion and the profundity, while leaving in the sex. 'Good,' he said."

Murdoch brought Graham King over from Southern Television in Adelaide, where he had become known as "the Prince of Promotion." King came up with the idea of celebrating the *Mirror*'s silver anniversary. Everything was silver: silver double-decker buses in Sydney, silver Rolls-Royces for winners of silver fox furs. "Everyone thought the idea was boring except for Rupert," said King. "He got on one silver bus and threw silver balloons at the crowd. It was a great success."

While Murdoch was developing and promoting the *Mirror*, his real ambition was to get into Sydney television. His station in Adelaide was already making good money; it showed profits of some 40 percent on paid capital in its second and third years of operation. As elsewhere, Australian commercial television was "a license to print money."

In 1962 he failed to gain a new TV license for metropolitan Sydney. So he tried to come into Sydney television on a curve—from the suburbs, as he had with newspapers. He went sixty miles south to the steel and coal-mining town of Wollongong and bought himself a share of an ailing station, Channel WIN 4. A whole swath of southern Sydney could, in theory, pick up WIN 4—but only if they adjusted their aerials. The station was on its knees because both Packer and Fairfax had forbidden their American distributors to sell to it any of the programming supplied to them, on pain of losing their business. Packer had been particularly ruthless.

Murdoch bought 320,000 Wollongong shares for £160,000. The solution, he understood by now, was programming. He called his friend Leonard Goldenson at ABC in New York and flew straight over. Packer realized what he was up to and flew after him, but too late. At that time there was a gentleman's agreement among Australian television companies that no one paid more than $6,000 for an hour. Murdoch told ABC to tear the agreement up.

Harry Plitt, who ran ABC's worldwide syndication, said that if he did that, he would never be able to sell another show in Australia. So Murdoch agreed to pay £1 million for everything that ABC produced or distributed for the next five years.

The challenge was immediately successful. Sir Frank Packer chose not to fight. Despite their personal antipathy, he offered Murdoch a quarter of the stock of his Television Corporation and two seats on the board. In return Murdoch would share his newly acquired American programs. Murdoch leapt at the chance. With this one bound he had broken the Fairfax-Packer monopoly of Sydney television. The episode confirmed to him that programming, which later came to be known as "software," was paramount. Ever since, he has been putting together a software empire to compete with the biggest European and American companies around the world.

* * *

In his ambition to grow, Murdoch had now taken on a financial adviser who was to remain with him for decades. Mervyn Rich was as solid as he looked, and talked as little as a clam in a cloister. He knew all about feeding the maw of the entertainment industry, coming to Murdoch from Hoyt theaters, the biggest cinema chain in Australia.

Rich was hired as News' financial controller, but quickly became Murdoch's business mentor and remained precisely that for more than twenty years. One of the key management devices he introduced was the weekly "Blue Book." Most media companies in Australia had only a monthly reporting system, so problems took two months to fix. At News from now on, every part of the company had to report its figures to Kippax Street every week, so that Rich and Murdoch could immediately see where any problems—in sales, costs, profits, circulation, advertising—were developing. "The crucial thing was having someone who could read and understand what the figures were telling you," said Rich. "Rupert and I both could. Rupert liked them very much because they were something he could have on his desk and read when he had the time, and circle something that hit him." These weekly reports still come to Murdoch from all over the world today.

Rich's second major contribution was to enhance and institutionalize Murdoch's relations with his bankers, particularly the Commonwealth Bank of Australia. "We always had very good dealings with them, and always kept our word to them," said Rich. "We always kept them informed."

Murdoch's first flirtations with the world beyond Australia were, sensibly enough, in the Pacific. In 1963, he bought a 28 percent share in a Hong Kong magazine publisher, Asia Magazines Ltd. He took only moments to consider and conclude the deal.

The next stop was New Zealand, where Roy Thomson, the Canadian press baron, was seeking to buy the *Dominion,* Wellington's major paper. The New Zealand government was nervous of any foreign owner, but in March 1964 Murdoch snatched it from the much larger and more prestigious Thomson group, quite a coup at that time.

CANBERRA

On July 14, 1964, Rupert Murdoch celebrated his finest hour to date. Off a secondhand press in Canberra, the nation's capital, rolled the first newspaper he had actually created. The *Australian* was a broadsheet and its declared purpose was "to report the nation to Canberra and Canberra to the nation." It was also the continent's first national daily and, as such, it was more than just a paper. It had a symbolic, emotional resonance. It was also a serious paper ("unpopular" rather than "popular" in Murdoch's parlance), and it remained so, losing money for Murdoch for many years to come. The courageous venture made Murdoch much loved, at the time, especially by Australian journalists, though many later came to dislike him.

Canberra was then a small town built specifically for government, a pretty, cardboard capital, a place without much life or soul. The only paper, the Canberra *Times,* was a gentle, sleepy affair owned and run by Arthur Shakespeare and his family. Advertising in Canberra was a rich seam, and the paper was a little gold mine, earning some £80,000 profit per year before tax by the end of the 1950s.

To Murdoch the Canberra *Times* was not an attractive family affair, but "a tiny little very underdeveloped rag." He said that his father had always wanted to buy it "and make it an important paper and maybe some sort of national," but he knew the Shakespeares would not sell it. In early 1964 he slipped quietly into town. He bought up a giveaway paper, the *Territorian,* which had been started by Ken Cowley, a former compositor on the Canberra *Times,* who stayed on to work for him. He also purchased a piece of land just down the street from the *Times.* When Parliament opened in February that year, Arthur Shakespeare and Murdoch met at a party. Shakespeare asked the young man what he wanted to do with his new land. "Run you out of business," said Murdoch without a pause.

Shakespeare was no fool; he had already made a secret agreement with Rupert Henderson of Fairfax, by which Fairfax could buy the Canberra *Times* should Shakespeare retire or die, or should any other company take steps to publish a paper in Canberra.

After Murdoch's threat, Shakespeare alerted Henderson. On May 1, 1964, the Canberra *Times* announced that it had been bought by Fairfax, and that the paper would be developed as a national daily. Fairfax at once began to fly high-powered teams of editors and journalists to Canberra. "They turned the paper from a shabby little tabloid, nearly all ads, into a very good-looking broadsheet in a month," said Murdoch. "It was a remarkable achievement. And a pretty rough welcome for us."

That was an understatement. It could have been a devastating blow to Murdoch's ambitions. His new paper would now never get the advertisements in Canberra needed to finance its publication. It looked as if Henderson, a brilliant operator, had taught Murdoch an expensive and humiliating lesson.

Murdoch would not be defeated. He decided that the only thing he could do was to go for the big time and publish a national paper at once, instead of in two years or more. "We never thought of pulling the plug. We just said, 'Well, we'll have to go national right away.' "

As editor Murdoch had chosen Max Newton, a legend among Australian journalists, described in one profile as "a man who rolled dice with governments and redirected the careers of Prime Ministers." For twenty-five years he flashed in and out of Murdoch's galaxy, a troublesome, brilliant, neurotic, burning comet.

Newton was the son of a lead burner in a sulfuric acid factory in Perth. He won a scholarship to Perth Modern School, and later, despite drinking, another to Clare College, Cambridge, where he became friends with a young American student, Norman Podhoretz, later the editor of *Commentary*.

Back in Australia Newton, a manic-depressive, held various unsatisfactory jobs before becoming political correspondent on the Sydney *Morning Herald* and then editor of the *Financial Review*. Early in 1964, he went to see Murdoch, who offered him the editorship of his new Canberra paper. Newton bounced into Kippax Street, where the paper was being devised, and then on to Canberra, in great spirits.

When the Canberra *Times* and Fairfax announced their alliance against Murdoch, Newton was convinced the game was up. But, he wrote later in the *Australian*, "in those terrible hours and days, when we realized our predicament, Rupert showed some of the steel, the gambler's recklessness and the foresight that have since grown to such immense maturity on the world stage."

Together they toured the country to find advertisers, and went to the Commonwealth Bank for further backing. The chairman, Warren McDonald, and the managing director, E. B. Richardson, told them, "You can have the money but you must not put the whole group into loss."

In less than four months they got the paper published and distributed across the continent—a remarkable achievement. The first few editions were, as with many newspapers, a mess. But the criticisms were quibbles. Murdoch had created not only a good paper but also an important paper to Australia.

The *Australian* was a fabulous adventure to all those who worked there in the early days. The editorial offices were unfinished when they started; the wind rushed leaves around the desks. It was magnificently exciting, and Murdoch was always at the center of every part of the paper. His energy seemed to *will* the paper into existence, and his courage sustained it.

The pressures of trying to run a national newspaper out of Canberra were immense. Circulation did not hold up as hoped. A total of 250,000 copies were printed at first and large numbers were given away free in the capital, but by November 1964 sales were down to just over 50,000 copies a day.

Losses rose and rose—to A$45,000 a week. Murdoch began to question his choice of editor. Newton was brilliant, but he was also erratic, and, most important, he was not producing the sales.

"Rupert and I drifted apart," said Newton later. "Rupert became more worried about his business." They also had serious political differences. At that time Murdoch supported protectionism, and still had some liberal views. "He was violently opposed to the war in Vietnam, which I thought was a very important thing for Australia," said Newton. "I remember recommending that we support the bombing of Haiphong Harbor. Rupert was appalled. . . . I don't blame him for being frightened, he had bloody good reason to be frightened."

Newton became more and more depressed, Murdoch increasingly worried. The survival of News Ltd. depended on the sales of the Sydney *Mirror*. It was the source which sustained the *Australian* (as, later, the *Sun* and *News of the World* in London were to sustain less popular and less profitable ventures). As the *Australian* continued to drain money, tensions on the paper grew unbearable. In March 1965 Newton resigned, or was asked to do so. He was upset, but later he said that Murdoch "did me a big favor. He sacked me because really I was an impossible bugger, wasn't a team player at all."

Murdoch appointed a new editor, but the paper continued to do so badly that, not for the last time, Murdoch seriously considered closing it. But in the end his fear of defeat was too great and he kept the paper going.

In 1966, he appointed Adrian Deamer assistant managing editor and placed him in charge of producing the paper. Deamer's father, Sidney, had been a distinguished and senior editor of the Melbourne *Herald* in the early 1930s, under Sir Keith. Adrian had inherited his serious aspirations for journalism, and he combined them with a mild manner and a waspish tongue.

By 1967, the circulation of the *Australian* had risen to a high point of about 75,000, but only 3,800 of these sales were in Canberra. Murdoch decided to move most of the editorial staff to Sydney.

Murdoch said later that the *Australian* was "an idealistic effort. You've got to look at the Melbourne *Age* and the Sydney *Morning Herald* and all those papers at the time we did it. They were being ground out by managers. Very poor papers. It was a way to open it up, have a national debate." He hoped that the *Australian* would give him a seat at the debating table, which it did. He deserved that reward. Merely by coming into being, the *Australian* had an important impact on Australia. It attempted to conquer "the tyranny of distance" which dominated Australian life in so many ways.

The *Australian* tried to give Australia a sense of nationhood. Even the Sydney *Morning Herald,* one of its greatest rivals, subsequently acknowledged that "the launch of the *Australian* was the most significant event in post-war Australian journalism. It was a force in opening up Australian society and preparing the ground for great changes in Australia after 1972." That force came from Murdoch.

CAVAN

As he established himself as a national force in Australia, Murdoch's life was changing. He was spending less and less time with Pat and their daughter, Prudence. They had remained in Sydney when he was starting the *Australian* in Canberra. When he was not building his empire—which took most of his time—he preferred to play with others. Later he said of his first marriage, "I was probably too young and married on the run. I was totally involved in the business—probably very inconsiderate. One grew apart, and outgrew, I think."

He had in those days a splendid wooden ketch named *Ilina,* which he used to sail with friends and courtiers. He competed in the Sydney-Hobart race on several occasions. There was a certain element of abandon in his yachting: *Ilina* once went aground on a reef off the Queensland coast and was stuck for two days. One journalist remembers Murdoch declaring, with characteristic bravado, "I bet, if I was going to be shot at dawn, I could get out of it." He also went horse racing, he took hair-raising flights in small planes all over the country, he went fly-fishing in the Snowy Mountains and he spent a lot of time with the boys.

Then he fell in love with an exquisite-looking young cadet (apprentice) reporter on the *Daily Mirror.* She was similar to Pat only in that she too came from a far poorer background than Murdoch. She had had to fight.

Anna Torv was the child of an Estonian father and a Scottish mother. Just before the Second World War, Jakub Torv left Estonia for Britain, where he served in the merchant marine. He married a Scottish girl, and together they ran a dry-cleaning shop in Glasgow. Anna, their eldest child, was born in 1944. In the early 1950s, they emigrated to Australia.

Life was hard for Anna's parents in Sydney too. They ran a picnic park which went bankrupt; they moved to a dreary high rise in Blacktown, a poor suburb in Sydney's outer west. Anna's mother left home, and she became surrogate mother to her two brothers and sister. "That's why I'm so bossy, because I had to do it from an early age," she has said. They had no money and Anna learned to slit open toothpaste tubes to avoid waste. They were Catholic, and Anna went to a school run by the Sisters of Mercy; she worked in a department store to augment the family income.

She left school at sixteen. She wanted to be an actress or a journalist, but her first job was in a suburban crematorium. Knowing no journalists, she could see no way of getting a cadetship on a paper. But she was lucky, or determined: "I decided that I would take any job in newspapers. I was seventeen. I got a call eventually and I became a clerk in the finance department at the *Mirror.* . . . The job paid seven dollars. So I made it happen."

Once at the *Mirror,* it was not hard for her to get to know the journalists, for she was both beautiful and ambitious. Douglas Brass, the editorial director of News Ltd., took her under his wing. Anna, says Blanche d'Alpuget, another cadet journalist and later a novelist, was determined to do well. Blanche introduced her to rich "yachties" (eligible yachtsmen), and attempted to wean her from her strict Catholicism.

With help from Brass and others, Anna became editor of the cadet newspaper and decided to interview the boss, Rupert Murdoch. He said later, "I thought she was a very pretty girl. Her writing skills were not going through my mind." She said later that she found him very attractive from the start: "He was like a whirlwind coming into the room. It was very seductive."

The parting and the divorce from Pat were unhappy, especially for their daughter, Prudence. Murdoch won custody of Prudence, who then went to London with him and Anna. When she grew up, she made London her home. Pat married a man who owned a chain of hairdressing shops and went to live in Spain, but that marriage broke up and she moved back to Adelaide, where Murdoch helped support her.

Murdoch and Anna married in April 1967. They spent part of their honeymoon in New York, where Murdoch rushed around seeing Leonard Goldenson of ABC and other television warriors. Like Rupert, she loved New York. It was a city bursting with the turbulence of the sixties, and to any young foreigner involved in communications it was clearly the cultural and technological center of the Western world.

During the decade, the ghostly glow of television spread, and Marshall McLuhan, almost alone, understood that it was the beginning of the most powerful revolution to hit Western man. The new media, he argued, were refashioning the world without boundaries. "Time has ceased, space has vanished. We now live in a global village, a simultaneous happening," he wrote in *Understanding Media*. This was a fantastic concept, but one which Murdoch was beginning to grasp.

In his own village, Murdoch had become a landowner. In the mid-1960s he had bought Cavan, an old one-story stone house with several thousand acres not far from Canberra. About twenty miles out of the town of Yass on a paved, narrow road winding though the foothills, the

estate sprawled along the banks of the Murrumbidgee River. It was a
lovely place.

In the late 1960s and early 1970s there were constant house parties
at Cavan. Murdoch was a generous host. The wine cellar was excellent,
and though by the late 1960s he rarely drank much, this did not deter
his journalist guests. He loved to play the country squire. Betty Riddell
recalled that once when she was staying there, Murdoch woke her up
at 7:00 A.M. and walked her all over the paddocks. There was frost on
the ground and he pointed out to her all the things he was going to
do with his land—a pool there, horses yonder. That same weekend
a News executive came down and Rupert insisted that they play tennis together. The man had no shoes, but did not dare to disobey the
command. Murdoch always played tennis as if the future of the world
hung on his winning. At the end of a typically aggressive match, the
executive's feet were raw; Riddell thought that Murdoch did not even
notice. Nevertheless, Riddell, in common with most of his journalists,
admired Murdoch. "He was always around, both at the *Mirror* and at
the *Australian*," she said later. "He knew us all, loved us all, and he
took our advice. When he made mistakes, he got rid of them fast. He
could always be talked to and argued with. Now it's all gone. Why?
Power, power, power, not money."

Part II

BREAKING OUT

2

LONDON

The door to Fleet Street opened for Murdoch in fall 1968, when the *News of the World,* one of Britain's longest-established popular newspapers, came into play.

The "News of the Screws," as it is often called, was Britain's most salacious Sunday paper, specializing in randy vicars, homosexual housemasters, threesomes in bed, stolen underpants, misplaced virginities. Although it published articles by politicians of all parties, it combined its interest in sex with devout support of the Conservative Party. It was an institution of a rather British kind, and successful, even though its circulation had fallen from 8.5 million in 1950 to about 6 million in 1968.

It was run on a shoestring, with only a handful of reporters under a Falstaffian editor named Stafford Somerfield. He was regarded as a genuine "Fleet Street character" who loved to pander to all the most chauvinistic of British prejudices. The company had been managed since the 1890s by one family, the Carrs, who were the largest shareholders. Sir Emsley Carr had been editor for fifty years and his son, Sir William, chairman for sixteen years by 1968. Sir William was a powerful man who had a long love affair with alcohol, which he indulged at midday at the Savoy Grill. Although difficult and complex, he was intensely proud of his position and had the capacity of inspiring loyalty among those who knew him well.

In the late 1960s, the assets had trebled, but the profits of the company had fallen, as had the share price. Nonetheless, the Carrs thought that they were impregnable, because they owned 27 percent of the voting shares themselves, while another 25 percent were in the hands of a cousin, Professor Derek Jackson. But in 1968 Jackson decided to sell.

William offered him the market price of twenty-eight shillings a share, but Jackson rejected this with contempt—he wanted twice that. Carr could not afford it. To Carr's horror, Jackson instructed his bank, N. M. Rothschild & Sons, to search for an outside buyer. They found Captain Robert Maxwell, M.C., M.P. No prospect could have been more terrible to the Carrs: Maxwell was a foreigner, a boor and a Labour member of Parliament. And there were other reasons why he aroused mistrust.

Maxwell had been born in Slovakia. After several name changes he became Robert Maxwell and served, with distinction, in the British army against the Germans. His first business coup came in occupied Germany after the war. He acquired a mass of German scientific documents owned by Julius Springer, brought them to Britain and began to sell them, very profitably, to librarians around the world. He then took over the bankrupt book wholesaling firm of Simpkin Marshall. He raised financing for the company, on which he paid interest, and then advanced substantial sums, interest-free, to his other private enterprises. He was effectively using Simpkin Marshall as a bank even though it was insolvent. When a director tried to raise the alarm, Maxwell silenced him with a "gagging writ." Throughout his life he used the law of libel to intimidate critics—unlike Murdoch, who nearly always allowed his critics to say their worst. After four years Simpkin Marshall collapsed, leaving debts, mostly to publishers, of £475,000. Many publishers never forgave Maxwell.

Maxwell renamed his own company Pergamon Press, and built up a successful trade in specialized scientific texts and magazines. He also ventured into the twilight zone behind the Iron Curtain, whence he had emerged before it descended, signing up Russian scientists to produce articles very cheaply, and using East European printing companies at very low contract prices. Having bought cheap, he sold dear. He would establish a near monopoly in a scientific discipline and then sell his works in small numbers at remarkably high prices; all that was required was that every library buy one Pergamon edition.

In 1959 he moved into British politics. He helped establish lotteries which transformed the finances of local Labour parties, and was elected to Parliament as Labour M.P. for Buckingham in 1964. By 1968 he had a reputation for being loud and domineering; he liked to compare himself to Beaverbrook, and played upon his position as an outsider, seeking to disarm criticism by complaining that it was anti-Semitic, which often led people to give him the benefit of the doubt.

On October 16, 1968, Maxwell made an offer of some £26 million. He was in a strong position. Not only had the company been doing badly, but he had already obtained pledges from Derek Jackson for his 25 percent of the voting shares.

Sir William Carr was seriously ill when the bid came in. He sent a message from his sickbed to the boardroom, describing Maxwell's bid as "impudent." He had no faith in Maxwell, either as an individual or as a businessman. The board advised shareholders to do nothing for the time being. But clearly a very serious effort would have to be made to resist Maxwell's money.

Enter Murdoch. As soon as he heard what was happening, the *News of the World* became his new obsession. He flew secretly to London. He and his financial adviser, Lord Catto, a director of the investment bank Morgan Grenfell, decided he should appear as a white knight to help the Carrs against Maxwell. It was quite clear to both of them that Murdoch wanted to control the *News of the World* when all was said and done. But Catto suggested that he be cautious and not frighten Carr. First, he must get Carr to agree to his becoming managing director in order to fend off Maxwell. Once that had been accomplished, he could issue a new block of shares in the name of News Ltd. to override Carr. It was a brilliant, assured and relatively cheap way to break into Fleet Street.

There was no way in which Murdoch could have raised the cash to match Maxwell's original offer, let alone to surpass it. But Catto proposed that some of News Ltd.'s Australian assets be transferred to the News of the World group. In exchange, the News of the World group would issue new stock to News Ltd. Sir William Carr could now call upon some 30 percent of the votes, and with the new ones issued to Murdoch they would be, jointly, unassailable.

Murdoch asked to be joint managing director with Sir William's nephew Clive. Sir William agreed. He had a seven-year contract as chairman and so felt secure. Moreover, he had long known and admired Murdoch's mother, and felt he could rely upon her son. (Not for the last time, affection for the irreproachable Dame Elisabeth swayed people in Murdoch's favor.)

They agreed that enough new shares would be created to give Murdoch 40 percent of the voting stock. Then he and Carr would jointly control over half of the stock. Murdoch also agreed that he would not buy further shares in the company to raise his stake above 40 percent, and that a member of the Carr family would remain chairman to support him in his role of joint managing director with Clive Carr.

By now news of Murdoch's presence in London had leaked. On the afternoon of Thursday, October 24, he gave a press conference to announce that he intended to acquire 40 percent of the News of the World group—he would buy 9 percent on the market and get the rest in exchange for Australian assets. He was asked many questions. Would not the minority shareholders suffer? Would the stock not soon fall well below its present value? Why would he not match Maxwell's offer? Because he did not have enough money, he replied. The man from the *Wall Street Journal* accused him of "watering the stock to swing this deal."

A special shareholders' meeting at which the offers would be voted upon was fixed for January 2, 1969. This turned into an extraordinary gladiatorial encounter, the first of many, between Robert Maxwell and the hitherto unknown young Australian.

The meeting took place at the Connaught Rooms, familiar, slightly déclassé territory for annual shareholders' meetings and chicken banquets.

The room was packed with about five hundred shareholders. They gave Sir William a long ovation when he appeared on the dais. He was clearly very ill. After him, Murdoch spoke briefly, modestly and nervously, stressing that News was a fine organization. He was delighted that Sir William would stay on as chairman.

It was almost like a masquerade, with the old king and his family, the crown prince from a far-off country and the big foreign villain, threatening in an electric blue suit. Maxwell was booed when he stood up. In his booming voice he stressed that his offer was now worth fifty-two shillings per share and that if it were refused—as by now he knew it would be—the shares would be worth only thirty-nine shillings and falling.

Carr replied, "What is money when you can get so much more out of life?" He compelled Maxwell to sit down. Maxwell accused the board of rigging the meeting. The audience needed no cue cards. Shareholders shouted, "Go home!" or "Go back to the Old Vic!"—a reference to Maxwell's theatricality.

Carr and Murdoch won the day overwhelmingly with 299 votes for the issue of the new shares and only 20 against. "The law of the jungle has prevailed," declared Maxwell. Most financial journalists agreed that he had been shabbily treated. But when it later became clear that Maxwell's company Pergamon was worth much less than he had claimed, the Carrs could show that their suspicions of him were justified. However, it was also evident that they could have defeated him without the help of Murdoch. The day after the meeting, Sir William was taken into the hospital for a series of major operations.

It was a bruising battle in which almost everyone had lost something. Maxwell had lost at least £200,000 and a lot of prestige, though he had gained some sympathy. The Carrs had lost some £2 million on paper and, more important, control of their company. The banks had lost, at the least, dignity, if not shareholders' money. Only Murdoch had won—he now had a beachhead in one of the most important publishing centers of the world. For him it was a famous victory.

Rupert Murdoch had no intention of being a mere partner. As soon as he had won the takeover battle, he unbuckled his knight's white armor and revealed a different person. As far as he was concerned it was just a question of getting down to work. But to the Carrs it was an appalling shock.

On the day after the takeover, he swept into the *News of the World* offices on Bouverie Street at 8:00 A.M. and found "cleaning ladies having tea on the chairman's desk." He also insisted that he found the real state of the company to be far worse than the Carrs had revealed. "It could have made us broke," he said later. He therefore had to embark on a radical overhaul. He began to buy more shares. Soon he controlled 49 percent of the stock.

He embarked upon a total transformation of the paper's structure and staff, explaining that this was urgently needed because of the Carrs' old-fashioned, unsuccessful management style. He said that as the new chief executive he had to answer to the shareholders and make sure that the company was properly and profitably run.

In fact, the decline of the paper could not all be blamed on mismanagement by the Carrs. The spread of commercial television was a major cause. A better-educated population and the growth of the middle class was arguably another.

Murdoch began to weed through the staff. Sarah Carr, Sir William's daughter, said, "It was a touch of the Carr brush. Anyone associated with us had to go."

On March 7, Murdoch wrote to Sir William to complain that now that he was out of the hospital, Carr was having too much contact with senior executives: "The plain fact, which I am sure you are as aware of as I am, is that a company of this nature can have only one executive boss." Although many of the executives were Carr's lifelong friends, Murdoch insisted that in the future he must contact them through Murdoch *alone*. He asked Carr to resign from the subsidiary companies in the group. He did not want there to be any confusion about the chain of command, he said.

Twenty-four hours later, Carr was dashed by helicopter from Sussex to London for emergency surgery. A plastic tube in his aorta had ruptured. It was removed, the aorta was sealed, and the blood supply to his legs was redirected through tubes which came down from under his arms.

Next, despite his written promises, and his assurance to the shareholders that Sir William would stay as chairman, Murdoch drove down to Carr's Sussex home, where he was convalescing, and told him that he wanted him to relinquish the job. Carr, too ill to fight, decided reluctantly to accept the ultimatum. He told Somerfield, "I had known our paper for many years as a happy place. It could not be happy if Murdoch and I did not agree. I decided to go." In June 1969, he resigned. At a meeting of the board, Murdoch was elected chairman. The Carrs felt that they had been betrayed. Murdoch had originally agreed that he would not raise his stock above 40 percent, and that a member of the Carr family would remain chairman. It was on this basis that the Carr family had voted its shares at the extraordinary meeting.

The editor of the *News of the World* was tougher than Sir William. Somerfield had been with the paper since the end of the war. Under Sir William he had been allowed to do things his way. Murdoch had no respect for Somerfield—he saw him as a pompous, complacent snob.

Murdoch did not have great sympathy for the idea of editorial independence. "As proprietor I'm the one who in the end is responsible for the success or failure of my papers," he said in 1969.

Since a paper's success or failure depends on its editorial approach, why shouldn't I interfere when I see a way to strengthen its approach? What am I supposed to do, sit idly by and watch a paper go down the drain, simply because I'm not supposed to interfere? Rubbish! That's the reason the *News of the World* started to fade. There was no one there to trim the fat and wrench it out of its editorial complacency.

Murdoch ordered Somerfield to fire some of the paper's columnists and reporters. He chose their successors. He started changing advertising posters that Somerfield had approved and told him not to send correspondents abroad without his agreement. When Somerfield complained, Murdoch said, "I didn't come all the way from Australia not to interfere. You can accept it or quit!"

In summer 1969, when Somerfield was away in Spain on vacation, Murdoch began to make large-scale changes to the layout of the paper. Somerfield rushed back to London and countermanded Murdoch's instructions.

They were, however, more or less united on the first big issue which involved Murdoch in a major controversy in Britain—and helped him to acquire from the satirical magazine *Private Eye* the name "Dirty Digger," which has remained with him since. It was a traditional *News of the World* story.

Christine Keeler was the beautiful call girl whose affairs with both the then secretary of state for war, John Profumo, and a Soviet naval attaché, Eugene Ivanov, in 1962 had seriously embarrassed the government of Harold Macmillan. Profumo lied to the House of Commons in denying the affair, then, when he had to admit it, he resigned.

The *News of the World* had paid Keeler £23,000 for her memoirs at the time of the scandal. For this it had been censured by the Press Council, the semiofficial body which was supposed to monitor newspaper conduct. In the summer of 1969, Keeler hawked around a new version of the story. To boost sales, as he knew it would, Somerfield wanted to run it again. Murdoch was at first concerned. Profumo had spent the last six years working among the poor in the East End of London; he was widely respected for this arduous and sincere penance. Nonetheless, the *News of the World* paid £21,000 for the recycled story.

There was an outcry. Murdoch was quoted as saying, "People can sneer as much as they like, but I'll take the hundred fifty thousand extra copies we're going to sell." This was certainly frank; the memoirs were bought precisely in order to sell newspapers. In one television interview he acknowledged that Profumo could be forgiven, but said that his actions should not be forgotten. His worst moment came when he was interrogated by David Frost for London Weekend Television.

At this stage of his career, Frost had developed the reputation as Britain's foremost television prosecutor. He interviewed his guests before a studio audience, which performed as a de facto jury.

Frost took the high ground and stayed on it. Murdoch tried to say that the articles would concentrate on the parliamentary side of the scandal, the role of the Labour Party and so on. But Frost pointed out that the first week's extract had been mere sexual titillation. Murdoch claimed that there were important new facts in the series—but he could not name them. Worse was to come.

After the commercial break, Frost screened an interview he had filmed earlier with Cardinal Heenan, the country's leading Catholic prelate, who had already made clear his distaste for the series. The cardinal expressed his shock at the *News of the World*'s cynicism and greed, and his concern for "this excellent man" Profumo.

Murdoch said the row had been "whipped up by some members of the Establishment that don't want to be seen with Mr. Profumo anywhere."

After the interview, Frost took the seething Murdoch to join Anna in the hospitality room. He offered them a drink, but Anna snapped at him, "We've had enough of your hospitality." Murdoch left the building vowing that he would buy London Weekend and dispose of Frost.

The incident hurt and angered Murdoch. He felt that he was once more a victim of British hypocrisy, as he had been at Oxford. It colored his whole attitude toward the British, and in particular toward that amorphous and uncertain entity, the British Establishment. Anna Murdoch felt that he had been outrageously abused by Frost. She was finding it hard to make friends in England, a fact which she attributed partly to the nature of the British and partly to the Keeler affair. Both of them began to nurture two seemingly conflicting ambitions—to get out and to get even.

From London they were often able to visit New York. They found it both more exhilarating and more friendly and were determined eventually to move there. But first there was another battle to be won in London.

FLEET STREET

At the end of the sixties, there was probably no British industry so arcanely and badly run as newspaper publishing. Production methods were archaic but the power of the print-union barons over management had grown enormously since Murdoch had last worked in Fleet Street in the early 1950s. Many newspapers were produced either at a loss or with far less profit than would have been possible if reasonable agreements had existed between management and unions. Instead there was a grotesque state of constant war, in which the publishers usually caved in to union demands.

In the *News of the World* building on Bouverie Street, Murdoch found a combination of expensive working practices and ancient machinery. "It was an unbelievable mess. We would have gone broke with all the bits and pieces of rubbish they had," he said later. He was desperate to get the presses and the men working all through the week. That meant buying or starting a daily paper.

The *Sun* was the worthy, left-wing child of Hugh Cudlipp, the chairman of Mirror Newspapers. It had been created in 1964 out of the corpse of the *Daily Herald,* a serious-minded left-wing paper half owned by the Trades Union Congress.

IPC relaunched the *Herald* as the *Sun* in 1964, in the belief that there was a brand-new market of upwardly mobile young people—"the growth generation"—longing to buy a new, more sophisticated popular paper to reflect their values. Apparently, however, they were not.

By 1969, the *Sun*'s circulation had fallen from 1.5 million to 850,000. Together with the *Herald*, it had cost IPC over £12 million, and the board was now free to sell it or close it.

Robert Maxwell made the first offer, but the print unions rejected him. So Murdoch entered the second round of the long contest between the two men.

In the end, he had a bargain. He paid only £50,000 down and further installments of £2,500 a week, up to a minimum of £250,000 that could only rise above that to a maximum of £500,000 if the paper continued to show a profit. Eventually, when he had won a circulation of over 4 million and a far greater readership than that, Murdoch could say that he had gained his readers at only a few pence each. By contrast, in the United States, newspapers have sometimes changed hands for as much as $1,000 a reader. Murdoch felt he was off to the races.

Murdoch needed no market research to tell him what the *Sun* should be: a daily version of the *News of the World*. He considered the *Mirror* the prime example of the "gentrification of the press." Cudlipp had tried to take it upmarket and it now offered serious investigative sections on contemporary political and social issues which Murdoch saw as pretentious. He thought that readers wanted more fun in their tabloid, and that they hated being preached at. The *Mirror* was the soft underbelly of the tabloid market. Murdoch was a true disciple of his father's old guru, Northcliffe, whose motto was "Explain, simplify, clarify!"

The first problem was overstaffing. The unions did agree to some cutbacks.

He insisted the paper had to be a tabloid. As editor he chose Albert "Larry" Lamb. The son of a Yorkshire colliery worker, Lamb considered himself a left-wing, boiler-room journalist.

Murdoch brought over from Australia some of the more hardbitten and experienced tabloid journalists who had made the Sydney *Daily Mirror* a financial if not an intellectual success.

In the last issue of the old broadsheet *Sun,* Murdoch published a signed editorial which promised, "The most important thing to remember is that the new *Sun* will still be a paper that CARES. . . . The new *Sun* will have a conscience. It will never forget its radical traditions. It will be truly independent, but politically mightily aware. . . . It will never, ever sit on fences. It will never, ever be boring."

Right from the start, there was British antagonism toward Murdoch and his *Sun.* The *New Statesman,* the voice of the established Left, referred to it as Murdoch's "shit sheet." When the *Sun* was criticized for having no principles, Murdoch stated what they were. It was opposed to capital punishment, apartheid, racism and the Vietnam War, and it was in favor of the permissive society. Some of these liberal positions were later to be renounced by Murdoch. But there was one attitude of his which remained constant: the *Sun* soon made plain his impatience with the British Establishment.

In January 1970 the paper called for the abolition of the honors system, by which thousands of people are annually awarded various medals or citations for their services to the country or to their profession. Murdoch had started attacking the honors system in the Sydney *Mirror* over a decade before. His theme song was and remained the boast "We are not going to bow to the Establishment in any of its privileged enclaves."

Murdoch was always as lavish on promotion as he was tight on editorial expenditure. He spent almost as much on the *Sun*'s launch as he had on the down payment for the paper—some £50,000. And he kept on spending thereafter. A lot of the *Sun's* success was due to clever promotion.

In January 1970, Murdoch sacked Stafford Somerfield, the editor of the *News of the World.* It was an expensive move, but it was worth it; Murdoch could now control the paper as he wanted. Somerfield was quite pleased too. He missed the good, easy, paternalistic old days of the Carr family in which he had ruled the paper.

Murdoch's politics were in a state of flux or redefinition at this time. He was still somewhere on the Left, but by now not very far off center. On election day, May 17, Murdoch published a front-page editorial which reaffirmed the *Sun's* traditional loyalty: "WHY IT MUST BE LABOUR." Edward Heath, leading the Conservatives, won an easy victory. The *Sun* was generous and used a racing analogy: "Well done, Ted Heath. The British love to see an outsider come surging up to pass the favourite." Murdoch had always liked to be on the same side as the party in government. Since the days of Rohan Rivett in Adelaide, his papers had rarely taken stands on political principle.

By the middle of 1970, the *Sun* was gaining readers in the hundreds of thousands. To begin with, the *Sun* gave more space to most subjects, apart from foreign news, than the *Mirror.* The *Sun* had more pictures, twice as many pinups (mostly clothed), more about TV and radio, more features, more local news, much more sports, even more City news—and many more competitions. "Win a champagne wedding" was a typical *Sun*-style giveaway.

Its extra feature space was filled with titillating articles like "The Affair" and "In Praise of Older Men." Sex was a great sales aid. There were numerous divorce reports, and articles on the pill and on sexual techniques: "HOW GOOD A LOVER ARE YOU?" Page-three girls were introduced to the world, with bras in place, in early 1970. They were known then as Sunbirds. The first bare-breasted pinup on page three was revealed to a breathless world on November 17, 1970. The caption announced: "From time to time some self appointed critic stamps his tiny foot and declares that the *Sun* is obsessed with sex. It is not the

Sun but the critics who are obsessed. The *Sun*, like most of its readers, likes pretty girls."

By the end of 1970, sales of the *Sun* had climbed to 1.7 million, only just behind the *Daily Mail*. Murdoch thought that the first important thing about its success was that it was a tabloid: "The broadsheet is just not part of modern life and the rush and the tubes and the buses. We were right to go for the *Mirror* of ten years ago. People wrote to say that they hadn't a paper they could understand until we came along." The *Mirror*, he said, had "turned their backs on the working class. We came along—brash, young and uninhibited."

Within the industry the *Sun* was named Newspaper of the Year at the beginning of 1971. To meet its challenges, the *Mirror* was forced to abandon its more serious pages. Hugh Cudlipp was bitter. "Someone will always be found to scrape the bottom of the barrel," he said. Many others were shocked by the *Sun's* sexual titillation. Richard Ingrams, editor of the satirical fortnightly paper *Private Eye*, embarked on a long-running campaign against "the Dirty Digger" for his "vandalizing" of the British press.

Murdoch himself complained that there was far more sexual innuendo in the upmarket papers than in the *Sun*, citing as an example an article in the *Observer* about women horse riders and masturbation.

At the same time as the *Sun* was "soaring away," to use its own words, Murdoch was taking his first steps into British television. Commercial television franchises were then awarded every six years by the Independent Television Authority. In 1968 two companies were given the franchise for London: Thames TV was given the weekdays and London Weekend Television (LWT) the weekend from Friday to Sunday night. Thames TV had two main owners. London Weekend's ownership was more dispersed: among the shareholders and leading lights were David Frost and Arnold Weinstock, head of General Electric.

The company had intellectual aspirations but little commercial skill. By 1969 it was losing money heavily. Weinstock sold his 7.5 percent of the voting shares to Murdoch, who thus became a nonexecutive director. True to form, Murdoch reckoned that viewers wanted relaxing weekend entertainment. He saw that the company was undercapitalized and offered to inject £500,000. The Independent Television Authority, alarmed by the thought of page-three girls on LWT, allowed him onto the board on the condition that he would not involve himself in programming. He agreed but, once on the board, found it impossible not to intervene. When he encouraged the board to remove the chief executive and tried to take over the job himself, the Independent Television Authority stopped him. Murdoch was denied the power he wanted and once again blamed the British "Establishment." But overall he had good reason to be delighted with his first two years of battles in Britain.

SYDNEY

Murdoch's empire has always had an odd shape. The nucleus of News Ltd. remained in the South Australian capital of Adelaide, but Sydney was now the real center of the antipodean operations. Murdoch was inevitably spending more time in London, where the real money was being made. Indeed, he often seemed an absentee landlord in Sydney. This is not to say that he left the place alone—he was constantly on the telephone from London, sometimes several times a day, giving orders, cajoling, flattering, seeking information and gossip.

The *Australian* was now quite a fine paper. Adrian Deamer had become editor and the circulation had risen to over 143,000. It was a coherent, national, slightly radical voice, much loved by journalists, and by its readers.

Murdoch said later he thought that Deamer had "great talent, and was a great technical editor. And he brought a lot of young people through." But Murdoch thought his tongue was too fierce, and he was uncomfortable with Deamer's politics. Deamer and his editorial director, Douglas Brass, saw to it that the *Australian* was the first serious broadsheet to demand the withdrawal of Australian troops from Vietnam. Brass wrote an impassioned column on "the shame" of My Lai. Murdoch was still against the war—but he was uneasy at the *Australian's* being seen as a voice of radicalism.

He began to worry that he could not depend on Deamer. He was too strong, too independent. As his empire grew, Murdoch felt increasingly that he needed men on whom he could rely—men whose judgment would not be different from his own. And thus, over time, he came more and more to appoint rather colorless editors who would not disturb the outposts of empire.

In July 1971 he told Deamer he was no longer producing the sort of paper he liked. Perhaps he would like to move to another part of the organization? Deamer replied that he would either edit the *Australian* or nothing. He left.

After Deamer, the *Australian* declined and lurched unsteadily toward the right.

In May 1972 Sydney journalism was subjected to a new upheaval. The Packers decided to divest themselves of the *Daily* and *Sunday Telegraph*, which were losing money—unlike the Packers' television and magazine interests. Murdoch bought the newspapers for the asking price of A$15 million. The purchase brought him Sydney's second morning paper (after the *Herald*) to complement his afternoon *Mirror.*

In December 1972, a national election was called. For the first time the Murdoch press showed its clout, coming out wildly in favor of the opposition Labor Party led by Gough Whitlam, and against the incumbent prime minister, William McMahon. The *Australian* declared that Whitlam's policy proposals were "exciting" and "a radical alternative to the Australia which exists today." Whitlam promised to take Australian troops out of Vietnam, a major issue at the time.

Whitlam won the 1972 election and Murdoch was quoted as claiming that he had "singlehandedly put the present government into office." Subsequently he asserted that he himself had become "far too deeply involved" in the election. "Looking back," he said, "we did some dreadful things to the other side." He also said that the *Daily Telegraph* in particular "went overboard." That had been a Liberal Party paper for a long time. "We all really threw ourselves into the fight, to get a change. It did break twenty years of conservative government. Not a bad thing to do."

TEXAS

In 1973, to Anna's delight, Murdoch made his first major move from Britain across the Atlantic. His first American purchases were three papers in San Antonio—the San Antonio *Express,* the *News,* and their combined Sunday paper.

He had been trying for years to establish a really firm beachhead in America. He did not believe he could have an English-language media empire without a strong presence in the States. Moreover, he and Anna were heartily sick of England. Although the *Sun* had continued to soar in Britain, they had both become increasingly irked by the continued intransigence of the print unions and what they saw as the snobbish hypocrisy of the British Establishment. After the *News of the World* published details about the liaison of a Conservative government minister, Lord Lambton, and a prostitute, the paper and its owner were even more widely censured.

The Lambton fracas coincided with another traumatic event for Anna. Driving her car, she knocked down and killed an old woman. It was an accident and the coroner's court found it to be so, but it was nonetheless shocking and distressing. Anna saw it as part of the misery that seemed always to attend her time in England. She was therefore relieved by the prospect of Rupert expanding into, and perhaps moving to, the New World.

Murdoch chose San Antonio only because it had properties available at a time when he had an ability—backed by the cash flow of the *Sun* and the *News of the World*—to buy. He had looked at a pair of free newspapers in California, at the Washington *Star*, at *Look* magazine and at other properties. None had seemed right. San Antonio was in fact an appropriate place for him to start in America, a Sunbelt town with enough elements of the Australian outback for him to find things familiar—it was raw, raunchy and growing fast. It was more advanced than Perth had been when he first descended on the *Sunday Times* back in the 1950s, but it had a similar frontier feel about it.

The San Antonio papers in which he was interested were the property of Harte-Hanks Newspapers. The morning *Express* had sales of about 80,000, the evening *News* sold about 63,000 and their joint Sunday paper sold some 135,000. The major competition for the *News* was the evening *Light,* a fairly lurid sheet which was owned by the Hearst Corporation and had a daily sale of about 135,000. So once again, Murdoch was doing what he liked and what was becoming a pattern: swooping on a town and buying the weaker paper in order to set it against the leader.

He paid $19.7 million for the three papers. This represented a multiple of fifteen times earnings, which was high, particularly given the amount he would have to borrow. On the other hand, the purchase gave him a foothold in the U.S., and any profits could be set against the losses he expected to incur on starting another paper.

Murdoch did to the papers what he almost always tried to do—he livened them up or dragged them down, depending on the viewpoint of the observer. He made them more sensational, more trivial, more readable, more commercial. He also backed them with his customary massive burst of promotion—television commercials and contests for the readers. Among the favored headlines of the new regime were "ARMIES OF INSECTS MARCHING ON SA," "UNCLE TORTURES PETS WITH HOT FORK," "HANDLESS BODY FOUND" and "ARMY TO POISON 350 PUPPIES." The most famous of all, which passed quickly into journalistic legend, was "KILLER BEES MOVE NORTH," written to describe an imminent invasion of monstrous bees flying up from Latin America to assault the good citizens of the United States.

Murdoch was not immediately successful. Despite all the hoopla, he managed, over two years, to lift the circulation of the *News* by some 12,000 only, to 76,000. American readers did not respond to his formula with quite the same enthusiasm as the British had done. Still, by 1983 he was well ahead of the Hearst *Light*, and the *News* and *Express* were set to earn over $5 million profit.

While he took over and remolded the San Antonio papers, Murdoch also prepared to launch his own national paper in the U.S.A. The *National Star* was a supermarket tabloid modeled deliberately on the *National Enquirer.*

The *Enquirer,* an American institution, was the creation of a former CIA psychological warfare officer, Generoso (Gene) Pope. Throughout the 1950s and 1960s, the *Enquirer* had sold over 4 million copies a week on a lurid, not to say fantastical, mix of crime, science fiction and the doings of Hollywood stars. For a time Murdoch had toyed with the idea of buying the *Enquirer* itself, but Pope refused to sell it for a price Murdoch considered reasonable.

Murdoch threw himself into the *National Star* with gusto. He was to be seen shifting desks, pasting pages on mock-ups and rewriting stories. He imported the legendary Steve Dunleavy from Sydney and, for a time, Larry Lamb from the *Sun,* as well as Graham King to mastermind promotion.

During the prelaunch publicity Murdoch abused and criticized mainstream American journalism, claiming that it was boring and complacent and that his new paper would be a fresh new *Time* or *Newsweek.* He was playing his favorite tune—that he was not an elitist snob. He would give the people what they wanted. "We are not interested in the publishing judgments of Madison Avenue or professors of journalism," he declared.

The first issue of the *National Star* carried the story "THOUSANDS KNEEL TO MIRACLE BOY MICHAEL," but the paper's launch was less than miraculous. Despite a massive budget for television advertising, Murdoch was unable to get space in supermarkets, and the *National Star* barely limped along. Murdoch himself was effectively the editor for the first few months; other editors came and went as if through revolving doors.

Murdoch had not realized that the *Enquirer's* audience had changed over the last twenty years—it had become more middle-class, and the *Enquirer* had moved (slightly) away from sagas of violent crime and sexual perversion and toward Hollywood gossip, diets and sexual self-help tips.

Graham King, his promotions wizard in both Australia and Britain, helped organize a relaunch. He worked with Marty Singerman, who had come from Triangle, which published *TV Guide.* Singerman ingratiated the paper with all the wholesalers, town by town, state by state. In 1976 the "National" was dropped from the title and the paper was given the subtitle "The American Women's Weekly." Most of its readers were indeed working-class women, and Murdoch, like the *Enquirer,* fed them a diet of fantasy about space, their weight and looks, Hollywood and their sex lives. Eventually the paper began to prosper; indeed, it became one of the most profitable parts of his empire—a cash cow as invaluable as the *Sun* in London. By the early 1980s it had a circulation of 4 million, 1 million less than the *Enquirer,* and was making about $12 million a year. But before that Murdoch had already established himself as the publisher of one of the oldest newspapers in America, the New York *Post.*

3

AMERICA

Conversation and communication across the United States and across other continents began in 1844 after Samuel Finley Breese Morse invented the telegraph, sending the message "What hath God wrought?" from Washington to Baltimore. He united the United States, shrank the old world and set the stage for the new one.

It was probably the telegraph which first made information into a commodity, something that could be bought and sold irrespective of its uses or meaning. Within four years of Morse opening the first telegraph line, the Associated Press was founded and news from everywhere, about anything and nothing, began to crisscross and entertain every state. People began to feel the first twinges of what became a serious disease in the twentieth century: a glut of information about crimes, wars, disasters and misdemeanors far afield that rendered them both horrified and powerless.

The American mass media as we now know them began in the first half of the nineteenth century in New York with the fierce competition among James Gordon Bennett's *Herald*, Horace Greeley's *Tribune*, Henry Raymond's *Times* and Ben Day's *Sun*. By the end of the century, mass production and mass marketing of all sorts of goods became the norm, and with them came a vast increase in advertising. In the early part of the twentieth century, almost all American city newspapers waged brutal wars with one another. The battles, vicious and ill tempered, pandered to the excitability and anxieties of a volatile immigrant society. William Randolph Hearst, Joseph Pulitzer and Colonel Robert McCormick were true barons who ran their papers as personal fiefdoms and propaganda sheets. They gave no quarter and they played by their own rules.

Bennett and Greeley in New York, McCormick in Chicago, and Hearst, whose kingdom had spread all over the nation, had personal visions which they wished to impose on the world. They talked about the public interest, but they wanted personal power. Their journalists were largely unknown, raffish, working-class, heavy drinkers, cynical, fun—or embittered. And so they remained until the Second World War—which was when Dorothy Schiff, known to everyone as Dolly, acquired the New York *Post*.

Schiff was the grandchild of Jacob Schiff, one of the most successful of the German-Jewish bankers whose wealth and power grew in New York throughout the industrial revolution of the nineteenth century. Despite her wealth, she was happily unconventional, within certain limits. She had a passionate relationship with Max Beaverbrook in the 1930s. Early in life she rejected her family's Republican affiliations and became an ardent supporter and friend of Franklin Delano Roosevelt; and in 1939 Roosevelt encouraged her to buy the *Post*.

Her then husband, George Backer, assured her that although it was losing money, the *Post* could be saved with an extra investment of only a couple hundred thousand dollars. That proved to be nonsense, and she began writing monthly checks for $100,000 for her husband, who had made himself the paper's editor. She did not at first think of herself as a newspaper owner at all—"I was just a woman who had gotten sucked into another sort of monstrous country house," she said. She grew disillusioned—but more with her husband than with the paper.

She became involved in the editorial side, and when she decided she would take over the paper, her husband went back to his mother in a fury. Next she married one of her editors, Ted Thackrey. Together they remade the paper, turning it into a tabloid with a liberal and indeed often left-wing slant. After the war, Thackrey became both passionately Zionist and increasingly left-wing. In the 1948 presidential election he supported Henry Wallace's newly formed Progressive Party. His marriage to Dorothy ended shortly afterward; but her relationship with the paper endured. Her money was constantly needed to save it. In the 1950s the paper took a lonely and courageous stand against Senator Joe McCarthy, and her editor, James Wechsler, was hauled before McCarthy's notorious Permanent Subcommittee on Investigations to name names.

The war had forced changes on newspapers, and television was now forcing more. During the war, radio had come into its own. Families received fast news of what was happening to their men on the other side of the world. Facts became more widely valued than sensation. News was complicated, but readers wanted it to be right. American journalists had to retrain themselves. From being drunken hacks, they had to become serious commentators, or at least serious reporters. Papers began to move upmarket. Then, after the war, commerce and advertising began to push papers even further away from their yellow origins.

Between December 1962 and the middle of 1963 New York newspapers were changed forever by a strike over, as usual, wages and hours. Print unions struck the *Times,* the *News,* the *Journal-American,* the *World Telegram* and the *Sun;* the proprietors of the *Post,* the *Herald Tribune* and the *Mirror* suspended publication in sympathy. However, Dorothy Schiff then broke with the other publishers and made her own settlement with the unions, thus coming back onto the streets well before her rivals, in March 1963. She tried but was unable to get union agreement to computerize part of the typesetting process.

In the early seventies, the *Post's* circulation fell away, and the morning *Times* and *Daily News* won the bulk of New York's advertising. One weekend in 1974 Schiff met Murdoch out in the Hamptons on Long Island. She was always susceptible to charming men. He told her what a rotten paper the New York *Times* was. The *Post* was just the sort of property for which he yearned, and in 1975 he asked her if it was for sale. It was not, but at age seventy-two, Dolly Schiff was clearly losing her enthusiasm for the newspaper business. She had tried to get good new editors, but was increasingly out of touch with the rates being paid. In the early 1970s, the story went, she even offered the job to Ben Bradlee, editor of the Washington *Post*, at $20,000 a year. "But Dolly," he replied, "some of my own reporters make more than that."

In the middle of 1976 she was told by her lawyers that new tax laws would mean that her children could not afford to keep the paper. Moreover, another strike by the print unions was looming. She decided she had had enough. Her lawyers made a number of calls to elicit interest. One was to the New York publisher S. I. Newhouse, but he was not interested in adding the *Post* to his empire, reckoning that the union problems of the paper made it a hopeless proposition. It had a circulation of almost 500,000 at this time, and was losing about $50 million a year. She asked Murdoch to lunch.

"I sensed she was very tired," Murdoch told Alexander Cockburn of the *Village Voice*. "She knew what was necessary to turn the paper and get it done right but she felt she just didn't have the energy left." Murdoch has always had a surplus of energy. At the end of 1976, the *Post* announced that Dolly Schiff would sell to Rupert Murdoch.

Schiff said she was happy. "Rupert Murdoch is a man of strong commitment to the spirit of independent, progressive journalism. I am confident he will carry on vigorously in the tradition I value so deeply," she announced.

For his part, Murdoch declared that "the New York *Post* will continue to serve New York and New Yorkers and maintain its present policies and traditions." Murdoch said he was "very happy" that Schiff had agreed to stay with the *Post* as a consultant for the next five years.

Many staff members of the *Post* regarded Murdoch's purchase as a reprieve. "If nothing else, I feel pretty good that the paper will survive. God knows in what form, but the guy is not pumping in millions to fold it," said one.

Others were apprehensive. "People who have the decent journalistic beats like government and politics are shaky," said one reporter. "They don't know if they're going to be asked to write stories about two-headed babies, or what."

Murdoch was immensely excited. He described having the *Post* as like having both the *Sun* and the *Mirror* in Sydney—and New York was many times the size of Sydney. He said that there were masses of changes to be made, columns to be scrapped, reporting to be improved. It would be his command post in America.

While his men in New York inspected the *Post*'s books, Murdoch attempted to buy the *Observer,* one of the oldest and most prestigious British Sunday newspapers. His bid was thwarted by the opposition of the *Observer*'s journalists, and the paper was sold to the American oil company Atlantic Richfield. The paper published glowing profiles of its new proprietor and congratulated itself on having escaped Murdoch's clutches. Murdoch was not amused. He thought that once again the British Establishment had rallied around to deny him one of its best-loved prizes. However, in the long term he had reason to be glad of it.

In New York the deal for the *Post* was masterminded by Stanley Shuman, a banker with Allen and Company, which Murdoch had chosen as his principal investment bank in New York. The final price was around $30 million; this was on the high side, but Murdoch wanted it. He said he would pay generously to satisfy himself.

He raised one third of the money in Australia, by the sale of investments and by borrowing. One third came from London—the earnings of the *Sun* and the *News of the World.* Merv Rich said later that at that time it was not easy for News to borrow in America—"We were not known there." The final third was an unsecured loan from the European American Bank and Trust Company. Murdoch explained that it was important that News International in Britain and News Ltd. in Australia each took only a half share—"In this way, a central bank in London or Australia can't order you to pay dividends, since you don't have control of the stock. It means you can plow back the profits."

On November 20, 1976, the day that the deal was finally agreed, Murdoch dined with Clay Felker, the publisher of *New York* magazine and the *Village Voice*, and a friend of Murdoch's for several years. Murdoch discussed his problems with the *Observer* and Felker told Murdoch that he was having trouble with the board of *New York* magazine. It was not for the first time. Felker was a gifted editor, but he was the despair of his more commercially minded colleagues. Felker considered this a private conversation between friends, but it soon became apparent that Murdoch had seen another prize.

With a small group of investors, Felker had started *New York* magazine in 1968; it was a lavish, glossy weekly whose writers included Tom Wolfe, Jimmy Breslin, Pete Hamill, Aaron Latham, Richard Reeves and Gloria Steinem. The magazine was a great success and Felker became a celebrity.

He was a connoisseur and an eclectic collector of information. He was obsessed with politics, film, art and style, and he liked to call himself an "information sponge." He was also volatile and could be irascible.

Felker did not own *New York* magazine—he had never had enough money. He had partners, the sort of people whom Murdoch loathed and would never tolerate. They did not all appreciate his social and editorial success, or the lavish spending in which he indulged. Alan Patricof, a venture capitalist and one of the original investors in *New York*, found Felker particularly irksome, according to an article in *Rolling Stone* by Gail Sheehy, who subsequently married Felker.

In 1974 *New York* acquired the *Village Voice*, the left-wing weekly published in Greenwich Village and devoted to the lives and causes of those who lived there. It was more of a merger than an outright purchase; two of the *Voice*'s controlling stockholders, Carter Burden and Bartle Bull, received 34 percent of the stock of the new company between them. There was an agreement that Burden had to give Felker first refusal on his 24 percent. Felker therefore felt he retained control of the publications. But Burden, a Vanderbilt heir, became an ally of Patricof in the struggle against Felker.

In 1976 Felker started a new magazine, *New West*, published in Los Angeles. It did well at once, but it did so expensively; the cost overruns were unwelcome. At the same time, Felker was negotiating for a large pay increase for himself. His partners were not amused. They did not feel part of the editorial enterprise. Patricof decided the only thing was to find a buyer for the magazine.

Sheehy believed that Murdoch had deliberately cultivated Felker since 1974—since he had learned that Carter Burden had received mainly stock rather than cash in the merger of the *Voice* and *New York*, and would be looking to sell. "His patience was rewarded," she wrote.

Three days after their dinner, Felker and Murdoch had lunch and Murdoch warned him, "You and I could never work together." Felker agreed—each of them liked to run his own ship. Murdoch also told Felker that what really mattered was 100 percent ownership—"then you don't have to take any crap from anybody." The next day, Stan Shuman called Patricof, who realized that he had a potential buyer.

On December 9, Murdoch astonished Felker by telling him he wanted to buy the company. He offered Felker $5 for shares that were currently quoted at $2. He offered to spin off *New West* and sell a third to Felker for $3 million. Felker refused and turned to Katharine Graham, owner and publisher of the Washington *Post*, for advice and assistance. She promised help if needed.

Meanwhile Stanley Shuman began what was called a "creeping tender": he contacted the stockholders one by one and obtained oral agreements that each would sell to Murdoch under certain circumstances. After Christmas, Carter Burden called Felker to tell him he had been offered $7 a share. Felker, anxious to exercise his right of first refusal, agreed to pay Burden that himself. The Washington Post Company would finance the purchase and would buy all the other outstanding shares for the same price. The company's investment banker, Felix Rohatyn, confirmed this offer to Burden's lawyer. Rohatyn thought he had a deal.

On the last night of 1976, Murdoch and Shuman and Burden's lawyer, Peter Tufo, flew out to Sun Valley, Idaho, to do a deal with Burden, who had been "on the slopes" whenever there had been inconvenient telephone calls from the Felker camp or the Washington *Post* camp in recent days. Tufo had told Shuman that there was a provision in the first-refusal clause which could become a loophole: Burden did not have to offer the stock to Felker if the company had had losses for four consecutive quarters. On January 1, 1977, a new quarter began and that condition was fulfilled. In Sun Valley the malleable Burden agreed to sell to Murdoch for $8.25 a share.

In New York Felker sought a temporary restraining order. He had another important weapon on his side: the writers. Like the *Observer* journalists in London, they had all recoiled in horror at the idea of being taken over by the obnoxious Murdoch. They met and were unanimous. Felker told them that he intended to fight, and they all agreed to support him. They were convinced that "the spirit" of the magazine would have no chance of survival under Murdoch. They called a news conference to announce to other reporters that they were a "talent package" that could not be bought or sold at will. The takeover became a major event, just the sort of media bonanza with which to launch the new year.

Suddenly the life and times of Rupert Murdoch were big news. In the first week of January both *Time* and *Newsweek* rushed to compile cover stories on the invader—an unusual double accolade. *Time* featured him as King Kong, seizing newspaper properties as he climbed skyscrapers.

On the night of Monday, January 3, a board meeting took place in the offices of Ted Kheel, a union negotiator and *New York*'s counsel. The journalists waited in an anteroom. Patricof had voted off the board two directors known to be on Felker's side, and then summarily disposed of Kheel. Then Patricof nominated two new board members—Murdoch and Shuman. Murdoch slipped calmly and quietly into one of the two empty chairs.

Eventually a delegation of writers from the magazines was allowed to present their views. The meeting exploded with shouts of "Fucking liar" and charges of illegal trading. The old hatred between the writers and the board was given full rein. Only Murdoch and Shuman remained calm and detached. Murdoch told Felker he was the most brilliant editor in America and asked him to continue editing *New York*. Byron Dobell, the managing editor, protested to the board: "You don't have the right to sell people," to which a board member, Thomas Kempner, replied, "You don't understand. In America, anyone can sell anything he wants, at any time. You're going to have to get that straight. That is just American capitalism."

Murdoch asked Felker to meet with him. The writers implored Felker not to, but a federal court, hearing his case against Burden and Tufo, ordered him to do so. Felker asked Murdoch to pull out, but Murdoch said he could not, for a reason which was both surprising and revealing: "I can't back down. After losing the *Observer,* I'd be a journalistic untouchable around the world. I can't lose."

Late that night Felker's lawyer met Murdoch, and in the small hours of January 7, Felker agreed to settle. He came out of it all with around three quarters of a million dollars. Later that day, he met with many of his writers gathered glumly in a restaurant across from his office. He was brief and bitter: "Rupert Murdoch's ideas about friendship, about publishing, and about people are very different than mine," he said. Close to tears, he continued, "He should know that he is breaking up a family, and he does so at his peril."

That night the next issue of *New York* magazine was due to go to bed. There were almost no staff members available to Murdoch. He put the magazine out himself, with the help of executives from the

Post and some of the board of *New York*. He canceled a cover by David Levine showing himself as a killer bee. About forty of the magazine's best writers and other members of the staff resigned. Murdoch installed his own editor, James Brady, and began to slash costs. The magazine continued to make money.

At the *Village Voice,* Murdoch tried to replace the editor, Marianne Partridge, despite a previous commitment that he would not do so. When some of the *Voice's* most valuable columnists, in particular Jack Newfield and Alexander Cockburn, threatened to make a great deal of trouble, he allowed Partridge to stay.

Murdoch did not renew her contract when it expired two years after the purchase. But he understood that the paper's radical views were essential to its success and he did not seek to impose a conservative editor. Instead he chose David Schneiderman, a journalist from the New York *Times,* who remained editor until Murdoch eventually sold the paper in 1985. The *Voice* ran frequent attacks on Murdoch and the New York *Post,* particularly in Cockburn's "Press Clips" column. For the most part Murdoch ignored them. Schneiderman received the occasional irate telephone call, protesting against the more savage criticisms, but otherwise Murdoch left the *Village Voice* alone. Its massive classified advertising base grew and the paper thrived.

Clay Felker went on to edit *Esquire* and then *Tonight,* the *Daily News'* evening attempt to challenge the *Post,* which failed. Subsequently he became publisher of *Manhattan, inc.* Much later he described himself as just one on the list of people damaged by Murdoch's advance. Felker thought Murdoch had two motives in all his actions: "To beat his father, Keith. And to run the world." But Murdoch did not destroy either *New York* or the *Village Voice* as Felker and the writers had predicted.

At the New York *Post,* Murdoch was a major presence from the start, and he immediately made that presence felt in the city. Within months Dolly Schiff's liberal backwater had become a roiling, clamorous torrent of news, mostly conservative opinion and hucksterish entertainment.

It was very much Murdoch's own paper; no one who worked there could have any doubt about that. He surrounded himself with a number of the Murdoch "mafia," those men (and a few women) who had charged with him through Sydney and London, and set about revitalizing the paper in his own particular fashion. He fiddled with stories and rewrote headlines. He was to be seen in the newsroom answering the phones and directing reporters. At once the paper became unsettled and changing, reflecting his own restlessness.

Stories became shorter, sharper and louder, the headlines garish. "BEHEAD THREAT!" told of an unfounded rumor during a Washington siege by Hanafi Muslims. A peaceful demonstration by less than a hundred people in Utah protesting against the execution of Gary Gilmore became "THREAT TO STORM GILMORE PRISON." Farrah Fawcett-Majors, the star of the TV series "Charlie's Angels," was chosen as a sexy mascot of the paper; story after story about her began to appear. Many of the paper's older or more reserved readers were appalled and left it.

The *Post* newsroom erupted in protests that were both general and specific. There was bad blood between many of the old Schiff reporters and the new men, in particular the Australians. A group of reporters sent Murdoch a petition complaining about the cartoons of Paul Rigby, an old colleague of Murdoch's, which they claimed were offensive to minorities and women.

Since he knew that there were some journalists who would always hate working for him, and since he wanted to bring in more of his Australian team, Murdoch extracted from the Newspaper Guild a once-only right to fire staff members he thought "incompatible with the new management." This became known as "the Auschwitz clause"; Murdoch used it to dismiss 122 out of 460 members of the guild.

By the 1970s newspaper economics throughout the land were

changing fast. Production and distribution costs had soared. Thousands of papers had folded. Some fifteen hundred cities still had daily papers, but almost all of them were local monopolies, and many of them were part of monopolistic chains belonging to Gannett, Knight-Ridder, Hearst and Times Mirror. Newspapers were becoming increasingly bland, centrist and dreary, all marching to similar tunes written by executives of the chains. Even in New York, the *Times* and the *News* were ostensible competitors, but each in effect had control of its own market.

Murdoch believed that the American media had become stuffy and self-satisfied. Journalists from the New York *Times*, particularly foreign correspondents, often behaved more like ambassadors than journalists. Too often the power and the glory turned into pomp and circumstance. Most papers, needing to attract the big advertisers like the New York department stores, were anxious to increase their share of upmarket readers at the expense of those lower down the scale. Murdoch insisted that the interests of blue-collar workers were being ignored. In 1977 he accused his fellow newspaper publishers of preaching "elitist journalism" and warned them against relying on the top end of the market: "A press that fails to interest the whole community is one that will ultimately become a house organ of the elite." This was a familiar Murdochian refrain.

Perhaps because the *Post* itself had no monopolistic security, Murdoch was determined not to accept what he saw as an insipid and prosaic formula. His blood-and-guts presentation had not yet proved very profitable in San Antonio, or with the *Star,* but he seemed determined to try it in New York. He came roaring into town and, as one writer, Chris Welles, put it, he was like "a throwback, a late nineteenth-century Hearstian figure who has seemingly materialized in the New York City of the late 1970s through some curious time warp." Most press barons of the time wanted merely to acquire comfortable monopoly papers with which to increase their cash flows and their dividend checks. Murdoch had, by contrast, always delighted in taking over secondary, ailing properties and turning them around by making them shout and scream as necessary.

No one made a louder noise than Steve Dunleavy, whom Murdoch transferred from the *Star*. Dunleavy came to widespread attention in New York soon after Murdoch acquired the *Post*. That year, 1977, had a long, hot and infamous summer, ideal for Murdoch and his new editor: there was a fiercely fought race for City Hall, Puerto Rican nationalist bombings, and in the midst of a July heat wave the New York power supply failed for twenty-four hours, during which there was some looting and arson. The *Post* capitalized with a screaming "Blackout Special"—"24 HOURS OF TERROR," the headline proclaimed, as an inside story described "A CITY RAVAGED."

Even more enticing that summer was the Son of Sam story, which might have been tailor-made for Murdoch's New York *Post*.

For a year a homicidal killer with .44 pistol had been on the loose in New York. It all began on July 29, 1976, when an eighteen-year-old girl named Donna Laurie was shot dead as she sat in a car in front of her home. Another girl was wounded at the same time. By March 1977 the maniac had murdered two more people and injured three others. The police dubbed him "Son of Sam," a sobriquet taken up with equal enthusiasm by the media and by the killer himself. In April two more people were murdered and the killer actually left a note signed "Son of Sam" by their bodies. It was clear that he was enjoying himself.

The *Daily News* understood and exploited the potential of the story before the *Post*. Its star columnist, Jimmy Breslin, began to write open letters to Son of Sam and in his column of June 5 printed what purported to be a reply from the killer himself. This of course excited considerable attention. Murdoch was determined to catch up, and Dunleavy was put on the case.

On June 26, Son of Sam struck again and wounded a young man and a young woman. As the first anniversary of the death of his first victim approached, journalists on all papers speculated that the killer would mark the day. The anniversary issue of the *Post* carried the headline "GUNMAN SPARKS SON OF SAM CHASE" and told the story of police pursuing a man over the Cross Island Parkway. It was mere titillation. Only in the penultimate paragraph did the paper reveal "police say the mystery gunman was definitely not Son of Sam."

On July 31, two days after the "anniversary," Son of Sam killed another woman and injured her escort. The *Post* ran the headline "NO ONE IS SAFE FROM SON OF SAM." Murdoch had insisted that there must be a new angle every day. On August 4 the *Post* declared, with no evidence, that New York's Mafia dons had declared that Son of Sam must be caught and had put their resources behind the chase.

Like Breslin, Dunleavy made a personal appeal to the killer to give himself up—to Dunleavy. Asked by the New York *Times* whether this was a good idea, Dunleavy replied, "There are no rules when it comes to appealing to a killer." He compared his "Open Letter to the Son of Sam" to an editorial that made an appeal to a head of state.

When the police arrested a man named David Berkowitz, the *Post* shouted triumphantly, "CAUGHT!" in bright red letters. Sales shot up by 400,000 to over 1 million for the afternoon.

The next day reporters and photographers from several papers, including the *Post,* were arrested for breaking into Berkowitz's apartment. All notions of guilt needing to be proven were cast aside—"INSIDE THE KILLER'S LAIR," read the headline over pictures of his room. Then the *Post* ran its most notorious headline in the case: "HOW I BECAME A MASS MURDERER by DAVID BERKOWITZ." Murdoch subsequently acknowledged that the headline was inaccurate. "I didn't write it," he said, "but I certainly approved it. I think it was wrong. But that's hindsight."

Later the *Post* published an improperly obtained photograph of Berkowitz sleeping in his cell. Murdoch insisted that he played no part in securing this picture and did not know how it was acquired. By now Murdoch had aroused the ire of his peers. The *New Yorker* attacked both the *News* and the *Post* for "transforming a killer into a celebrity." The *Times* published a front-page article questioning the *Post's* propriety. The magazine *New Times* called Sam "Murdoch's favorite son," and the writer Pete Hamill now likened the *Post* to a guest who throws up at a dinner party: "He is looked upon with alarm and pity, but no one really knows what to do to help."

Murdoch was not going to let him get away with that. Hamill at that time was escorting Jackie Kennedy Onassis, and, in revenge, Murdoch reprinted in the *Post* excerpts from an unflattering column Hamill had written about her some years before. Hamill, Murdoch said, was suffering from sour grapes because he had wanted to be editor of the *Post:* "Pete's a nice guy, but I don't think he'd make an editor. I don't think he'd make an editor's bootlace."

Post journalists began to complain, as their counterparts had in Sydney, about their paper's political bias. Soon after Son of Sam was caught, the *Post,* like other papers, wished to endorse a candidate for mayor. Murdoch took the election seriously and looked over all the candidates. He was impressed with Herman Badillo, the Hispanic candidate, and thought of endorsing him. He was less enamored of Mario Cuomo, the liberal secretary of state of New York. The New York *Times* came out for him. Three weeks later, the *Post* endorsed Ed Koch, in an unprecedented front-page editorial. Murdoch's choice was, as always, pragmatic. When he was asked why he chose Koch over Mario Cuomo, he was reported to have replied, "It's very simple. There are two and a half million Jews in New York and one million Italians." He told *MORE* magazine that he had been impressed with Koch and found him "very specific."

Murdoch's choice showed in the paper's coverage of the election. A subsequent analysis confirmed that the front-page stories up until the primary were far more favorable to Koch than to any other candidate. Indeed, there were quite simply no unfavorable stories about Koch.

The Koch experience was instructive for American politicians. They came to understand that an endorsement by Murdoch was not just a peck on the cheek, as it would be from the New York *Times,* but a bear hug. As Mario Cuomo said, the *Times* might, after long deliberation, give you a column. "With Rupert, he turns the whole paper over to you." Koch understood this, and Murdoch had a grateful friend in City Hall almost from the day he took over the *Post.*

Then came the incident which earned Murdoch the enduring anger of his peers: the 1978 newspaper strike.

The dispute, which afflicted many newspapers in the 1970s and 1980s, centered on the introduction of new, computerized technology to replace the old Linotype system, which had been in operation for almost a century.

Dolly Schiff had not been prepared to form a united front with the other publishers in demanding concessions from the unions. Now the *Times* and the *News* were anxious to have Murdoch on their side. The *Post* stood to gain less from a successful deal with the unions than its rivals. Nonetheless, Murdoch agreed to lead the publishers and appear as their spokesman. He later said that he did this because it gave him "a chance to be seen a lot on TV in a different role, instead of always having to answer first about some crappy headline in the *Post.*"

However, at the end of September 1978, Murdoch broke with his colleagues. He agreed that if the unions would print the *Post,* he would settle eventually on the terms they managed to get with the *Times* and the *News.* On October 5, the *Post* was on the streets with a run of 1 million copies. "WELCOME BACK!" it shouted to itself. While he left the painful and costly bargaining to the other proprietors, Murdoch spent hours on the telephone cajoling and charming major advertisers. For a time, he cornered some of those that had previously eluded him. On the spur of the moment he decided also to start a new Sunday paper to compete with the *News.*

Eventually the publishers did obtain concessions on featherbedding from the union pressmen (described by Murdoch as "an ornery bunch of bloody Irishmen"). And when the other two papers came back onto the street in November, they went after his advertisers like piranhas. The *News* ad department organized a "Bury Murdoch" campaign. *News* salesmen were given hefty bonuses for every *Post* account they could lure back as an exclusive *News* account. Within weeks the *Post* had shrunk and Murdoch was forced to concede defeat. He closed the Sunday edition.

The *Times* was as savage as the *News*. And *Newsday*, the suburban daily published on Long Island, New York, put up a fierce fight against Murdoch in Queens, where the *Post* was threatening to make inroads into *Newsday's* readership. Otis Chandler, the principal owner of *Newsday's* parent company, the Los Angeles–based Times Mirror Company, announced, "We are waiting to see how long it's going to take him to fail in this country."

By the end of the 1970s, Murdoch was regarded as a fiend by some in New York publishing. It was as if Dracula had come to Gotham and was sucking newspapers dry. Josef Barletta, the general manager of the *Daily News,* acknowledged in 1979 that New York newspaper publishing was not a gentleman's club.

> But you still don't have to become a dirty street fighter. I and my associates feel that there are some rules of good behavior. In Murdoch's world there are no rules. His world is amoral. . . . Now that he has shown how he works, we'll do it too. We're willing to play the game with him by his rules if that's what he wants.

Abe Rosenthal, the outspoken executive editor of the *Times,* announced that Murdoch was "a bad element, practicing mean, ugly, violent journalism." Even an airline magazine wrote of him: "MURDOCH—the very name triggers chills and palpitations among many members of the American press, as if it were some dark, evil, contaminating presence slinking out of the night—the Grendel, the Blob." A writer from the *Daily News* complained in the *Washington*

Journalism Review about the *Post's* "S curves of Sex, Scandal, Sensation and Screw the facts." The *Columbia Journalism Review* claimed that the *Post* had turned white against black, the comfortable against the poor, the First World against the Third World: "The *New York Post* is no longer merely a journalistic problem. It is a social problem—a force for evil."

Murdoch's response was combative: "If these people are going to get up and score off me all the time," he said, "if they want to have a fight with me, they may as well know before they're through that they've been in a fight."

THE CLARKE RING

After his youthful flirtation with Lenin, Murdoch did not honor many prophets. He was not known for reading books. His life was too packed with opportunities and buying and running companies to allow time for great reflection. But there was one man whose vision fascinated him, the science-fiction writer Arthur C. Clarke. He was fond of quoting Clarke's prediction that "in the struggle for freedom of information, technology not politics will be the ultimate decider."

There is an area of the galaxy named after Clarke. Circling the equator 22,300 miles above the earth are satellites parked on the Clarke Ring. It is a place of great importance to Murdoch.

Clarke was the man who first conceived the idea of satellite communications. In doing so, he redefined sovereignty.

Long before the technology existed to build satellites, Clarke worked out what in theory they could be. He calculated that at precisely 22,300 miles above the earth a satellite would take just twenty-four hours to orbit it. Since the earth itself spins on its axis once every twenty-four hours, a satellite above the equator at that height would seem to be motionless above the ground. Clarke later downplayed his vision. There was nothing new about the geosynchronous orbit, he said. "Any fool since Newton could have seen that. . . . My contribution was to realize that the satellite was the answer to the global broadcast distribution problem and that that was the place to put it." Despite such modesty, Clarke is a genius.

In 1945, Clarke had thought that realization of his idea was at least half a century away. Even he had not foreseen the fantastic pace of technological change that the next few years would bring.

The first low-orbit satellite was *Sputnik 1,* launched by the Russians on October 4, 1957, to the horror of the United States. *Telstar 1,* the first international communications satellite, went into orbit in 1962. Reception dishes could track it across the sky for only an hour or so before it dipped below the horizon.

Australia's clear sky and vast deserts were crucial to the new science of rocketry and satellites. By the early 1960s Australia provided locations for satellite communications systems and deep-space tracking stations that enabled the United States to orbit the earth and send missions to the moon.

In 1964 Intelsat, the International Telecommunications Satellite Consortium, was formed in Washington to organize the world around the new technology. By the end of the 1970s Intelsat had almost one hundred member countries and controlled fourteen satellites in various positions on the Clarke Ring. It channeled television, telephone calls and other data among 171 countries and territories around the world. The organization carried two thirds of the world's international communications traffic and almost all international television transmissions. Intelsat offered over thirty different services, from telephone calls to sophisticated computer-to-computer exchanges and videoconferences across the world.

The system was dominated by the West and the U.S. in particular. A large proportion of American military and diplomatic communications was carried by Intelsat, as was the hot line between Moscow and Washington.

In Washington, the Nixon administration recognized the potential of the new generation of satellites, establishing an Office of

Telecommunications Policy in the White House, run by Clay T. (Tom) Whitehead, a graduate of MIT and a researcher at the Rand Corporation. One of his tasks was to fulfill the White House's long-standing responsibility for the allocation of government frequencies in the communications spectrum.

Whitehead was ambitious. He tried to sort out the tangles into which cable television was developing and drafted a new satellite policy within the United States. He wanted to introduce competition into the entire communications business. So the White House pressed the Federal Communications Commission to allow an "open skies" policy for domestic communications satellites. As a result, in the next few years, dozens of privately funded and operated satellites were blasted up to the Clarke Ring to provide a host of domestic services, from television to mail order to banking. In Washington, direct broadcast to the home was seen as a fantastic opportunity to footprint Western broadcasts all over the Soviet empire.

The first country to use direct broadcasting by satellite was India. A one-year experiment in 1975–76 using American satellites was billed as an attempt to see how far the service could be used to provide isolated rural communities with information and instruction. The antennae were literally chicken wire and sticks. Technically the short-lived experiment was a success, and was seen as such by the CIA.

In 1976 Canada and Indonesia both began to experiment with direct satellite broadcasting. The Russians also started direct broadcasts to the inhabitants of Central Siberia and the far north when they launched the *Ekran* spacecraft up to a position of ninety-nine degrees east. Japan conducted similar trials.

In January 1977 the World Administrative Radio Conference met in Geneva to carve up the Clarke Ring, allocate national satellite spots and divide the spectrum into broadcast frequencies for different countries.

European governments were nervous. They knew perfectly well that the footprint of any satellite 22,300 miles up would cover more than one country. French programs would be beamed into Britain, and British jokes into Germany. The French in particular were frightened of their airwaves being swamped by American imports beamed at them by one of their neighbors. It was already becoming apparent—and not very welcome to governments—that the telecommunications revolution was, as Clarke predicted, redefining the nature of sovereignty.

Six hundred delegates from 111 countries attended the conference. They drew up an international plan for broadcasting satellite services. The satellite world of the Clarke Ring was divided into three regions. Region One contained Europe, Africa, the U.S.S.R. and Mongolia. Region Two covered the Americas and Greenland. Region Three embraced Asia, Australia and the Pacific. WARC 77, as the conference was inelegantly known, developed into a fight between those who favored regulation, led by France, and the advocates of open skies, led by the U.S.A. and Canada. The French insisted on a very rigid plan for Europe, whereby each country had only five channels. The Americans thought such restrictions absurd, if only because the technology was racing ahead.

The Americans were right. By the end of the decade it appeared that almost any satellite could be used to transmit directly into the home of anyone who had a small dish—and, of course, a television. The transnational opportunities that this offered to an international media empire like News Corporation appeared to be limitless. To Murdoch, satellites offered the same prospects that the railroads had provided for the barons of a previous era. This time the tracks led around the world.

AUSTRALIA

On the morning of Tuesday, November 20, 1979, Rupert Murdoch strode into his father's old office at the Melbourne *Herald* on Flinders

Street—the office where, as a child, he had first been entranced by newspapers and by his father's power—and told the chairman that he intended to buy the paper. It was an emotional moment.

Murdoch's move to recapture his childhood memories came at a time when he was trying to expand his group hugely. His acquisitions were being financed principally by profits from the *Sun* in London. Its racy formula of snappy news, pungent editorials and bare-breasted girls on page three continued to win readers. In 1978 the paper finally managed to overtake the *Mirror*'s circulation of 4 million a day. Despite the ceaseless problems between management and unions, the *Sun* was now the financial engine of Murdoch's empire. In 1979 pretax profits rose by £7 million to £25 million.

Under pressure from Anna, Murdoch had turned his attention back to Australia. He was planning to settle there—or at least to make it more of a permanent base. Asked whether this was for business or personal reasons, he said,

> Purely personal. I think it is a lottery whatever happens to your children, but quite a compelling reason is not to have my children educated in the public-school system in England because I feel they could never get the old school tie off their necks. If they want to lead a life in newspapers, if they choose that, they will grow up with better values in Australia than anywhere else I can think of.

He intended to send them to boarding schools in Melbourne and to treat Cavan as home.

By this time, Murdoch had become a much more controversial figure in Australia—largely because his politics had shifted. In 1972 his papers had supported Gough Whitlam, whose Labor Party had won the election. But Murdoch had grown disillusioned with Whitlam's socialist policies and anti-Americanism. In 1975 a constitutional crisis arose when the governor-general dismissed Whitlam and installed his opponent, Malcolm Fraser. There was widespread fury on the left in Australia, and there were allegations of CIA interference against Whitlam. In the subsequent election, the News Ltd. press took strong positions against Whitlam. Journalists went on strike in protest at what they saw as deliberate slanting of the news to hurt Whitlam. The rows seriously damaged the *Australian* and its standing in the country. Many people never forgave Murdoch and from now on saw him as an American agent.

Murdoch was now developing investments in gambling. By the end of the 1970s, gambling—previously the territory of crooks and gangsters, at least to some people—was beginning to acquire big-business respectability, largely because of the technological revolution. It was always a passion for Murdoch, the grandson of Rupert Greene. For decades he has been seen by headline writers as a gambler: "RUPERT MURDOCH—THE GAMBLER'S ROLLING HIGH"; "MURDOCH, THE GAMBLER WHO CAN'T BEAR TO LOSE"; "MURDOCH, THE GAMBLER WHO ALWAYS WINS."

In the 1970s his newspapers became involved in the simplest forms of gambling—soccer pools, lotto and, for readers of the Sydney *Mirror,* the *Sun* and the New York *Post,* some form of bingo.

By the early 1980s, gambling was a huge and vital part of the international entertainment industry. Vernons, one of Britain's biggest betting firms, had made its mark in Australia. Its principal owner, Robert Sangster, made a deal with News Corp. "With his distribution system, his knowledge of marketing and his printing plants, Murdoch was the natural partner," said Sangster. By 1974 they were granted licenses as sole operators of soccer pools in four states, the Northern Territory and Canberra.

In 1977 they expanded into the United States. New York State was anxious to develop a new low-stakes, long-odds game. Sangster and Murdoch competed for the contract, choosing as their U.S. partner Mathematica Inc., a Princeton think tank founded by the games theorist Oskar Morgenstern. It had produced many mathematical designs for the U.S. government, including blueprints for the space shuttle.

Together they won the right to operate lotto—a new version of the old game which was becoming a worldwide craze—throughout New York State.

Back in Australia, Murdoch and Sangster then went into partnership with a far more seasoned gambler, Kerry Packer, to form Lotto Management Services. They planned to compete in every area of long-odds gambling across the continent. The stakes were high: in Victoria alone the right to run lotto meant a revenue of some A$30 million. The consortium first won a partnership with the government of New South Wales to run lotto there. Next it obtained the rights to an instant numbers game in Queensland. In 1983 Australians alone spent $12 billion on gambling, the British $20 billion and the Americans $80 billion.

Murdoch was also expanding his television interests. He still had his stations in Adelaide and in the steel town of Wollongong, near Sydney. Now he made a play for one of the three Sydney commercial stations, Channel 10. His bid was fiercely resisted by the Australian Journalists' Association and the Labor Party, which had been united against him since the 1975 election. But after lengthy hearings before the Australian Broadcasting Tribunal, he won his application. Then, in November 1979, he made his assault on his father's old paper, the Melbourne *Herald*, bidding for 50 percent of the stock at A$4 a share.

In panic, the *Herald* management turned to its old rival and partner, John Fairfax and Sons. Fairfax was determined to deny Murdoch the 51 percent he was after, and started to buy shares in the *Herald*. In just two days Fairfax spent over A$52 million to acquire 15 percent of the *Herald*. Murdoch had not anticipated quite such effective opposition and began selling shares. But he hid what he was doing. "I employed a different broker to sell," he later recalled. "They were still buying, thinking they were buying against me." In fact, they were buying the shares that Murdoch was secretly selling.

Suddenly the *Herald* and Fairfax brokers realized the full horror of what they had done. In a matter of moments, Murdoch made a profit of more than A$3 million. He then declared that his bid was at an end. The share price immediately fell. Even so, Fairfax management apparently felt that its enormous losses were worth carrying for having kept Murdoch out of Melbourne newspapers. Murdoch denounced the Fairfax-*Herald* partnership as "two incompetent managements throwing themselves into each other's arms at the expense of their shareholders."

LONDON

As the seventies ended, the Western world began to shift toward the right—the direction Murdoch now favored. In the 1979 election the *Sun* came out resoundingly in support of Margaret Thatcher and the Conservatives. They won the election. For the next decade and more the paper remained astonishingly loyal to her, and that loyalty was rewarded. Throughout the 1980s Murdoch and Thatcher encouraged and reinforced each other. The Thatcherite revolution and the Murdoch revolution strode hand in hand across the decade.

By the end of the 1970s, production of the *Sun* was constantly being stopped by union disputes. The unions complained that, despite the profits the paper was turning in, Murdoch refused to invest in improvements to the plant. There was some truth in this. The pressroom, the newsroom, the canteen, the latrines and almost all the other facilities at the *Sun* were among the filthiest and most primitive on Fleet Street. But, as more millions of copies were lost each year through strikes, Murdoch became more and more impatient.

Neither the *Sun*'s editor Larry Lamb nor Murdoch liked to call himself a Tory. But they both considered the Labour government of James Callaghan a disaster. By 1978 Lamb was persuaded that "there was no alternative to Thatcher."

In the winter of 1978–79 public-sector strikes led to garbage overflowing on the streets and bodies being left unburied. Lamb borrowed from Shakespeare a headline which stuck to the government—"THE WINTER OF DISCONTENT." In early 1979, when Callaghan returned from a summit in Guadeloupe seemingly unaware of the extent of the discontent, Lamb had him say, "CRISIS? WHAT CRISIS?" in the paper's banner headline. The fact that he had said no such thing did not diminish its effect.

Mrs. Thatcher came to Bouverie Street. Lamb said she "accepted a glass of whisky, kicked off her shoes and engaged us all in spirited debate for several hours. We were all impressed, not least by the fact that she listened."

On Election Day, May 3, 1979, the *Sun's* massive editorial, covering the entire front page and continuing inside, was headlined "VOTE TORY THIS TIME. IT'S THE ONLY WAY TO STOP THE ROT." Murdoch had had reservations and had asked Lamb to substitute "THIS TIME" for Lamb's first preference "TODAY"—arguing that this would suggest that the *Sun* was not committed to the Tories forever. The editorial asserted that the *Sun* as a radical paper was urging a vote for the Conservatives.

The biggest swing to the Conservatives was among the lower-income group, known to market researchers as C2s, which included many *Sun* readers. In 1980, Mrs. Thatcher gave Lamb a knighthood. Murdoch disapproved of all such honors.

Like everyone else, Lamb was still trying to decide what made Rupert run. In the end he too came back to Keith Murdoch: "Some people live for ever in the shadow of distinguished fathers. Whatever else, Rupert was always determined that he would cast the longer shadow."

Lamb also tried to explain that despite the page-three girls, Murdoch was something of a Calvinist. At the same time, Lamb recalled, Murdoch was unable to understand the hostility that he aroused in Britain. He was a good husband and father, a patron of the arts and the employer of thousands of people. Yet he was regarded as a monster. Why?

Lamb himself sometimes thought Murdoch a bit of a monster. Especially in the early days, he found Murdoch's criticisms painful. "Eventually we reached an unspoken truce," said Lamb. "He ceased to be so unrelentingly critical, and I tried harder not to take offence when he was." Perhaps most disconcerting of all for an editor was the fact that Murdoch knew far more about every aspect of newspaper publishing than anyone he ever employed. And his determination could be ruthless.

WASHINGTON

The 1980s, the decade in which the technological, political and financial revolution enabled Rupert Murdoch to transform his company into one of the world's most important media empires, began for him with two significant adventures: the rescue of Maxwell Newton, the first editor of the *Australian*, and an interrogation before the United States Senate. Both were hugely enjoyable successes: Newton once again became entranced, and the senators were charmed by Murdoch.

The roller coaster of Max Newton's life had taken him down rather more often than up since he and Murdoch had parted company in Canberra in 1964. After being denounced as a Japanese spy and raided by Australia's Commonwealth Police in 1969, he had tried to build up his own small newspaper empire. He started a mining newspaper and purchased a small country paper, the *Daily Commercial and Shipping News,* and then the *Sunday Observer* in Melbourne.

The *Sunday Observer* made Murdoch's tabloids look tame. "I WAS THE POPE'S BOYFRIEND," "BILL'S NOT A HOMO" (this allegedly from the wife of the prime minister), "THANK BLOODY CHRIST" (when the Whitlam government fell) and "PREMIER'S POOFTER SCANDAL" were some of the front-page banner headlines that screamed at the citizens of Melbourne in the early 1970s. The paper was also sustained by pages of advertisements for sexual services.

Newton continued to live in style, with his pompadour hair, his sharp shirts with their metal wing tips, a large house in the Melbourne suburb of Toorak and a Rolls-Royce. He existed on borrowing and bartering.

His business prospered for a couple of years, but Newton was unable to control it. He became addicted to Mandrax, and his marriage, which had weathered so much, collapsed. Newton had always lived on the brink of despair; these misfortunes drove him close to insanity. Suddenly, after twelve years as a teetotaler, he started drinking again.

He married once more, but his addictions and his sexual meanderings soon took their toll. In 1976 receivers moved into the *Sunday Observer* and began to repossess his personal property. One day he called a friend. "The world has ended," he said in a voice of doom. "They've taken away the Rolls."

By now he was publishing straight sex papers. Through one of them he met Olivia Mader, who became his third wife. They diversified into sex shops and then into brothels, and they began to make a lot of money, all in cash.

This Hogarthian life led Newton nearly to suicide, and he developed cancer and diabetes. In 1979, he backed slightly away from the abyss when he wrote a series of political and economic analyses for *Penthouse*. They were well received. He became a television pundit, and when Murdoch made his move for the Melbourne *Herald* that same year, Newton praised him. Murdoch invited him to dinner, and they discovered that their friendship was renewable. They now shared a conviction that only right-wing politics and totally free markets could make the world both safe and prosperous.

Murdoch decided to rescue Newton. In 1980 he invited him to America to advise him on economics and on the direction of the New York *Post*. Newton never went back to Australia, partly because the tax men were still chasing his spoor around Melbourne.

In America his life began again. Murdoch made him chief business columnist for the *Post,* and he began to write like a fanatic. His passionate promotions of Reaganomics were a great success, and his punditry began to give the *Post* a presence (and sales) on Wall Street. His column was syndicated throughout the Murdoch empire. He also started writing private financial newsletters, as he had in the 1960s, and a book on the Federal Reserve.

In 1982 he suffered agonizing operations for cancer of the prostate. This, said Olivia, made him work all the harder; words were a substitute for sex. The 1980s were Newton's most productive decade. He stayed sober and he knew he owed his salvation to Murdoch—who continued to treat him generously. Newton made the best of his new life and enriched himself from his prodigious output, but the black dog of despair was never far from his side.

After his 1979 retreat from the purchase of the Melbourne *Herald,* Murdoch turned his attention to acquisition of ATI, the company which owned Ansett Airlines and Channel 0 in Melbourne. In a complicated but swift series of steps, he acquired enough shares to be appointed chief executive of ATI. He then made a deal with the other suitor for the company, Sir Peter Abeles of Thomas Nationwide Transport, whereby they each ended up with 50 percent of ATI shares. Abeles, a resourceful businessman, had arrived in Australia as an immigrant from Hungary, and since built TNT into a successful transportation company. He and Murdoch became joint chiefs. Abeles was always full of praise for Murdoch: "I am a normal businessman, but he is a phenomenon. Rupert is well above all of us in capacity and speed. I have never seen anyone working so fast and so precisely. He can cover so much ground—no other human being in the world could do it."

At the end of 1979 both Australian domestic airlines, Ansett and TAA, were renewing their fleets. In the past they had flown the same equipment, and in December 1979 TAA ordered Airbus 300s, the main European competitors to American medium-range passenger jets. In the past Ansett would have done the same, and indeed Airbus promised to supply the planes to Ansett at the same time as to TAA.

Murdoch, as usual, had his own ideas. If the terms were comparable, he wanted to buy American.

Boeing, the company from which Murdoch wanted to buy the jets, recommended that he pitch his case personally to the Export-Import Bank. Murdoch asked if the meeting could be held on February 19, when he had to be in Washington anyway for a lunch with President Carter. This was a date which Murdoch had already twice rescheduled to suit his own plans. Carter wanted the support of the *Post* in New York's Democratic presidential primary, in which Teddy Kennedy was challenging him.

After telling Ex-Im Bank officials that the loan must be at a rate of under 8 percent, Murdoch went to lunch with President Carter. He insisted later that the loan was not discussed between them. He told Carter that the *Post* would endorse him for the New York primary, but he refused to commit the paper to him for the general election. Three days later, on February 22, the *Post* did indeed endorse Carter.

In the end the bank offered Ansett a total loan of some $290 million, less than half what Murdoch was asking. He won his 8 percent rate on the purchase price of only five aircraft, not twenty-five as he had sought.

But the speed of the deal, the low rate of interest and the coincidence of Murdoch's lunch with and support for Carter led to intense speculation. In Washington journalists and congressional staff alike attempted to find evidence of a corrupt deal—cheap money for political support. They were unable to discover any such thing.

Murdoch volunteered to testify before the Senate. He explained that it was Boeing's idea that he should meet with Ex-Im Bank officials. The fact that he lunched with Carter the same day as meeting with Ex-Im Bank officials was pure coincidence. Finally, he pointed out that the *Post*'s endorsement of Carter in the primary was no surprise. His opponent was Edward Kennedy, and Kennedy was not one of the *Post*'s favorite politicians.

Senator William Proxmire pointed out that the media's influence on the public was enormous. Senators had an ethics code designed to avoid even the appearance of a conflict of interest. Did Murdoch?

"Of course we do, sir," Murdoch replied. "And I sympathize with you in what you're saying about the media, in particular watching television and what a job they did on me the last couple of days. There is no conflict of interest here unless it's in the eye of the beholder." He said he admired Boeing, and Australians trusted Boeing airplanes.

In conclusion, Proxmire threw Murdoch a bouquet: "Well, I want to say that you are a remarkable man, Mr. Murdoch. We have had a lot of witnesses before this committee, but I was especially impressed with what a quick study you are. You seem to know a whale of a lot about an industry you've just gotten into. You are very refreshing, intelligent and an effective witness, and responsive."

In the end the Senate committee chided the Ex-Im Bank, saying that the application had been handled sloppily, that not enough care of public money had been shown and that too much of the bank's money went to the aircraft industry anyway. But Murdoch had already been given the loan. The whole investigation seemed to have been fueled more by fervor than by facts. There was never any likelihood that the *Post* would support Kennedy in the primary; "Teddy Is the Toast of Teheran," the paper had declared early in the Iran hostage crisis—a switch from its usual emphasis on his drinking and womanizing. Carter did not need to ask Murdoch to lunch to have his support in the primary, but neither lunch nor the Ex-Im Bank loan was enough to win him Murdoch's support in the general election.

Murdoch thought Carter was an ineffectual liberal and he thought it high time that liberalism be decently buried. A sense of crisis gripped America in 1980. America's ally of thirty-seven years, the shah of Iran, had been driven from his country. American diplomats had been seized as hostages and the Carter administration seemed unable to do anything about it. Since OPEC's second oil-price "shock" of 1979, the price of crude oil had risen by over 50 percent in six months. Cars were lined up at gas stations for hours. Inflation had soared over 10 percent and was still rising. Carter made what came to be called his "malaise" speech, in which he talked about a "crisis of confidence . . . that strikes at the very heart and soul and spirit of our nation's will." But he appeared to many Americans to be inadequate. The Soviets marched into Afghanistan and Carter's response was an embarrassing declaration that Brezhnev had betrayed him personally.

Ronald Reagan was the only person selling what has been called "pure strength." He told the Americans what they wanted to hear, and his election seemed to be, in the end, America's final rejection of the 1960s solution to the great problems of the 1970s—economic stagnation, social fragmentation and the continuing drama of the Cold War.

Carter seemed to many to represent a scaled-back America, a nation that would live modestly, renouncing its restless mobility, withdrawing from full engagement with politics around the globe, focusing only on issues of international importance. Carter's vision did not appeal to the American imagination. Reagan's did. It appealed also to Murdoch.

With the election of Ronald Reagan in November 1980, Murdoch had kindred spirits in both the White House and 10 Downing Street. The 1980s turned out to be the era of Reagan and Thatcher—and Gorbachev. It was a decade which shook the world. Murdoch liked to see himself as part of that process. He was.

4

LONDON

In February 1981, Rupert Murdoch, in direct succession from his father's friend Northcliffe, became owner of the *Times* of London. When the deal was completed, he called Anna, who was in Australia—at home, as she thought. She still detested England.

She asked him where they would spend most of their life from now on. "He thought about it and said, 'More than half in the Northern Hemisphere.' So I thought: Well! That narrows it a little bit."

The battle for the *Times* and the *Sunday Times* and their subsequent evolution have been crucial to perceptions of Murdoch. This happened in particular because of his well-publicized rows with one of Britain's most famous editors, Harold Evans.

The *Times* and the *Sunday Times* were, in different ways, two of Britain's most distinguished papers, but they were blighted by the atrocious state of relations between Fleet Street management and unions.

The *Sunday Times* was bought by Roy Thomson, the Canadian press baron, from Lord Kemsley in 1959, when its sales were under 1 million. Thomson appointed a fine editor, Denis Hamilton, and allowed him to recruit a first-rate staff. In 1967 the paper's circulation touched 1.5 million, far ahead of each of its rivals, the *Observer* and the *Sunday Telegraph*.

Before Thomson was allowed to buy the paper, elaborate safeguards were devised to prevent him from abusing its editorial independence. The avuncular Thomson was happy to accept the conditions; he described the purchase of the *Times* in his memoirs as "the greatest thing I have ever done."

In many ways Roy Thomson was the journalist's perfect proprietor. He was creative, and yet he never interfered. He had fairly pronounced right-wing views of his own, but he reckoned that it would be absurd to try to impose them upon all the newspapers that he owned. He allowed his editors freedom.

After Thomson acquired the *Times*, Denis Hamilton became editor in chief of both the *Times* and the *Sunday Times*. William Rees-Mogg, an erudite writer on the *Sunday Times*, became editor of the *Times*, and Harold Evans was made editor of the *Sunday Times*.

Evans, the son of a railroad engineer, had been a journalist all his working life. He first edited the *Northern Echo*, where he distinguished himself by successful crusading journalism. Denis Hamilton spotted him and in 1966 brought him to London as his chief assistant. One year later Hamilton handed over to him a superbly functioning, profitable newspaper with as gifted a team of journalists as was to be found. The *Sunday Times* was a paper, as Evans himself later said, "vivid with personality and excitement."

Under Hamilton and then Evans, the *Sunday Times* developed a technique of journalism by a team of reporters. They were collectively known as Insight, and the fruits of their labors came to personify the paper. Evans made Insight into a full-time investigative unit, and throughout the late 1960s and 1970s the paper published massive inquiries into areas of public concern. These included the life and crimes of Kim Philby, the Soviets' most important agent inside the British Secret Intelligence Service, MI6; an inquiry into the McDonnell Douglas DC-10 disaster in northern France; and an analysis of how the company Distillers came to market the drug thalidomide. This investigation was accompanied by a sustained and ultimately successful campaign for generous compensation to the victims of the drug.

Evans saw journalism as a social weapon, and it was one which he deployed with enthusiasm, forever taunting the government and trying to push back the laws of contempt, of libel and especially of governmental secrecy. His *Sunday Times* had many critics who saw its style as abrasive, pinchbeck journalism with more glitter than substance. But Evans and his supporters argued that his paper saw the citizen as a victim in need of defense, and that it was politically neutral, assuming a critical, quietly radical suspicion of all administrations.

It was, for all these and more reasons, a paper with a certain esprit de corps. Evans hired skillful journalists and allowed them their head. Among the most brilliant and combative was Bruce Page, editor of Insight and then features editor, a man who would study eighteenth-century German history or molecular physics in order to get a story right.

The paper's serious investigations continued. But by the end of the 1970s, some of the spirit had faded. Evans could be as capricious as he was stimulating. He was not good at delegating and yet he was often too distracted to make a decision. He was a bundle of nervous energy, often on the run—or on his motorbike, or on his skis or on a squash court. His own life was changing. He was in the process of divorce and remarriage. He had coauthored a successful picture book on skiing, and he later helped edit the memoirs of Henry Kissinger—which some thought an odd extramural activity for an editor who prided himself on his independence from politicians.

While the *Sunday Times* prospered, economically and journalistically, in the 1970s, its sibling, the *Times,* did not.

When Thomson died in 1976, everyone at Grays Inn Road, where the *Times* and *Sunday Times* were published, wondered what would happen next. Whereas the Old Man was tickled pink by owning the

Times even if it lost him money, and loved England, his son Ken had no such romantic notions. He lived in Canada and found London much less congenial than his father had.

In October 1980, after endless confrontations with the unions over the introduction of new technology, and a prolonged shutdown of the papers, Ken Thomson put them up for sale. Bids had to be submitted to the investment bank S. G. Warburg by December 31. If no sale was agreed to, then the papers would close between March 8 and 14, 1981. Thomsons was anxious to avoid that because it would mean the company would have to make severance payments of some £36 million.

Among the possible buyers were Lord Rothermere, descendant of Northcliffe and the owner of Associated Newspapers, which included the *Daily Mail;* Lord Matthews of the Express group; Robert Maxwell, the owner of Pergamon Press and perpetual suitor of any likely newspaper bride; and Atlantic Richfield, the American oil company which had bought the *Observer* when Murdoch had hoped to buy it. Then there was Murdoch. In the past he had said he would "never" buy the *Times.* When the sale was announced, he said that he had no real interest; he had a lot on his hands already, and Times Newspapers was "a snake pit."

He also knew that the rules had changed since he had bought the *Sun* in 1969. He was already a British newspaper owner, which meant that if he sought to buy another paper, his bid would almost certainly have to be examined by the Monopolies and Mergers Commission. That could be lengthy and disagreeable. There was, however, one loophole. If the paper concerned was clearly commercially unviable and was otherwise threatened with closing down, a bid by an existing proprietor could go ahead unchallenged. On this crucial question much came to hang.

Rees-Mogg and Evans each tried to put together consortia to rescue their papers and searched for backers.

In early December Murdoch came to London for a Reuters meeting. He met Gordon Brunton, managing director of Times Newspapers, at the apartment of Lord Catto, Murdoch's London investment banker. Brunton had encountered Murdoch often at meetings of the Newspaper Publishers' Association, the group of owners which had tried vainly for years to unite the defense of its interests against the print unions. He used to say that Murdoch was one of the few publishers who would keep his word. Brunton was a manager, not a journalist; he admired Murdoch's business acumen, and saw him as an honorable man. He wanted Murdoch to buy the papers. By contrast, he loathed Maxwell and distrusted Rothermere, two of the other obvious candidates.

Murdoch made a bid of £1 million, just to get his foot in the door before the December 31 deadline laid down by Thomsons. Like the other bidders, Murdoch knew that if a deal was not done and Thomsons closed the papers in March, it would be liable for the massive severance payments.

Among the bids were those from both editors. But the unions decided they preferred Murdoch. He had saved jobs on the *Sun* and created more; he was tough but he was reliable.

Evans now realized that for the Thomsons board, too, Murdoch was the favorite. "It was a bitter thought that they should favor an outsider, and one for whom they had expressed contempt in the past," he wrote later.

Then Murdoch called Evans.

"It's all mine," Murdoch said at once. "Unless Harmsworth [Rothermere] comes up with a bigger offer. What do you hear?" He told Evans he was going to make a clean sweep of management and asked Evans to lunch the next day. Evans says he was unhappy to accept, but did so because he wanted to know what was going on. "Murdoch had become a prime source," he wrote in his memoir, *Good Times, Bad Times*.

"Would you like to edit the *Times*?" Murdoch asked Evans over lunch. In his book, Evans wrote that he ignored the question and that he was "quietly angry" at the way in which Murdoch was ignoring his consortium bid. He says he told Murdoch that the consortium wanted to continue to run the *Sunday Times* as a campaigning, investigative paper. "Sure, sure," said Murdoch.

Asked later (in an interview for this book) how Evans reacted at that lunch, Murdoch said, "I want to be fair to Harry. When I said it to him, he did not jump at it. He said he was thinking about his future. I thought he was just being coy. I think he wanted it as much as anything. . . ."

On Saturday, January 17, Murdoch invited Harry and his fiancée, Tina Brown, to his Eaton Place apartment. In his book, Evans quotes at some length from the relevant passage in Tina Brown's diary, in which he says Tina noted Murdoch's "alarming charm."

> I had to admit I liked him hugely. He was in an American country gentleman's three-piece suit and heavy shoes, and was by turns urbane and shady. His face seems to have been made for the cartoonist's distortion—the gargoyle lips, deep furrows in the brow, the hint of five o'clock shadow that gives him such an underworld air when he's sunk in thought. But when he was standing by the fire with one foot on the fender laughing uproariously he seemed robust and refreshing. There's no doubt he lives newspapers. They are not merely seen by him as assets, as Ken Thomson sees them. At eight o'clock, when the first editions arrived, he fell upon them with childish excitement. I warmed to him when he read the *Observer*'s hostile account of his bid and instead of being cross burst into gales of laughter: "The bastards!" he shouted, throwing it to the floor.
>
> The truth is that, although he'll be trouble, he'll also be enormous fun and H. has had so many years of Thomson greyness this vivid rascal could bring back some of the jokes. "I sacked the best editor of the *News of the World*," he said at one point. "Stafford Somerfield was too nasty even for me!"

What had happened in the space of two days seemed clear to those who knew Murdoch. Harry Evans had fallen in love, and so perhaps had Murdoch. There was nothing unusual about that. Murdoch would become immensely, sometimes disproportionately, enthusiastic for a new recruit or adviser. For such a person his attention could be overwhelming. His charm was so intense and yet so unaffected, so natural and yet so strong, that few people came away from their early meetings with him other than mesmerized. Harry Evans was susceptible.

When his associates in the consortium urged Evans to lead a Stop Murdoch campaign, he refused. Later he wrote, "In the light of events they were right, and I was badly wrong to resist them." But at the time he argued that the thing to do was to tie Murdoch's hands as they had never been tied before. Evans' decision, in effect if not yet in public, to throw in his lot with Murdoch was important. It is likely that if Evans had publicly opposed Murdoch's bid, it would, at the very least, have had to be referred to the Monopolies Commission.

On January 20, Denis Hamilton had Rees-Mogg and Evans to lunch to ask which of the possible buyers they preferred. They said that on margin they favored Murdoch, but that he would have to give guarantees of editorial independence. So they had to decide what guarantees they wanted and then to extract them from him.

On January 21, less than a week after Murdoch had offered Evans the editorship of the *Times,* a committee created by Thomsons met to vet Murdoch's journalistic attitudes. It included three of the four national directors: Lord Dacre, better known as Hugh Trevor-Roper, the historian; Lord Roll, an economist and chairman of S. G. Warburg; and Lord Greene, who, as leader of one of the rail unions, had been Sid Greene. (Lord Robens, the other national director, was abroad.) With them were Denis Hamilton, Evans and Rees-Mogg.

When Murdoch came in, Evans said he noticed for the first time the thick black hair on the backs of his hands. According to Evans, Murdoch walked quietly and spoke softly, "like someone visiting a friend in hospital."

Hamilton set the discussion rolling by telling him what high standards they set at the *Times.* Murdoch then told them all about himself.

According to Evans' account, he said he had learned the traditions of editorial freedom from his father and was used to producing different papers for different markets. He stuck with papers that were losing money—look at the *Australian*, he said. He would expect the national directors to be a court of appeal for the editor. He spoke self-confidently but not arrogantly; altogether, he gave a good account of himself.

He agreed to everything they asked him. He then went back upstairs to talk money. His was by no means the best offer Thomsons had received. Rothermere had offered £25 million for the *Sunday Times* alone, and £20 million if he had to take the *Times* as well. But he also insisted that he must retain the right to close the *Times* if he wished. Meanwhile, Murdoch's original offer of £1 million had increased to £12 million on the understanding that apart from the buildings on Grays Inn Road, the company had almost £18 million worth of assets.

In the end, soon after midnight, the deal was closed at £12 million. Murdoch was jubilant. And well he might have been. The *Sunday Times* building on Grays Inn Road alone was worth at least half of what he had paid for the whole company. Murdoch also retained the right to pull out if the deal was referred to the Monopolies and Mergers Commission.

Purchase was contingent on Murdoch's making a deal with the unions. But they were eager for him. He did not push them far; in the end they agreed to some seven hundred layoffs and to the *Times* literary, educational and other supplements' being printed outside London.

A few weeks later Murdoch revealed to an Australian trade paper how well he thought he had done. The constraints imposed by the national directors were no problem: he could still appoint his own editor and a veto would be "highly unlikely if I go about it in a sensible manner." He confirmed that the price had been a steal: "We paid less than half the book value of its tangible assets, so we can always close it down and still be ahead."

The only remaining hurdle, but the highest one, was the possibility of a reference to the Monopolies Commission, which had a special responsibility for newspaper takeovers. Under the 1973 Fair Trading Act, all, or almost all, newspaper mergers must be referred to the commission.

If the Monopolies Commission had taken up the issue, its investigation would inevitably have delayed the purchase beyond the deadline set by Thomsons. Both Brunton and Murdoch had already been to the Department of Trade and Industry to argue that the sale should not be referred. Brunton had warned that if it were, the papers would both close. "I had thirty-six million pounds' redundancy [severance] payments to worry about. I told the government I would rather close the papers than go through a referral. Murdoch told them he would withdraw in those circumstances. I got him to do that." On behalf of Thomsons, S. G. Warburg presented the ministry with figures which showed that not only the *Times* but also the *Sunday Times* was losing money.

The matter of referral was considered by an informal meeting of cabinet ministers. There was apparently tension at the top. Unconfirmed gossip began to circulate on Fleet Street that his own departmental lawyers had advised John Biffen, the secretary of state for trade and industry, that the sale might have to be referred to the commission, but that Mrs. Thatcher had decided otherwise. Evans later alleged he heard of "Mrs. Thatcher's determination to reward Murdoch for his political support, especially at the 1979 election." But Biffen himself said, in an interview for this book, that he had no reason to believe that this was so.

Biffen said that he would approve the sale providing that the editorial safeguards which the vetting committee had proposed be written into the Articles of Association of Times Newspapers. They would have the force of law and Murdoch would risk going to jail if he broke them. Evans praised this move and told the Press Association: "No editor or journalist could ask for wider guarantees of editorial independence on news than those Mr. Murdoch has accepted and which are now entrenched by the secretary of state." Biffen said that he was greatly influenced by Evans' remarks. But later he privately conceded that there were political arguments either way about a decision to refer.

Harry Evans said later that as the deal went forward he was still unhappy that the *Sunday Times* had been portrayed as a loss-making paper. In his memoirs he recalled being deeply upset as he sat in the House of Commons on listening to John Biffen describing the *Sunday Times* as not a going concern: "It was for me, sitting gagged and bound in the Press Gallery, perhaps the most bitter and frustrating moment of the whole affair."

But Evans, with Murdoch's assistance, seemed to have gagged and bound himself. As Magnus Linklater, a senior editor on the *Sunday Times*, later contended, "Evans knew in advance that the whole object of the exercise was to steer Biffen in that direction. He knew the figures would be shaped to portray the papers as lossmakers. If he felt so strongly about it, did he not have a duty as editor of that paper to reveal them?" Evans subsequently disputed Linklater's supposition that he knew the figures. But at the time Evans appeared committed to Murdoch; some of his associates on the *Sunday Times*, still anxious at the idea of the wolfish Murdoch taking over their paper, were disappointed in his attitude.

The *Sunday Times* journalists voted to use legal action to force a referral to the Monopolies Commission. They hired solicitors, put together a dossier on Murdoch and prepared a financial prospectus to show that the *Sunday Times* was definitely a going concern.

On the evening of Friday, February 6, a committee of the journalists met Murdoch and found him impressive and straightforward. He appeared to make some concessions. The national directors could have a special voting share to protect their status, and to give them some "teeth." He would allow two journalists on the board, but he refused to give journalists any say in the appointment of the editor. "I'm not having elections," he said.

After agonized debate, the *Sunday Times* journalists voted to accept Murdoch as the next owner. One of them, John Barry, said of Murdoch, "The man's charm is *lethal*. One minute he's swimming along with a smile, then *snap!* There's blood in the water. Your head's gone." Nonetheless, Barry, along with Hugo Young, the political editor, now advised voting for Murdoch and dropping the court action.

Their change of heart swayed many people. One of the few executives to stand out against Murdoch was Magnus Linklater. Almost in tears, he argued passionately against caving in. In the end, however, the journalists voted to accept Murdoch as the next owner.

Rees-Mogg had made clear that he would not stay as editor of the *Times* under any new proprietor and on February 17 Murdoch formally offered the job to Evans. "I wanted to get the energy of the *Sunday Times* into the *Times*," Murdoch said much later.

Harry Evans accepted. "Ambition and conceit were two of the elements," he admitted later. "I wanted to edit the *Times* of London. It was the most famous paper in the world. Nobody could resist it." He also thought that he could deal with Murdoch. Revealingly, he later said,

> Every editor, and many a politician who deals with Murdoch, thinks that they're the one who is going really to change him. They're like a woman who goes out with a womanizer. She thinks, "This time, this time he really means it. He really loves me. He'll really marry me." Well, Murdoch's like a womanizer in that sense. He has this fatal capacity to instill the confidence in you that you and he have a special, exclusive relationship. It's a wonderful con trick.

Enraptured, Evans went to lunch with Murdoch at the Savoy and prepared to leave the *Sunday Times*. Murdoch still had to persuade the *Times* board of the wisdom of his choice.

Hugh Trevor-Roper, who disliked Evans and felt he had lowered the tone at the *Sunday Times,* believed he was quite unsuitable as editor of the *Times*. Hamilton agreed. He later wrote that he had told Murdoch "it would turn out disastrously," but he did not speak out forcefully at this meeting. Murdoch was granted the man he described as "the best journalist in Britain."

There was no problem about the man whom he wanted to edit the *Sunday Times*. Murdoch chose Frank Giles, the honorable sixty-two-year-old deputy editor of the newspaper.

The Village

With Times Newspapers, Murdoch had also bought himself 5 percent of a gold mine. "I did not know it at the time," he says, "nor did Thomsons."

The gold mine was Reuters, the traditional news agency, suddenly transformed in value through its importance as a tool of the international financial services market.

In the first half of the 1980s, Reuters was floated as a public company, with the purpose of enriching its owners, newspaper proprietors of Great Britain, Australia and New Zealand, Murdoch prominent among them. "Reuters," says Murdoch, "is a key story in the information revolution. A real key." And it was a key to much more than newspapers. It was also integral to the arguments promoted by UNESCO in the 1970s and early 1980s about "cultural imperialism" and "information sovereignty."

Reuters was created in the 1850s by a German Jew who became a Christian and changed his name from Israel Beer Josaphat to Paul Julius Reuter. Telegraph cable had just been laid under the English Channel and Reuter saw an opportunity to link the London and Paris stock exchanges. But he did not restrict himself to share prices. He used the cable to transmit other news as well and thus soon became a power in British journalism. He insisted on limiting news to verifiable facts. As a result, Reuter's organization soon developed a reputation for terse accuracy on which it prided itself ever after.

The news agency was not itself profitable—at any time in its history. Reuter made money by supplying commercial information to private subscribers and by a private telegram service. Reuters became a public and rich company.

During the First World War, there were fears that it could fall under German influence, and a group was formed to privatize it again. In the 1920s, rather than being refloated on the market, it was sold to the news agency the Press Association. A new crisis arose during the Second World War when the loss of its Axis subscribers put the operation in financial jeopardy. Despite parliamentary misgivings, the Fleet Street press barons of the Newspaper Publishers' Association agreed to buy 50 percent of the company for £170,000, and created "the Reuters Trust" to manage the agency.

After the war, Reuters continued to build on its reputation as a safe, sober and reliable purveyor of the news from around the world, but made very little money. In 1963, Gerald Long, a former correspondent, became chief executive as the company teetered on the edge of bankruptcy. There was talk of accepting a subsidy from the British government. Long rejected that and decided to follow the lead of the company's founder—"Follow the cable."

At the end of the 1950s, a new generation of international cables had been laid, much more reliable than shortwave radio transmissions, which were crackly and apt to break. Reuters had already leased land lines over Europe, and in 1960 it leased its first transatlantic cable circuit. It was able to transform its transatlantic circuit to carry telephone as well as teleprinter traffic. The circuit could be split into twenty-two teleprinter channels in each direction. But now technical changes followed one another with dizzying speed; within a year the number of circuits was doubled. By the end of the decade Reuters was leasing two million miles of teleprinter line. Soon even that was a tiny number.

Until then ticker tape had been the standard means of transmitting stock exchange prices; it was reliable, but cumbersome and slow. The nascent computer industry was beginning to change all that. Long bought the rights from a U.S. firm to supply stock market quotations to subscribers through video terminals linked to a central computer.

After the 1971 collapse of the Bretton Woods pegged-exchange-rate system, money became a commodity to be traded like any other, and the volume of trading grew enormously. Commercial firms needed to hedge their positions. Speculation became a growth industry. Long realized that banks and money traders needed faster information on market movements, and Reuters devised a computerized system called Monitor, which would use computers to make currency trading instantaneous worldwide, creating a global marketplace.

The system was launched in the aftermath of the 1973 Middle East War, during the Arab oil embargo, when currencies were unusually volatile and trading volume high. Within a few years Reuters' financial services had more than 15,000 subscribers in 122 countries and carried quotes on more than 100 currencies, more than 135 commodities and more than 40,000 stocks and bonds. In 1980 Reuters refined the service to allow hundreds of its subscribers to negotiate confidential currency deals on a one-to-one basis. Dealers all over the world could conclude transactions on their screens in just four seconds—at least eleven seconds faster than by telephone. Within a decade, Reuters' revenue had grown from £13.8 million a year to £180 million. Reuters was spinning money for itself and the world's financial markets.

When Murdoch bought his share with Times Newspapers in 1981, there was already discussion among the other shareholders, the Fleet Street proprietors, of taking the company public so that they could all profit from their suddenly very valuable holdings. The most eager was Lord Matthews of Express Newspapers.

Glen Renfrew, who succeeded Gerald Long as chief executive of Reuters after Long went to work for Murdoch as managing director of Times Newspapers, recalled speaking to Murdoch about the profit potential in early 1981. Murdoch was fascinated by the whole business of information services, and by the use that Reuters was making of satellites; in New York he would visit Reuters' satellite farm outside the city. He was eager to see Reuters grow as fast as possible and for it to go public, so that he could offset the losses from Times Newspapers. But unlike some of the other barons, he did not seem to Renfrew to be merely intent on stripping the assets of Reuters for his own company. Renfrew found Murdoch a useful ally on the board in the face of the greed of some of his peers.

Reuters' sudden new profits coincided with increasingly polemical attacks, from the Soviet Union and some Third World governments, upon the role of the international news agencies and the spread of information from the West. In the 1970s and early 1980s they mounted a campaign against "Western cultural imperialism" and in favor of "information sovereignty." In retrospect it could be seen as a desperate Soviet attempt to halt the spread of information carried by computerization and by satellites. But concerns were also expressed in many developing countries.

It was true that Western organizations dominated the news flow. At least 80 percent of international "news" was supplied by Reuters, Associated Press, United Press International and Agence France-Presse. The daily output of these four agencies was vast. They were increasingly accused of selecting and distorting news about the Third World in order to pander to the prejudices of their predominantly Western markets. To Third World governments which controlled their own media, it seemed absurd to allow Western news organizations unlimited freedom. By the midseventies more and more such governments, encouraged by the Soviet Union, were insisting that news was a commodity which they should control. Their demands took form in a series of polemical UNESCO resolutions which were to prove disastrous for that organization, if only because they were contrary to the basic tenets of freedom of information enshrined by the United Nations after the Second World War.

The Russians also saw satellite broadcasting as a threat to their sovereignty—or rather to their ability to deny information to their citizens, and the citizens of the states they dominated. UNESCO agreed, over the opposition of the U.S., Britain, Canada and West Germany, that there should be no satellite broadcasts without the consent of receiving countries. All programs should "respect . . . the right of all countries and peoples to preserve their cultures."

One study conducted for UNESCO in the 1970s showed that while Western Europe imported a third of its television programs, Africa, the Middle East and Latin America imported about half. Asian countries, apart from Japan and China, imported more. The bulk of all imports came from the United States, which even then was exporting some 150,000 hours a year, most of it TV series and feature films.

The idea that television was a form of American "cultural imperialism" was widespread as early as the 1970s, and not only in the communist bloc and Third World. There was also concern in Australia. And in France, Jack Lang, the minister of culture, accused the U.S.A. of advocating "the freedom of the fox in the barnyard."

A UNESCO report, directed by Sean MacBride, suggested ludicrously that while journalists should be free, they must understand that their duty was to uphold friendly relations among states, enhance national dignity and promote peace, disarmament and other worthy causes. And so it continued. UNESCO seemed unable to understand that with information being more and more important a world commodity, governments would impoverish themselves all the more by cutting themselves out of the loop.

Rupert Murdoch's guru, Arthur C. Clarke, was sanguine about such attempts to stop the tide. In 1983 he suggested, in words which were prescient of events in China and Eastern Europe at the end of the 1980s, that the debate on the free flow of information would be settled by engineers, not by politicians. Governments would not for long be able to conceal the evidence of their crimes.

The very existence of new information channels, operating in real time and across all frontiers, will be a powerful influence for civilized behaviour. If you are arranging a massacre, it will be useless to shoot the cameraman who has so inconveniently appeared on the scene. His pictures will already be safe in the studio five thousand miles away and his final image may hang you.

That was somewhat optimistic, as the history of the rest of the decade showed. But Clarke did predict the way the communications revolution reported on, and in part created, images and events such as the young man facing the tanks in Tiananmen Square at the end of the decade.

AUSTRALIA

One of the happier events in Murdoch's fiftieth year was the birthday party which Anna organized at Cavan, soon after he acquired Times Newspapers. A small plane circled overhead, trailing a banner reading "HAPPY BIRTHDAY RUPIE." But from then on, 1981–82 was an unnerving year. Interest payments on Murdoch's holdings shot up from the equivalent of 36 percent of operating income to 80 percent. News Corporation's pretax profits crashed from £26.1 million to £3.2 million. Earnings were poor and the income from Ansett became essential.

Times Newspapers was the big new drain, but the New York *Post* was still shedding money fast. Circulation had increased, but not enough for the paper to become profitable. The strike-prone *Australian* continued to provide an object lesson in labor relations at their worst.

The Australian newspaper operations were overseen by Ken Cowley, the compositor who had joined Murdoch in Canberra—he was now the managing director of News. Cowley was utterly loyal to Murdoch and rarely questioned his judgment. Working for him was "an adventure that eclipsed all my little dreams," Cowley said much later.

The years since the 1975 strike had been turbulent, partly because of the hatred of Murdoch that had been engendered. Editors came and went quickly, and the paper's continued losses were irritating to News Corporation's managers, who saw the paper, in Cowley's words, as "a bit of an indulgence by Rupert." The culture of News was resolutely profit driven. The *Australian* was also constantly hit by strikes, because, as Cowley pointed out, "it was the most vulnerable paper, and the closest to Rupert's heart."

In the late 1970s Murdoch had nearly closed the paper. Cowley had persuaded him to keep it going. Many of the journalists who had remained since the early, heady days of the paper had grown disillusioned with its lack of any direction except toward the right ever since.

Everywhere, there were problems. To alleviate them, Murdoch was always on the phone, calling London, calling New York, calling Sydney, calling San Antonio, calling Adelaide—asking, demanding, shouting, ordering, soothing (sometimes), threatening with long silences (at other times). The empire was run, as one of his editors later put it, "by phone and by clone." Complications inevitably arose. In London, the problems at the *Times* became insupportable to almost everyone involved.

LONDON

Harold Evans assumed his duties as editor of the *Times* just as Murdoch celebrated his fiftieth birthday. He was suffering from flu, but he visited the various departments and addressed the journalists in the reporters' area, making a powerful and, on many, a favorable impression.

In answer to questions, he promised that he would not make it look like the *Sunday Times*, which had a more theatrical layout. It would be wrong to inject similar drama into the *Times;* he wanted to reassert the paper's authority. His relationship with Murdoch was very good. The most impressive thing about him, said Evans, was his enthusiasm and his excitement about Times Newspapers. "In those first months Murdoch did everything and more to support me editorially," Evans later acknowledged in his book *Good Times, Bad Times.*

Although Evans promoted some of the *Times'* journalists—notably Charles Douglas-Home, who had hoped to be editor and who had become his deputy—he also imported a number of close colleagues. Among them was Anthony Holden, a former *Sunday Times* journalist and biographer of Prince Charles, who became features editor. From outside journalism, as an adviser and editorial writer, came Bernard Donoughue, an associate of former Labour prime minister James Callaghan, whom Gerald Long described as a "saloon bar Machiavelli." Their arrival, their close relationship with the editor and their generally higher salaries were widely resented by many of the old *Times* men and women, who felt they were being shifted aside by a new mafia. The new men made no secret of their intention to change everything by yesterday. As Evans began to impose his ideas and his vigorous if somewhat chaotic methods, the division between old and new blood increased.

There were undoubtedly major problems on the *Times* staff in 1981. Whole areas of interest were poorly or inadequately reported. Stories, according to Evans, would be lost in some Bermuda Triangle in the newsroom. Many journalists on the paper feared changes even before they began. Some of the opposition to Evans was from traditionalists who disliked the larger photographs and headlines he introduced as part of a major redesign which survives to this day. But some of it was more considered. Murdoch felt that the editorials had become erratic, even inconsistent. Gerald Long said: "Harry lacked the mental and physical stamina needed: the pressure of running a daily paper is enormous." When editions of the *Times* missed the trains, Evans became rather unpopular among News International's circulation managers.

By the autumn of 1981 many of the *Times'* journalists were very unhappy, Charles Douglas-Home among them. At one stage, Edward Mortimer, an editorial writer of the old school, went to Hugh Trevor-Roper, one of the independent directors, to complain. Trevor-Roper, who disliked Murdoch and Evans with equal intensity, said: "Our job is to protect the editor from the proprietor if need be. What can we do if the editor himself is ruining the paper?"

More and more people volunteered to take the severance payments Murdoch was offering in order to cut staff—one month's pay for every year worked—and leave the paper. By the end of 1981, over fifty people had gone. That was fine with Murdoch; the trouble was that Evans hired as many new people—some of them on higher salaries than those they replaced. That had not been Murdoch's plan. Although circulation started to rise, Murdoch began to have doubts about Evans' vaunted brilliance. He felt that Evans was spending freely but not always consistently. For his part, Evans was frustrated by the fact that Murdoch had still not given him his formal editorial budget, an important issue as the guarantees allowed the editor independence within a set budget. Evans complained that Murdoch gave him no idea what the figures of the paper really showed. Gerald Long was critical of both men: "Harry's idea of a budget was having the accountants on the floor below, pushing up five-pound notes through the cracks. Rupert had his own ideas of financial control which, in my view, did not produce true control or reliable forecasting. Rupert is a gambler: he had a martingale and it worked, most of the time."

Evans became both more suspicious of his proprietor and yet more anxious to please him. Murdoch, Evans said, created an aura—one of scorn for the Social Democrats and bleak hostility toward the Tory "wets" who did not like Mrs. Thatcher's toughness. The Labour Party was of course beyond the pale. He would send Evans right-wing articles marked "Worth reading!" and would jab his finger at *Times* headlines which he thought should have been more supportive of Mrs. Thatcher, saying, "You're always getting at her!" According to Evans, he hated "balance" and "objectivity" and kept calling for more "conviction," which, Evans thought, meant more Tory cheerleading. "None of this," wrote Evans later, "represented a reasonable exchange of views between editor and proprietor, unexceptional in any newspaper. The tone was assertive and hostile to debate."

Murdoch, who had never accepted the Divine Right of Editors, remembered the problem differently. "Harry used to come to me and say"—he mimicked a fast and mouselike whisper—" 'I'll do anything you like. Just tell me what you'd like.' And I'd say, 'Harry, nothing. Please get on with it. But please be consistent.' " Evans, he claimed, was forever switching the paper's policy on big issues. "The only thing I did say, and I put it into writing, was: 'You must have some underlying philosophical direction and follow it. Consistency is what we need.' " Evans claimed that by "consistency" Murdoch meant pro-Thatcherite views. Not so, said Murdoch. "I never discussed politics. I used to complain if it was anti-American, which it wasn't, much."

Deprived of the glow of Murdoch's affection, Evans became more and more nervous. Murdoch later told an Australian journalist that Evans would come into his office and speak rapidly and disjointedly: "You've done all this and what can we do . . . you don't know . . . what we are. . . . You must come here more often. It's wonderful to have you here." Murdoch then imitated Evans returning to his own office, laying his head in his hands and saying, "My God, the *pressure* I'm under. You don't know."

When Murdoch was not in town he often dealt with Evans through Gerald Long. Long was to become an instructive casualty of the News Corp style. A cultivated, military-looking man, he indulged a passion for French wine, food, language and literature, was highly opinionated and did not suffer fools easily.

At Reuters he had been an inspired, if maverick and gruff, chief executive. With a small group of expert colleagues he had brought the agency to the front lines of the information revolution. He considered Murdoch a friend and had joined him as managing director of Times Newspapers on a handshake and a brief word about salary and pension rights. Now, on Grays Inn Road, he became Murdoch's doppelgänger. Murdoch exerts such a strong force that those around him constantly try to please him and to foresee his wishes. Long became aggressive, suspicious and cantankerous. Richard Searby commented, "It's pretty difficult being one of Rupert's direct line managers, when he is involved on a daily basis. Gerry was used to being really chief executive, but he couldn't run Times Newspapers like Reuters." Murdoch's presence was too powerful. Edward Pickering, whom Murdoch had chosen as national director, suggested that "perhaps some of Rupert's boundless energy and aggression rubbed off on Gerry." Another thing which rubbed off was the kick-butt management style which seemed to characterize so many Murdoch operations yet which Murdoch, by virtue of his remote-control techniques, often appeared to be above.

The butt that all were free to kick belonged to Frank Giles at the *Sunday Times*. According to Evans, Murdoch allegedly declared on one occasion that Frank Giles and his wife were "communists." They were as unlikely a pair of revolutionaries as has ever graced a London dinner party, but they were certainly more prodétente and less passionately anticommunist than Murdoch. To Murdoch, this looked like limp-wristedness.

Giles never received explicit instructions about the political direction of the *Sunday Times*. But, like all Murdoch's editors, he soon came to know the proprietor's views. On a Saturday night, he would often tear through the paper, growling at anything he disliked, criticizing headlines, pictures, layouts, shouting, "What do you want to print rubbish like that for?" When reading a piece critical of Reagan's policies in Central America, Murdoch would complain of the reporter, David Blundy—a fine war correspondent who was eventually killed in El

Salvador—"That man's a commie." If there were others in Giles' office, Murdoch could appear even more aggressive. Giles said that in front of such an audience, "Murdoch's bitter animus, stridently voiced, became especially hard to bear."

But Giles also insisted that Murdoch was capable of acts of private kindness. When his chauffeur was diagnosed as dying of cancer, Murdoch did everything possible for him and his family. When the other drivers thanked him, he seemed embarrassed by their knowledge of his generosity.

Throughout 1981 the fortunes of the Thatcher government, and of News, were ebbing. Britain was experiencing one of the worst recessions since the Second World War. Murdoch and Long were at pains to impress upon both Evans and Giles how much money the company was losing. Crisis hit in September when the *Sunday Times* branch of one of the two main print unions, the National Graphical Association (NGA), threatened "to withdraw cooperation" in support of its demand for another pay increase. Murdoch had not acted aggressively against the unions when he took over the papers. Now, however, he declared that if the NGA would not work normally, then everyone who worked for the newspapers would be locked out. No one would be paid, not even the horrified journalists, who were used to being cosseted by Thomsons.

In the event, one issue was lost and the NGA climbed down. But the gulf between many journalists and Murdoch grew.

He demanded that the unions agree to shed six hundred jobs within "days." The papers were "bleeding to death," he said, and without such cuts he would have to close them. At the same time, to protect the trademarks in that event, Murdoch was quietly trying to remove the titles of the *Times* and *Sunday Times* from Times Newspapers Limited to News International, which owned the *News of the World* and the *Sun*.

On February 5 Murdoch met with senior *Times* executives to brief them on the financial crisis and to warn them that the papers might have to close if the unions were not more cooperative. Charles Douglas-Home asked if the titles would be available to a liquidator. Murdoch replied simply that they "might not be." This elliptical answer rippled around Grays Inn Road and *Sunday Times* journalists went to Companies House to check the Times Newspapers mortgage register. They found that in the list of Times Newspapers assets there was now no mention of "titles and copyrights." They had been transferred to News International. The effect of this transaction was to strip Times Newspapers of its principal assets, the titles. If the company were liquidated, the titles would remain part of the Murdoch stable, to be dusted off and republished at will.

Searby later said,

> The losses we were sustaining at Times Newspapers were huge for News to bear at that time. We were smaller then. The unions thought they had us over a barrel. So we thought, Suppose we take the trademark and simply transfer it to News. Then if there was a terrible strike, we could simply close Times Newspapers and then at once start up a new subsidiary called New Times Newspapers. We wanted to preserve the papers, not destroy them. Our solicitors, Farrers, told us in writing that this would be OK.

Both Evans and Giles had been at the board meeting in December 1981 at which the removal of the titles had been approved. Neither of them had then objected. However, when their journalists pointed out the significance of the matter, Evans authorized the *Times* to investigate. In February 1982, the paper published a detailed story. Trevor-Roper declared that the lack of previous consultation was a prima facie violation of the terms under which Murdoch had acquired the papers. The previous editor, William Rees-Mogg, called for the transfer to be canceled. The government said that it was studying the affair.

Murdoch asked Richard Searby to come over from Melbourne and sort out the mess. On February 17, News International announced that the titles were being transferred back to Times Newspapers.

In his memoirs, Evans subsequently accused News International of "fraudulent" behavior over the titles, a charge which the company categorically denied. The affair marked the death of the relationship between Murdoch and Evans. Rumors to this effect began to circulate on Fleet Street and Evans demanded that Murdoch publicly deny them. Murdoch did so, praising the improvements Evans had made to the *Times*.

There had been improvements, but the last year had wrought havoc among the staff. Their discontent coalesced around Charles Douglas-Home, Evans' deputy. In his memoirs Evans accused Douglas-Home of conniving with Murdoch against him; Douglas-Home denied this and Gerald Long maintained: "Charlie was loyal to the paper, not to Harry, but he never connived with Murdoch against Harry—he was an upright and honest man."

Communication from editor to proprietor now tended to take the form of barbed memos loaded with surface flattery. On February 21, Evans wrote, "May I say how much I admire and support the battle which I feel sure we are going to win [with the unions]. . . ."

Evans' note was written with an eye to Murdoch's prejudices. Commenting on a rise in circulation, "We collect the usual cheap sneers for being competitive and wanting readers." He went on to drop a name, and a possible opportunity for the proprietor. "By the way, Henry Kissinger offered to write pieces (for paying his fare or something like that). He is president of the US football league and knows a lot about the game. If you like the idea I'll take it further—or you can meet him when he comes here in April on his delayed trip."

Evans wanted to recruit "an intelligent polemicist." "I did talk to Alexander Chancellor [the editor of the *Spectator*] but came to the conclusion he represents part of the effete old tired England"—the class Murdoch most despised.

Evans concluded, "There's more but you have a lot on your plate.

Thank you again for the opportunity and ideas. We are all 100 per cent behind you in this great battle and I'm glad we're having it now."

Murdoch replied coolly, complaining that several well-known journalists had recently decided to leave the *Times*. He went on:

My chief area of concern about the paper is one I have raised with you several times: the paper's stand on major issues. Of course it takes attitudes, but I fail to find any consistency in them, anything that indicates unmistakably the clear position of conscience that a great newspaper must be seen to hold. Just what that position is, it is your duty to define, and it cannot be mine. But it must be defined with clarity and authority and even repetition.

In a formal "Dear Chairman" reply, Evans was combative, though he ended: "But of course, while being consistent in our editorial position, we have deliberately opened the paper to a diversity of views in the belief that truth will triumph and that our readers, especially, want a fully informed debate rather than a monolithic line of propaganda." The letter was signed "Yours loyally, Harold."

On February 24, Evans sent a memo asking Murdoch for his views on how the paper should cover the impending budget, which all British papers always covered extensively. Murdoch replied cordially enough:

Dear Harry,

I don't see why we should be writing notes to each other when my door is always open to you. . . . The sports pages look terrific. . . . I don't know how to advise you about the budget. . . . Surely you need to know the size and content of the budget statement before committing the exact amount of space.

The staff was in turmoil. Both Charles Douglas-Home and John Grant, the managing editor, decided to resign, but stayed at Murdoch's request.

On March 1 Harry Evans' father died. He was deeply affected. Murdoch wrote him a note of condolence saying that it was thirty years since his own father died and he remembered it as if it were yesterday. "A good father-and-son relationship is one of the best experiences in life. You must take any time you need to attend to the necessary family arrangements."

Then, four days after the funeral, on March 9, budget day, the busiest day of the year for any British newspaper, Murdoch called Evans to his office and asked for his resignation. Evans said he refused and asked Murdoch why. Murdoch said, "The place is in chaos. You can't see the wood from the trees. . . . Your senior staff is up in arms."

Murdoch had already seen Douglas-Home for breakfast that morning at his flat on St. James's and had asked him if he would take over the editorship. Douglas-Home had accepted. Later that day Evans went to his deputy and told him he had no integrity, no honor. According to Evans, Douglas-Home replied, "I would do anything to edit the *Times,* wouldn't you?" Douglas-Home also allegedly told Evans that he was "too close to Murdoch, too desirous of his approval, too ready to do his bidding."

By now, having secured almost three quarters of the reduction in the work force he had demanded, Murdoch announced that the *Times* was safe after all. But the newspaper was now riven by rumor. On March 12 a *Times* report on the successful outcome of the talks with the unions noted: "Mr Harold Evans, the editor of the *Times,* said he had no comment to make on reports circulating about his future as editor. He was on duty last night as usual." However, according to Searby, he had decided to leave, and the only thing being discussed was the size of his golden handshake.

Next day, Evans agreed to resign, but then reconsidered and went back to the newspaper. Crucially, however, he made no attempt to rally the staff. If he had done so, and had challenged Murdoch directly for interfering with the paper's independence, he might have secured the support of the journalists, though many were as dissatisfied with him as others were with Murdoch.

Murdoch made a statement denying all reports of editorial disagreements between Evans and himself.

Evans was continually on the phone to the national directors for advice. One of them, Lord Robens, pointed out in a radio program that he was "the most protected editor in the world." He could not be forced to resign if he thought he was under improper pressure. He had only to complain formally to the directors. In fact he made no formal complaint on which they could act.

Murdoch flew back to New York for a fifty-first birthday party, leaving Gerry Long and Richard Searby to negotiate Evans' terms. Searby said later, "I told Rupert that it would be hard for Harry to get another job comparable to the *Times,* and it was basically our mistake for hiring him in the first place. We wanted to be generous and to make the payoff as tax efficient as possible."

Evans was understandably emotional and uncertain what to do. His talks with Searby were painful. He described the Australian lawyer as having the debonair charm of a riverboat gambler. Long, however, found Searby meticulous and totally honest.

On Saturday, March 13, a group of *Times* journalists representing Journalists of the *Times* (JOTT) issued an extraordinary statement calling for Evans to resign and for Douglas-Home to take his place: "Our concern is that the gradual erosion of editorial standards from within might leave us with no paper worth saving. The way the paper is laid out and run has changed so frequently that stability has been destroyed." Only a few of the journalists had approved this statement, but it was clear that at least a part of the staff sided with the owner against the editor. Others, said Edward Mortimer, "were as dissatisfied with Murdoch as anybody. But Harry's fault was the greatest. He never asked for our support because he never made a decision to fight. Most of the damage Murdoch had done to the *Times,* up to that point, he had done through Harry." Evans was in a lonely place—rejected by both his proprietor and a large number of his staff.

Evans hung on through the weekend, wrestling with his nerves and his conscience. On Monday, March 15, he signed. News International paid £120,000 into the company's pension plan, gave him another £150,000 in cash, extended an interest-free mortgage for another year and gave him his company car. He read a short statement to the press and went home, where Tina had organized an impromptu party, filled with friends who toasted Evans and cursed Murdoch.

Tony Holden left the paper in solidarity with Evans, without a payoff. Bernard Donoughue was fired with a severance payment. He subsequently went to work as a financial adviser to Robert Maxwell, whom he used to praise, while condemning Murdoch. Gerald Long, whom Murdoch removed as managing director of Times Newspapers soon after Evans' dismissal, also retained unhappy memories, and said that working for News was the worst time of his professional life. He thought Evans did not have the necessary talents to edit the *Times,* but he too found Murdoch's management methods unbearable.

THE FALKLANDS

A few weeks after Evans resigned, Argentina invaded the Falkland Islands, and Britain went to war.

Murdoch shared Mrs. Thatcher's determination that the islands be recovered. On April 22, when he was made the first "Communications Man of the Year" by the American Jewish Congress in New York, he told the audience that the conflict between Argentina and Britain should be taken as a reminder of what might happen in the Middle East: the issue was democracy versus dictatorship and the case for supporting Britain was the same as that for supporting Israel.

All of Murdoch's editors reacted in character. At the *Sunday Times,* Frank Giles published a measured response in which he said he hoped that a peaceful solution could be negotiated, and he tried to exonerate the Foreign Office, which many others were blaming for having failed to predict the invasion.

At the *Times,* Charles Douglas-Home called the attack "Naked Aggression," unparalleled since the days of Adolf Hitler, and then declared, "We are all Falklanders now." The paper questioned the ability of the foreign secretary, Lord Carrington, to carry on in the face of Foreign Office failure to predict the invasion. That same day Carrington resigned. The *Sun* declared that the Foreign Office had been a haven of appeasers since Munich.

The *Sun* fought a famous war which clearly reflected the personality of its editor, Kelvin MacKenzie, whom Murdoch had appointed in place of Sir Larry Lamb. Murdoch was looking to MacKenzie to liven things up, and he was not disappointed.

MacKenzie was born in 1946; he was a man of stout suburban origins who liked to affect a working-class loutishness in person and in print. Like Murdoch, MacKenzie had a fearsome temper, and he would bawl out his reporters in the most ferocious "bollocking sessions." His public persona was one of manic brutishness and a disdain for Murdoch's pet hate, the Establishment. Next to that, he despised the socialist sympathies of the *Daily Mirror* and the liberalism of the *Guardian,* which he called "the world's worst newspaper"; other "upmarket" papers were merely "the unpopulars." His motto, and one by which he abided tenaciously, was "SHOCK AND AMAZE ON EVERY PAGE."

Murdoch seemed to treat him like a wayward son, an erratic genius who had to be humored. For the *Sun* reporters, the MacKenzie era was like being on a roller coaster with a crazed fiend at the controls.

He began to move the paper further downmarket or, as Murdoch would put it, made it more popular, in pursuit of the *Star*, which Express Newspapers published to undercut the *Sun*. MacKenzie soon became a legend among journalists for his abusive, scatological language and for the crude, witty, sometimes untruthful and sometimes brilliant paper he edited. Sex, violence, sports, xenophobia and Thatcherism were the essential ingredients of his brew.

Falklands War fever gripped the *Sun* as nowhere else. *Sun* reporters gave themselves military ranks, a picture of Winston Churchill was hung up in the newsroom and, when the British military task force set sail for the South Atlantic, a new slogan was coined: "The paper that supports our boys."

Many soldiers in the Falklands were offended by the ghoulish jingoism of the *Sun*'s reports and headlines. It accused the BBC of "treason" for its evenhanded reports. Its rival, the *Daily Mirror*, denounced the *Sun* as "the Harlot of Fleet Street." It was censured by the Press Council for fabricating an interview with a war widow. All the same, MacKenzie was happy with his war record and the backing given by his proprietor.

In May 1983, less than a year after her triumph in the Falklands War, Mrs. Thatcher asked the country for a renewed mandate. Given that there were three million unemployed at the time, this was anything but a foregone conclusion.

The *Sun* featured Thatcher as the Falklands heroine, contrasting the decisive nature of her leadership with the chaotic condition of the Labour opposition. The Tories were said to be making a new Britain: it was "GOODBYE TO THE OLD SCHOOL TIE" under Maggie. The Conservative manifesto was spread over two pages with the headline "MAGGIE'S VISION OF GREAT DAYS FOR BRITAIN." In 1979 the paper had advised "Vote Tory," but now it was "VOTE FOR MAGGIE . . . Carry on Maggie! All the way to the GREAT Britain that a great people deserve." Similar if slightly more judiciously worded sentiments were expressed in the *Times*. The *Sunday Times* was less enthusiastic about Mrs. Thatcher; Frank Giles said Murdoch never interfered, and, in the end, it too endorsed the Conservatives. Thatcher won.

Soon after the election, Murdoch called Giles and told him that he wanted him to make way for a younger man. Murdoch proposed that Giles should assume the title of editor emeritus for the two years until his retirement. It was said that Giles had asked Murdoch exactly what his new title meant. "It's Latin, Frank," Murdoch was reported to have replied. "*E* means 'exit' and *meritus* means 'you deserve it.' " The story is apocryphal.

In place of Giles, Murdoch appointed Andrew Neil, a relatively unknown thirty-four-year-old journalist from the *Economist*.

Neil, a man with a rough-hewn face and a substantial but tender ego, was very much a man after Murdoch's heart. First of all, he was a Scotsman, and Murdoch liked to say that the Scots were the only decent Britons and, in America, the only decent WASPs. Like Murdoch, Neil saw himself as a leader of the new Conservative meritocracy, forever jousting with the effete English Establishment. He soon set about remaking the image and the behavior of the *Sunday Times,* destroying, in effect, the last vestiges of the reign of Harry Evans which Frank Giles had elegantly retained. In doing so, Neil aroused dissatisfaction among the staff and among a section of the paper's readers.

Eighteen months later Evans brought out his book *Good Times, Bad Times,* of which the latter were almost all spent with Murdoch. The proprietor appeared, in Evans' account, to be the incarnation of evil.

The story was well paced and many reviewers praised the narrative, as well as Evans' courage in resisting and now denouncing the ogre. Even Murdoch's own papers were generous. But to some critics, the book seemed bitter and flawed. In his review, Magnus Linklater complained, "At vital moments, it shies away from the truth"—in particular the truth about the early courtship of Evans and Murdoch. In response, Evans wrote an angry letter to Linklater, accusing him of a pusillanimity similar to that of intellectuals in the Weimar Republic. Evans was equally upset by other criticisms made in the Washington *Post* by Patrick Brogan, who had resigned from the *Times* when Murdoch bought it. Evans wrote to Brogan to denounce his comments as "the product of a mean and fatuous mind . . . so frivolous . . . second hand smears . . ."

Murdoch was much cooler about the whole matter. He largely ignored the book. In an interview in the Sydney *Morning Herald,* he said, "Harry wanted to be loved by everybody. But he ended up being loved by nobody."

At the *Times,* Evans' successor, Charles Douglas-Home, was regarded with more affection. The literary editor, Philip Howard, once pointed out that Douglas-Home had taken over the *Times* "in a raging storm, with mutiny and panic below decks, and the ship in danger of foundering." As captain, he had quelled the mutiny and quietly calmed the staff after the trauma caused by the bitter contest between Evans and Murdoch. He tried to give the paper a renewed sense of itself. Most of the journalists liked him, but not everyone approved the Thatcherite and more populist course on which he tried to steer the ship.

According to some of the staff, Douglas-Home found it easier than Harry Evans to be robust with his proprietor. Instead of being appalled or terrified by a suggestion from Murdoch, he would either accept it or say simply, "Rupert, I'm sorry, but I just won't do that." This has always been the best way for editors to deal with Murdoch; he responds better to a show of decisiveness than to floundering. However, like many others, Douglas-Home often found Murdoch remote and used to say, "Rupert's not on receive." Murdoch's constant air of preoccupation could mean that even while he was talking his mind had already moved to another problem, perhaps thousands of miles away.

The relationship was eased by the fact that, like Murdoch, Douglas-Home was a Conservative who admired Mrs. Thatcher far more than Harold Evans had done.

Murdoch rarely gave Douglas-Home direct instructions. As always, his wishes and views merely emanated from him, rather like ectoplasm. His editors knew his opinions, and they knew his financial interests also. Many of them were constantly anxious to please him and there is no doubt that one way of doing so was to anticipate his views. Thus, from the mid-1980s on, the *Times* and the *Sunday Times* not only would be generally in favor of Mrs. Thatcher (which they might have been anyway, whether or not they were owned by Murdoch), but also would carry constant sniping criticisms of such Murdoch *bêtes noires* as the BBC and the British television establishment in general.

Perhaps the crucial fact about Douglas-Home's editorship, and certainly the most tragic, was that throughout it he was suffering from an excruciating and incurable bone cancer. Many editorial meetings were conducted with the editor lying on his back on the floor.

He died in October 1985 and was buried near his home in Gloucestershire. News was generous to Douglas-Home's widow, Jessica, and paid for the education of their sons. Jessica Douglas-Home remained devoted to Murdoch—as a man, as a proprietor and as a friend. She later became involved in helping dissidents in Eastern Europe, and solicited Murdoch for assistance, which he gave.

5

BOSTON

In the early 1980s Murdoch was determined above all to build up his presence in America. Just as he was fortunate in his relationship with Mrs. Thatcher in Britain, so he was blessed in having Ronald Reagan and his free-market philosophy reigning in Washington. Murdoch's political views continued to move further to the right. The process, he said, was "accelerated by five years in London watching the welfare state and watching what's happening in New York, which has a welfare state without being able to print money."

Murdoch cherished his relationship with the White House, though once, when he went to lunch with Reagan in the early 1980s, he was surprised by the president's age and fragility. Reagan actually fell asleep during the meal; the other guests went on eating and the waiters continued to take the plates away. Eventually Reagan awoke, bright and cheerful, as if on cue. Murdoch later described the experience as "awful."

Murdoch was also becoming friendly with Richard Nixon. Murdoch believed that Watergate-type investigations were not the purpose of journalism. "I differ from the vast majority of my peers in this country in that I believe the new cult of adversarial journalism has sometimes been taken to the point of subversion," he told a group of Boston businessmen. "It is a disgrace that we can and do read thousands upon thousands of words about our national defense and our foreign policy every day without so much as a nod of recognition to the enormous risks to our freedom that exist today—to the terrifying consequences of Russian and Cuban bases on this continent. . . ." He also argued, "It is a sorry fact that the media as a whole . . . unquestioningly embrace a welfare state which divides and embitters our society without helping the truly poor and needy."

Murdoch's family holding company, Cruden, still owned 40 percent of Australia's News Ltd., which in turn owned 49.3 percent of his British company, News International. These two public companies were partners in the News America publishing company. At this stage News America was not required to publish its results, because it was not traded on the New York Stock Exchange.

In America, Murdoch had taken on Donald Kummerfeld as president and chief operating officer of News America. Kummerfeld had previously been first deputy mayor and budget director of New York City. As a Democrat, Kummerfeld was a little uneasy with some of Murdoch's friendships, particularly that with Roy Cohn, who had acquired a sleazy reputation since he had first become famous as Senator Joseph McCarthy's aggressive chief counsel during the Army-McCarthy hearings in 1954.

Through the 1970s, News had been globally run by Murdoch on a wing and a prayer. As it grew in the early 1980s, it was clear that a more structured organization was needed. Kummerfeld, with his budgetary experience, attempted to supply this.

When Kummerfeld started with News America in 1978, the company was worth some $300 million. By the time he left in 1985 its value was nearer $2 billion. He insisted on stricter budgets and quarterly budget reviews. A financial committee consisting of Merv Rich, Kummerfeld, Murdoch and Stan Shuman of Allen and Company, Murdoch's principal American banking adviser, was created. With Jeff Leist, an American accountant, Kummerfeld helped set up a computerized system for dealing with all the currencies in which the company traded. (Murdoch loved to gamble on the foreign exchange markets.) With Bruce Matthews, Murdoch's powerful manager in London, Kummerfeld also set about coordinating the purchase of newsprint for papers around the world. The News group became the world's largest newsprint consumer.

Kummerfeld also worked on Murdoch's image, enlisting the help of Howard Rubenstein, one of New York's most successful public relations wizards. Together, they tried to turn Murdoch into a social force in the U.S., as well as a supporter of the Zionist cause. He and Anna became involved in civic events in New York, where she felt easily at home. "I belong here," she said to Kummerfeld's wife, Beth.

As their life changed, Murdoch had less time for some of the original colleagues he had brought from Australia. Or, at least, so it seemed to them. Paul Rigby, the cartoonist, had been a friend since the wild Sydney *Mirror* days. "He expected a lot of patriotism from his Oz mafia, but he wouldn't pay much for it," said Rigby later. "I had five kids at school but Rupert would never recognize that." This parsimony with old-timers contrasted with his tendency to offer large salaries to new recruits. Eventually, Rigby accepted a more lucrative offer from the New York *Daily News*. The *Post* reacted by employing his son, also a cartoonist, so that it could still proclaim that Rigby was in its pages.

On a public level, Murdoch used the paper as almost every baron of the media has done, to exert political influence. The *Post* gave him a unique and valuable platform in one of the most important cities of the world. He had used it to help elect the mayor of New York and he had wholeheartedly supported Reagan for president in 1980.

Later Murdoch said that when the *Post* endorsed Reagan "we expected a firestorm. In fact, the letters began running very strongly, first fifty-fifty for and against, then within a week they were running three to one in our favor. It was then I knew there was something on. It was not such a brave thing to do after all."

After Reagan's victory Murdoch was almost as supportive of Reaganism as he was of Thatcherism. Max Newton's enthusiastic encomiums to the "Reagan Revolution" were influential. In a way, Murdoch helped both Reagan and Thatcher define the spirit of the 1980s. He was in a sense their amanuensis. Reagan responded. When he visited New York in spring 1982, he gave the *Post* an exclusive interview. It was only one of many favors from the administration.

Murdoch also continued the *Post's* enthusiastic support for Ed Koch in New York, and in 1982 urged the mayor to run for governor. Once again reporters grumbled that their stories were edited to reflect the paper's endorsements, that balancing quotes were removed, that new and slanted leads were added. It was Steve Dunleavy of whom they complained most often. He was described in the *Columbia Journalism Review* as Murdoch's point man in the city room.

"The *Post* became what amounted to a political pamphlet for thirty days," observed Koch's opponent in the Democratic gubernatorial primary, Mario Cuomo. "That has to be important. The small political community that controls the early stages of every campaign is disproportionately influenced by something like the *Post* campaign; they read everything." Nonetheless, Cuomo won the primary and then the general election.

In fact, there was nothing new about the massive support that Murdoch extended to his preferred candidates. American publishers like Hearst, Greeley and Pulitzer had behaved even more brazenly.

Murdoch believed that tabloid journalism had to be alive to thrive, and he quoted H. L. Mencken's warning to tabloid papers: "Every tabloid, as soon as it gets into safe waters, begins to grow intellectual. The bold, gaudy devices that launched it are abandoned and it takes on decorum. I know of at least two that are actually liberal. This, I fear, is a false form of progress. The tabloid, so lifted by its bootstraps, becomes simply a little newspaper." And little papers, Murdoch added, disappear in big markets.

But he was wrong about the New York market. Despite his love for the wilder shores of journalism, the *Post* was not working properly. Whereas most British and Australian tabloids were only thirty-two pages, and had relatively high cover prices, Americans were used to fat papers at low prices. Advertising revenues were vital to American dailies, to offset the costs of low circulations. In almost all cities the local stores were crucial advertisers, but the stores were concerned not so much with numbers of readers as with their buying power. Although the New York *Times* had half the circulation of the *Daily News* in the mid-1970s, it carried almost twice as much advertising. Thus the *Times* was profitable while the *News* was always on the verge of going under. In San Antonio, Murdoch found that gains in circulation were actually losing him money—advertisers were not interested because they thought that most of the new readers were Mexican Americans too poor to buy the goods advertised.

In New York he never managed to win for the *Post* the better-heeled readers the advertisers wanted. There was a widely quoted story that a senior executive of Bloomingdale's explained to Murdoch why the store did not advertise in the *Post:* "Rupert, your readers are our shoplifters."

This tale was only just apocryphal. A man from Bloomingdale's did indeed tell the *Wall Street Journal,* "It's immaterial to us if the *Post*'s circulation is six hundred thousand or six million. Our customers are sophisticated and urbane and don't want to hear about the violence and sex the *Post* touts." By 1982, the *Post* still had only 6 percent of the advertising in New York papers—the *Times* had 56 percent and the *News* 38 percent. Even the supermarket chains, which cared less for demographics, on the grounds that everyone has to eat, were doubtful about the *Post*.

Murdoch was forced to acknowledge that what he called "the cheeky working class" who bought the *Sun* in Britain did not exist in quite the same form in New York. In fact, he came to the conclusion that New York did not have a working class at all:

This is a middle-class city. Everybody in this country wants to get ahead, get a piece of the action. That's the fundamental difference between the Old World and the New World. There's not the self-improvement ethic in England that there is in this country. If you drop below that level, you're talking about the ghettoes. And there's a question as to whether those people can even read, let alone afford a newspaper.

Murdoch still had his sights fixed upon the New York *Daily News*. He intended to launch a morning tabloid, the *Daily Sun*, against its soft underbelly—just as he had launched the *Sun* against the *Daily Mirror* in London. Despite his realization that New York was different from Britain, he still argued that the *News* had become too respectable, edited by people "who wish they were working for the New York *Times*."

Murdoch's analysis was not dismissed at the *News*. Its editor, Mike O'Neill, acknowledged that after the disastrous 1962–63 strike "we decided to move closer to the *Times,* occupying the center." It was a mistake. "We'd love to get back irreverence without sacrificing credibility," said O'Neill.

Soon after Harold Evans' stormy departure in London, Murdoch offered to buy the *News*. The Tribune Company of Chicago, which owned the paper, was then negotiating its sale to the Texas financier Joseph Allbritton. The idea that Murdoch should buy it was not appealing. They expected that he would close it to ensure the profitability of the *Post*. The company said no to Murdoch, which enabled the *News* to display the headline "TRIB TO RUPERT: DROP DEAD," an echo of its famous headline "FORD TO CITY: DROP DEAD." In the end the *Tribune* held on to the paper—and it went on losing money.

Undeterred, Murdoch continued to search for more North American papers. Later in 1982 he made a lunge at the *Courier Express* of Buffalo, New York. But the unions refused to agree to the scale of cuts in the work force he thought essential to stanch its losses. The paper was closed. One reporter was quoted as saying, "We voted to die with dignity," an odd endorsement of suicide. Murdoch continued his quest in Boston, where the city's second paper, the Boston *Herald,* was the underdog to the established, mighty and somewhat preachy Boston *Globe.* This was a situation made for Murdoch.

The first Boston *Herald* had been founded in 1846 by printers in the city. In 1912 it had absorbed the Boston *Traveler* to become the Boston *Herald-Traveler,* and was until the end of the 1950s the preeminent broadsheet in the city, outselling and outclassing the *Globe.* But in the 1960s it had declined and in 1972 it was bought by the Hearst Corporation, which merged it with its tabloid *Record American.* This marriage of a blue-collar tabloid with a blue-blooded broadsheet produced an ever thinner and drearier paper. Editors came and editors went. Advertisers just went. The paper had no idea of its readers or of itself.

In 1979 a gifted editor, Donald Forst, was transferred across country from Hearst's Los Angeles *Herald Examiner.* He improved it, but circulation continued to fall—below 200,000 on weekdays and to 329,000 on Sundays in 1981. The *Globe* now had almost half a million in daily sales and almost 800,000 on Sundays. The *Herald-American* was losing at least $10 million a year.

Forst induced Hearst to make one last attempt to save the paper by investing another $3.5 million and turning it into a tabloid. The paper became sprightlier, running headlines such as "HINCK'S SHRINK STINKS"—about John Hinckley's unsuccessful insanity plea during his trial for the attempted murder of President Reagan—and "CLAUS IS A LOUSE," referring to Claus von Bülow's celebrated trials for the attempted murder of his wife.

Circulation rose—but only by a few thousand. The Hearst Corporation began to cut costs and it seemed clear that it wanted to get rid of the paper. Forst contacted Murdoch, who had once offered him the editorship of *New York* magazine.

After a lunch in Boston, Murdoch invited him to his house at Chatham in upstate New York, and pumped him for information on the paper. Like so many others, Forst was disarmed by Murdoch. "He charmed me out of my underwear," he said to Murdoch's biographer Michael Leapman later. But Murdoch took Forst for a walk in the woods with his children and told him that, notwithstanding Forst's valiant efforts for the paper, he would want a new editor if he bought the *Herald-American*.

Even so, Forst retained fond memories of Murdoch: "He was wonderful with his kids. . . . And he seemed to have a nice relationship with his wife. . . . How can I get angry with him? If a man pulls a rabbit out of his hat, he's entitled to do with it what he will. Make stew or skin it or turn it into another felt hat. That's the ball game."

Murdoch offered Hearst $1 million for the *Herald-American,* plus another $7 million from future profits, if any. Since the paper's building alone was thought to be worth $8 million, he believed he had another winner. On November 17, 1982, Hearst announced the negotiations, describing Murdoch as "the buyer of last resort." Murdoch insisted that he would go ahead only if the unions agreed to significant work-force reductions by midnight on December 3. The *Globe* at once tried to wrest similar concessions from the unions and Murdoch accused the paper of trying to sabotage him. He threatened to sue the *Globe*.

As so often, the talks went right up to the wire, so that each side could demonstrate its resolve. Right till the end, it looked as if at least one union would hold out and spoil the deal. "MURDOCH AND THE UNIONS. GOING DOWN TO THE WIRE," ran the last headline of the Hearst ownership. Just ten minutes before the deadline on December 3, 1982, Murdoch got the concessions he wanted and acquired the paper.

He agreed to invest some $16 million, while cutting staff in all departments. He changed the paper's name to the Boston *Herald*—which was what most readers called it anyway. He brought in new editors from New York, put bright yellow *Herald* vending machines all over town, spruced up the building, installed computers and changed the layout from four broad columns to seven narrow columns a page. And, of course, he took the paper into that netherland where he always goes—downmarket. More sports, a bit more sex (not too much in Catholic Boston), more competitions—in particular Wingo—more bizarre reports, more of everything that Murdoch thought Boston working-class readers should like. Stories were made shorter and were given fancy borders. Often the entire front page was given over to a headline designed to seize the reader by the scruff of the neck. It was all part of a deliberate effort to convince people of the truth of the headline on the day Murdoch clinched the deal: "WE'RE ALIVE."

The *Herald* gained over 100,000 readers in the first year Murdoch owned the paper. Tom Winship, the editor of the *Globe,* dismissed the *Herald* as "circus journalism." But the competition was good for the *Globe,* which began to cover more local stories and expanded its foreign reporting. David Greenway, the *Globe's* associate editor, took a more considered view: "Murdoch saved a paper, he found a whole lot of new readers in Boston and he kept us on our toes." He thought Murdoch had benefited Boston.

Murdoch hoped to outsell the *Globe.* He thought that in some ways Boston would be an easier city for him to succeed in than New York. "Boston is a very passionate city. It's a very direct, no-nonsense city. You don't have the fakery and glitter here of Madison Avenue. . . . I think it will be easier for us to find an identity here than it was in New York."

Many of the journalists on the *Herald* enjoyed working under Murdoch. Andrew Gully, the city editor, said later:

> The great thing about Murdoch is that we are left completely free to assign stories as we want to. There's no one ringing us from New York telling us, "I want this covered," or "I want that

covered." We do what we think is best and that is a real luxury in any kind of business. . . . The image is that Rupert is very heavyhanded, but it just hasn't been the case here.

When Murdoch bought the paper he said that it would not try to influence political life as strongly as the *Post* had endeavored to do in New York, but "our politics will certainly be a lot less liberal than the *Globe*'s." That naturally extended to strident criticism of Massachusetts' senior, liberal Democratic senator, Edward Kennedy. He was to be a dangerous enemy for Murdoch.

THE CLARKE RING

While he was negotiating for the *Herald,* Murdoch also climbed aboard the Clarke Ring. In November 1983 the space shuttle *Columbia* launched a private communications satellite owned by Satellite Business Systems (SBS), a combine which included the Aetna Insurance Company, IBM and Comsat. Murdoch bought into Inter-American Satellite Television Inc., a company which leased five transponders from SBS for six years at a total cost of $75 million. There were to be a movie channel and a sports channel and subscribers would pay a monthly fee for the programs which were to be beamed to backyard dishes. Murdoch called his company Skyband, and declared optimistically that it would soon be broadcasting to one hundred thousand subscribers.

At this time cable was snaking across most of the United States, but Murdoch made a conscious decision not to invest in any franchises. He found the whole idea of cable television boring, and this disdain led him to ignore its huge commercial potential. By the end of the 1980s, the cable operators were mining gold from the monopolies they had established.

Satellite broadcasting seemed much more exciting to Murdoch. It did have promise. In the United States one of the huge steps onto the Clarke Ring had been taken by a Time Inc. executive, Gerry Levin, who had risked putting Home Box Office "on the bird"—onto a satellite. A whole new era in communications and media began at that moment. Home Box Office was a regional pay-TV service in the northeastern U.S. till the mid-1970s. Once aloft, it was suddenly national, broadcasting its signal to regional cable systems all over the continent. And all because Levin had understood the magic of satellite television. The idea apparently came to him with the broadcast of a few seconds of the Frazier-Ali fight from Manila—the so-called Thrilla in Manila.

Levin was taking a considerable gamble. When he began, there were not many cable companies with satellite dishes. But once Home Box Office was up there, they began to proliferate. In 1977 there were some five hundred cable-system dishes in the country. By 1982 there were five thousand. Cable was driven across the land by Home Box Office and by Ted Turner's superstation, WTBS. Like Levin, Turner was a pioneer. The fact that each of them had low-power satellites to transmit to cableheads transformed the economics of cable. WTBS eventually spawned CNN, the station that transformed the reporting of the world. One of Murdoch's most serious misjudgments was to ignore cable.

He believed that there was a large market for satellites because, while there were eighty-three million TV households in the United States, only fifty-five million of them were in areas being wired for cable. The others, mostly in rural areas, would probably never be wired. He expected Skyband to gross almost $325 million a year by 1986. The market was entirely new but, he said, "there was never any doubt it was going to happen. The real question is, Are the advantages of being first in very great? We think they are."

Only after the deal was done and the first payments were made did Murdoch discover that his thinking was premature. The dishes required were still large and it was hard to persuade people to accept them in their yards. There were not enough programs to attract viewers, and furthermore the satellite itself was already becoming obsolete. A new generation of more powerful satellites and smaller dishes was on its way. Jim Cruthers, an Australian television pioneer who was one of Murdoch's close advisers on the project, said, "The more we looked at it, the more we realized that it was extremely difficult to get programming of a sufficient quality that would make us competitive in the U.S., where there's so much TV."

In 1983 Murdoch backed out of Skyband, taking losses of $20 million. But he was still determined to take to the skies, in America and elsewhere; at the same time, he was making his first move onto the European section of the Clarke Ring. He bought into Sky Television, the system that was ultimately almost to destroy his empire.

Sky Television was born in Europe in 1981, as Satellite Television plc. It was fathered by a British television producer named Brian Haynes who had become interested in satellite broadcasting at the end of the 1970s. Haynes' vision was of a pan-European satellite-delivered TV service, first through cable systems and then eventually direct to dishes at home.

Haynes persuaded the European Space Agency (ESA) to allow him to use its Orbital Test Satellite (OTS)—which had been intended for telecommunications only. With some difficulty he then induced Eutelsat, an intergovernmental organization which controlled European satellite use, to allow him to broadcast.

The investment bank Guinness Mahon helped Haynes raise some £4 million of risk capital, and he began broadcasting to Malta in 1981. The whole operation was run on a shoestring, but on its own tiny scale, Satellite, as the channel was called, began to work. Haynes thought it should remain a minute system, but by 1983, as expected, Satellite had burned up its first £4 million. Haynes then discovered that a second round of £6 million in risk investment capital was not so easy to find.

The banks put out feelers, and Murdoch responded. He paid an initial £10 million for a controlling interest in Satellite Television plc and renamed the channel Sky to give him a global link to his American Skyband satellite venture, which he hoped might one day fly again. He immediately set about enlarging his new acquisition with more people and further infusions of cash.

Costs rocketed to near £20 million. The problem was that Murdoch had bought a distribution system, not a television company. At that time there was only a small number of pan-European brands which wished to advertise on an international basis.

In the early days, Sky was a tax loss. Meanwhile, the technology was whirring ahead. The French and the Germans were trying to enter the market, but American companies were now developing much smaller, cheaper medium-powered satellites whose signals could be picked up by smaller dishes, and which could transmit more channels than the direct broadcast satellites (DBS).

Tom Whitehead, who had run President Nixon's Office of Telecommunications Policy, now appeared. By 1983, Whitehead was running the satellite communications department at Hughes Aerospace. He went to Luxembourg to persuade the government that it should fill the slot it had been given on the Clarke Ring at the WARC 77 conference with a medium-powered satellite rather than a high-powered DBS. He chose Luxembourg partly because it had a tradition of international broadcasting and because it is, in effect, an offshore banking center.

But there was still massive opposition from other European governments, including France and West Germany, to the concept of an international and private "bird" on the Clarke Ring. What Whitehead called "the most violent and the most ridiculous" opposition came from François Mitterrand, who angrily dismissed the Luxembourg plan as "the Coca-Cola satellite" because it had Whitehead and other

American business interests behind it. He declared that the French government would do everything it could to obstruct Luxembourg's plans, in order to protect the integrity of French borders and French television culture. At the same time, France and Germany signed an agreement to manufacture two direct broadcast satellites to service their two countries with national programs.

Threats came from other governments, from Eutelsat and from the post offices. Nonetheless, Whitehead and the Luxembourgers set up a medium-powered satellite broadcast system called Coronet. But negotiations broke down, and Whitehead moved back to America. A consortium led by Luxembourg banks stepped in and kept Coronet afloat, until it was renamed Astra. It was this enterprise that eventually gave Murdoch his big platform in the sky, later in the 1980s.

CHICAGO

In the winter of 1983–84 Charlie Wilson, a former marine from Glasgow who carried himself like a lightweight boxer, arrived in Chicago. He was expected, he said, "to sodomize" Murdoch's latest acquisition, the Chicago *Sun-Times*, on his master's behalf. That, he was sure, was how the journalists on the paper expected Murdoch's commissar to behave. And indeed, he was met by a gale of loathing with a chill factor at least as painful as the winds which roar through the Windy City off the Central Plains and Lake Michigan.

Chicago is a robust and vibrant town, with a history of fearsome newspaper wars, yet in early 1984 the arrival of Murdoch and his men provoked an extraordinary amount of whimpering. This was strange, if only because he was Chicago's kind of man, ruthlessly and single-mindedly building an empire of information rather than of steel or railroads.

Through the city the El thunders along, a steeplechase ride that brushes up against bedroom windows as it passes stockyards, iron buildings and one ethnic neighborhood after another. It speeds past rooftops you can virtually touch with your hand, behind three- and four-tiered back porches crisscrossed with lumber braces.

At the beginning of the twentieth century, Chicago had twenty-five or more newspapers competing for readers in ruthless ways. Some of their unscrupulous methods were illustrated in Ben Hecht and Charles MacArthur's famous play *The Front Page*. The most violent struggle took place between William Randolph Hearst's Chicago *Examiner* and Colonel Robert McCormick's Chicago *Tribune:* each paper dispatched thugs onto streetcars to grab its rival's pages from passengers' hands, and they would throw the papers and sometimes even the readers into the gutter.

The *Sun* was founded by Marshall Field III, heir to the first Marshall Field, who had established one of the first and most successful of American department stores in Chicago in 1856. Its legendary motto was "Give the lady what she wants." The Marshall Field store became and remained a byword for service—and was famous for its shoppers' dining room.

Marshall Field III created the *Sun* on December 4, 1941, as a New Deal alternative to the isolationism and right-wing policies of Colonel McCormick's Chicago *Tribune*. Three days later came Pearl Harbor and isolationism died. In 1947, Field bought the Chicago *Daily Times,* an afternoon tabloid, and soon merged it with the *Sun*. From then on a state of fierce war existed between the *Sun-Times* and the *Tribune*. Their offices were at either end of the bridge over the Chicago River, the *Sun-Times* in an ugly modern slablike building at the south end and the *Tribune* in a glorious gothic tower on the northern bank. All through the 1950s and 1960s there was ferocious competition—Chicago journalism had quite a lot in common with Murdoch's Sydney. The order of every day was blood, guts and deception; reporters thought nothing of impersonating policemen by flashing phony badges; they stole photographs of dead relatives; they did whatever they needed to do to get The Story.

In the 1970s some of these excesses were abandoned across America as the profession of journalism became, post Woodward and Bernstein, a fashionable activity, and one which attracted thousands of college graduates. The game was cleaned up and the job became more genteel—far too much so, in the opinion of Rupert Murdoch. But the memory lingered on.

In 1980 James Hoge, a graduate of Yale who had been editor of the *Sun-Times* since 1968, was appointed publisher. He moved the paper upmarket to compete more directly with the broadsheet *Tribune*. He favored both aggressive reporting and stylish writing, and he made the *Sun-Times* a vigorous, crusading local paper. He even took on the Cardinal—a historic act in a town where the Catholic Church wielded enormous power. He assembled a good and, by Murdoch's standards, a lavish staff. By 1983 the *Sun-Times* had a daily circulation of some 640,000, with 30,000 more on Sundays; the rival *Tribune* had sales of 751,000 on weekdays and well over 1 million on Sundays.

The *Sun-Times* was clearly the second paper in Chicago, but it inspired much loyalty in a city of immigrants where loyalty was important. It was not dying—but its profits were unspectacular. In 1982 it made only $3.5 million on revenues of $161 million.

By now the paper was owned 50 percent by Marshall Field V, grandson of the founder, and 50 percent by his half brother Frederick "Ted" Field, who was not interested in newspapers. Frederick was described by the New York *Times* as "a bearded amateur race car driver who lives in southern California and invests in real estate and movies." By 1983 he wanted a much greater return on his inherited capital than the *Sun-Times* was providing and decided to sell out. Marshall Field V resisted him for a time, but the trust devised by their father's lawyers provided that in the event of a purchaser being found for the paper, one brother would have to buy out the other at top dollar—or agree to the sale.

Marshall was not happy, but neither did he wish to fight his half brother. Various buyers sniffed around but decided that the *Sun-Times* was not profitable enough; the conventional view was that it would always remain the number-two paper in a highly competitive market. The Washington Post Company was interested. So was Murdoch. This struck horror into the hearts of the journalists, and Jim Hoge began to put together a consortium, based in Chicago, to buy the paper.

In the end, the Washington Post Company offered $50 million and Hoge's consortium offered $63 million. There was also a syndication service, which was worth $20 million. Murdoch offered $90 million for the paper and the service together, making his bid some $7 million higher than the consortium's offer. This was not a huge difference, but Field Enterprises president Lee Mitchell rejected Hoge's offer "without explanation or bargaining."

The Fields had agreed to consider Hoge's counterbid if it was over $55 million. Now that promise looked like a sham. Company officials had even told Hoge that they would not actually sell to Murdoch—his reputation was too awful—but would allow him to bid the price up. Later they qualified this by saying that they would sell to Murdoch, but only if his price was disproportionately higher than that offered by anyone else—high enough to compensate for his bad name, in other words.

On November 1, 1983, Murdoch signed a letter of intent to buy the paper. He wrote to the Field brothers to assure them that he had no intention of changing it significantly and pledged to uphold the highest standards of journalism. He said that he was "approaching the task of continuing the work of the *Sun-Times* with great seriousness and no little humility." The final documents were to have been signed on December 15, but this was delayed by a dispute over the valuation of the pension plan. Belatedly, another Chicago group tried to save the paper from Murdoch. Marshall Field first stalled, then made himself unavailable—rather as Carter Burden had done during the sale of *New York* magazine. He finally admitted through his lawyers that he feared court action by Murdoch if he entertained the new offer.

Murdoch had a deal. For $90 million he had the paper and syndicated news and feature service, producing annual revenues of some $200 million. The buildings alone were worth $30 million.

At a press conference after the purchase was concluded, he was asked what he had to say to counter his reputation as someone "who sends chills up the journalistic spines." He replied, "Nothing at all. I'm very happy to stand on my record." Asked again about the "sleazy" reputation of his papers, he retorted, "You ought to look at them before you spout those myths."

The journalists on the paper were furious, especially with the behavior of Marshall Field. One reporter was quoted as saying that Field was far worse than Murdoch "because he was so duplicitous. There's a moral defect in leading people on and appearing a civic figure. . . . Here he has a legacy, a community trust, and he violates it." The paper's eminent movie critic, Roger Ebert, said Field "betrayed hundreds of people."

Nick Shuman, a senior editorial writer with thirty-two years' service on the paper, wrote a letter of resignation to Field, saying, ". . . the legacy left you by Marshall Field III and Marshall IV was honorable, creative service to their community. You have pissed on that legacy."

Murdoch made several visits to the paper. The New York *Times* reported that when he appeared in the fourth-floor newsroom, he received scattered applause for his promise to keep the paper "substantially" the same. He hosted a small dinner for the paper's editorial stars at a Chicago restaurant and repeated assurances that the *Sun-Times* would not be compromised. But he also told Jim Hoge that he wished to be able to intervene editorially—he hadn't spent $90 million to let someone else have all the fun. Hoge replied that he had heard that this was how Murdoch operated. Each doubted he could work with the other, but they agreed to try.

Donald Kummerfeld visited Chicago and told Hoge that the way *News* functioned was that Murdoch made flying visits, altered budgets, provided a million dollars here if he felt generous and trimmed a bit there if he did not. "My job is to come in with my executives and clean it all up," Kummerfeld explained. Around the world, editors and journalists often found the attitudes and orders of Murdoch's managers much harsher than his own.

Murdoch's acquisition of the *Sun-Times* came shortly after the publication of Harry Evans' memoir, *Good Times, Bad Times,* in which he portrayed Murdoch as restless, brooding, moody, aggressive, manipulative, petulant and very right-wing. This assault on the new boss was widely read in the newsroom of the *Sun-Times.* "It was a deterrent to everyone to stay," said Hoge.

One of those who decided to leave was Mike Royko, the paper's star columnist and a Chicago institution. His column, which often featured an ordinary worker named Slats Grobnick, was widely read and much loved. Royko was seen as a defender of the little guy against authority.

After the deal was completed but before Murdoch moved in, Royko started to refer to Murdoch in his column as "The Alien," and painted a picture of a kind of journalistic terrorist. For years Royko had said he would never work for the *Tribune*—that he could not stand the right-wing legacy of Colonel McCormick—but no self-respecting dead fish would want to be wrapped in a Murdoch paper, he said, and he went across the bridge to the competition. Murdoch immediately sued him for breach of contract. The action was big news in Chicago; teams of cameramen stationed themselves outside the courthouse and sales of the *Tribune* increased notably.

Royko relished the drama. In his first column for the *Tribune,* he said that the thing he liked best about his job was that he could do it sitting down.

Until today, I've been doing my sitting at another place about a block from here. And I was content until this fellow came into town with a large sack of money and decided to buy that place.

As sometimes can happen between boss and employee, we didn't see eye to eye on a few things, so I decided to do my sitting over here. . . .

But now this international tycoon's aides say they are going into court to prevent me from doing my daily sitting here.

What a problem. I don't want to do my sitting there. But he doesn't want me to do it here. Can you imagine a guy coming all the way from Australia just to tell me where to sit?

After a couple of days of massive publicity, the case was thrown out. Royko thought that Murdoch had brought this action just to create a news story.

Some *Sun-Times* journalists were prepared to be more openminded about Murdoch. Irv Kupcinet, the columnist, wrote that journalists should wait and see what Murdoch actually did. Movie critic Ebert opted to stay because

I would rather have Murdoch as an owner than Marshall Field. Murdoch is a newspaper man, a height to which Field never truly ascended . . . he could not have told you how many columns his paper ran to the page. . . . [Murdoch] is smart and cynical, like all the publishers legends are based on. . . . He is like [Citizen] Kane in inheriting a small family fortune of which the only part that interested him was the newspaper.

In the first days of 1984 Murdoch was in London. He called Charlie Wilson, the deputy editor of the *Times,* up to his office on Grays Inn Road and told him he needed someone in Chicago he could trust, and he needed him there immediately. Wilson thought he would be away about two weeks. He was gone three months.

Wilson was the antithesis of Jim Hoge. Hoge was handsome and

Ivy League. Wilson was a rough-edged, aggressive Glaswegian, given to brackish oaths. Both were smart, but in very different ways. When he arrived in Chicago, one local paper quoted Patrick Brogan, late of the *Times,* as saying, "Murdoch is always looking for tough, aggressive, unpleasant people to bring into his papers to whip them into shape. Wilson is very tough, unpleasant, rude to his subordinates. He puts the fear of God in them." Wilson pointed out later that Brogan had never met him.

Wilson himself said he was astonished by the wall of hostility with which he was confronted in Chicago. "It was a classic Murdoch-monster-myth situation," he said. But it was beyond even the classic—it was hysteria. The hatred bubbled off the desks, it seethed from the video terminals, it bounced off the walls. Wilson said he felt like the running dog of a Cyclops. It was as if Murdoch were some foul fiend that stalked and ravaged the earth, chewing up newspapers for breakfast and expelling them covered with filth later in the day. Among the questions the *Sun-Times* staffers asked—when they could bear to speak to him at all—were: Would there still be a sports page? Was the Washington bureau going to be closed? What about photographs?

The center of the cauldron of hatred was the newsroom of the *Sun-Times,* and from there the hatred spread through Chicago and beyond. Wilson's job was made more difficult by the "window" that the Fields had opened, which gave journalists two weeks after the change of ownership in which to decide whether to take high severance pay and leave the paper. "It was very tempting—the choice, after all, was to be sodomized or to do the sodomizing," said Wilson. "I spent my time trying to convince the staff that Murdoch was not Satan, that we were not going to make the *Sun-Times* into the *National Enquirer* and that when the window closed life would still be bearable."

Many journalists refused to be convinced. For them the obvious "moral" course seemed to be to leave rather than to work for the Monster. In all, over sixty people leapt through the "window" and out of the *Sun-Times.*

Wilson lived in a penthouse nearby and spent about eighteen hours a day at the office. He recalled:

> It was one of the most exciting periods of my life, a terrific challenge. People hated me. I worked out that the only way I could change them was by convincing them about my journalism. I had a deputy and a managing editor who helped. When people took the window, I promoted people from inside the paper to get their loyalty.

Together with two News America executives—Robert Page, who came from the Boston *Herald* to be publisher, and Roger Wood from the New York *Post*—Wilson immediately began to apply some of the Murdoch prescription. He shortened stories, used more graphics and photos and paid more attention to the front page. He increased crime coverage, especially of murder and rape. Every day he changed the front page as often as possible between editions in order to give the readers at least the illusion of freshness. He frequently called the circulation department to see how different headlines had fared on the streets.

Wilson thought he finally won acceptability in the newsroom with the death of the Soviet president, Yuri Andropov, in February 1984. He heard the news at 6:00 A.M. and realized that the morning edition had already been gone an hour. "I instantly thought that we must do a special, a slip edition," Wilson recalled. Knowing there was a lot of background on Andropov in the computer, Wilson woke up two editors from Murdoch's San Antonio *News* who were working on the *Sun-Times* and told them to get in. He telephoned the night production manager and found there were enough people still cleaning the presses to start them rolling again. By breakfast time he had a special edition out on the streets. The first three pages were devoted to Andropov. "I made sure it was on sale outside the *Tribune* building by the time its staff arrived for work."

"From being a sodomite, I was now a hero," said Wilson later. "Chicago loves to think of itself as fulfilling the *Front Page* tradition. It takes itself very seriously. It had not seen a special for twenty-five years. I was being toasted by lunchtime."

In the end, those who feared the worst may have been surprised. After an expensive, self-congratulatory and ultimately ineffective attempt to boost circulation through a million-dollar Wingo game, the *Sun-Times* changed far less than had been predicted. "Gradually the hatred faded because the paper never became the *Sun*-type rag which had been feared," said Wilson. "But the image of Rupert did remain. The other media were always on at us; everything we did was construed as badly as possible. Many sources would as a matter of course go to the *Tribune*."

The Medill School of Journalism in Chicago made a serious attempt to assess Murdoch's impact. It compared randomly selected final editions of the 1984 *Sun-Times* with others from 1980 and from 1976, and made a similar analysis of the *Tribune*. The students also interviewed almost a thousand readers and dozens of *Sun-Times* employees.

The survey found that readers of the *Tribune* tended to be better educated, more liberal and better off than those of the *Sun-Times*. *Sun-Times* readers were more conservative on the issues of abortion and prayers in school. "These findings suggest that the paper's shift to a more conservative editorial stance under News America's management may be well received by a large proportion of its readers," the Medill report concluded.

Sun-Times readers were asked what changes they had noticed. "Sensationalism" was mentioned in more than one fourth of the answers, but those polled were unable to tell the difference between headlines of the *Tribune* and the *Sun-Times* and also thought that the headlines from the earlier years' samples were more sensationalist than those of the Murdoch era. The survey showed that 13 percent more of the editorial space was being devoted to graphics and photos than in the earlier papers. Similarly, there had been an increase (2 percent) in the space devoted to crime news plus a 15 percent jump in the number of crime-related items, but the average length of stories had decreased. The number of crime items in the *Tribune* had also increased.

Coverage of government affairs declined, while the space devoted to "*Sun-Times* self-promotion" increased enormously. There were 20 percent more stories about the Chicago area under Murdoch, and there was more coverage of celebrities, entertainment, accidents and disasters.

In both Boston and Chicago, the hysteria about Murdoch was misplaced. Under him the Boston *Herald* and the Chicago *Sun-Times* were effective tabloid newspapers. The *Herald* continued to keep the Boston *Globe* on its toes; in Chicago the *Tribune* continued to be the more comprehensive paper, but it was no longer the only "acceptable" paper in town. After Charlie Wilson went home to London in the spring of 1984, Murdoch brought in Frank Devine, a cheerful, radical right-winger from *Reader's Digest,* as editor. He did away with such headlines as "RABBI HIT IN 'SEX SLAVERY' SCANDAL" and "MEN BEAR CHILDREN?" and began to let his reporters loose on local scandals. The paper became much more of an aggressive local watchdog—the kind of paper that Chicago had always known. And then, in order to move into American television, Murdoch sold it.

Part III

THE NEW WORLD

6

1984

In 1984 Murdoch began to burst upon public consciousness in the United States. In a cover story, *Forbes* declared that he was "building the greatest communications empire the world has seen," and was "on the way to world leadership."

George Orwell's nightmare vision notwithstanding, the year 1984 marked the turning point in the totalitarian nightmare; the Soviet Union began the process of reform which led to its collapse. But there are those who argue that the state of society in 1984 should not be measured against Orwell's fears but against those of Aldous Huxley's *Brave New World*. Huxley's fear was of the world destroyed by trivia. In *Brave New World Revisited*, he proposed that those who were alert to the dangers of tyranny were often asleep to the dangers of distractions. He warned that people would be controlled by pleasure, not by pain; their cultures would be made essentially inconsequential.

As Murdoch well understood, entertainment was more and more the staple of Western and particularly American culture. In the global village, television was taking the place of the village green—a tiny but enticing green in every house. Visual images were beginning to replace arguments. Information was being presented as entertainment, and there was no one more skilled at marrying and mixing the two businesses than Rupert Murdoch.

Politics, too, was becoming a form of entertainment. "Politics is just like show business," Ronald Reagan had announced as far back as 1966. By 1984 it was possible to argue that television controlled and trivialized the flow of public discourse in America. As Neil Postman put it, "By ushering in the Age of Television, America has given the world the clearest available glimpse of the Huxleyan future."

The other world revolution which took place throughout the decade of the 1980s was that of computers. It utterly transformed the nature of government and information; one cannot exaggerate the scale or the importance of this change. In the 1960s the computing industry still relied on IBM mainframes or other electromechanical monsters. It was thought that there might be a market for some fifty of these machines in all the world; they would sit at the center of enterprises in their own huge sanctuaries, guarded and tended by a multitude of keepers, and they would dominate and control the world. The computer was then seen "as a leviathan instrument of Big Brother."

In the event, the opposite happened, and in a flash. Thanks to the development of the silicon chip, computers became smaller and smaller, cheaper and cheaper, and more and more powerful. The firms that developed these personal machines were not the big corporations but smaller companies, such as Fairchild and Intel, which developed the first microprocessors and computer arcade games in the early 1970s. By 1976, dozens of companies had joined the competition, microcomputer conferences were being held and the Apple I was born in its garage.

But it was in the 1980s that the explosion took place. When Ronald Reagan was inaugurated, the IBM PC had not even been announced. But from then on a vast new software industry grew exponentially to meet the possibilities that the new hardware had created. It was software that transformed the computer from a machine into an integral part of more and more homes and almost every business.

In 1977 nearly 100 percent of the world's computer power had still been commanded by mainframes and other large computers in government or corporate hands. In the flash of ten years all this changed. By the mid-1980s less than 1 percent of the world's computer power was in mainframes. The vast bulk of it was not in government but in private hands. U.S. companies controlled two thirds of a vast new global computer market of some ninety million personal computers, more than half in the U.S.A. "The resulting array of personal computers, engineering workstations, database servers, desktop publishers and silicon printers emerging in the real year of 1984 unleashed forces of liberation that would foil every tyrannous portent of *1984* and other industrial fictions," noted George Gilder, the writer and apostle of technological liberation. The pace of change was barely credible. Between 1961 and 1989 the speed of a computer operation increased 230,000-fold.

This fantastic revolution was accompanied by widespread deregulation of finance, telecommunications, trucking, energy and air transportation in the United States. The supporters of such liberalization argued that it had massive and overwhelmingly beneficial effects on the U.S. economy, helping to create fifteen million new jobs during the 1980s.

By 1984, another consequence of the computer revolution was becoming apparent. The first industrial revolution vastly increased the value of raw materials. The coal and steel of the Ruhr basin had been crucial to the balance of power in Europe. No longer. Gilder suggested that whereas a steel mill was the symbol of the first industrial age, a similar symbol today is that of one man alone at a single computer workstation, with access to databases all over the world. Information was becoming one of the world's most valuable commodities.

At the same time, the combination of scientific and technological advances had by the mid-1980s produced a totally new kind of international financial market, quite unforeseen by either Orwell or Huxley. Computers and satellites meant that the world was now awash with new waves of money. As we have seen, Reuters, with its fantastic instant flow of information across the screens of the world, was leading the revolutionary changes of the 1980s. So were the banks, and among them one of the most important in New York was Citibank, where the chief executive officer, Walter Wriston, was a close friend and supporter of Rupert Murdoch.

Through the 1980s, the decade of debt, Citibank was marching alongside News. The one was building a global banking empire, the other a global news and entertainment empire. Citibank became one of News' principal bankers. Wriston believed that the vast new financial trading market which grew in the 1980s "is not just more of the same: it is something new in the world. It has changed the world." The longbow had changed the course of military history at the Battle of Crécy. "Today, the financial longbow is the linking of the satellite, the computer and the cathode-ray tube." Wriston and Murdoch shared (with Reagan and Thatcher) an absolute, almost obsessive belief in the virtues of the free market, and in its eventual triumph, largely through its technological superiority, over communism.

This possibility was by now understood in the Soviet Union, where Mikhail Gorbachev, the new secretary-general of the Soviet Communist Party, came quickly to understand the U.S.S.R.'s desperate failure to benefit from the information revolution which was driving Western progress in the 1980s. Soviet leaders had always had a terror of communications technology and had sought to control it. Trotsky had apparently proposed a modern telephone system to Stalin, who had dismissed it, saying, "I can imagine no greater instrument of counter-revolution in our time." In *Cancer Ward*, Aleksandr Solzhenitsyn described at great length Stalin's attempt to record telephone conversations. The legacy of Stalin's paranoia had had a disastrous effect on Soviet scientific advancement.

The simple telephone was crucial to the computerization on which the West was embarked in the 1980s. When Gorbachev came to power the Soviet Union's telephone system was one of the most primitive in the industrialized world; there were only ten telephones to every hundred citizens, a far lower ratio than in any other industrialized country.

Gorbachev quickly began to lay plans to double the telephone system by 1990, to start to computerize the society and to make the next generation of Russians halfway computer literate. He understood that such policies would inevitably lead to the government losing its control over information. But he also understood that the exchange of information is crucial to a modern society. By 1984, as we have seen, the West was rushing helter-skelter through a technology-driven period of extraordinary expansion. It was undergoing the sort of creative destruction which Joseph A. Schumpeter, the economic historian, identified as characteristic of periods of major technological change. The Soviet Union was experiencing nothing of this.

There were then almost no computers in Soviet society outside of large institutions. The society was starved of the resource it most desperately needed: information. The Western world, by contrast, had almost a surfeit of it.

While Gorbachev was first grappling with the disaster of the Soviet Union, News Corporation was becoming one of the most important and most interesting of the stateless, international corporations of the Western world. Murdoch now owned a truly multinational media corporation. News Corporation's worldwide revenues for the fiscal year 1984 were expected to be $2.1 billion, only just behind the Times Mirror's $2.5 billion and not very far behind Time Inc.'s $2.8 billion. And it was by far the most international of the world's media companies. It owned some eighty magazines and newspapers and was the Western world's largest newsprint consumer. The company was entirely a reflection of Murdoch himself and of his intuitive business genius. But there was a monkey on his back. Its name was Debt. So far, however, it seemed a friendly creature—indeed, one which was essential to Murdoch's method of operation.

He had a reputation among his business peers for honoring his commitments. Editors and journalists might distrust him but he inspired confidence among his brokers and his bankers. Everyone wanted to give him concessions and favors. He had the smell of success, and he could be trusted. His reputation was that once he shook hands on a deal, that deal would stick. Even if he had made a mistake in the figures, he never reneged.

Murdoch started to appear regularly on the covers of American financial and news magazines. In America, public television made a critical two-part series informed by the attacks of Harold Evans. For the first time people began to understand that Murdoch owned as a personal fief one of the world's largest media empires, stretching across three continents. But if it was large now, it was less than half the size it would be by the end of the decade.

With his papers in San Antonio, with the New York *Post,* the Boston *Herald* and the Chicago *Sun-Times,* the *Star,* the *Village Voice,* and *New York* magazine, Murdoch was by 1984 a major American publisher. He approached Hearst to see if he might acquire the Baltimore *News American,* an afternoon paper which he considered making into a morning paper for distribution in Washington, which lies only an hour away by road or train. He also considered buying the Los Angeles *Herald Examiner.* Neither purchase went through. He claimed that he had no more newspaper peaks to climb; there were no more Boston *Heralds* that interested him: "I'm not going to run around buying little papers in little country towns all over America." Like many other people, he would have liked to buy the Washington *Post* and change its liberal policies, but he could not afford it and, moreover, he said, "It ain't for sale."

American pundits were beginning to compare him with Pulitzer and with Hearst. The *Forbes* cover story was written by Thomas J. O'Hanlon, one of the first American journalists to spot the implications of Murdoch's imperial ambitions and business genius. "WHAT DOES THIS MAN WANT?" asked the headline. The answer was "Lots."

O'Hanlon praised him, saying, "While most media corporations today are run by relatively colorless, numbers-oriented businessmen, Rupert Murdoch . . . almost alone among them combines a zest and a feel for the product with a shrewd sense of the bottom line."

He described Murdoch as "part accountant, part gambler, part brilliant marketer, part shrewd journalist. . . . By the time Rupert Murdoch retires to his Australian farm in the twenty-first century, his current vulgar image will have faded, and he will be regarded as a sage who followed opportunity where it led and put together a global empire in what may be the twenty-first century's greatest industry, communications."

Fortune magazine was more critical: "Murdoch's tabloids luridly depict a world in which fiendish criminals prey on women and children, evil immigrants menace the natives, and most government affairs are too tedious to note." Murdoch was quoted as saying,

> I don't know any better than anyone else where the electronic age is taking us, or how it will affect a large newspaper company. But I do know that . . . you will have to be a major player in the production of entertainment programming.

Anna Murdoch remarked, "I don't think Rupert has finished yet. I don't think he has any plan that he follows, but I do believe that he still has things he wants to accomplish. I wish he would stop. I wish it would all slow down—we could have more time together. But I don't think that's going to happen."

Murdoch agreed in 1984 to authorize an official biography by Thomas Kiernan, author of books on Jane Fonda and Yasser Arafat. Kiernan wrote a detailed synopsis in which he said Murdoch was more controversial than any other media baron since Hearst. He had been called "a sinister force," "a piranha," "an evil element," "a foul odor"; he had affected millions of American sensibilities and made no secret of wanting to shape American culture. He had star quality. He was a throwback, the stuff of "Dallas" and "Dynasty." "He is the personification of all the fundamental contradictions of the American experience: selfishness vs altruism; ambition vs reticence; publicity vs privacy; daring vs caution."

Murdoch had agreed to give Kiernan total access in return for merely being able to comment on the accuracy of the manuscript. But the collaboration collapsed, and Kiernan's unauthorized *Citizen Murdoch* portrayed Murdoch as monstrous.

No man sees himself as a monster. Murdoch considered himself a newspaper publisher and a crusader against established pieties, rather than as a mere businessman.

He was interested above all in cash flow. He needed to have revenue flowing all the time to finance expansion and to feed his monkey. It was fair to say that News was driven by economics rather than by journalism, as well as by opportunities rather than a plan. Synergy between the various elements of News, if synergy there was, happened by chance, not by design.

In Australia, Fairfax, his main competitor, was very different. It had always been an innovative company with a strong journalistic tradition, and it had frequently created new journalistic products. It looked at the market to see where new products could be launched. Once Murdoch had been like that in Australia, but he was no longer so.

His editorial or journalistic policy was oriented toward the market. His papers tended to be gray broadsheets or racy tabloids. Neither attracted excellent journalists. The ethos of News discouraged independent investigation or troublesome journalism. As a landlord who was absent everywhere most of the time, Murdoch was generally disinclined to upset the established order, especially if it was an order from which he benefited.

Measured in Australian dollars, News Corp's revenues had jumped by 41 percent over the previous two years, and the share price had increased by five times between early 1983 and early 1984. The debt-to-equity ratio was much higher than in most large publishing companies. Richard Sarazen, News' financial controller, explained that this was because Murdoch was still absolutely refusing to dilute the 46 percent of News owned by his family company, Cruden Investments (a stake worth some A$340 million). To explain this, Sarazen summoned the ghost of Sir Keith: Murdoch had seen his father make a fortune for others without much benefit to himself and he was determined not to make the same mistake. In fact, the family's share of News was probably even greater than the 46 percent owned by Cruden Investments. Another 14 percent of News equity was held by nominee companies, including 2 percent owned by News Nominees.

Other companies were vulnerable to shareholder pressure to produce short-term results at the expense of long-term strategy. This was never a problem for Murdoch. He was able to borrow as much as he wished and to ignore short-term problems because of Cruden's control of the group. He did not risk either shareholder discontent or exposure to a predator. But he claimed that he was nonetheless still accountable: "If you screw up, the shareholders may not throw you out but the bankers will. Whatever happens, you're subject to the disciplines of the marketplace. What it does mean is that you can take long-term risks, like the *Times,* and back your judgment, take a bad year or two, and nobody's going to run at you." His competitors had no such luxury.

At that time it was Murdoch's policy to try to keep long-term debt equal to or preferably below the level of shareholders' funds. Even so, News' ratio of over $80 debt to every $100 of net worth was about twice as high as that of most publicly owned publishing groups. Sarazen told the *Economist* that long-term debt had sometimes exceeded shareholders' funds by as much as 50 percent. Murdoch said that a ratio of 1:1 was the ceiling.

His bankers were sanguine and said that instead of concentrating on News Corp's debt-to-equity ratios, they looked at its ability to pay interest charges and to make capital repayments if it ran into trouble. The beauty of newspapers, which generated most of

News Corp's revenues, was that they were the supreme cash-flow businesses.

The empire was still administered personally by Murdoch using the weekly reporting system devised by Merv Rich over twenty years earlier. Every week Murdoch received the key figures for every business in the group, and he was thus able to tell at a glance where costs were rising too sharply and where revenue was falling. He would give instant instructions by telephone throughout the world to get the numbers back up to where he thought they should be.

Murdoch was spending less time in Australia. He said, "If a company grows a lot, as we've done, there's got to be a limit to how much you can grow in Australia. For practical, political, social reasons, and everything else." In 1982 he had been there four times; in 1983 he spent only around eight weeks there altogether. However, he still said that he would retire and die in Australia—"Even if I semiretire, I would start spending half my time in Australia." Asked when that might be, he replied, "When I'm 133 or something. . . ." He could not bear to think about handing over to a chief executive. "It makes me quite miserable. But that's human and everyone has to face that sometime in their lives."

The profits on his Australian newspapers and television stations were fair but not fabulous. He did not own any of the richest sources of classified advertising. These still belonged to Fairfax and the Melbourne Herald group. He would not be allowed to own more than the two television stations he already had, and competition in newspapers was fierce and very expensive. Ansett Airlines was his most profitable Australian investment; he had bought it for A$80 million and it was now worth some A$500 million. His flagship, the *Australian,* was still in an unhappy state. It had inadequate journalistic resources—thirty-nine journalists had been fired in 1982—and was not encouraged to upset the status quo. A Labor government was riding the international political wave to the populist radical right, and Murdoch was becoming an ever closer "mate" of Bob Hawke, the prime minister.

All over the world News had become a political company in the eighties, embracing the deregulatory policies and ethics of the Reagan-Thatcher era.

In the United States, News America had lost money till 1983, largely because of the *Post; New York* magazine, the *Village Voice,* the *Star* and the Texas papers were all profitable. But to Murdoch the losses on the *Post* were worth taking for the thrill of owning a paper in New York—a city of enormous power and patronage and one of his principal homes. He could not contemplate living in a city in which he did not publish a newspaper.

The *Post's* sales had soared as high as 960,000—an astonishing rise from the 485,000 when he bought the paper—but they were no longer rising. Its share of the advertising market had continued to fall, from 11.3 percent in 1977 to 7.6 percent in 1983. The *Daily News'* share, by contrast, had grown from 25 percent to 32.7 percent, while the share of the *Times* had fallen from 63.6 percent to 59.7 percent. The *News'* advertising revenues in 1983 were over four times those of the *Post*—$225 million, as against $50 million. Murdoch acknowledged that the *Post* would never make money unless he managed to launch and sustain a Sunday edition.

His problem in Chicago and Boston as well as New York was that whereas most American city papers were profitable monopolies, the three he had bought were all locked in competition with bigger and better-positioned rivals. That was the way he liked to operate, but given the overall decline in newspaper readership, there was little reason to suppose that he would make much money from them.

Nonetheless, he seemed to have no liquidity problem. The previous year he had raised some $68 million by selling off oil interests. Ansett Airlines was providing significant revenues. And Reuters was, amid great controversy, about to go public. News Corp's share of that would be worth some $150 million. In November 1984 he spent $350 million on buying Ziff-Davis' travel publications.

The biggest money-maker in the empire was still the *Sun* in London; it earned a staggering $50 million in 1983—British working-class readers were providing 40 percent of News Corp's worldwide operating profit. When the earnings from the *Star* and the Sydney *Telegraph* were added to that, almost 60 percent of the company's operating earnings were accounted for.

However, in 1984 the *Sun's* position was a little less secure. Its circulation had fallen by 51,500 in 1983, while that of its main rival, the *Daily Mirror,* had risen 90,000. This had happened partly because the *Sun* had cut its promotional advertising. Seventy percent of the *Sun's* revenue came from its cover price and Murdoch was loath to raise that for fear of losing readers. In 1984 the *News of the World* was also in decline and Times Newspapers continued to lose money, largely because of the labor problems which Murdoch had inherited from Thomsons, and which he had till now failed to confront.

Like Roy Thomson before him, he had agreed not to interfere in the editorial policy of the *Times* and *Sunday Times.* He expected his other papers to stay within certain guidelines, but he did not demand that they obey daily instructions from him.

He hated the allegation that he had bought the *Times* to buy respectability. "All newspapers are run to make profits," he said. "Full stop. I don't run anything for respectability. The moment I do I hope someone will come and fire me and get me out of the place—because that's not what newspapers are meant to be about." He predicted—wrongly—that in five years the *Times* would be the most profitable asset in News.

He was puzzling his way through the new technology maze and bazaar that confronted everyone in the 1980s. "Let someone else *own* the satellites," he said. "I wish someone else would own the printing presses." He believed that satellites had an immense role to play in the delivery of entertainment, in the future if not now.

He argued that the *Sun* was a testament to the success of the printed word in an age in which television was becoming more and more dominant. The *Sun* could and did handle all the big news, but it tried to do it in a way that was entertaining as well. He thought that popular papers did so well in England because television was so elitist that the English were deprived of choice on the screen and needed popular papers more than did the Americans.

In New York he had to take on the *News* because there was no room for a second New York *Times.* It was not hard to compete with the *News,* he said, because American journalists simply did not know how to compete — "They all go to journalism school and listen to failed editors dressed up as professors."

Perhaps the most revealing statement he made at this time was to Barbara Walters of ABC television. When Walters asked him if his newspapers did not appeal to the baser instincts of their readers, he replied, "Well, there's nothing wrong with talking to the masses. You know, William Shakespeare wrote for the masses. I think if he was writing today, he'd probably be the chief scriptwriter on 'All in the Family' or 'Dallas.' They'd certainly be a little bit bawdier."

HOLLYWOOD

In the beginning was the photograph. Then came the phonograph, the radio, the moving picture, the talkies, television, VCRs, satellite broadcasts, and more movies and more television.

By the mid-1980s, entertainment was the second-largest export business in the United States, after aerospace. Each technological advance increased the power which American entertainment products exerted over an increasingly large portion of the world's population. It was indeed J. R. Ewing, not Hamlet, who was the symbol of international culture.

Entertainment was one of the few really global industries. There were other international products—especially foodstuffs like Coca-Cola, Pepsi-Cola, and McDonald's hamburgers—but music and images, from the Beatles to Michael Jackson, from Luke Skywalker to Indiana Jones, were beamed over large parts of the world. And almost all those images came from America. As the *Economist* put it, America was to entertainment what Saudi Arabia was to oil. And the Hollywood studios were among the biggest gushers of all.

By 1984 Murdoch had come to realize that his future lay in America. He thought like an American, saw his values as American. He also believed that entertainment and the electronic media were becoming more vital to his empire than news and publishing. News alone was commercially unviable; it had to piggyback on entertainment. And the Rupert Greene in Murdoch was more interested in entertainment than in education.

He became increasingly eager to acquire one of Hollywood's major film studios. Twentieth Century Fox had eluded him at the beginning of the decade. In 1983 and early in 1984, he made a lunge at Warner Communications, which owned the old Warner Bros. studio and film library. His assault upon the company and the angry response of Steve Ross, Warner's chairman, did more than anything else to draw Murdoch to the attention of Wall Street.

In 1982 Warner Communications shares had been as high as $63.25, but by early 1983 their price had fallen to under $20. The main reason for this fall was the collapse in the sales of Atari, Warner's video-games division. The company was vulnerable.

In August 1983 Stanley Shuman took Murdoch to see Steve Ross at his vacation home. Ross did not object to Murdoch's proposal that he buy a holding. He therefore began to do so, financing the purchases through short-term capital borrowings—which meant monies available to News through short-term banking facilities in the U.K.

In September Murdoch announced that he had purchased a million Warner Communications shares; this amounted to less than 2 percent of the company, considerably less than the 5 percent threshold at which the Securities and Exchange Commission required a buyer to disclose his interest. As Warner's losses accumulated in the last quarter of the year, Murdoch went on buying. In December 1983 he revealed that he had spent another $98 million and now owned 6.7 percent of the company—much more than Steve Ross or indeed all of Warner's management together. He stressed in his filing to the Securities and Exchange Commission that he was not trying to control the company, nor did he even want a seat on the board. It was merely "an investment," he told the New York *Times;* he did not want to take over Warner.

Nonetheless, Ross became alarmed. Meeting with Murdoch on December 9, he tried to warn him off, telling him that his purchases "might adversely affect Warner's relationship with certain of its creative personnel." In other words, some of the company's Hollywood stars and directors might not want to work with a man of Murdoch's reputation. Murdoch was not impressed; he did not think very much of Ross' own reputation.

Ross was also concerned lest Murdoch's growing share in the company jeopardize its cable television franchises in New York and Boston. The Federal Communications Commission did not allow cross-ownership of newspapers and television stations or cable franchises in metropolitan areas and Murdoch owned papers in both cities.

Ross immediately devised a complicated scheme to prevent Murdoch from increasing his stake. At the end of December Chris-Craft Industries announced that it was planning to buy over 25 percent of Warner while Warner would acquire a 42.5 percent stake in a Chris-Craft subsidiary, BHC. This was the fourth-largest nonnetwork television company in the country. The beauty of the transaction lay in the fact that aliens like Murdoch were not allowed to own more than 20 percent of an American television station. So the arrangement not only diluted Murdoch's existing share in Warner, it also precluded him from pursuing any hostile intentions toward Warner at all.

Murdoch responded at once, filing a complaint with the Federal

Communications Commission and then went to court in Wilmington, Delaware. He complained that the share swap between Warner and Chris-Craft was a breach of the commission's cross-ownership rules because Warner already owned cable television services and BHC owned six television stations.

In court, News argued that the deal was against the interests of the shareholders, including News, and that Chris-Craft derived far more benefit from the swap than Warner. A highly incompetent and vastly overpaid management was quite improperly protecting itself, the suit declared. News also charged Warner with engaging in "a pattern of racketeering"—this derived from the claim that Warner executives had been guilty of insider trading when they sold their own stock in the company just before the losses of Atari became public.

Warner filed its countersuit, describing Murdoch as a disreputable and untrustworthy Australian scandal-sheet printer. Drawing on Harold Evans' memoirs, Warner accused Murdoch of being "deceptive and manipulative" and asserted that he was well known for changing papers "into a sensationalist format, emphasizing violence, scandal and sex. Murdoch has already destroyed the journalistic reputations of the [New York] *Post* and the [Boston] *Herald*."

Before the Federal Communications Commission Warner argued: "What is really involved here is the effort of News International and its controlling individual, Australian newspaper publisher Rupert Murdoch, to maneuver themselves into control of Warner." Warner quoted Harold Evans as saying: "Murdoch issued promises as prudently as the Weimar Republic issued marks."

Murdoch preferred Swiss francs. He flew to Geneva to discuss with his bankers the bond offering he intended to issue to finance the purchase of further Warner stock. There he told the press, "We feel very hardly put upon by what has happened there. We're extremely critical of that management. We're going to go on and our present plan is that if we're successful in the courts or before the regulatory authorities we will certainly have a proxy fight to remove that management."

Richard Sarazen told the court in a sworn deposition that, until the Chris-Craft deal, Murdoch had intended only to be a passive investor, but after this public insult he decided to seek to exercise some influence, if not control, over the company.

Both the Delaware court and the Federal Communications Commission found for Warner; neither saw any need to stop the asset swap between Warner and Chris-Craft from going ahead. Murdoch vowed that he would continue to fight. Ross shrugged off the threat. Each of them continued to collect as much dirt as possible on the other. Ross hired a team of investigative lawyers in Washington. Murdoch's method was less orthodox. He deputed Steve Dunleavy to lead a team of reporters from the New York *Post* to investigate Steve Ross' background.

In public, Murdoch struck his usual combative attitude. In one speech he vowed that he would "oppose and expose gross mismanagement, racketeering and abuse of shareholders' funds." To the New York *Times* he said, "When someone's trying to run you down, you try to protect yourself. So that, the next time, someone else doesn't try to run you down."

However, in March a settlement was reached. To get rid of him, Warner paid Murdoch $31 a share for all of his stock. Thus he emerged with a profit of $40 million. Soon the price of Warner stock collapsed, to the dismay and in some cases fury of the other stockholders.

Shortly afterward, Murdoch went after another company, St. Regis Corporation, a producer of paper and building supplies, whose share price had fallen sharply. Because it was burdened by long-term debts of about $900 million, its prospects were being downgraded by analysts, and it was an obvious takeover target. Having bought just under 6 percent of St. Regis for some $65 million, he denied that he was interested either in "greenmail" or in acquiring the whole company. Nonetheless, the board of St. Regis filed a lawsuit to prevent News from acquiring any further stock or attempting a takeover. The company lost that legal battle in July 1984 and Murdoch then told the board that he was willing to pay $52 a share or $757 million in cash for 50.1 percent of the company. The money had been provided for him by a consortium led by the Midland Bank of London. To escape him, the board rushed into the arms of Champion International Corporation, another forest products company. The two companies merged in a $2 billion deal—entirely through fear of Murdoch—and Murdoch himself made a profit of about $37 million on the stock he already owned.

He later said that he had not liked the bad publicity that he received for his attempt at a hostile Warner takeover. "I'm about building a company," he said. "I'm not about making money in the stock market. I thought I was getting quite the wrong reputation."

He told the *Economist* (which published another cover story on him) that he had wanted to diversify from newspapers into another branch of the entertainment industry. He claimed: "We didn't want to get control of Warner. We wanted to come along and have a look at it, take a ride and see, and maybe in our wildest dreams—if someone had made a run at it and given it to us. . . . But the major thing is the studio, and they've got a great film library. . . ."

But the failure to diversify into Hollywood was short-lived. Once again Murdoch's extraordinary luck held. A few months later an equally fabulous slice of the legend and reality of Hollywood became available: Twentieth Century Fox was on the block again. The company, founded by Hungarian-born William Fox, started as one nickelodeon on Broadway just after the turn of the century. Fox then went into making movies and newsreels. William Fox was an early forerunner of Murdoch in that he understood well the potent combination of news, film and entertainment. The company had a typically Hollywood checkered history; among its most famous postwar films were *The Robe, Gentlemen Prefer Blondes, Cleopatra, The Sound of Music* and *Star Wars.*

By 1980 the company's overall assets were worth far more than

Fox's current stock market value of around $35 a share. The board decided to try to effect what later became commonly known as a leveraged buyout, but the deal came unstuck in January 1981. The publicity generated put Fox "in play" and made it vulnerable to a takeover bid.

This came from an oilman, Marvin Davis, and his silent partner, an oil and gas broker named Marc Rich. In April 1981 they bought the company for about $70 a share, or $703 million in all.

Davis had struck lucky as a wildcatting oilman in Wyoming in the 1960s, and his riches were vastly enhanced by OPEC oil price rises of 1973 and 1979. He was a mixture of shrewdness, even toughness, and joviality. He had always loved movies and enjoyed "fun" businesses. In 1981 he sold about 850 of his oil wells and had a pile of cash worth some $630 million.

His partner, Marc Rich, was less straightforward. He was under investigation by the Justice Department for tax evasion and for illegally selling oil to Iran, which had been under embargo since its seizure of the American embassy hostages in 1979. In 1982, he fled to Switzerland and the U.S. government froze all his assets, including his half share of Fox.

Davis established himself as a flamboyant presence in Hollywood. Though he became disillusioned by the failures of Fox's films in the early 1980s, he and Rich did well out of their purchase. By 1984 Davis had taken out of the studio most of the money he had put in and millions in profits as well. The studio was still deeply in debt.

In 1984 a key figure arrived. Barry Diller was brought into Fox from Paramount, where he had had an extraordinarily successful ten-year reign as chairman. Diller terrified many of the people who came into contact with him, and made others perform very well. When his relationship with the chairman of Paramount's parent company, Gulf +Western, deteriorated so much that he decided to leave, Diller called Marvin Davis and asked him to sell him half of Fox. Davis refused, but said he might sell him 25 percent if he would agree to run it. They began to negotiate.

By October 1984, Diller had secured himself a splendid contract. His basic salary was to be $3 million, together with 25 percent of any increase in the equity value of the studio during his tenure. Davis also lent him $1.5 million interest free, to pay off a similar loan from Paramount. His expense account was vast. The contract also stated that Davis would step aside and allow Diller day-to-day control of the studio. Davis was not even allowed to talk to Fox employees "in such a manner as shall derogate, limit or interfere with Diller."

Once the deal was done, Diller and Davis found they could not tolerate each other, let alone collaborate. Davis was a raunchy, emotional, bluff man who did not know much about films beyond the fact that he liked them—especially *The Sound of Music,* to which he wanted to make a sequel. Diller was cool, crisp and fearsomely aggressive toward his staff. And he knew a lot about the movie business. In Hollywood the relationship became known as "the Hitler-Stalin Pact."

Moreover, by early 1985 Diller had begun to realize the size of the studio's financial problems. Its debt of $430 million required $70 million a year just to service it. There was not enough money to make good new products and Davis was unwilling to invest more. He suggested that Diller approach Mike Milken at Drexel Burnham Lambert to arrange additional monies.

Part of the enormous process of expansion and change in the communications industry in the 1980s was financed and made possible by the creation and sale of junk bonds, in particular by Milken and others like him. Indeed, his supporters claimed that by the mid-1980s Milken had become an extraordinary force in American business life.

Drexel Burnham Lambert was attracting some $2 billion to $3 billion in foreign funds every year into America—thus doing something to reverse the capital flight from previous decades. Milken's activities were crucial in the development of the new industries which were transforming communications—fiber-optic networks, the growth of Ted Turner's empire and Fox itself. Milken later pleaded guilty to six felony charges and served a sentence in a federal penitentiary. Nevertheless Milken understood more than almost anyone else (save perhaps Murdoch) the speed at which technology was transforming the world, and in particular the world of communications. In ten years he transformed junk bonds into a vast and mainstream financial instrument which he used to open the capital markets to clever and aggressive entrepreneurs.

Despite Fox's problems, Milken agreed to try to raise $250 million by selling junk bonds. But that deal misfired because Diller demanded that Davis give him real equity in Fox. When Davis refused, Diller scotched the Drexel issue.

In early 1985 the Justice Department agreed to allow Davis to buy the 50 percent of Fox which the U.S. government had seized from the fugitive Marc Rich. Because of Fox's atrocious results, Davis was able to persuade Justice that the half share was worth only $116 million. Although he also had to shoulder Rich's half of the debt, it was the sort of bargain which Marvin Davis was famous for making.

Then, after further rows with Diller, Davis decided to resell Rich's half share. There was one man interested in buying: Rupert Murdoch. He agreed to pay Davis an effective price of $250 million. Davis clearly made a large profit, and the general perception was that Murdoch had paid a premium price because he considered this a rare opportunity to acquire a major film library which could both provide the foundation of a fourth major American television network and supply programs for his television enterprises abroad. Murdoch described Fox as "one of the world's great film and television companies" and said that he was confident that it was about to grow significantly.

Murdoch had never been very interested in partnerships of any kind; it is a relationship that does not suit him. Nonetheless, he felt that half of Fox was better than no part of any studio at all. He reckoned that for all Fox's obvious problems, Diller was a good bet, and that he could help sort the studio out. Diller, however, was concerned about his own position. He did not know Murdoch well, but knew that his reputation was as fearsome as his own. He demanded the right to be able to terminate his contract at any time within the first year of Murdoch's ownership. Davis was alarmed that this might frighten Murdoch away. But Murdoch was blithe about it. He understood that, given Diller's dislike of Davis, he himself would soon be in an overpowering position at Fox. Diller told Murdoch that as he did not know him well, he wanted "exit rights" in case things did not work out. Murdoch gave them.

For Murdoch the purchase of Fox was a triumphant and essential step toward creating a worldwide media and entertainment empire. "A really integrated media company has to be in the production of entertainment," he said.

> It also has to be in news reporting. For both, the question is one of how do you present it? In magazine form or television form? For all those things, you've got to have a foot in the creative processes. Making movies is part of that. I went to entertainment not to get into entertainment. It was part of a broad strategy to get into the media industry, the heart of the media industry. I know you can't really talk about one global economy, but there really is. There are certain things that are common. Hollywood is still the magnet for the most talent. Studios here still have the preeminent position. So if one owns a studio, it's a great opportunity.

Now what he needed were television stations. A few weeks after he had purchased his half share of Fox, they came his way, by an extraordinary stroke of serendipity.

In the spring of 1985, Murdoch went to China. His herald was the Australian prime minister himself; a few weeks before, Bob Hawke had visited Peking and spoken warmly to the Chinese leadership of his friend Rupert Murdoch and his projects. When he arrived, Murdoch was treated like some new capitalist demigod by the Chinese communist authorities, who at that time were moving China toward a market economy while attempting to sustain political orthodoxy. Like many anti-Soviets, Murdoch came away from China enthusing about the country and its progress. He also understood its unique commercial potential: eight hundred million new consumers. He wanted to extend his empire behind the Great Wall.

His first idea for an international hotel and media center was eventually dropped, and he pursued a more primary interest—tapping the vast, untouched Chinese market for entertainment. The Chinese evening television news reached over five hundred million people. There were hundreds of millions of homes in China. What they needed above all was a bit of fun. The problem was that they had no money to pay for it. To get his foot in the door, Murdoch made a deal for Fox movies to be shown all over China. A committee of official censors came to Hong Kong to vet the films and to choose those which were deemed politically, culturally and socially "acceptable." The most popular in villages all over the country were subsequently said to be *The Sound of Music* and *Patton.*

On his return from China, the weekend after Easter 1985, Murdoch stopped off at his newly acquired Fox lot, where he met a friend, John Werner Kluge, the owner of a chain of independent television stations called Metromedia, which had rented a studio at Fox for a financial presentation. They talked and, said Murdoch, he decided within minutes to buy Metromedia.

John Werner Kluge's was a great American Dream story. He had come to America from Germany as a fatherless child of eight, and had since made himself one of the richest men in the world.

He started as a food broker and bought into radio. By 1959, when television was beginning to expand hugely, he had made enough money to buy the controlling share of Metropolitan Broadcasting Corporation, a poorly run company which owned TV stations in New York and Washington and two radio stations. He changed the company's name to Metromedia and began to acquire independent television stations in large metropolitan areas. Kluge swiftly built Metromedia into a corporate empire which grossed over $100 million in 1964.

He hoped to start a fourth national TV network himself. The first half of the 1970s was comparatively lean, but in 1976 advertisers began to deluge both the networks and the independent TV stations with money. Kluge's stations did well. By this time the three national networks, ABC, NBC and CBS, were beginning to lose their audience share, as cable TV encouraged people to switch channels more frequently. Kluge had Metromedia begin to buy up some of its own shares. In 1978 Metromedia offered ten-year nonconvertible debentures for 1.5 million shares. By the early 1980s the price of the shares had risen from under $40 to over $150. Metromedia was now the nation's largest independent broadcasting company.

In many ways Kluge operated like Murdoch. He kept a firm control over costs—his headquarters were in New Jersey rather than New York in order to avoid the city's taxes. Like Murdoch he also insisted on receiving weekly profit-and-loss reports from each division of the company. He liked to act alone, without a big board or an excess of executives to hamper him. Thus in 1983 he negotiated the purchase of WFLD in Chicago in just one day—though the station was not even for sale. He paid $140 million.

By the early 1980s he was much richer and had bought, among other things, the Harlem Globetrotters. In 1981 he married his third wife, Patricia Gay, who was part English, part Iraqi, wholly Catholic and a former model for men's magazines. They had a splendid society wedding at St. Patrick's Cathedral in New York; the groom converted to

Catholicism for the occasion and Anna Murdoch was one of the ma-
trons of honor. (When they were divorced in 1990 Patricia Kluge was
said to have been given $80 million a year.)

At the end of 1984 Kluge embarked on his most astonishing deal
to date. He made a leveraged buyout of Metromedia and, while
pocketing $115 million in cash and securities, increased his share of
the company from 26 percent to 75.5 percent.

The banks agreed to a loan of $1.3 billion and the Prudential In-
surance Company, which led the way by buying $125 million of the
preferred stock, seemed delighted to help him. The deal enabled the
banks to place large amounts of money at a rate which was pegged to
the prime, which was more than most corporate borrowers were willing to pay. The only snag for Kluge was that this allowed the banks, led
by Manufacturers Hanover, to keep Metromedia in line—not something he enjoyed. Under the banks' terms, he had to pay back a first
installment of $200 million by June 1985. The idea that he should meet
his interest payments from Metromedia's cash flow and pay back the
principal in stages was not unusual, but it did not appeal to Kluge. It
might mean that he had to sell some property, perhaps even one of
the TV stations.

He began to replace his bank debt with $1.3 billion of new junk
bonds created by Michael Milken and Drexel Burnham. Drexel issued four kinds of junk bonds with a total value of $1.35 billion against
all the assets of Metromedia, including the radio stations and the
cellular telephone systems in which Kluge had become interested.
Metromedia was worth more as a private company, in which Kluge
could manage to maximize cash flow, than as a public company which
had to maximize reported earnings. It was clever. Allan Sloan pointed
out in *Forbes* that Kluge was in effect doing "a leveraged leveraged
buyout."

Kluge had to pay a higher rate on the new paper than he was paying the banks, but Metromedia's cash interest payments were lower
because $300 million of the new money came from zero-coupon

bonds. The original bank loan had cost Kluge $14.5 million in front-end fees—and he had kept it for only six months. But he probably reckoned it was worth it to rid himself of his shareholders. Now he was also rid of the banks, had deferred his principal repayments and had improved his tax position. He was, said *Forbes,* well on the way to his first billion.

He was betting that the value of the stations would compound faster than securities Drexel sold for him were accruing interest.

By the time he met Murdoch and then Barry Diller on the Fox lot, Kluge wanted to get out of television and concentrate on new technological products such as cellular phones and a paging device. He thought that cable, pay television and video recorders would all conspire to devalue television networks. He also felt that the demand for television stations would never be as great again, because the Federal Communications Commission had just changed the rules to allow a single company to own a maximum of twelve stations, as opposed to seven, provided that together they did not cover more than 25 percent of the national market. And so he told Murdoch and Diller that he might sell some of the Metromedia television stations, but not the one in New York.

The next day, at a meeting also attended by Michael Milken, Kluge said he wanted $1.05 billion for his stations in Los Angeles, Chicago, Dallas–Fort Worth, Houston and Washington, D.C. The Boston station was already pledged to the Hearst Corporation and he again insisted on keeping New York. The price he asked for the other stations was about fifteen times cash flow, whereas the standard ratio would have been ten to twelve times earnings. (This meant that Murdoch would have to pay $15 for every $1 a year that the stations provided. He would then pay 14 percent to borrow the $15, which worked out to $2.10. Add another 20 percent for transaction costs, also financed by borrowed money, and he was paying something like $2.50 for every $1 of station cash flow.)

Diller thought this price absurd, but Murdoch told him not to worry about it. Murdoch saw that to get a group of stations in major American cities was a unique opportunity. He realized this was a key moment in the development of News. His overwhelming ambition now was to be a force in global communications, and to achieve that he needed U.S. television stations at the core of his empire. To seize them, he would pay whatever was the going rate. He argued, "You're paying a premium for them all coming together. It's the one time in life when wholesale is more expensive than retail." Never again would there be a chance to buy such a string of well-placed stations, offering the chance to start a fourth network. But he had to have New York as well. He told Kluge that no deal was possible without it, and Kluge conceded.

Marvin Davis presented difficulties. He was reluctant to expand his commitments, and he too thought Kluge's price was exorbitant. He told Murdoch he would only go into Metromedia on a short-term basis and would want Murdoch to buy him out soon thereafter. However, he kept changing his mind about the price at which he would want that to happen.

Apart from the price and Davis, there were two other obvious and serious problems. The first was the rule preventing cross-ownership of television stations and newspapers in the same city. The second was the law that no alien could own an American television station. Murdoch was undisturbed by either problem. He would apply to the FCC for a temporary waiver of the cross-ownership rule, and he would deal with the citizenship problem in the only possible way.

The agreement between Metromedia and Fox was announced on May 6, 1985. Murdoch and Davis (who remained on the masthead, but was little more than a name) agreed to buy Metromedia's seven television stations for just over $2 billion. They formed a separate company, Fox Television Inc. (Fox TV, formerly News America Television Inc.), to make the purchase. At the same time Murdoch also established Twentieth Century Fox Holdings Inc. (Twentieth) as the

umbrella company for Fox TV. Both new companies were incorporated in Delaware. Twentieth would buy and keep WITG in Washington, D.C., WNYW in New York, WFID in Chicago, KTTV in Los
Angeles, KRIV in Houston and KDAF in Dallas. The Boston station,
WCVB, would be immediately sold to Hearst.

It was the second-largest deal in the history of media so far, after the
purchase of ABC by Capital Cities just one month earlier. With the
resale of the Boston station for $450 million, the effective net price
was about $1.85 billion, including all the fees and transaction costs.

Fortune magazine said that the sale could be "the worst deal yet"
in a spate of high-cost U.S. TV takeovers. But the financial writer
Allan Sloan pointed out in *Forbes:* "When you have ambitions like
Murdoch's, and when you have his grasp of media realities, you don't
worry about quarterly earnings or even annual earnings. You fix on
the big picture. Which is another way of saying that, yes, Murdoch
overpaid in the short run but not necessarily in the long run."

Richard Sarazen gave another reason for Murdoch's branching into
television and away from his first love, newspapers: "If you are an arch-
conservative, fighting a world of left-wing journalists, particularly in
this country, wouldn't you want to have another influence, another
say?"

Murdoch himself acknowledged that he was betting News on the
success of the deal. It was a gamble he could make because he, not
institutions or shareholders, controlled News. "Apart from the normal
motives of greed, it's the stability of the company. We've been able
to take the years when we've got things wrong, and not look over our
shoulders . . . thinking someone's going to take us over."

In its first filing with the FCC after buying the stations, Fox said
that it believed the stations reached 22 percent of American television homes and 23 percent of the U.S. advertising market. But some
of the stations Fox had purchased were UHF stations, and FCC rules
allowed them to be discounted by 50 percent for the purpose of accounting market shares. Therefore, the six Fox stations were said to

cover only 18 percent of the U.S. advertising market (the total had to be less than 25 percent). Fox estimated that after the purchase of WXNE in Boston, this would rise to 19 percent. Fox could therefore buy up to five more TV stations provided that their aggregate market share was 6 percent or less.

Another problem with the purchase was how to deal with the junk bonds that Drexel Burnham had issued. These bonds were secured by the television stations, and some other assets as well. This meant that Murdoch had to satisfy the holders of Kluge's debt that the television stations alone, without Metromedia's other properties, would be adequate collateral for their bonds. They would need to give their permission for the sale. Only Drexel knew just who had the bonds, and that knowledge was an expensive commodity.

Drexel informed Murdoch that it could not get the agreement of all the original Metromedia bondholders, and that he could not simply assume Kluge's junk bonds. This put Murdoch at Drexel's mercy. Milken suggested instead that Fox TV issue $1.15 billion in convertible preferred stock. Then came the knife. Murdoch was offering the holders of Kluge's paper either a cash payment or an exchange of his preferred stock for their bonds. Assuming that Kluge bondholders wanted to roll their investment over into Murdoch paper, which many of them undoubtedly did, it made no difference to them whether they sold the Kluge bonds to Murdoch and used the proceeds to buy Murdoch preferred stock, or swapped the bonds for the Murdoch preferred. But it made a big difference to Drexel and to Murdoch. If Kluge bondholders took the exchange, Murdoch and Drexel paid a fee of 1 percent of the preferred stock thus swapped. If new preferred stock had to be underwritten, Murdoch would pay Drexel a fee of 3.5 percent. As it turned out, all the Kluge bondholders took the cash—including Drexel, whose trading desk seems to have owned several hundred million dollars of the Kluge bonds. Thus Drexel got a 3.5 percent fee for virtually the entire issue, rather than a mix of 1 percent and 3.5 percent fees. Drexel made many extra millions out of Murdoch—altogether,

Drexel's fees came to around $50 million. Milken was one of the few people who had outsmarted Murdoch on a financial transaction, and that angered Murdoch.

He was also angry that the preferred stock was three-year stock, and if not paid off in those three years it would convert into News Corp stock. Such an idea was anathema to Murdoch. He had always refused to dilute his stock, because he wished to retain his family's share, just under 50 percent. The risk of losing this control if Fox did not develop as well as he hoped in the next thirty-six months was enormous. He was furious with Milken for having, as he saw it, misled him.

Richard Sarazen devised clever tax advantages in this series of transactions. In the United States the dividend payments on the Fox preferred shares were considered debt, and were allowed as tax deductions, almost as if they were interest payments. In Australia, by contrast, preferred stock was treated as equity rather than debt and Australian banks lent money on the basis of that equity. So in Australia News Corp's assets had now increased by A$1.6 billion. Australian accounting rules, unlike American rules, also allowed companies to revalue their intangible assets, like mastheads. This could automatically and almost miraculously transform a company's debt-to-equity ratio overnight.

To raise some cash to put toward the Metromedia purchase, Murdoch began to sell assets that he considered tangential to the global empire he was building. He had never been comfortable with the radical political and sexual philosophies of the *Village Voice* —but he had known better than to interfere with its successful formula. Now he put it on the block. One of the people keenest to buy it was John Evans, who, as the publisher of the *Voice*, had built up its classified ads and therefore its vast profits. He was now head of Murdoch Magazines. When he asked Murdoch if he would mind if he put together a consortium to buy the *Voice*, Murdoch gave a rather grudging consent. But Evans was unable to match the $55 million offered by Leonard Stern of Hartz Mountain Industries. Even though some of this payment was deferred, it represented a fabulous profit on the $7.5 million which he had paid for *New York* and the *Voice* in 1978. Murdoch was amused when the *Voice's* staff asked the new owners to promise the same editorial independence as they had enjoyed under Murdoch.

Murdoch also agreed to a management buyout of the Chicago *Sun-Times,* which was put together by the paper's publisher, Robert Page. Murdoch had bought the paper for $90 million in January 1984; just two years later, he sold it for $145 million, another substantial profit. At the same time he also disposed of a part of his Reuters stake.

Then Marvin Davis struck a blow at the whole scheme. In June 1985, he pulled out of the deal. "We have decided not to exercise our option," he said. "Instead we will concentrate on the development of our other investments, including Twentieth Century Fox." This left Murdoch to find another $775 million to pay the full cost of $1.85 billion for Metromedia, which would increase News Corp's debt burden by six times, from the $408 million in the 1984 annual report to over $2.3 billion.

On top of that, there was the problem of what to do with Davis. He said he looked forward to continued association and partnership with Murdoch at Fox. But that, of course, was hardly to be expected. Murdoch now liked him no more than Diller did. "You can't rely on anything he says," he complained later. Davis came to realize that he was powerless against the combination of Murdoch and Diller and had best get out.

According to Murdoch, Davis suggested that they flip a coin to see which of them should buy the other out of Twentieth Century Fox. Murdoch said he accepted the challenge but Davis then backed out. Throughout the summer of 1985 they argued, with increasing dislike for each other, over the price which Murdoch would pay Davis for his 50 percent of Twentieth Century Fox. Eventually they agreed on $325 million, but that included the $88 million he had already put in as a loan to the studio.

Davis kept 2.7 acres of the 56.7-acre lot in Hollywood, the Aspen Skiing Company and the Pebble Beach resort in Carmel, California, assets with an estimated value of some $100–$150 million. He subsequently sold Pebble Beach at a huge profit.

Quite apart from the financial cost, Murdoch had to pay a heavy price to establish a TV network. First he would have to renounce the New York *Post*—because the cross-ownership rule prevented one person from owning a television station and a newspaper in the same town. Despite its lack of commercial success, Murdoch was almost besotted with the *Post*. It was his paper in his town, and that town was the hub of the world media. A major newspaper office, with the roar and the smell and the grime of the presses and its power in the community, had exhilarated him all his life: it reminded him of his childhood and of Keith. Indeed, he derived the essence of his personality and his power from a newspaper's environment. As Alexander Cockburn put it in the *Wall Street Journal*, for Murdoch to sell the New York *Post* "would be like Dracula selling his coffin."

Second, there was the obligation to revoke his Australian citizenship and become an American. The U.S. Communications Act was quite specific: No corporation could hold a broadcasting license if any officer or director were an alien or if more than one fifth of its capital stock were owned of record or voted by aliens, or if it were directly or indirectly controlled by any company with alien management, ownership or control.

To Murdoch even such high prices were worth paying. The acquisition enormously increased the reach of News Corp. Murdoch's venture was seen as one of the most ambitious that any media magnate had ever attempted. No one else had managed to build a fourth U.S. national TV network. And no one before had ever attempted to build a global communications empire as large and as complex as News was becoming. With the stations, he now controlled ninety-three publishing, broadcasting and other operations with assets of $4.7 billion and annual revenue of $2.6 billion. He would reach a quarter of the world's English-speaking population.

But first he had to make a similar journey to that which millions of immigrants had made before him, through today's equivalent of Ellis Island.

"ELLIS ISLAND"

For two centuries now, America has seemed the best and the bravest new world, the lodestar, the safe haven, the El Dorado for millions of people around the globe. That is still so today, just as it was in the nineteenth century. No other country in history has exerted such a fierce gravitational pull.

At the end of the twentieth century, the world is on the move as never before. Before the Second World War there were just two million international travelers. Now four hundred million people travel abroad every year. At the beginning of the 1980s there were ten million refugees in the world. At the beginning of the 1990s there were over seventeen million. There were many millions more migrants, both legal and illegal. For millions of Asians, Latin Americans and citizens of the Soviet empire, the United States was the dream destination, with Europe, Canada and Australia trailing behind. Migration has always been one of the great enigmas of human history, as the poor, the wretched and the tempest-tossed flee poverty and persecution in the hopeful pursuit of human happiness and wealth.

In one sense Murdoch was doing the same; he too believed in the American Dream. But to his critics his motives seemed so material that he was merely a caricature of the millions who had landed in the New World with optimism and trepidation, and of many of those who were with him in the district court in lower Manhattan, on September 4, 1985.

The ordinary immigrants, dressed in their best clothes, waited in the corridors. As the time for the ceremony drew near, they were shepherded into the courtroom, clutching their copies of the oath of allegiance.

Rupert Murdoch, Anna and their children Elisabeth, Lachlan and James, now aged seventeen, fourteen and twelve, arrived in two limousines and drove straight down into the underground entrance of the court. From the parking lot, they rose into the courthouse by elevator, avoided the press, and were ushered into the courtroom where everyone else was waiting. They were shown into the jury box. Judge Shirley Wohl Kram entered, took her seat and made a rather moving speech about the rights and responsibilities of new citizens.

The Australian papers recorded that at exactly 10:55 A.M. New York time on September 4, 1985, Rupert Murdoch became an American by placing his hand over his heart and pledging allegiance to the flag of the United States of America and to the republic, so renouncing the Commonwealth of Australia, where he had been born in 1931.

After the ceremony, the New York *Post* took pictures for that day's edition, as Murdoch and his family (who had not changed their citizenship) shook hands with Judge Kram and slipped out of the courthouse the way they had arrived. Murdoch climbed into one limousine; Anna and the children took another.

The reporters, mostly Australian, foiled so far, rushed after the cars. Say a word to Australia, Citizen Murdoch! How does it feel not to be an Aussie, Rupert? Bye-bye, Bondi Beach! For a moment it looked as if the traffic would bear the Murdochs away upon its flow, but their cars were caught at a red light. An Australian television reporter dashed up to Murdoch's limousine. Murdoch's window was tightly closed. The Australian banged on the roof of the car to make the American inside open up. Murdoch smiled, but his car drew away.

Anna Murdoch was less prudent; she had her window down. Microphones were pushed into her face. How did she feel about her husband's change of citizenship? the jostling reporters shouted. "I'm very happy for him," she said.

Others were outraged. Jimmy Breslin, the tempestuous columnist for the *Daily News,* described Murdoch not as a man for all seasons, but as "a man for all occasions. He regarded New York as a town without sense, a place of damaged palates where nobody can taste, and he presented the great city with headlines about killer bees and newspapers filled with pictures of blacks in handcuffs. He gave you thuggery and called it a newspaper."

Breslin thought that Murdoch had incited racial hatred in the city. "We are a mixed population and he tried so blatantly to use race to sell his newspapers that he became known as 'Tar Baby Murdoch.' I can't believe that we're so easy in this city that an act like Murdoch's can get by. You have more right to own a television station in this city than Murdoch does."

In a similar vein, William Safire had already expressed his misgivings in the New York *Times.* Safire acknowledged that Murdoch "is just the sort of entrepreneurial type the country wants to attract—one who will generate jobs and pay taxes and challenge the powerful." (In fact, Murdoch's critics charged that he usually befriended the powerful rather than challenging them.) "Isn't it true that his main reason for becoming a citizen is simple greed and lust for power?" Safire had no problem with that, but he felt that Murdoch was in fact the opposite of a nationalist. "He is the multinational man, a true 'citizen of the world.' He is at home in London, New York and Sydney and he pays homage to no political prince. . . . Americans should remind him that allegiance means loyalty, sometimes passionate loyalty."

Mike Royko, the Chicago columnist who thought Murdoch's papers unsuitable even for dead fish, demanded to know how Murdoch could be welcomed so easily when poor Mexicans and Haitians were turned back at the frontiers or on the high seas. He was not fleeing communism or any other kind of tyranny. "Nor does he have a skill that is in short supply. By profession, Murdoch is a greedy, money-grubbing, power-seeking, status-climbing cad. Since when is that skill in short supply?"

To Royko, Murdoch's only motive was to get even richer and more powerful. He was "a bloated millionaire," a sacker of American workers and breaker of unions, "a proven ingrate," "a proven liar." Murdoch obviously had contempt for Americans.

> In his heart, if such an organ exists, Murdoch thinks we're boobs. That's why he publishes boob-mentality newspapers. He thinks that's all we can understand. . . . So, if Murdoch is allowed to become a citizen while we're turning away people who are running from death squads or starvation, then we should make one small change in the plans to renovate the Statue of Liberty. Get rid of the torch. Just have the lady hold up her hand with the middle finger extended.

On the other side of the political spectrum, the views were rather different. Within the Reagan administration, Murdoch's move was widely welcomed, nowhere more so than on the Federal Communications Commission, which was undergoing its own Reaganite revolution at the hands of its chairman, Mark Fowler.

From Murdoch's point of view, there could have been no better chairman of the FCC than Fowler—they were ideological soul mates, united in their love of the free market and their abhorrence of regulations. Fowler admired Murdoch's own freebooting philosophy and welcomed his desire to create a new television network. Indeed, he did everything he could to ease Murdoch's passage. Murdoch later called him "one of the great pioneers of the communications revolution" and "perhaps the most successful of any Reagan appointee."

Fowler was a forty-three-year-old communications lawyer who had worked in Ronald Reagan's 1980 campaign and was then given the chairmanship of the Federal Communications Commission. He was a jovial fellow, a showman, who kept in his office a Mao cap, adorned with a red star, which he used to put on the head of any of his officials who came up with a suggestion he deemed "collectivist." He was an unabashed Reaganite and defined his mission as "pruning, chopping, slashing, eliminating, burning and deep-sixing" as many as he could of the regulations which the FCC had created and imposed upon communications throughout America in the half century of its existence. Fowler's enemies, many of them public-interest groups concerned with broadcasting, saw him as "the mad monk of deregulation." One former commissioner complained that Fowler saw regulation "as a kind of evil empire, and he's Luke Skywalker."

In the first four years of Fowler's chairmanship, the commission had allowed many more automatic renewals of broadcast licenses, and had begun to deregulate radio and television. It had authorized direct broadcast satellites and raised the number of AM, FM and TV stations a single owner might have from seven to twelve of each. This last change was important in the takeover of the ABC network by Capital Cities, and in Murdoch's purchase of Metromedia.

Fowler thought Murdoch an exciting challenger of the entrenched networks. He was coming in "to provide new choices." Fowler commented, "That is something we certainly want to encourage as a generic matter." If Fowler had had his way, Murdoch could have had the Metromedia stations without the inconvenience of becoming an American citizen; after all, his nationality had not prevented him from buying his American newspapers, and Fowler wanted the freedom of print to be extended to the air.

Fowler had forced the commission to catch up with the technological revolution. But the change went deeper than merely adjusting to the revolution in computers and telecommunications. It was ideological. Under Fowler the commission sometimes appeared to be no more than a mere bystander in private industry disputes. Even some of the other commissioners thought this could go too far. James H. Quello, the dean of the five-member board, warned that "the FCC is not here to serve fastbuck artists who buy broadcasters to bust them up."

It was upon Quello that Murdoch and Kluge had together made a formal call to inform the commission of the intended sale. Quello said afterward that he liked Murdoch, whom he found soft-spoken and persuasive. He did not think Murdoch was going to "bust up" Metromedia. "There was a good feeling at the commission about having an Australian turn American and becoming a big player in the communications industry," Quello said later.

Murdoch now saw himself above all as an American international citizen. His expansion promoted his worldview and reinforced the power structures of which he was a part. He considered that he had a mission, or at least an opportunity, to spread and to propagate the free-market-version American Dream wherever his empire stretched.

Nations are now increasingly defined by the extent to which knowledge is a tradable commodity in their economies. In America by the end of the 1980s, half of all jobs were related to information processing of one kind or another. In developing countries like the Soviet Union, and many in sub-Saharan Africa, primitive communications were inimical to development. Mark Fowler asserted: "Just as coffee beans will be grown in the most conducive environment, communications and computing traffic will move to those nations that can handle it fastest and cheapest."

This argument held that communications determined national identity. But at the same time communications were making national identity "less significant." Murdoch's belief, and Fowler's, was that the spread of communications around the world was in itself a good, but this conviction tended to ignore two corollaries of the communications revolution: its threat to national identity is making that identity all the more jealously guarded, particularly in the Islamic world, and, conversely, the revolution is attracting more and more people toward its center. In the years to come, mass movements of people toward the United States and Western Europe, the communications hubs, will become overwhelming.

In Australia, such perceptions were secondary, and reactions to Murdoch's change of citizenship were emotional. Dame Elisabeth admitted to the Sydney *Morning News,* "It was quite a bit to swallow at first blush." Murdoch himself insisted, "I am not severing any links with Australia. I continue to have the same emotions and feelings about Australia. If I have to change the color of my passport, then so be it. I don't put the same stress on it as some other people do." Many Australians certainly did.

Anna Murdoch, too, was privately dismayed by her husband's abandonment of his Australian citizenship. "I was shocked. I never thought he'd do it. I realized then how strong his ambitious drive was," she said later.

She too had her ambitions, and as her husband changed citizenship, she attracted attention to herself by publishing her first novel, *In Her Own Image.* It was a book about women and the courage that they need in a world of men. It was written with passion; in it the fear of loss dominates the lives of two sisters straining for places in a world structured by men. Anna's women had passionate emotions; her men merely had ambitions and fears.

Anna Murdoch was now a beautiful woman in her forties, elegantly dressed, with an air of coolness and a shyness that concealed determination. Her tongue could be sharp. It was clear that her life had made her very independent. When she was publicizing the book, some of her interviewers commented that although Murdoch was well known and seriously vilified, his family was kept surprisingly secret. She said that they had guarded their privacy jealously. "We have a very strong sense of ourselves. We don't need that sort of recognition that some appear to look for. . . . I don't want to be a partygoer. I don't want to be a shopper. I don't want to be going to charity things all the time. . . . You can take us or leave us," she said, "and we prefer it if you leave us." It was clear that they were able to protect themselves much more effectively than the victims of her husband's papers.

She had to face a lot of questions about the *Sun*. "We *are* [good people]," she told the Washington *Post* rather defensively. She insisted that the criticisms had no effect upon them as a family: "We know what he is like. People who work with him know what he is like. Of course, he has enemies. He doesn't suffer fools gladly. But he is a very good and moral human being, and we are bringing up our children that way."

Anna was practiced at defending her husband. "He's very much misunderstood, he's much nicer than he seems," she had told *Time* in 1976. "I know in board meetings he can be very tough. I guess you could say that I'm a softy, but I can come over very tough and he's the other way around." He could be very impetuous, and sometimes he regretted his actions.

He was not always a very patient father, she said. "He's not a wrestly daddy. He'd rumple his tie." He could seem remote even at home. His son James sometimes asked her, " 'Is Daddy going deaf ?' 'No,' I say, 'he's just not listening.' "

His children sometimes complained that Murdoch's aggressive competitiveness intruded even into his games with them. Nonetheless, Murdoch was a committed family man, and enjoyed, when he found the time, taking his children on summer camping expeditions, as well as skiing with them in winter at Aspen, where they had bought a house.

In New York in the mid-1980s Anna had decided that the children were old enough for her to do something of her own, to be more of Anna and less of Mrs. Murdoch. She also needed to assuage the loneliness: Rupert spent so much time hop, skip and jumping around the world, and when he was at home he was usually on the telephone. "I suppose I could have just complained . . . and become a whining wife," she said. "But I didn't want to do that, so why not make it a positive thing and use the time?"

Through the end of the 1970s and the early 1980s she studied mythology and then literature, first at Fordham and then at New York University. Along with other ladies of New York society, she attended a literature course run by John Gross, a former editor of the *Times Literary Supplement;* he was impressed by her diligence. She started writing short stories, but Murdoch's criticisms were, she said, "devastating. Here was someone who was not only my best friend and my husband and everything else, saying things about something I was really trying to do and not in a way that was helpful to me." She added, "What he said was so mortifying that I could never touch it again."

Despite his lack of support, she was determined to write a book before she was forty. She decided never to show him anything else until it was finished. On her fortieth birthday, the book was in type, though not yet in print. She finally gave it to Murdoch. He read it all the way through and, since his attention span was notoriously short, she was pleased.

The book, which Anna said was "about forgiveness," was well received, but some reviewers and interviewers were especially excited by its fairly raunchy sex scenes. Anna told Philip Oakes of the *Sunday Times* that these were difficult for her: "I'm a modest person, but I wanted to be honest in describing how women feel about things. And the difference between love and lust would have been completely lost if I'd stopped at the bedroom door and not gone inside. But there are special difficulties for a woman writer because there are some words used about parts of the body which are particularly male. A woman is limited in her use of verbs and nouns because they sound pejorative and sexist."

She said she thought it was a question "to which feminists could address themselves."

The Melbourne *Age* had fun with this dilemma. At the end of a sympathetic interview with her, the *Age* quoted from the book.

Overcoming her modesty, Anna wrote, "They were slipping and sliding on each other up and down. His hands, her hands, his chest, her breasts, his face, her mouth, his buttocks, her lips. They were lost until he said, 'Now. Now.' And it was time.

"He bit her left breast with his teeth and they were bucking and rolling with each other, his arms no longer wandering over her but holding her firmly, one on each side of her hips, until he was pounding into her, and she could not shake him loose and she cried out, 'Harry. Harry. At last, at last.' "

She had shown it to Rupert.

"Who's Harry?" Rupert asked.

"It's you, darling," she said.

7

WAPPING

None of Murdoch's endless battles was more ferocious than the one he waged at Wapping in London's Docklands through 1986.

By the end of 1985, the debt from the takeover of Fox and Metromedia meant that he needed to milk his British cash cows more than ever. He was exasperated by the intractability of the Fleet Street unions. If the *Sun, News of the World* and *Sunday Times* were produced efficiently, Murdoch knew they could be wildly more profitable.

What he needed was agreement on uninterrupted production and new technology. New technology, for Murdoch and other publishers, meant "single keystroking," by which journalists and advertising staff could set words in type without the help of printers.

In 1982 he began to build a new London plant, far from Fleet Street, in Wapping, east of the City of London. At first he expected this new building to be merely a very modern printing plant. Pages would be typeset and made up in central London as before; the journalists would still not have access to the terminals. The unions insisted that if they were ever to move into this new plant all the old rules and practices of Fleet Street must move with them.

By the middle of the 1980s almost all London papers were suffering financially. Telegraph Newspapers was in an especially parlous condition. Like Murdoch, the Telegraph management was building a new plant out of Fleet Street, on the Isle of Dogs, which in terms of distance from "the Street" was Peking to Wapping's Moscow. By 1985, the company was practically bankrupt and its proprietor, Lord Hartwell, was forced to turn to a Canadian entrepreneur and newspaper owner, Conrad Black, for salvation. Exhausted by the struggle, Hartwell almost casually turned his family's business over to Black.

Murdoch liked to quote the *Times* columnist Bernard Levin, who said that Fleet Street newspapers were "produced in conditions which combined a protection racket with a lunatic asylum." He once complained that within his empire he employed four men to a press in San Antonio, five men in Chicago, six in New York and Sydney, and in London—eighteen! "And all were paid salaries at least one hundred percent above the national average."

Early in the new year of 1985, Murdoch decided to try to break the unions. It was a hard decision, because his whole empire depended upon the cash flow from Britain and the initial disruption was bound to be immense. The time seemed propitious. The government was setting its own example by resolute resistance to a miners' strike. At the *Times,* circulation was edging up and nudging the circulation of the *Guardian* at just under 500,000. But to print more copies, the machine room staff on Grays Inn Road demanded an extra seventy "jobs"—which would have cost another £1 million a year. Murdoch's innate caution when dealing with the unions was finally overtaken by his exasperation. He agreed to start planning a move to Wapping, and soon became totally committed to it.

He wanted a legally binding no-strike agreement with just one union. The closed shop would be killed. Management would have the right to hire and fire as it wished. Journalists and telephone-ad saleswomen would have direct input to computer terminals. In other words, the unions would have to drop everything upon which they had insisted over the last forty years. Management was demanding the right to change all the existing habits and actually to manage. And this time, that management had an escape route.

Murdoch worked two tracks. Ostensibly negotiations went on with the established unions. Secretly a team at Wapping set to work equipping the factory to produce not only a new London daily paper but all four of Murdoch's national titles.

In Wapping the first thing that Murdoch decided on was the computer system. Despite his interest in technological progress, he was a man who could hardly change a lightbulb, let alone change a fuse or insert a cassette into a tape recorder. Perhaps for that reason, he held the practical view that it was up to others to make the trials and suffer the errors associated with new equipment, as Eddie Shah had done. For himself, he wanted the most commonly used, off-the-shelf computer technology that had so far been developed for newspapers. This was Atex, a system created in 1972 by three men in a loft in New England. It had been bought in 1982 by Kodak for some $80 million, sold to over five hundred customers around the world, and was especially well tried in newspapers across the United States.

In February 1985, Murdoch made a secret agreement with Atex to install a system at Wapping to cope with at least four papers.

An Atex team of about a dozen people was selected from regional offices around America. They began to arrive in London and lived anonymously in houses in Belgravia and Chelsea. Atex set up a separate company in London and News International activated a small company so that these two unknown firms could do business with each other without either name striking a chord anywhere. News even asked that Atex purchase about $3 million worth of extra equipment, such as typesetting machines and graphics cameras, from other American companies and ship them over by the same secret system. Atex changed its usual shipper so that this link would not be a risk, and used spray paint the color of cardboard to delete the company's name on the outsides of cartons. The Atex team worked in an unused shed—which they called "the Bunker"—in east London. There they began to put together the system.

Murdoch insisted on equal secrecy from his own people. Meetings of the key executives took place in different London hotels. There were usually no minutes; agendas were destroyed.

By early May, just as Murdoch agreed to buy Metromedia in the U.S.A., the men and women in the Bunker in London had assembled the entire new system. It was broken into pieces again and put into boxes to be shipped to Wapping. Contractors were banned from the factory. Three large trucks came to the Bunker, picked up the crates and carried them surreptitiously into Wapping. The rooms in which the computers were installed became the holiest of holies, off limits to all except the few who knew the extent of the revolution which Murdoch hoped to bring about. By the end of the first week of June the computers were all fired up and on line.

Murdoch was equipping Wapping with presses that were even less modern than the computers. He had bought them more than a decade earlier, when they happened to be for sale cheap. They were Goss Mark One machines which had been kept in their crates. Now they were literally dusted down and greased up and fitted with new electronics.

At the same time the building's original heating oil tanks were cleaned and filled with ink—enough for three months.

Everything else—string, glue, wire, pencils—came in under cover. Paper was the biggest item. Convoys would come in with one driver and manager. By the end of the year there were about four thousand reels of paper available. But this was less than it appeared to be; it would last all the papers for about a week.

The most difficult problem was to decide who was to run the machines. Murdoch and Matthews decided to use the electricians' union. The electricians began to recruit men in Southampton on six-month contracts. They were bused about a hundred miles every day to Wapping and were sworn to secrecy about what they saw and what they did. It was deemed especially important that they not understand the huge power of the Atex system. Astonishingly, they never did. Even though gossip began to run through the pubs on Fleet Street as to what Murdoch might be secretly planning behind the walls and wire of Wapping, no one really understood.

Murdoch then decided to create a completely new distribution system—by truck, not by unionized trains. The trucks themselves were provided by "my friends and partners in Australia," Thomas Nationwide Transport. Murdoch paid £7 million toward the capital costs of eight hundred trucks and vans.

As usual, Murdoch was spending his time flying by Concorde back and forth across the Atlantic, often with his invaluable assistant Dorothy Wyndoe, who had been at the center of his operations for years.

As the prospect drew nearer that Wapping would begin operating, News began to worry about the security of its staff. Key executives were advised to inform their local police who they were: "There are among us people who may be regarded as targets for terrorism. . . . Be sensitive to persons behaving in a suspicious or unaccountable fashion." They should avoid regular patterns of behavior, at home they should have locks put on all doors and windows and remove trees or shrubs that could give cover, they should worry about car bombs and letter bombs and they should shred all documents and letters and discuss nothing confidential on the telephone.

In the last quarter of 1985 the print unions began to shift closer to a deal, but not with any sense of urgency. They believed they still had the upper hand and that, with his new American acquisitions, Murdoch could not afford a strike, which would stop the cash flow from Bouverie Street and Grays Inn Road. They had not yet grasped that Murdoch planned to move all four titles to Wapping.

Then a crucial element in the secret strategy leaked in the Communist Party daily, the *Morning Star,* just before Christmas. It had been outlined in a letter from one of News Corp's lawyers, who gave detailed advice on the most expedient method of getting rid of the London work force: "The cheapest way of doing so would be to dismiss employees while participating in a strike or other industrial action." A striker would be in breach of contract, and "can thus be dismissed instantly." A striker would not be entitled to severance pay and would have no claim in the event of unfair dismissal, "provided *all* the strikers have been dismissed and *none* selectively reengaged."

The picture was coming into sharper focus, but the print unions still could not entertain the idea of Murdoch being able to produce *all* his newspapers without them.

Murdoch went skiing in Aspen after Christmas 1985. Early in the new year, he flew to London. He had reserved four whole weeks for the Wapping campaign. News International announced that he was to take charge of the talks for the London *Post,* for which publication was said to be anticipated on March 17.

On January 19 the *Sunday Times* published a special supplement produced at Wapping. Among a series of articles entitled "The Future of Fleet Street," Murdoch himself was interviewed and insisted that there was no dispute with the unions. "They have refused to work at Wapping and agreements are in place at our existing plants," he said. He rejected claims that he was a union basher: "We don't have a print plant anywhere in the world which is not unionized. . . . News Corpo- ration employs more trade unionists than any other publishing com- pany in the world." The supplement deliberately repeated the fact that Wapping could produce "more than one" newspaper. The unions knew that the gauntlet had been thrown down.

If they had been wise, they would have done nothing. Then Murdoch would have had to pay the men on Fleet Street as well as the new men in Wapping. If they went on strike instead, Murdoch could at once fire them and so escape the obligation to make severance pay- ments of about £40 million. The unions knew this. Nonetheless, they voted to go on strike.

By now Murdoch was no longer interested in any compromise. "It's all too late," he said. Now the fences at Wapping were topped with coils of razor wire bought from Germany. More guards were stationed

Rupert Murdoch on the Fox back lot. Murdoch took personal control of
Twentieth Century Fox in 1992, consolidating News Corp's position as
one of the world's most far-reaching and diversified media conglomerates.

Ann Lane, the Citibank vice-
president who helped assemble
the refinancing package that saved
News Corp from disaster.

3

4

Rupert Murdoch's maternal
grandfather, Rupert Greene,
in 1936.

Murdoch's paternal grandfather, the
Reverend Patrick John Murdoch.

5

Keith Murdoch's official farewell from Lord Northcliffe in London.
Keith, holding his presentation golf clubs, is in the front row at Northcliffe's right. Billy Hughes, the Australian prime minister, is on Northcliffe's left.

Rupert Murdoch, age five, in a train window with Sir Keith.

6

Sir Keith and Lady Murdoch, returning from a trip to Britain and the Middle East, 1942.

7

The day of Rupert Murdoch's marriage to Anna Torv in April 1967.

8

9

Rupert Murdoch addressing the vital meeting of *News of the World* shareholders at the Connaught Rooms on January 2, 1969.

Max Newton, the first editor of the *Australian*, onetime pornographer and later economics pundit at the New York *Post*.

The front cover of *Time* during Murdoch's conquest of
New York.

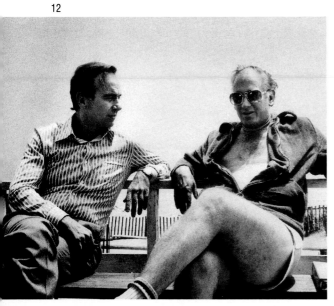

Murdoch with Clay
Felker, publisher of
New York magazine and
the *Village Voice*, before
the bruising battle that
ended with Murdoch's
acquisition of both pub-
lications.

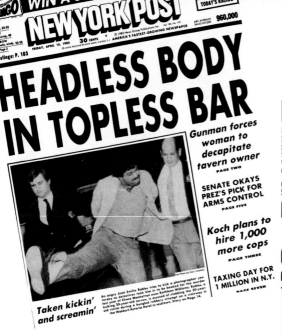

During the early years of Murdoch's reign at the *Post*, the paper fueled its bid for increased circulation with eye-catching "grabber" headlines.

Murdoch with Dolly Schiff, from whom he bought the New York *Post* in 1976.

NEW YORK POST

METRO
TODAY'S RACING

JUNTA GOONS KIDNAP N.Y. TV MAN

He's stripped & threatened with execution: Pages 4 & 5

'MY BABIES ARE DEAD,' MOM SCREAMS

GRIEF-STRICKEN Mrs. Anna Garcia is restrained by neighbors after returning from a trip to the grocery yesterday — and discovering that her two youngest children, ages 1 and 2, had died in each other's arms during a fire in her sister's Bronx apartment. But a courageous tenant managed to save Mrs. Garcia's 3-year-old twins. Story: Page 7.

NEW YORK POST

METRO
TODAY'S RAC

'MY 7 DAYS IN SEX DEN'

Kidnaped L.I. teen tells of her nightmare

PRETTY 17-year-old student Debra Sagers who was kidnaped, raped and held in a "sex den" for a week, yesterday told of her bizarre ordeal at the hands of a crazed couple with a baby who at times treated her "like family," then abused her. Debra, pictured here with her mom and dad after the ordeal, said the experience was "one endless blur." FULL STORY PAGE 4.

Politically partisan headlines were also a Murdoch favorite at the *Post*. Senator Edward Kennedy was a favorite (liberal) target.

DESPERATE TED STORMS NEW YORK

TED BLOWS HIS TO...

16

17

Rupert Murdoch scans a copy of his latest acquisition, the *Times* of London, on January 23, 1981. At his left is Harold Evans; to the right, William Rees-Mogg.

The *Times* bicentenary celebration, July 11, 1985. Rupert and Anna Murdoch greet Prime Minister Margaret Thatcher and her husband, Denis.

18

A security guard patrols behind the barbed-wire fence at "Fortress" Wapping, just before the presses rolled on January 25, 1986, to produce the first copies of the *Sunday Times* and the *News of the World* to be printed at the new headquarters.

OPPOSITE, BOTTOM—The proprietor holds the first copies of the *Times* and the *Sun* to be printed at Wapping. The date is January 27, 1986.

Perhaps the classic
Sun headline.

Rupert Murdoch is congratulated by his mother, Dame
Elisabeth, after his successful
bid for the Melbourne *Herald,*
the paper his father built. The
date is December 3, 1986.

Rupert and Anna Murdoch with
their children—James, Lachlan
and Elisabeth.

Press barons of the world. From left, Viscount Rothermere, Rupert Murdoch and Robert Maxwell at a Reuters lunch in 1987.

23

24

John Evans, futurologist and head of Murdoch Magazines, relaxing with the Murdochs in Aspen in 1989.

Rupert and Anna Murdoch at their meeting with President Gorbachev in Moscow, May 1991.

25

Murdoch with John Kluge, from whom he bought Metromedia Television in 1985.

26

27

Murdoch with Diane von Furstenberg, fashion designer and friend of Barry Diller, and Mort Zuckerman, publisher of the *Atlantic* and *U.S. News & World Report*.

Marvin Davis, from whom Murdoch bought Twentieth Century Fox in 1985.

Steve Dunleavy (right), the Australian journalist who became a regular reporter on Fox Broadcasting's "A Current Affair" and helped bring Murdoch's tabloid style to television.

Murdoch and Anna at their new home in Beverly Hills, their headquarters after Murdoch took full control of Fox in 1992.

Murdoch with Joe Roth, whom he appointed as head of the Fox film division in 1989. Among his successes: *Home Alone*; among his failures: *For the Boys.*

As head of Twentieth Century Fox, Barry Diller (right) succeeded in creating a fourth successful television network. His departure from Fox in the spring of 1992 caused industry shock waves. Diller is pictured here with Ted Turner, founder of CNN, the service Murdoch hopes Fox will ultimately top.

Murdoch with the Simpsons, the cartoon family whose travails reflected American working-class woes in the nineties. Their series was one of Fox Broadcasting's biggest hits.

The Last of the Mohicans, starring Daniel Day-Lewis, was a huge hit for the Fox film division in the fall of 1992.

"Studs," brainchild of Steve Chao of Fox Broadcasting, ruled the Nielsen ratings but seemed to its critics to be the epitome of "lowest common denominator" programming.

Murdoch with Steve Chao, whom he fired as president of Fox Broadcasting after Chao hired a male stripper to entertain at an Aspen News Corp retreat in 1992.

Murdoch with a satellite dish, the essential element in his attempt to build an international news and entertainment network.

around the site. The government was briefed; Thatcher was said to be delighted with Murdoch's plan. The police sealed off side streets and practiced tactics to defeat picketing and to keep the trucks running out of Wapping every night. It was the duty of the police to keep the highways open, but Murdoch was fortunate to have friends in high places. A Labour government would have given him far less support.

In the final weeks of 1985 and the first days of 1986, Murdoch was at Wapping as often as he could manage, cajoling, bullying, flattering the men who were struggling to get the plant ready to produce four newspapers a night. "Bloody exciting, ain't it? Bloody exciting," he would say when he was on a high. When he felt lower, because something was going wrong, he would shout, "Fix it," and would curse people, crying, "You're bloody incompetent. You've let me down." The key question now was whether the journalists would do the same.

FLEET STREET

Going to Wapping without printers was no problem—indeed, it was the whole point—but going there without anybody to fill the pages would be disastrous. The National Union of Journalists was instructing its members not to go until a deal with the print unions had been concluded, and the message had percolated down through the ranks. On January 22 the journalists' committees at the *Sun* and the *News of the World* voted to obey their union's instruction. Then talks between management and the printers broke down and the print unions called a strike on the evening of Friday, January 24.

It was one of the few times in the industrial history of newspapers when the journalists possessed real power. The novelty of it was reflected in their bewildered response. In fairness, many were genuinely divided between their suspicion of Murdoch and their distrust of the printers.

Murdoch flourished both carrot and stick: if the journalists agreed to go to Wapping, they would be generously reimbursed. If not, they would be considered to have gone on strike and would therefore be dismissed. The legality of this ultimatum was very much in question, and many of the journalists were infuriated by its tone. It seemed to them to betray, more than any previous action, the contempt Murdoch had always felt for journalists.

Much unhappiness might have been dissipated if Murdoch had addressed the journalists himself and made them feel he cared for them. But there were problems with this, which Sir Edward Pickering, Murdoch's old friend and now a director of News, put his finger on later: "The trouble was that Rupert was regarded as the Supreme Satan."

At Bouverie Street, Kelvin MacKenzie called a meeting of the *Sun* journalists. He made an astonishing but characteristically boisterous speech in which he appealed for the journalists to abandon the print unions. They were not all happy, but they voted to go to Wapping. So did the journalists of the *News of the World*.

Up on Grays Inn Road, the new editor, Charlie Wilson, apologized for not having spoken to the journalists earlier—it had been impossible. "The storm has broken tonight," he said. "The *Times* will only survive and continue production if it can be from Tower Hamlets." Tonight's paper would be lost, but no more. Monday's paper would be written and published on Sunday at Wapping. "I am here to invite you to come along and help us do it." Those who did not would be fired. The journalists hesitated. The printers' SOGAT called its members, who included secretaries and researchers as well as machinists, out on strike.

Murdoch was now at Wapping full-time. Wearing old trousers, a cardigan and sneakers, the owner and boss was totally in charge of the operation. Adrenaline pumping through his small, lithe frame, he was everyone and he was everywhere, cajoling, cursing, praising, rushing about like a kid with a complicated toy which he was assembling for the first time. He had lost Friday night's *Sun* and *Times;* on Saturday he was determined to get the Sunday papers out. The *Sunday Times* and the *News of the World* were being written by a handful of journalists who had already agreed to come on board or from stories prepared earlier and brought in by executives. That Saturday evening at about eight o'clock, he stood with his senior executives and pushed the button to set the presses into motion. Everyone clapped and cheered.

Shortly after 9:00 P.M., the first TNT trucks came down the ramp and roared through the East End of London. Others left News' new plant in Glasgow just after 10:00 P.M. That night, January 25, 1986, News published four million papers without any help from the traditional craft unions. The papers were distributed around the country by fleets of TNT vehicles which bypassed the rail network and its unions. The Wapping revolution had begun.

On Sunday, at a hotel in Bloomsbury, the *Times* journalists' chapel met again for passionate, angry debate.

Some fifty *Times* journalists did go to Wapping that Sunday to prepare Monday's paper. At another meeting that Sunday evening, they were denounced by some of their colleagues, but after more emotional argument that evening they voted, by three to one, to move to Wapping. Many journalists were in tears; no one was happy.

Next morning, Monday, January 27, the front page of the *Sun* read, "A NEW SUN IS RISING TODAY," and announced underneath it, "WE BEAT STRIKE THUGS." The story began, "Good Morning Britain," and described how the papers were being produced "despite the biggest print strike since the war." The *Sun* said Murdoch was jubilant. The *Times* story described him as "relaxed and cheerful" and "delighted with the success" of the move.

Now it was the turn of the *Sunday Times*. Of all his newspapers, the *Sunday Times* was the most iconoclastic and independent of Murdoch, and the one most at odds with its own editor. Since his appointment as successor to Frank Giles over two years earlier, Andrew Neil had made no secret of his contempt for the liberal traditions established in Harry Evans' day.

When Neil announced to his staff that Monday morning, "I am one of you," many of those who remained just didn't believe him. There was a widespread suspicion that Neil had been deeply involved in the Wapping schemes from the start and was therefore coming before them not to share a response but to manipulate one.

At the end of the day, a slim majority of his journalists voted to go to Wapping. Altogether, only sixty journalists from the four titles refused Murdoch's inducements and instructions to do so. The others went along, though some regretted the fact that they had not fought harder. They could have realized how important they were to the papers, if not to Murdoch. They could have felt more sympathy for other workers. They could have asked for time. Or for more money.

WAPPING

At first the pickets came slowly to Wapping. But it soon became clear that Murdoch had embarked on the most significant challenge to the British unions since the government faced down the miners' strike in 1984–85, and that he would enjoy the government's full support in the struggle.

Those journalists who first made it through the lines were astonished by the spectacle of their new workplace—by the fierce fencing topped with razor wire, the gigantic gates, the floodlights, the ramp for the trucks, and the huge, hideous newspaper factory itself towering over the middle of the compound, alongside the old rum warehouses, which were to house the *Times* and *Sunday Times* editorial offices.

On every desk inside the old warehouse where the *Times* and *Sunday Times* were now based were the new Atex terminals, and bright American trainer/hostesses—"Hi, I'm Cindy"—who were there to lure the hacks into the late twentieth century.

Most industrial disputes start fiercely and tend to ebb away. Wapping, in contrast, seemed to grow progressively uglier.

The strikers, almost five thousand strong, were desperate from the outset. In industrial terms, the battle was over almost before it had begun. Murdoch had quite simply outwitted them, and in holding on to what he had achieved he had the backing of the prime minister.

By 1986 Mrs. Thatcher saw her reform of the labor laws as among her most significant accomplishments. She had provided management with the weapons—secret ballots and strict limits on picketing—to fight the unions. Nonetheless, few private-sector employers had yet taken advantage of their right to fire striking workers; they preferred to have a labor force at the end of the dispute. Murdoch, by contrast, did not, at least not the same labor force with which he started. Murdoch simply took the law to its logical conclusion, as employers throughout the nation looked on in amazement and, usually, admiration.

While Murdoch could count upon all the resources of government and, in particular, of the police, the printers could not even count on the other unions. They might be admired for their skill in getting their own way and, sometimes, for the skill of their craft, but this did not translate into sympathy. They had for years made so much money, and had behaved so arrogantly toward fellow unionists as well as toward their employers, that around the country union members refused to support their London colleagues by blocking the distribution of Murdoch's papers.

Murdoch's careful preparations—in terms of both the physical and the legal defense of Wapping—meant that the strikers had little room

for maneuver. He had shrewdly diversified his operations under a series of newly registered, separate companies to maximize the difficulty
of secondary picketing.

The striking printers wanted reinstatement, something that
Murdoch had no intention of giving them. Money, or its equivalent,
was a different matter. In early April, he offered to give the unions the
Times and *Sunday Times* plant on Grays Inn Road to produce their
own newspaper. In the end the proposal died.

By now the roads around Wapping were closed even to local resi-
dents and, at night, the traffic lights were synchronized on green to
give the trucks a straight run out of the area. Nonetheless, on the night
of May 3 there was violence outside the plant. Over 250 people were
injured.

Next weekend the violence was repeated. It was horrifying, but it
was quite clear that the new machinery of production and distribution could withstand any weight of picketing. Secret talks between
Murdoch and SOGAT leaders in Los Angeles failed. On May 26,
Murdoch flew in from New York and met with national union leaders
at a hotel near Heathrow Airport. He told them that he would never
tolerate at Wapping the different chapels and closed shops that had
flourished on Bouverie Street and Grays Inn Road. "I have just been
released from that nightmare," he said. "I don't intend going back."
He made a "final offer" which proffered severance payments totaling
£50 million.

That evening, he said in a television interview: "We are under no
obligation to pay any money at all and we are putting this forward in an
attempt to close down the picketing." It was an "extremely high price
for bringing the dispute to an end."

On June 6, the London branches of the unions rejected the offer. Murdoch described their decision as "a second suicide." The first
had been when the unions had gone on strike in the first place. The
printers were now left with nothing, he said, "no jobs, no recognition
and now no money."

So the bloody dispute dragged on. Murdoch became more detested by the political Left in Britain than any other employer had been for decades. He seemed to many to personify all that was most ruthless about the Thatcher revolution. He was already despised by the liberal intellectual establishment. Now he became the ultimate demon, with a forked tail and cloven feet for all to see. His newspapers were banned from college common rooms and by Labour local authorities all over the land, and leaders of the Labour Party refused to give interviews to journalists from Murdoch newspapers. His effigy was everywhere. One protest group called "Women Against Murdoch" marched on Wapping chanting, "Burn, burn, burn the bastard." Publicly, Murdoch was cool. "It's a very localized thing," he said. "And it's become very emotional. And it's natural, when things get emotional, they get personalized." Privately, such reactions confirmed his dislike of "soft-centered" and "appeasing" British attitudes.

More serious for him was the hemorrhage of journalists from Wapping, particularly from the *Times* and *Sunday Times*. Some left because they could not abide their editors and the politics they were imposing. Others had long been uncomfortable about working for Murdoch, and Wapping was the last straw.

Many now sought new jobs on a new paper, the *Independent*, which three former journalists on the *Daily Telegraph*, were planning to launch in the autumn. The new paper promised to live up to its name. By July, a third of the 115 journalists it had hired came from Wapping; many more followed later.

Murdoch claimed to be delighted by the exodus—it "was probably twenty years overdue"—but the drain of journalists became too fast even for him. Huge salary increases were offered as an incentive to those who would stay in Wapping. Some journalists accepted; many did not.

Although a Murdoch victory would benefit all Fleet Street managements, other newspapers were slow to praise, let alone support, him. The *Observer* even bowed to union pressure to deny work to part-time staff who also worked on other days for Murdoch. It also refused to publish a review by Bernard Levin, a long-time contributor to the paper, merely because he was a columnist for the *Times*. The *Daily Telegraph* refused to accept an advertisement from News.

In January 1987, Murdoch obtained the final settlement he wanted at a cost of £60 million and the pickets trudged away. When the money was divided, the strikers received no more than a half of what their entitlement would have been if Murdoch had been obliged to lay them off in the first place. For him it was a famous and fantastically inexpensive victory. And he could proudly claim that he alone had broken the noose the unions had tightened around the industry, and had liberated all of Fleet Street.

Drexel Burnham estimated that the value of Murdoch's four London papers rose from $300 million to $1 billion just by moving out of Fleet Street and into Wapping. By the end of 1986, Wapping and Glasgow were producing almost 33 million newspapers a week. Murdoch had reduced the number of print workers from over 2,000 to just 570; 132 people now packed the papers in the publishing room—a task for which in the old days 1,469 men had been employed. The factory was said to be generating £2 million a week. His U.K. profits were up 85 percent, to £34.5 million. Bankers throughout the world were full of admiration for his ruthlessness and his success. Their accolades were important to Murdoch. He said, "The financial world, the industrial world and a lot of the rest of the world are impressed that we've been able to change the industrial environment in Fleet Street. And of that we're very proud."

He could fairly claim that Wapping brought a new "Silver Age" to British journalism, and he pointed out that not only could the *Independent* not have begun but for Wapping, but it also benefited in other ways. "The *Independent* was a total beneficiary because we became the public enemy of the Left and the Labour Party. Also, the soft center didn't like us. I don't mean the Liberal Party or the Social Democrat Party. There's a soft center there in Britain. Always has been. There were the appeasers—the sort of Tories I don't like . . . they saw our actions at Wapping as a measure of enormous harshness. This gave the *Independent* a bit of a break."

The battle of Wapping was a strategic defeat for the labor movement in Britain, and a victory for Thatcherism. The profits that derived from it would flow like blood through the arteries of Murdoch's empire all around the world.

8

MELBOURNE

On the morning of December 3, 1986, Rupert Murdoch marched once again into the office of his father's old paper, the Melbourne *Herald,* and announced to the chairman, John Dahlsen, that he was making another bid for the company.

Before nightfall, the board of the Herald and Weekly Times group recommended that shareholders accept the offer "in the absence of a more attractive offer from anywhere else." The *Herald,* an afternoon paper, printed a special final edition that day announcing the news with a banner headline.

That evening Murdoch gave a press conference with his mother, Dame Elisabeth, beside him. He said that he had been welcomed by the Herald board "somewhat like Father Christmas." When he said he had only decided to make the bid over Thanksgiving in America, someone asked him if this was the biggest turkey he had ever swallowed. He laughed.

Murdoch admitted that the deal had great emotional significance for him. When asked the perennial question "What makes you run?" he replied, "It's the challenge of the game. It gives me a great thrill and it would be very wrong to deny that it is emotional."

He and his mother were photographed alongside the bust of his father in the lobby of the *Herald* building. Dame Elisabeth said that

Rupert was "a modern-day version of my husband. . . . He's very much like his father."

"Rupert is not ruled by his heart, but there is a great deal of heart in everything he does, particularly in this instance," she said in a television interview. "It is naturally sentimental. I am very happy that Rupert has managed to take his place back in that organization. That is what his father might have wished for him."

She went on to propose a motive for her son's ceaseless, frenetic, acquisitive activity: "His father dying so young was a great challenge to Rupert. Subconsciously, he wanted to prove he was worth all his father's trust and worth all his praise. It was a challenge. And that is probably the secret of his success."

A writer in the Melbourne *Age* compared Murdoch with Citizen Kane: "It may be drawing a long bow, but with his mother by his side, there seemed to be a feeling yesterday, that just as the tycoon in Orson Welles's film pined at his death for his childhood toboggan, so Rupert Murdoch had always believed the *Herald* was his by birthright."

Others pointed out that if the deal went through, Murdoch would have control of major daily newspapers in every Australian capital city, more than 60 percent of the total daily newspapers throughout the country. Why should Australians tolerate such power in one man's hands, just so that he could prove himself to his father's ghost? Among a wide section of the Australian population Murdoch's ambitions became more feared and disliked than ever.

This particular battle in his personal, unending war of the worlds had begun on the slopes of Aspen. The Australian government gave him advance warning that it was planning a radical change in its broadcasting and press policy. In the words of the government's treasurer at the time, Paul Keating, it was offering media owners the choice between being "princes of print or queens of the screen." In Australia Murdoch would take the role of the prince.

After dozens of his usual daily phone calls to New York and to Australia, he ended his vacation on Saturday, November 29. He flew to Los Angeles, where he was met by a secretary who had flown posthaste from New York with his new American passport. From Los Angeles Murdoch took a commercial flight to Melbourne, and began to plot his strategy in the Regent Hotel.

Since his change of citizenship, Murdoch had been fighting to hold on to his Channel 10 television stations in Sydney and Melbourne. Problems of citizenship and ownership had always been among the most intractable that Murdoch faced everywhere while trying to build his international empire. This was particularly true in regard to television stations. Governments take television much more seriously than they take newspapers, and the price of having a TV station is usually paid in accountability and agreement to serve the public interest. And so Australian broadcasting law, media and even politics had been in turmoil ever since Murdoch's decision to become an American.

When he had first sought to buy Channel 10 in 1979, one clause of the Broadcasting Act had prevented any company from holding a television license if 15 percent of that company was controlled by someone who was "not a resident of Australia." The Labor Party had endeavored to show that Murdoch in 1979 was certainly not such a resident. Murdoch had put up his usual self-defense of being the little man taking on huge established interests.

Eventually, the tribunal decided that he was adequately resident and could legitimately have the Channel 10 license. Then the law was changed. It was no longer necessary to be *resident* in Australia—instead, an owner of a television station had to be a *citizen* of the country. This was advantageous for Murdoch and seen as an example of his influence over the government of the day. It was widely called the "Murdoch amendment." But by the middle of 1986 it seemed clear that, as an American citizen, he would have to sell off his two television stations in Australia.

Nevertheless, Murdoch sought to retain them. He saw them as an important if not crucial part of the global news and entertainment web he was weaving around the world from its center on the Fox lot in Hollywood.

In Australia, that was seen as part of the problem. "Our cross-ownership rules were vital because they stopped Murdoch having both papers and TV all over the world," said Deirdre O'Connor, the chairwoman of the Broadcasting Tribunal. "It broke the circle. I think Murdoch was very anxious to keep Channel 10 at that time. He had just bought Fox and said it would be of great mutual benefit to Australia and the U.S.A. That's what we feared—we didn't want to be swamped by U.S. material." Once again, fears of omnivorous American culture had been raised.

Prime Minister Hawke was reported to be strongly in favor of changes that would assist the Packer and Murdoch organizations. Hawke's declared motive was "national reconciliation"—almost as if Murdoch were a sovereign state.

Like the United States, Australia had become more and more deeply in debt in the 1980s; assets were shuffled and redealt. One industrialist called it a "casino mentality." The Australian macho concept of "mateship" between Labor leaders and tycoons was an insidious part of this process. Murdoch and Kerry Packer were among the mates. Hawke called Packer "a close personal friend and . . . a very great Australian." Fairfax and the Melbourne *Herald*, by contrast, were seen as representing the old Establishment and being irredeemably pro-Liberal and anti-Labor.

When he became an American citizen, Murdoch's Australian lawyers had announced plans to transfer control of the Channel 10 network to the public shareholders of News Corporation and to a new trust. The purpose was to quarantine Murdoch's personal interest in the two stations and keep it below the maximum 15 percent allowed to an alien. Under the proposal a new company called Network 10 Holdings would own the two stations.

News Corp proposed that it would have less than 1 percent of the voting rights of Network 10 Holdings. Then, the government suddenly announced its "princes of print or queens of the screen" choice for media owners; the changes in the broadcasting system were modeled on American cross-ownership rules.

From now on, owners could buy as many television stations as they wished—but could not also own a newspaper with more than half its circulation in the same market.

This scheme would not hurt Murdoch or Packer, but it would penalize the Melbourne Herald and Weekly Times group and the Fairfax group. The Herald group had daily newspapers in many markets and these would prevent it from developing a national television network.

Kerry Packer had no newspapers, only magazines, so the new rules were of no concern to him. For Murdoch the situation was different. Assuming that his attempt to keep his Channel 10 stations failed, and he had to sell them, he was now likely to get a much better price. If there was no longer a two-station rule, the value of leading stations in both Melbourne and Sydney would increase enormously to anyone seeking to establish a national network. One analyst reckoned that the changes increased the value of Packer's and Murdoch's stations from A$800 million to A$1.8 billion.

On November 24, the Labor cabinet finally approved the Keating proposal. At a subsequent meeting of the Labor Party caucus, Keating attacked the Herald group and said that it would be good if it were split up because it was not "one of us."

Keating had had dinner with Murdoch in New York several weeks beforehand and told him of his plans. Murdoch said later that they sounded so fantastic he thought they would never get through the cabinet. Keating also alerted Packer, but gave no such advance warning to either the Herald group or the Fairfax group. When the cabinet agreed to the Keating plan and it was announced, Murdoch knew that this would be the best possible time to sell his television stations and to become an even more powerful prince of print. He made his dash from the slopes of Aspen back to Australia to try to buy the *Herald*.

The Herald group had been vulnerable to a takeover for some time. It was an old, established company with valuable assets and a cautious management. Its flagship, the Melbourne *Herald,* had once been the biggest-selling newspaper in the city, but its circulation was in decline. Its chief executive, John D'Arcy, realized any threat was most likely to come from Murdoch. News was not financially strong in Australia now—Murdoch's papers did not have the classified-advertising market that Fairfax and the Herald group enjoyed. A large part of Murdoch's cash flow came from the earnings of Ansett Airlines.

D'Arcy tried to defend the group with a series of cross-shareholdings with other companies, the Brisbane-based Queensland Press and Adelaide-based Advertiser Newspapers, two of the largest shareholders. But rumors of takeover abounded.

At 7:00 A.M. on December 3, 1986, Murdoch's Australian managing director, Ken Cowley, called D'Arcy asking if Murdoch could meet with him and the Herald group's chairman, John Dahlsen, at 9:00 A.M. "I knew what it was, obviously," said D'Arcy.

When he came in, Murdoch was friendly, but he insisted on an answer by 5:00 P.M. The board discussed it all day. Some felt they could reject the offer, but they had to consider their duty toward their shareholders. "It was a bloody bonanza. He was paying forty times earnings!" said D'Arcy later.

That evening the board recommended acceptance of Murdoch's offer of A$12 per share, in the absence of a better offer. This was deliberately phrased in order to bring the Perth businessman Robert Holmes à Court into play. After the Herald group's announcement, Murdoch told the press that his price was fair and generous. He said he would sell off the Herald group's interest in the Melbourne and Adelaide TV stations if the bid succeeded. That was necessary under the proposed cross-ownership laws, but it also suited Murdoch financially. Although Ken Cowley had warned him that the *Herald* might not be savable, he committed himself to taking it upmarket to make it once more "the quality act" in town.

If the takeover succeeded, it would give Murdoch unprecedented power over Australia's newspaper business. His Australian empire was already wide. With the Herald group as well, he would control major daily newspapers in every Australian capital city and would have a monopoly in Perth, Brisbane and Adelaide. Seventy-five percent of daily circulation would be in Murdoch's hands.

His bid was therefore widely greeted with both fury and concern. His biggest rival, Fairfax, felt especially threatened. An editorial in the Sydney *Morning Herald* warned that Murdoch would transform the group from a "benign, loosely managed media giant to an extension of Mr Murdoch's ego and a very closely managed instrument of his ambition." The *Financial Review* complained: "The Government was encouraging a near national monopoly—and an absolute monopoly in some places—by an American citizen who has a history of using his newspapers to manipulate politics as it suits him." Murdoch denounced this as "a filthy libel."

Despite the criticisms, it became clear that the government had no intention of standing in the way of the bid. Hawke said that the old Herald management was "viciously anti-Labor, so if Mr Murdoch were to fire a few salvoes at us, it couldn't be worse than what we have been enduring." The only body which could step in to prevent the bid was the Trade Practices Commission, which did not do so.

Murdoch did not get his way at once.

On Christmas Eve 1986, Robert Holmes à Court made a A$1.95 billion offer, or A$13 a share, for the Herald group. When he increased his bid to A$13.50 a share, the board recommended the offer to shareholders.

On January 4, 1987, Fairfax entered the contest. It did not launch a bid for the Herald group, but for Queensland Press Ltd., which had a vital 24 percent stake in the Herald group. This was a relatively cheap but somewhat uncertain method of putting pressure on Murdoch. Fairfax bid A$20 cash for Queensland Press shares, which had closed the previous trading day at A$17.20. It was a condition of the offer that Queensland Press should accept Holmes à Court's offer of A$13.50 per share for the Herald group. This condition suggested that Fairfax and Holmes à Court were working together to fight off Murdoch and carve up the Herald group.

Murdoch responded by increasing his offer to A$15 a share.

On January 15, Holmes à Court and Murdoch made a deal, despite Murdoch's earlier insistence he would do no such thing. Holmes à Court agreed to drop his bid for the Herald group in return for being allowed to buy the Herald group's TV station in Melbourne for A$260 million and West Australian Newspapers Ltd., publisher of two news-papers—the *West Australian* and the afternoon *Daily News*—for A$200 million. He would also make A$100 million in trading profits from the sale of his shares to Murdoch.

Fairfax then made another offer for the Herald group, topping Murdoch's bid and proposing to carve up the group. However, the Herald group's management decided that this offer had come too late and that Murdoch was now unstoppable.

Murdoch finally had the house his father built.

Once the Herald deal was finalized, Murdoch moved quickly to divest the group's television assets to avoid another threatened hearing of the Broadcasting Tribunal. He sold them to Northern Star, a small media company which had links with News.

❖　❖　❖

Murdoch made John D'Arcy chairman as well as chief executive of the Herald group. He appointed his sister, Mrs. Janet Calvert Jones, a director. She was the first woman on the board and said she shared her mother's and brother's excitement "about the *Herald*, about something that Dad built up." Reviving the *Herald* would be a major task. Its circulation, once over 500,000, had since fallen to some 238,000. "We're going to turn it around, get it back into the homes of Melbourne. It will have authority, polish and professionalism," Murdoch said. The *Herald* would be "the best written paper in Melbourne . . . a young middle-class paper."

Murdoch raided Fairfax. Eric Beecher, the editor of the Sydney *Morning Herald*, was made editor in chief of the Herald group and editor of the *Herald*. Beecher regarded himself as a serious journalist, not a popular one in the prevailing News Corp tradition. Murdoch gave him considerable financial freedom and Beecher said he was not intimidated by stories of interference from Murdoch, whom he found "extremely charming and intelligent." He began to poach top Fairfax journalists.

In July 1987, Murdoch officially "relaunched" the *Herald*. There was to be a multimillion-dollar advertising campaign. Edition times were to be brought forward to 10:00 A.M. It was a brave effort. In the months to come Beecher certainly succeeded in taking the paper upmarket to rival the *Age*. Melbourne society was approving; Dame Elisabeth was delighted. But the relationship between owner and editor soured and Murdoch's hope of restoring his father's flagship to the glory that he remembered as a boy proved forlorn.

THE VILLAGE

In those days Murdoch was bursting with self-confidence. Bankers from all over the world were falling over themselves to praise his victory at Wapping. They were almost begging to recycle their money through his miraculous machine. In the heady financial atmosphere of the mid-1980s, over which the clouds of the October '87 crash seemed to pass quickly, Murdoch appeared, to others and to himself, invincible.

By early 1987 News Corp was one of the world's largest communications groups, with some 250 subsidiaries. Apart from newspapers, books and television, the company had interests in aircraft, oil, bauxite, wool and gambling. Turnover and profits of the group had both risen enormously fast after Wapping—they were up 56 percent and 83 percent respectively in the second half of 1986. But debt was beginning to burgeon as well—by September 30, 1986, it was close to A$3 billion, a total approaching the company's annual revenues. (By contrast, CBS Inc., which many people considered overburdened by debt, had debts amounting to less than a quarter of its revenue.) News' debt was serviced by the cash flow of the company's newspapers, particularly those from Wapping. In fiscal year 1986 the interest payments doubled, to more than US$160 million, but cash flow was up to US$364 million.

In 1989 loan maturities and redemption of preferred shares would total US$425 million, in 1990 US$560 million, and in 1991 US$1.2 billion. Nonetheless, Richard Sarazen, News Corp's financial officer, was sanguine. He had said early in 1987 that the principal could be renegotiated when the time came, and if interest rates started rising, "we are prepared to swap into fixed-interest debt at a moment's notice. We have lines of credit and standby agreements to do that when we think it is appropriate."

Murdoch and Sarazen also constantly played the foreign-exchange markets, in effect gambling on the prices of the various currencies in which the company traded. They usually did this to good effect; in 1986 the company recorded currency-exchange profits of A$64 million.

Nothing could keep Murdoch still. Even as he completed the purchase of the Herald and Weekly Times group in Melbourne in early

1987, he was planning a Sunday edition of the New York *Post*, despite the fact that the FCC was requiring him to sell the paper to comply with U.S. cross-ownership rules. In fact, he was still doing everything he could to find his way around these rules, or to obtain another temporary waiver. He detested the idea of losing the *Post*.

At the end of 1986 Murdoch outbid Pearson plc, the publisher of the *Financial Times*, and paid A\$260 million for the *South China Morning Post*, Hong Kong's most profitable daily newspaper and one of the best in Asia. Michael Sandberg, the chairman of the Hong Kong and Shanghai Bank, said that Murdoch had told him that he saw the *Post* as "the *Times* of Southeast Asia."

More than that, perhaps. Murdoch had long had his eye upon China, since his first visit there in 1985; he understood that English was the second language in China and that a vast market for books and films beckoned there. Hong Kong's economy was booming, and so were its commercial links with the coastal cities of China, especially in Guangdong Province, which was increasingly becoming an extension of Hong Kong industry. The classified advertisements of the *Post* seemed to Murdoch to be an almost bottomless mine of gold. Moreover, quite apart from China and Hong Kong, the entire Pacific was economically the fastest-growing region in the world and the *Post* gave him a media presence on a fourth continent. The fifth, Africa, was being left almost entirely out of the information revolution, because it seemed incapable of generating the wealth necessary to make it attractive to international corporations.

In America, Murdoch had managed to lower the cost of financing his infant network, Fox. News Corp had already redeemed most of the \$1 billion–plus preferred-stock issue, and the rest of it was expected to be bought in soon. Interest on the borrowed funds had been reduced from about 13 percent to 7 percent. The seven television stations were underperforming against earlier projections, but Richard MacDonald, an analyst with First Boston who followed News Corp stock, reckoned that their cash flow was already much greater than their financing costs. Part of this success was due to skillful accounting.

Fox Broadcasting, carried by the seven stations, had already cost at least $50 million, but was still too young to have made a real impact. In Hollywood, Barry Diller was talking of "counter-programming." "Anyone looking for an edge will try to offer what isn't being offered," he said. He was looking for shows that appealed to the young. New sitcoms like "Small Wonder" and "9 to 5," which Fox produced for its network affiliates and also sold into syndication, had had some success, though neither was as popular as the reruns of the old series "M*A*S*H," which Fox had produced for CBS in the seventies and early eighties—it was still the king of situation comedies, and was responsible for between $20 million and $30 million of News Corp's cash flow.

Richard Sarazen declared that Murdoch would now consolidate rather than expand further. But Sarazen knew that Murdoch had spent his life saying that he had now bought enough. He never meant it. He simply could not escape, ever, the seduction of a deal. He had no game plan, no carefully devised strategy. It was just Murdoch against the world, trying to score whenever he could. He never stopped pulling in pieces and people as they were needed, in his everlasting attempt to create some extraordinary machine that straddled the globe and fed the world what he knew it wanted. Just as Sarazen said Murdoch had stopped, he dashed after the New York publisher Harper & Row.

This was, according to his banker Stanley Shuman, another last-minute decision. The public reaction showed how American views of Murdoch had improved since he had become a citizen. He was now seen much more as the man trying to build a fourth national TV network than as the publisher of downmarket newspapers.

Murdoch considered book publishing an essential part of his growing global network of publishing, film and broadcasting properties. He had long wanted to have an American publishing house to be a partner to Angus and Robertson in Australia and William Collins, the

British house, of which he had owned over 40 percent since 1981. The story of his interest in Collins is crucial to the purchase of Harper & Row.

Collins was one of Britain's oldest family publishers. Collins authors included Alistair Maclean and the Holy Ghost, for Collins published the Bible in Britain and in British overseas markets. In the late seventies, the company ran into difficulties and had to be put through painful restructuring which lessened the family's control.

Ian Chapman, the deputy chairman, and David Nickson, the vice-chairman, set about putting Collins back on its feet. Much cost-cutting ensued. By the end of 1979 the company was breaking even. In 1980 it was scheduled to make £2 million in pretax profits, and the company was worth about £10.5 million.

In early 1981 rumors of an impending takeover by Robert Maxwell spread. Murdoch expressed an interest and, after an initial rebuff from the board, bought 31 percent of the stock from a member of the Collins family. This holding obliged him under law to make a bid for the entire company. Meanwhile, Maxwell had increased his shareholding to about 9 percent. Although he said he would never sell this stock "to that Australian bastard," he did so.

Murdoch made a £25 million bid for the company. Chapman mobilized his authors—Alistair Maclean, Jack Higgins, Hammond Innes, Ken Follett—against it. They all urged the shareholders to reject Murdoch, and in July 1981 the shareholders did so. However, Murdoch was left with 41.7 percent of Collins' voting stock and two seats on the Collins board. Chapman persuaded him to take one for himself, and he gave the other to Sir Edward Pickering.

Murdoch took his defeat gracefully and, said Chapman, promised he would behave as nonexecutives should behave, representing all the shareholders, monitoring the performance of the executives, playing a part in the board's decisions, but beyond that not interfering. In Lord Goodman's presence, Murdoch assured Chapman he would not make a hostile bid for the company.

And that, according to Chapman, was how Murdoch behaved for many years. Under Chapman's direction, and with Murdoch's support, Collins thrived during the early 1980s. Profits rose from £4 million in 1981 to £15 million in 1986. Throughout all that time, said Chapman, "Murdoch was as good as his word. He didn't interfere, nor increase his holdings, as he was entitled to do, at two percent a year."

In 1983 Chapman acquired Granada Publishing for Collins and renamed it Grafton Books. By the mid-1980s he was eager to acquire an American publishing arm for Collins. In 1985 he came close to buying New American Library, but it was considered overpriced. Then in early 1987 Harper & Row came into play.

Founded in 1817, Harper & Row had published Herman Melville and Mark Twain. By the mid-1980s, it was one of the last independent publishers in New York but, despite its fine backlist, the board was attempting to devise a defensive structure against takeover. The company's largest stockholder, Theodore Cross, a lawyer and editor who held 5.3 percent of the stock, made a surprise bid of $190 million for the company on March 9 — $34 a share against the market price of $24. That was followed at once by an offer of $220 million from Harcourt Brace Jovanovich.

Murdoch immediately saw this as the perfect opportunity to buy the American trade publisher he thought the News empire needed. He called Chapman, who had been talking to Brookes Thomas, the chairman of Harper & Row.

Chapman shared Murdoch's enthusiasm. He had personal connections with Harper & Row and agreed to call Brookes Thomas and suggest Collins as a white knight. Thomas replied that Harper & Row would be delighted to have Collins ride in. After negotiations involving Harper & Row, Collins and News, a deal was struck, but then Chapman and Murdoch agreed that News would buy Harper & Row outright and that Collins would have an option to buy 50 percent of it after three or four months. Chapman, delighted with this deal, persuaded

Harper & Row executives that Murdoch was not to be feared—he had been a perfect partner at Collins.

Murdoch's bid of $300 million valued the company at $65 a share—fifty-five times earnings, a generous multiple by any standards. Thomas said, "If somebody offers you more money than you think you could ever make through earnings, you have to take it." Murdoch seemed less of a risk than Harcourt Brace Jovanovich, which was expected merely to take over the list and dismantle the company. After a meeting at Murdoch's apartment on Fifth Avenue, Harper & Row's management accepted Murdoch's offer. A few months later Murdoch, as agreed, sold 50 percent of the company to William Collins for $156 million. By linking Collins and Harper & Row, he was creating one of the largest and most powerful publishing companies in the English language.

The deal brought fever to the American publishing industry. "Anything that isn't pinned to the wall is being bought," said Roger Straus, president of Farrar, Straus & Giroux, one of the few companies that remained in private hands.

By the 1980s, book publishing was becoming more and more dominated by large conglomerates. William Morrow had been bought by Hearst, Scribner's by Macmillan, Simon & Schuster by Gulf+Western. Bertelsmann bought Doubleday for $475 million and merged it with Bantam and Dell. The International Thomson Organization (the former owner of Times Newspapers in London) had been making acquisitions in the U.S., including South-Western Publishing, for which it had paid $270 million. Harcourt Brace paid $500 million for CBS Educational and Professional Publishing. Time Inc. paid $520 million for the academic publisher Scott, Foresman.

The sale of Harper & Row to Murdoch seemed to many to be another blow to "quality" publishing. Fears were expressed that with fewer and fewer publishers, there would be an increasing demand for blockbusters of clear commercial but not much literary merit. Even Brookes Thomas, who had favored the sale of Harper & Row to Murdoch, agreed that being owned was not the same as being independent: "If somebody has your string—even if they never pull it—maybe it has some effect on you."

LONDON

Murdoch's next acquisition brought him into direct conflict with his old rival. On Saturday, June 27, 1987, in Los Angeles, he received a telephone call from Robert Maxwell in England. It was a costly mistake by Maxwell.

For almost twenty years Maxwell had been consumed by his rivalry with Murdoch, who regarded Maxwell with bemused contempt. Privately Murdoch said Maxwell was a mad crook. Maxwell's ambition was to build an international media empire bigger than Murdoch's. He had not succeeded, but his own empire had certainly expanded since he had lost their first battle over the *News of the World* in 1968.

In 1969 Maxwell had lost his company Pergamon after Saul P. Steinberg of Leasco pulled out of an agreement to buy it, insisting that Maxwell had misled him as to its real worth. The shareholders then ousted Maxwell from the board and a Board of Trade inquiry concluded that Maxwell "is not in our opinion a person who can be relied upon to exercise proper stewardship of a publicly quoted company."

Nonetheless, in 1974, after reaching an out-of-court settlement with Steinberg, Maxwell persuaded the board of Pergamon that only he could save it, and was invited back. He claimed, falsely, that he had been exonerated of the Board of Trade charges against him. He issued writs against anyone who suggested otherwise.

In 1980 he had another success—he convinced the British Printing Corporation and its unions that, since it was nearly bankrupt, the company could be saved only if jobs were cut from thirteen thousand to seven thousand. With its name changed to Maxwell Communications

Corporation, it became profitable. But he was still after a newspaper. So far, he had been thwarted in his bids for the *News of the World,* the *Sun,* the *Observer* and the *Times.* Three out of four of these had gone to Murdoch.

Finally, in 1984, he was able to buy Mirror Group Newspapers from Reed International. At last he had a daily tabloid and two Sunday papers. And not only that—he also had the tabloids which were pitted most directly against his rival's *Sun* and *News of the World.*

At once he dominated the *Mirror* far more completely, and far more crassly, than Murdoch had ever aspired to do with his own newspapers. He himself was a constant subject of stories, whether he was conducting fawning interviews with East European dictators or flying on a "*Mirror* Mercy Mission" to Ethiopia. Although he continued the paper's support for the Labour Party, it became, for a time, a vehicle for the blatant promotion of Maxwell.

In the spring of 1987 Maxwell and Murdoch both became interested in buying *Today,* the paper which had launched the revolution in modern newspaper publishing that was completed at Wapping.

When Maxwell thought he had virtually clinched the deal, he made the crucial mistake of phoning Murdoch in Los Angeles. "It's all over," said Maxwell. "Congratulations," said Murdoch. But as Maxwell talked, Murdoch suddenly became aware that the deal was not yet finally signed.

He now realized that either he could let Maxwell buy a paper that was losing nearly £30 million a year, or he could try to acquire it himself and make it into a success, just as he had done eighteen years earlier with the *Sun.* The challenge, added to the thrill of frustrating Maxwell, was irresistible. Murdoch was not obsessed with his rival, but he was irritated that they were so often compared and confused in the public mind—the two indistinguishable evil barons dominating the British media. And it was in Murdoch's nature to compete. He swooped, and on June 29 he grabbed the paper away from Maxwell for a payment of £38 million in cash.

The deal gave Murdoch his fifth national newspaper; he now controlled about one third of the British press. The government decided not to intervene to consider the monopoly implications. The Labour Party was furious and Labour members of Parliament denounced government acquiescence in the takeover as the payoff for Murdoch's all-out support for Mrs. Thatcher.

Murdoch appointed David Montgomery, editor of the *News of the World,* as the new editor. The paper aimed itself more squarely at the young men and women who were doing well in Thatcher's Britain. Business coverage was improved. There were more gossipy stories about TV personalities. Politically, the paper abandoned the Social Democratic–Liberal Alliance—easy enough now that the group was imploding—and adopted Murdoch's loyalty to Margaret Thatcher. Early in 1988, Granada TV awarded the paper the title "Newspaper of the Year," for its preference for news coverage rather than topless models, sex scandals and lurid details on violent crime.

In July 1988, *Today* announced that its sales had topped the half-million mark. This rise was phenomenal, but it was still losing £150,000 a week, and its circulation was only a quarter that of its main rivals, the *Mail* and *Express.* Murdoch himself remained dissatisfied. He did not know what, if anything, the paper stood for, he said.

The battles for Harper & Row and *Today* had scarcely been won when Murdoch opened yet another front. He staged a dawn raid on the shares of Pearson plc, the financial and publishing conglomerate whose most prestigious property was the *Financial Times,* arguably the world's best financial paper. Frank Barlow, the chief executive of the *Financial Times,* who thought Murdoch an honest man but a compulsive interferer, was adamant that Pearson should not cooperate with its new shareholder.

The news of Murdoch's raid aroused horror in some quarters. The

Labour Party, which still refused to speak to Wapping journalists, was aghast.

The affair reached the States. Anthony Lewis declared in the New York *Times* that the *Financial Times* was a superb independent newspaper, whereas Murdoch's name was "synonymous with slippery journalism." Commenting on Murdoch's support for Thatcher, Lewis concluded that "those who believe in a free press" should support Pearson.

Throughout the winter of 1987–88, speculation about Murdoch's intentions continued. Murdoch was anxious at that time to become a major force in the booming new field of information services and was seeking to buy the 55 percent of Australian Associated Press that he did not already own. With AAP's 13.5 percent of Reuters added to News Corp's stock, he would be Reuters' largest single shareholder. Then he would be halfway toward being able to beam the contents of the *Financial Times* around the world on Reuters' screens. Unlike Pearson's management, he thought the *Financial Times* could and should be transformed into the principal daily price list of the global village. He was confident he would get his way. "You can't ignore your largest shareholder," he told *Forbes* magazine early in 1988. "It's not possible." But it was possible. Pearson formed a series of defensive alliances against him, and after being snubbed for two years, Murdoch decided to sell his shares and move on. It was a setback.

New York

In 1980, Murdoch had charmed the U.S. Senate. In 1988 he suffered at its hands another of his rare defeats: he was compelled to sell the New York *Post*. The sale caused him greater grief than almost any other business transaction in his life. He blamed it on Senator Edward Kennedy—and never forgave him. Max Newton said later that in fact Teddy Kennedy did him a favor in forcing him to dispose of the *Post*. But that was certainly not how Murdoch saw it at the time.

"We had never before lived in a town where we did not have a paper," said Anna afterward. Murdoch was attached to the paper because it was the first major property he had bought in America, and because it afforded him invaluable entrée into American political life. As such it was a continuing source of power, a base from which to mount all other operations. Moreover, a newspaper office is a very invigorating environment, and Murdoch was never happier than when he was immersed in the hubbub of a newsroom. Sitting in an ordinary, anodyne office would never compare to presiding over the roar of the presses.

Under the American law governing the cross-ownership of television stations and newspapers in the same city, Murdoch was bound sooner or later to sell the *Post* after he bought New York's Channel 5 TV from John Kluge, but he had intended it to be later rather than sooner. Ever since the purchase was completed in 1985, he had searched, with some success, for loopholes in the regulations, and for some device by which he could continue to own both the paper and the station. It was Kennedy who put a final stop to that.

By the mid-1980s, the *Post* displayed the layers of Murdoch's life in New York. Some of the old Australian "mafia" had left, but others were still on good terms with the boss. Steve Dunleavy was the most prominent. His louche career continued to flourish. He had had a radio show in New York, which he called "Radio Dingo." He would sometimes pass the night drinking in bars in the fish market area of New York (the sort of place where one is apt to hear Frank Sinatra played on the jukebox) and would then straighten his tie and go right into an editorial conference at the paper. In 1986 he left the *Post* and moved to Fox, where he became famous as a "tabloid TV" reporter. Murdoch, in whom the Rupert Greene element still celebrated Dunleavy, spoke glowingly of him at his farewell party at the *Post*.

The formula which Murdoch had applied so well at the Sydney *Mirror* and had adapted with such success on the *Sun* in London had not worked in New York, and furthermore Murdoch had serious labor problems on the paper. The paper handlers' union at the New York *Post* was heavily composed of Irishmen recently arrived from County Kerry. If a union member retired or died—or was murdered—within days the union produced a young replacement fresh from Ireland, complete with green card. "It's all quite charming—except that they're being paid a thousand dollars a week to do a job that could easily be mechanized," said Murdoch.

Later Murdoch said that he should have put more resources into the *Post*. "Should have kept a steadier course with it. It was such a difficult, impossible position being the third paper out of three." He said that the problem was not one of getting advertisers but of getting more of the right kind of readers. "If we had more readers than the *Daily News,* we would have taken all their business away. No problem about that at all." Circulation had risen, but never enough. He had never been able to get enough middle-class readers in Queens. "This is not a melting pot, this place, it's a landing ground. I mean, it's very ethnic. It's very settled in its attitudes."

Among those attitudes were the city's politics. It remained, just, a Democratic town, while Murdoch ran a Republican paper. Ever since 1980, the *Post* had been supportive of Ronald Reagan. In its 1984 endorsement the *Post* said that he had "unleashed the boundless energy, innovation and enthusiasm of America." The corollary of that support for Reagan was denigration of his opponents. The *Wall Street Journal* quoted a Washington official as saying that Murdoch was very useful: "He's a great supporter of this administration and of the Western alliance. He has a great deal to contribute." For his part, Murdoch also benefited, in particular at the Federal Communications Commission.

In 1986 he brought Frank Devine over from the Chicago *Sun-Times* to edit the New York *Post*. Devine, a large and jovial man, thought the basic problem was that "Rupert was trying to run a lumpen proletarian newspaper in a country where there is no lumpen proletariat. He hid this from even himself, because he is such a good salesman." He also hid from himself the fact that the chances of keeping both the *Post* and Channel 5 were slim. He hired the political consulting firm of Roger Stone, the northeastern director of the Reagan-Bush campaign, a man close to the heart of the Republican Right, to help him bypass the cross-ownership rule.

The rule, introduced by the Federal Communications Commission in 1975, was controversial. There is no doubt that the rule, designed to prevent unscrupulous owners from having too great a stranglehold upon local opinion, had led to the closure of some newspapers which had previously been subsidized by the greater profits of local television. The Freedom of Expression Foundation, a conservative Washington lobbying group which Murdoch helped fund, claimed that the rule had forced the closure of well over one hundred papers. It argued that newcomers like Murdoch were penalized because they could not use broadcasting to subsidize print.

When Murdoch had first proposed buying Metromedia in 1985, he was challenged by public-interest groups concerned about his reputation for managing to bend rules to suit himself. Before the FCC approved the transfer of the stations, he had been compelled to give repeated assurances that he would not seek a permanent change or waiver to the cross-ownership rule.

In July 1986 he sold the Chicago *Sun-Times* to a consortium led by Robert Page, the paper's publisher. In New York, where he had Channel 5, and in Boston, where he had more recently acquired station WXNE (now known as WFXT), his tactics were different. He sought and obtained temporary waivers from the FCC—it gave him two years in which to sell the *Post* and eighteen months for the *Herald*. Later Mark Fowler, chairman of the FCC, remarked that these waivers were among the best things he had done at the FCC. (Later still, he said this remark had been made jokingly.)

Murdoch considered Boston borderline. He would try to keep both the *Herald* and the TV station, but would not kill himself in the attempt. New York, however, was his town, and he wanted to do everything he could to keep the *Post*. "Instead of getting on with it and selling it then, we delayed and said maybe they would change the law," he acknowledged.

The *Wall Street Journal* reported that he intended to have the waivers extended further or even made permanent. The *Post* stopped all the giveaways and other circulation-boosting gimmicks for which Murdoch had always been famous. Promotion budgets were cut and the eight editions were reduced to two. Circulation began to fall, from 700,000 to under half a million, and by 1987 the paper was losing $100,000 a day. Buyers did not line up, and the closer Murdoch moved toward the end of the waiver, the more it seemed as if the *Post* might be unsalable. The Federal Communications Commission would then be faced with the choice of either seeing the paper close or letting Murdoch keep it.

In August 1987, the commission repealed the fairness doctrine, which demanded that television, unlike newspapers, attempt to be evenhanded. Many Democrats in Congress, led by Senator Ernest Hollings, the chairman of the Senate Commerce Committee, which oversaw the commission, were greatly opposed to this move. In November 1987 the Freedom of Expression Foundation filed a petition with the FCC to eliminate the cross-ownership ban. The president of the foundation, Craig Seaton, said that the petition was not intended to help Murdoch as such, but it did have News Corp's full support. The FCC at once asked for comments. Fowler's successor, Dennis Patrick, appeared to share his deregulating philosophy.

However, under pressure from Edward Kennedy, Senator Hollings decided that the FCC should now be prevented from lifting the rule and thus giving Murdoch a permanent waiver. On December 15, 1987, Hollings inserted a rider into an appropriations bill which prohibited the FCC from repealing the cross-ownership rule and from extending any waivers to it. News America's was the only waiver outstanding at the time. The bill passed the floor late at night on December 22, with the new wording at first unnoticed by almost everyone.

Murdoch was in Los Angeles when he learned the news. William H. Meyers, a New York *Times* reporter who was with him, wrote,

A fiery-red Lotus roars out of the driveway of the Bel-Air Hotel in Los Angeles. Knees tucked under the dashboard, Rupert Murdoch guns the low-slung two-seater through the twisting turns on Stone Canyon Road—simultaneously shifting, steering and tracking down his subordinates on the car telephone. At precisely eight o'clock on this balmy January morning, the Lotus rolls through the gates of Twentieth Century Fox, Murdoch's television and motion picture studio.

Murdoch storms into his office, his double-breasted blazer flapping, and confronts the stack of letters and faxes on his mahogany desk. . . . Normally Murdoch would devour these documents, but he impatiently shoves them aside. He wants to concentrate all his considerable energies and anger on the target of the day: Senator Edward M. Kennedy, Democrat of Massachusetts. . . . Over the next days, Murdoch will mount the kind of brass-knuckle attack that has made the Melbourne-born publisher the most intimidating media mogul since William Randolph Hearst.

Murdoch told Meyers, "The process was an outrage." It was "liberal totalitarianism," an attempt by Kennedy to kill off his critics.

It was the Patrick Murdoch, not the Rupert Greene, in Murdoch who hated Teddy Kennedy. He was appalled by Kennedy's drinking and womanizing. But there was also an important political agenda. Kennedy was one of the mainstays of liberalism in the Senate; he was an effective senator and a leader in the fight against the Reagan revolution.

For years the Boston *Herald,* the *Post* and the supermarket tabloid

Star had published editorials and columns revealing Kennedy's sexual misadventures, or reexamining the worst of them, the death of Mary Jo Kopechne at Chappaquiddick. Steve Dunleavy had written a muckraking book about the family. Kennedy was now becoming a target of Fox's "tabloid television" investigations as well. Howie Carr, a columnist on the *Herald*, delighted in calling Kennedy "Fatso" and, when space allowed, "that fat rich kid."

The language in the appropriations bill, which finally closed the door on Murdoch's *Post*, was seen by Murdoch as Kennedy's revenge. It led to a classic brawl. "Fat Boy versus the Dirty Digger," chortled *Time*. "Was it something I said, fat boy?" asked Howie Carr. Murdoch lined up his friends and supporters.

He called his friend Charles Z. Wick, the head of the U.S. Information Agency, a member of Reagan's kitchen cabinet. Wick offered his help and Marlin Fitzwater, President Reagan's spokesman, said that Reagan would have deleted the amendment, had he had the power to do so.

Murdoch also spoke to Mayor Edward Koch, who declared publicly that the handling of the appropriations bill revealed a "character flaw" in Kennedy, and, with more than a hint at Chappaquiddick, he said, "In the dead of night, and then by the way not to immediately own up to it. We've seen that before."

Kennedy acknowledged that he had encouraged Hollings to insert the waiver language in the appropriations bill. He explained, "The signals were abundantly clear that history was about to repeat itself"—just as the FCC had repealed the fairness doctrine, so it was now about to repeal the cross-ownership rule, and he and Hollings "were not about to be burned again." He claimed that "right-wing ideology is dictating policy and deregulation is running amok." The important question, he said, was whether Murdoch was "entitled to be the only publisher in America who can buy a television station and obtain an exemption to keep his newspaper under the antitrust laws." He said that Murdoch had not seriously tried to sell the *Post*.

Murdoch replied that he was "shocked that the rules were changed in the middle of the game." He insisted that he had been looking for a buyer for the *Post*. Mark Fowler, who was now practicing law in Washington, said that Murdoch was "a local businessman being intimidated and bullied by a politician." The First Amendment, he added, "was precisely designed to protect against that." Kennedy said he would agree to a further waiver only if a buyer for the *Post* had already been identified and more time was needed to complete the sale. Hollings insisted that he would continue to fight the legislation being prepared by New York's senators, Daniel Patrick Moynihan and Alfonse D'Amato, to repeal his appropriations bill amendment.

On January 19, 1988, the FCC decided to abide by the legislation and deny Murdoch's request for an extension of the waiver. On January 25, the Senate defeated the Moynihan-D'Amato bill by a vote of 60–30 after a heated debate in which Senator Lowell Weicker, a liberal Republican from Connecticut who was often attacked by the *Post,* called Murdoch "the number-one dirtbag" in communications.

Senator Hollings wrote an op-ed piece for the New York *Times* in which he complained about the "unholy alliance" between Murdoch and the FCC. This, he said, had begun with Murdoch's purchase of Metromedia, and it had allowed him to delay the sale of the *Post* thus far. "The FCC and Mr. Murdoch need to be reminded of three important principles of our democracy. The airwaves belong to the public. Concentration of media ownership threatens free speech. No man is above the law."

Murdoch responded with a full frontal attack upon Hollings and the way in which the amendment had been surreptitiously slipped through Congress. He asserted that at first only Kennedy had really known what effect his amendment would have and that many of the senators who voted on the appropriations bill were quite unaware of the wording that had been covertly inserted and of its effect. This was undoubtedly true. Murdoch asked a federal appeals court to rule on his charge that the Kennedy-Hollings amendment was unconstitutional because it singled him out.

Even though he knew now that he would have to sell the *Post*, Murdoch still delayed. Frank Devine recalls that Murdoch became more and more depressed as the awful day approached: "He tried everything possible to hang on to it. His spirits would rise when some scheme seemed possible." One escape route he considered was to turn the *Post* into a national paper. He had often regretted that he had not started a paper such as *USA Today*.

By now, no one on the News Corp board wanted him to keep the *Post*. Nor, really, did Anna. But Murdoch still found it almost impossible to let go. He was dismissive of most of those who sought to buy the paper, like a father rejecting his daughter's suitors. He considered that one bidder was untrustworthy, another was out for a payoff, a third was merely seeking publicity. Eventually he entered into negotiations with Peter Kalikow, a New York real-estate developer and landlord. Given the losses of the *Post*—$17 million in 1987, according to Murdoch—Kalikow wanted to force the best possible deal from Murdoch. He demanded sweeping concessions from the unions.

As with the Boston *Herald*, it was uncertain till the last minute whether the unions would make adequate concessions and the sale would be completed. A deal was finally concluded on March 5, 1988. "WRITE ON," declared the banner headline on the front page. Murdoch could hardly bring himself to sign the final papers.

Just three weeks later, the Washington, D.C., Court of Appeals ruled in Murdoch's favor on the waiver issue. Two judges appointed by Reagan were on his side; the third, a Johnson appointee, dissented. Part of the majority decision read, "The Hollings amendment strikes at Murdoch with the precision of a laser beam." It was by now too late for the *Post*, but Murdoch said he would still press for exemption for the Boston *Herald* and his station WFXT. In June he filed an application with the Federal Communications Commission to have the station placed in trust and beyond his editorial control. This was eventually approved.

Murdoch thought that the loss of the *Post* would be seen as a failure and, worse, a defeat at the hands of his enemies. It was "a nightmare," he said. In the Murdoch war of the worlds, it was one of the most significant battles he had lost. He said that it sent him into a deep depression. The only way out of it that he knew was to go on what he called "an expansionary lunge." This one was to be almost fatal to his empire.

ASPEN

If there was a high point in the spread and the confidence of the News Corp empire, it was marked by two conferences which Murdoch hosted for his employees and colleagues in the Rocky Mountain town of Aspen.

They were high councils of war, strategy sessions at which the officers of the News Corp army were summoned from their posts around the world, fitted out with uniforms, debriefed and rebriefed, inspired and invigorated and sent back to their commands filled (it was hoped) with renewed loyalty to their commander in chief and the sense of purpose of the worldwide organization.

The 1988 session began in Los Angeles. The general staff was welcomed by the Murdochs at their new hilltop house in Beverly Hills, the former home of Jules Stein, the founder and head of MCA. Murdoch impressed many of those whom he knew only slightly. He instantly recognized them and recalled their names. The next day everyone was handed color-coded boarding cards for one of several Learjets which were to fly, in formation, across the Rockies to the ski resort of Aspen, where Murdoch owned a house.

Aspen '88 had two parts. To start with, outside speakers who represented different aspects of Murdoch's view of the world addressed the group. Norman Podhoretz, editor of *Commentary*, was there. So was Paul Volcker, former head of the Federal Reserve. The star performer was Richard Nixon. The former president flew in on Murdoch's plane, stood stiffly at the lectern and impressed listeners with a cogent speech on the way in which the world was changing, particularly under the impact of *perestroika*. Murdoch glowed.

There were obvious similarities between Nixon and Murdoch as they stood together, Nixon in his plaid jacket and tie, Murdoch in a short-sleeved blue T-shirt bearing the News corporate logo. Murdoch was more relaxed than Nixon, but they shared a certain brooding quality. Both men were guarded and shy, both restless. Each had a global vision, some parts clear, some parts flawed, and was ruthless in pursuit of it. Each saw himself as an outsider attempting to force an established world into new patterns. Nixon believed that the Establishment (by which he meant liberals in the Washington press and their allies) had destroyed him; Murdoch agreed with that. His own fight against his enemies in what he called the Establishment was continuing relentlessly.

Murdoch could now see himself as an essential piece of the structure of Western power, as close to the Republican leadership in the States as he was to Thatcher in Britain. His influence, and the power of the resources he deployed, was recognized in America by his appointment to the board of the Hoover Institution, an increasingly conservative think tank based in Stanford. He was also on the board of United Technologies, a major defense contractor.

This marked an important transition for Murdoch. A decade earlier in America he had been seen as an alien gutter-press lord and his New York *Post* had been denounced as "a force for evil." Now, as the American leader of a new army, a transnational media force, he was welcomed into the drawing rooms and councils of state of the American Right.

❖   ❖   ❖

After the speeches by Nixon and the other visitors, editors presented their papers to one another so that everyone could understand a little better the deployment of the different corps commanders in the international army.

Such a session was certainly needed, because the size of the army had been increased enormously in the last three years. In terms of assets, by the end of 1988 the company was six times the size it had been in 1985, and was now worth about $13 billion. Sales in the year 1988–89 were expected to be about $4.8 billion, not far behind those of Bertelsmann, the largest media conglomerate in the world. From now on the American properties would account for the majority of News Corp's total revenue, almost $3 billion.

Murdoch still ran this vastly expanded empire by studying the figures for each company and each property every week, though Merv Rich was no longer responsible for the weekly book. The old wizard from Sydney had been replaced by Richard Sarazen, who was at Aspen to explain just how the system worked.

One hero of the 1988 conference was Andrew Neil, the editor of the London *Sunday Times*. His paper's circulation was increasing and the profits it was generating from Wapping were enormous. Its critics saw it as raucously right-wing, a broadsheet version of the *Sun*. Neil would retort that he employed left-wing columnists and allowed them total freedom of expression. That was undoubtedly so. But many of the papers' attitudes—criticisms of liberals, the royal family and the BBC—were similar.

Philip Crawley, editor of the *South China Morning Post,* was there. Crawley ran a serious paper, perhaps the best English-language paper in Southeast Asia. It was also increasingly profitable—as more and more people sought to leave Hong Kong before its return to Chinese rule in 1997, the classified-ads section was growing exponentially.

Eric Beecher, whose attempt to take the Melbourne *Herald* up-market had resulted in a further loss of circulation, was present, but starting to reconsider his position. News Corp's Australian managers were beginning to question his decisions, as was Murdoch. Far more bullish was Max Newton, resplendent as ever in his metal wing-tipped collars. He was still ideologically close to Murdoch; each was convinced that a brave and wonderful new world was being fashioned by communications technology.

One of the senior executives at Aspen was Carolyn Wall. Few women were promoted very high in the News Corp army. (Even Murdoch's closest admirers have acknowledged his difficulty in dealing with women as senior executives.) She had been the publisher of *New York* magazine since 1984. Although she had no experience in television, Murdoch had given her the job of running his New York television station, WNYW, a business with a staff of 450 and annual sales of $150 million. "Working for Murdoch is like being thrown into the water without knowing how to swim," she said, with obvious delight, to the New York *Times*.

Also at Aspen was John Evans, head of the magazine division and probably the only one of Murdoch's entourage who could boast of having been a hippie. Like many who worked for Murdoch, Evans said that it was hard to explain his task: "In true Murdoch style, no one ever tells you what your job is. You make it up as you go along. You may be given a title but you have to define the job yourself." Evans told a New York weekly paper that News was "a very large family business" which worked on trust. "None of us have contracts, none have written financial security. All of us are given amazing amounts of trust and we pass that along. It's an amazingly elevating feeling to know you're trusted."

Evans was known as the futurologist in News. In terms of technology, Murdoch was almost a blind man, and Evans was his seeing-eye dog. He rhapsodized about the great marriage to come—the coupling of the TV and the personal computer. The PCTV of the near future would be programmed, he believed, with its owner's personality profile, and would behave accordingly throughout the day, so that when you came home at night the TV would say, "Hi, there's been seven minutes of news that you will be interested in. I expected to record the game between the Mets and the Phillies, but it was rained out. The good news is that *Citizen Kane* was playing on Channel 42, so I've got that for you."

"Civilization is equal to bandwidth" was one of Evans' favorite lines. He talked about fiber-optic cables' vast capacity for transporting information, which he reckoned would transform the world. He was trying to create electronic databases for News, and believed electronic publishing could double the value of the magazine division. News, he felt, was technologically still looking toward the past.

Aspen demonstrated that News Corp was an eclectic collection of companies, a reflection more of Murdoch's will and opportunities than of any business plan. All arteries led through Murdoch. Only he knew what everyone and every company was up to.

At the closing dinner, one Australian editor who had been hired, fired and rehired by Murdoch made a rather emotional speech in praise of his employer, who responded by saying that "we all share certain values." Barry Diller, the head of Fox and perhaps the only registered Democrat in the room, muttered to his neighbor, "Like what?"

Soon after his lieutenants had returned to their posts, Murdoch announced a new deal which staggered almost everyone. It was the deal too far, the one that created so much debt that it subsequently crippled his entire empire. He intended to buy *TV Guide* and other properties of the Triangle group from his friend Walter Annenberg.

Murdoch and Annenberg had known each other since the late 1960s, when Murdoch first arrived in Britain and Annenberg was American ambassador to the Court of St. James's. They liked each other; indeed, it seems hardly fanciful to suggest that each saw something rather special in the other. Annenberg had lost his son. Murdoch had lost his father. Annenberg was in his eighties and, like Sir Keith, had made an extraordinary success in the publishing industry.

Murdoch was doing just what Annenberg would have liked his own son to do.

Like Murdoch, Annenberg was born into media riches. Moses Annenberg made a fortune with the *Daily Racing Form,* the bettors' bible, which he had purchased in 1922 for $400,000. The previous owner, Frank Brunnel, had insisted on cash and Walter, then aged fourteen, later recalled: "I carried this huge package, one foot square, all wrapped in old newspapers, to Brunnel's office." Mo Annenberg also ran other racing papers, and a wire service which reported racing results. In 1940 he was jailed for tax evasion, but the *Racing Form* continued to flourish. Walter recalled that in the family it was known as the "Old Cow" because it gave such rich milk.

After Walter Annenberg took over the company, he spent much of his career trying to live down his father's reputation. He started *Seventeen,* a magazine for teenage girls, which became known as "The Acne and the Ecstasy," and in 1953 he was one of the first publishers to understand the coming power of television: seeing that independent television guides were springing up in New York, Philadelphia and Chicago, he had the idea of making them national.

In 1974, *TV Guide* became the first magazine to sell over a billion copies a year. By 1988 one of every five magazines sold in the United States was an issue of *TV Guide.* The magazine, costing seventy-five cents, had 106 regional editions and a new cable edition. Weekly circulation was around seventeen million. In the first six months of 1988 it had advertising revenue of $162.8 million. Even so, 70 percent of its total revenue came from circulation sales.

At the same time, *Seventeen*'s circulation had grown to 1.8 million, and it was thought to generate profits of some $10 million on annual revenues of about $150 million. The group also owned *Good Food*—a new creation which lost money—and the *Racing Form.* The circulation of the *Racing Form* was not audited, but it was thought to sell about 140,000 copies a day, at the huge price of $2.50 a copy. The *Form* was said to make $40 million profits on just $80 million in revenue.

There were, as Murdoch was to discover to his cost, alternatives to *TV Guide,* but for racegoers there was no alternative to the *Racing Form.*

By the end of the 1980s, Annenberg was a prominent figure in the conservative Republican Establishment in America, a friend of both Richard Nixon and Ronald Reagan. Since representing the United States in London, he was known as "the Ambassador."

When Annenberg decided to sell Triangle, he immediately thought of Murdoch. He said later that since his son, Harry, had died, "I had no one to carry on, and it was a family business. Rupert occurred naturally to me. He had Fox and Metromedia, and I sensed he was after the whole ball game."

Almost twenty years earlier, Murdoch had asked, through an intermediary, if Annenberg would sell *TV Guide.* For $1 billion, came the reply. In those days such sums were far beyond Murdoch, but their friendship developed. Annenberg said to this author, "I thought him very attractive and an immense gambler. A determined, dedicated fellow and a fearless competitor." He said he thought the outstanding thing about Murdoch was "the courage he had displayed at Wapping."

The midwife of the deal in 1988 was John Veronis, the chairman of the New York investment banking firm Veronis, Suhler and Associates. Annenberg wanted a fantastic sum, $3 billion in cash, for Triangle. Murdoch agreed. The profits were gushing in from Wapping. Mrs. Thatcher had been reelected and there seemed no threat to his British businesses. Interest rates were low. But even that sense of security would not usually lessen his attentiveness. Normally he subjected all potential purchases to close scrutiny. In this case, the biggest media purchase in history, he appeared to do nothing of the sort. It was all over very quickly.

"Maybe I was a bad buyer, too keen," acknowledged Murdoch later. "I should have beaten him down a few hundred million. He's a hard dealer. Wants his pound of flesh. Said he could sell to someone else, that the Japanese wanted to pay more."

Astonishingly, it seems that Annenberg had more doubts than

Murdoch. He asked Warren E. Buffett, the legendary investor from Omaha, if he should sell for $3 billion. Buffett replied, "Run to the bank, Walter, run to the bank."

Veronis said, "It was an understandable, natural conversation between two professionals, two giants in the field who have enormous respect for each other." Murdoch's public-relations man, Howard J. Rubenstein, added, "There is a circle of friendship here that really helped in this deal, because they had mutual respect and trust for one another."

The deal aroused front-page astonishment throughout the United States. The Washington *Post* commented, "No drawn-out negotiations. No takeover threats. No white knight defenses or greenmail to complicate matters." Just two hugely successful entrepreneurs shaking hands. One question debated was whether Murdoch was an ideologue bent on taking over the world or merely a gambling man with an eye to the main chance. The Washington *Post* delivered itself of the view that, despite appearances, he was "not a wizard." The Los Angeles *Times* asked if he was "a global Citizen Kane." Another Los Angeles *Times* piece began, "In science fiction books, a handful of global corporations whose pursuits transcend any nation's interests or borders emerge to control modern society's most prized and powerful resource. The resource is information. This week, Rupert Murdoch took what many consider another step, whether intentional or not, into that science fiction fantasy."

Murdoch himself said that the deal made him the largest publisher of consumer magazines in the States. There were then about 3,000 magazines on the nation's newsstands, but only around 120 of them sold more than 100,000 copies an issue. Curtis Circulation, with *Penthouse* and *Ladies' Home Journal*, was the leading distributor, with Warner Publisher Services, which distributed the Condé Nast publications, coming second. Both of these sold many magazines with circulations below 100,000. By contrast, Murdoch, together with Triangle, sold relatively few titles, but they were large-volume titles.

What Murdoch bought with *TV Guide* was not only the magazines but also Triangle's distribution company, which handled *Reader's Digest, Newsweek* and *Woman's World.* This huge clout would mean space at the supermarket counter and the newsstand shelves. The association with *TV Guide* would "piggyback" weaker Murdoch titles like *Elle* closer to the front of the rack.

Norman Lear, the television producer and publisher of the industry magazine *Channels,* was outraged. "This is one of those events that makes me think that the last great war will not be fought between two countries but between two giant conglomerates that have already gobbled up all those countries," Lear said.

Such concerns were understandable. The deal extended Murdoch's reach within the United States enormously. David Wagenhauser, an attorney at the Telecommunications Research Action Center, warned, "One of the best ways to influence public opinion without holding a political office is to control the media, and from past experience it does seem that Mr. Murdoch wants to influence public opinion." Similarly, Andrew Jay Schwartzman, executive director of the Media Access Project, a public-interest telecommunications law firm, said that joint ownership of Fox and *TV Guide* gave Murdoch too much power.

Too few different voices is a threat to the democratic process. If there are several Murdochs out there, fine, but if there is only one Murdoch, look out. Murdoch has a bias for incumbency and an old-boy network. The broadcast medium has enormous power shaping public taste ... Murdoch has not kept all his promises. He is someone for whom citizenship is matter of business convenience.

While Murdoch's potential "threat to democracy" was being debated, many of his colleagues saw the purchase more pragmatically as a commercial disaster, though John Veronis said later that Murdoch had studied the numbers very carefully.

If, as was thought, Triangle had revenues of $700 million and an operating profit of some $200 million, he had paid some fourteen to fifteen times cash flow—a high multiple. Time Inc.'s board had looked at Triangle and decided that it was not worth more than $1.5 billion—half what Murdoch was paying. But Murdoch argued that *TV Guide* was unique. It went into seventeen million homes every week and took in $12 million in gross revenue. After the supermarkets and others had taken their cuts, this probably left about $6 million revenue. Then there was another $6 million a week in advertising. The magazine would also provide an enormous database for the electronic publishing company he was planning; it had computerized summaries of 20,000 movies and 150,000 programs. In the future, he might be able to use the listings as the basis for an international television magazine. He already owned his own version of *TV Guide, TV Week,* in Australia.

Despite this, many of those who knew anything about the finances of Triangle and of News were aghast. One colleague who said he tried to talk him out of the deal was John Evans, head of Murdoch Magazines. He and others at News thought Murdoch was captivated by Annenberg, "the Ambassador."

Evans argued that *TV Guide*'s day was over. Its circulation had already fallen from twenty million to seventeen million and there was nothing to stop it from dropping further. Readers were dying off. "You had to grow up with *TV Guide* to use it. Even Rupert couldn't use it." There were now so many channels that the magazine needed to be larger, but then the advertising rate per column inch would fall, and it would lose its slots at the supermarket checkout. Evans told Murdoch that the price was at least $250 million too high, but Murdoch would not hear of offering a lower price. He had made his agreement with "the Ambassador." In those days, Murdoch appeared sanguine, almost cavalier, about his level of indebtedness. He said of *TV Guide*'s purchase, "Dick Sarazen fixed it with short-term debt. I don't know where the money is coming from." News Corp spokesmen said that he would raise about half the purchase price by selling existing assets and the other half by increasing his debt. The purchase would probably increase the company's overall debt from $5.5 billion to $7.6 billion, requiring annual interest payments of some $760 million. In addition to that, the company had $960 million of convertible notes on which annual interest payments totaled $48 million.

Murdoch raised some $320 million by the sale of a building in Los Angeles, and in London the treasurer of News International, Colin Reader, rounded up another $2 billion. "I went to our good friendly bankers and arranged for ten of them to provide two hundred million dollars each," Reader said. "It was done on the basis that half the money would be repaid by the following June. The other half we did with a general bank syndication"—which meant inviting any interested bank worldwide to participate. Despite a last-minute hitch with the financing, the deal was completed on November 7, 1988. (The $1 billion repaid by June 1989 came primarily from the sale of travel magazines to Reed International.)

After the purchase had been completed, and when Murdoch had begun to realize that Triangle would not in fact make enough to service its own debt, Evans suggested that he should resell the company promptly—perhaps along with a couple of magazines like the *Star.* Murdoch would not consider it.

Publicly he remained enthusiastic. "These publications are the most valuable and prized publishing properties in the world," he said. Perhaps he believed it, but perhaps for Murdoch there was a sense of pleasure in paying Ambassador Annenberg, the friend of presidents and a pillar of the information society and the conservative elite, what he had asked.

9

SUN COUNTRY

Stepping out of the elevator on the sixth floor of the factory at Wapping, the visitor would be advised by a sign which read, "You are now entering Sun Country."

This was a fantastic place. At its heart (if it had one) lay the legendary gold mine which Murdoch had discovered in 1969. Ever since then he had hired gangs of more or less wild men and women to excavate its precious seams. They had dug, lower and lower, but still the ore came out. For over two decades Sun Country had been Murdoch's El Dorado, a place of fable and riches, where fantasy passed for real life, jokes for news, falsehoods for facts, and nothing was as it seemed. Only one thing was certain: as Mae West said with a wink at her cleavage, "There's gold in them thar hills."

Many of Murdoch's critics would claim that, although he was born with silver type in his mouth, and was bred with the ambition to be at least as great a newspaperman as his father, he had rarely been able to produce outstanding newspapers, or even outstanding journalists. There was a mediocrity about the papers in every corner of his empire. The *Sun*, however, became a paper touched by genius, both commercial and editorial—it was the genius of the late, mad Lord Northcliffe, the inspiration to Rupert's father, Keith.

At the end of the 1980s and in the early 1990s the *Sun* was the largest-selling English-language daily in the world. It carried a good deal of news, though some of it was so succinct as to be almost invisible; its editorials were crisp, its headlines often superbly inventive. It was witty, it was ideological and it was often cruel.

On any day, and at almost any hour, its remarkable editor, Kelvin MacKenzie, could almost be guaranteed to be in Sun Country, and on the rampage around his terrain.

Through the 1980s, MacKenzie established himself as Murdoch's favorite editor. Murdoch considered the *Sun,* along with the *Australian,* his original creation, and felt that it was in good hands. For his part, MacKenzie was always reverential about "the Boss." To him, Murdoch was a man who "achieves more in half an hour than any other human being achieves in a whole day," and who was "as smart as a wagonload of monkeys."

The Press Council, which monitored the behavior of the British press until the end of the 1980s, frequently censured the *Sun's* approach to the news. At various times this was found to be sexist, racist, xenophobic, exploitative and just plain fabricated. Many people sued the *Sun,* among them Queen Elizabeth II. But the most spectacularly successful action was brought by the pop star Elton John, who earned libel damages of £1 million—a British record.

Opinion divided over whether MacKenzie was an ogre or a manic genius. One could argue that he was both. His authority for his actions, aside from Murdoch, was a near mystical understanding of "the readers." He would invoke them much as Richard Nixon invoked the "silent majority" in the United States. MacKenzie, and MacKenzie alone, was the great arbiter of their tastes, desires, fears and frustrations.

Like his proprietor, MacKenzie had little sympathy for homosexuals, whom he described as "poofters" when he was not calling them "shirtlifters" or "bum bandits." Reporters who had the temerity to protest that AIDS, the so-called gay plague, was in no way confined to homosexuals merely invited his ridicule.

Never trammeled with ideas about the need to "educate" readers, he gave them what his gut told him they wanted—sex, scandals, TV soap operas and the royals. There was nothing especially original about this formula, but the zest with which it was pursued and the punchy brilliance of the packaging had not been previously equaled. "Don't worry about the fucking writing," MacKenzie snarled to a new reporter agonizing over a piece. "We've got subs to do that bit."

Apart from homosexuals, MacKenzie's *Sun* targeted the Labour Party and the trade unions with ferocity. The royal family also came in for increasingly rough treatment. Indeed, much of the hatred for Murdoch in Britain stemmed from the constant intrusion into the lives of the royal family that his tabloids practiced. Not that other papers were far behind.

Sometimes MacKenzie went too far even for Murdoch. But most of his reproaches of MacKenzie were of a fond, parental nature. Kelvin appealed to the Rupert Greene side of his nature, much as Steve Dunleavy did in New York. And MacKenzie instinctively knew that Murdoch liked him to be naughty. The only thing he could seriously do wrong would be to cease to be entertaining. This in itself was a stern discipline.

MacKenzie found Wapping liberating. There were no printers around to refuse to print words they found offensive. And the new technology had the charm of making it much easier for senior executives to re-write copy. His new office and those around it bristled with motivating slogans along the lines of "Do it to them before they do it to us" and "Make it first, make it fast. Make it accurate." Alongside this an office sage inked in "Then go and make it up."

For some years, under MacKenzie's guidance, the *Sun* had been cutting the lead established by the *News of the World* as Britain's main kiss-and-tell paper, detailing the sex romps of celebrated persons. This was high-sales material, but also high-risk. In 1987, the year after both newspapers moved to Wapping, they faced a combined total of fifty lawsuits.

Murdoch's view of tabloid excesses, which led to parliamentary demands for legal restraints upon the press, was ambiguous. He told an American interviewer who asked him about the *Sun's* sensationalism, "You have in Britain a society that is becoming extremely decadent. You don't have the underlying puritanical history that this country's got, an influence that is still there." Others would argue that tabloid excess contributed to any such British "decadence." The cruelty they inflicted on ordinary citizens was often unforgivable.

On the back benches of the House of Commons the eagerness to curb the tabloids reached new levels of fervor. The press, "populars" and "unpopulars" alike, was becoming thoroughly alarmed, and with good reason. The great concern of the "unpopulars" was that the process of sanitizing the tabloids could undermine hard-won press freedoms. The government was also disturbed. Murdoch's paper had been among the strongest supporters of the government, and it was Murdoch papers that were most under threat.

Preempting the possibility of legal controls on them, the government announced its own review. It gave notice to editors and proprietors that they were now all "on probation." David Mellor, the Home Office minister who took on the oversight of the review, announced: "The tabloids are now drinking at the Last Chance Saloon." In Sun Country, they began to tidy up their act—a little. But it remained a bizarre, alien territory, a wild West in Wapping, a place where wit and dross, pornography and cruelty, were equally traded, where only the strangest people could thrive. Patrick Murdoch would have hated it. But Rupert Murdoch defended it against almost all criticism.

SPRINGFIELD, U.S.A.

At the very end of the 1980s, the respectable suburb where Mr. and Mrs. Jim Anderson and their clean-cut children, Betty, Bud and Kathy, had lived their perfect American life in the 1950s TV sitcom "Father Knows Best" was invaded. The wretched Homer Simpson and his unhappy, alienated family moved in and took over the American imagination. Fox Television had launched its animated sitcom, "The Simpsons."

With his perpetual five o'clock shadow and slovenly ways, Homer Simpson was an unmotivated worker at Springfield's nuclear plant, just down from the town's toxic waste dump and prison. He and his good-natured, eccentrically coiffed wife, Marge, had three children: melancholic, existential Lisa; Maggie, a baby glued to her pacifier; and above all the incomparable Bart. Bart was the Dennis the Menace of modern TV, a renegade who would not tolerate conventional rules. He was cantankerous and determined. He was street-smart. He was aggressive. He took no hostages and suffered fools very ungladly. He also had a kind and charming side to his character and he could use that charm to manipulate people. In many ways he was a miniature Rupert Murdoch. Only in one respect were the two characters unlike: Bart was an "Underachiever—and Proud of It."

Within months of the Simpsons' premiere on prime-time Sunday-night TV, young people—and many older ones—across America were trading Bartisms and donning Bart T-shirts. The family pushed Fox television to the top of the Nielsen TV ratings, just three years after the fledgling network had begun to make its bid for a share of a dwindling national television audience. Bart and his parents spoke a language that viewers apparently wanted to hear, at a time when the American Dream seemed at least on pause, if not on rewind.

"The Simpsons" was the brainchild of a counterculture cartoonist, Matt Groening. In his America, values were not clear-cut, feelings were often thwarted or, worse, ignored and family relationships collided. In short, life was a struggle. Instead of being the "normal" American family, reconciling all of life's difficulties and getting what they want, the Simpsons battled and often lost. "The Simpsons" was the show that fanned Fox's flame and gained it the respect of the television industry.

On one hand, the show seemed to display the cynicism that Americans had begun to feel about their country by the end of the 1980s. On the other, it represented Fox's daring in putting together a slate of provocative programs designed to target the baby boomers and their progeny. Either way, programs like "The Simpsons" made Fox the darling of media buyers. By the autumn of 1990, 49 percent of Fox's audience was aged twelve to thirty-four, compared to 37 percent for ABC, 31 percent for NBC and 25 percent for CBS. These figures helped Fox rack up $550 million in advertising sales for the 1990 season, up 75 percent from 1989. Bart Simpson had done the impossible. He had created a fourth national network.

Bart had help. The credit for Fox's success lay principally with the strange partnership of Barry Diller and Rupert Murdoch. Diller was a special kind of Hollywood creature. Aggressive and touchy, he could be both charming and psychologically overbearing. Powerful motorcycles, heavy skiing and Democratic Party politics were his style. Politically, he was the sort of person Murdoch might have detested. But he came with Fox and Murdoch realized that he knew his job. "Barry is one of those rare people who have a combination of great creative talent and a very sharp business head," he said. It was rare, he thought, to find in Hollywood someone so energetic and so honest as Diller. At Fox, Diller was Murdoch's Murdoch.

Diller was short, slight and meticulously dressed. He seemed aloof and had been described as having "the sly manner of a leprechaun," but he could cut people to pieces with his tongue. "Killer Diller" ran a tough ship, and not many of his colleagues could take life before his mast for very long. He demanded full commitment. "Don't just nod your head," he would say. "Go bananas if you like something. Don't take no for an answer. Do you love it? How much do you love it?" (One correct answer was "Enough to lie down on barbed wire.") But Diller worked people effectively as well as hard, and many came to admire him. What he did, he did with flair. He did Hollywood.

Like Murdoch, Diller had always had money; his father was a Beverly Hills real-estate developer. Diller had started in the mail room at the William Morris agency. Later he said this had been his school—he had read all the files on every star the agency represented. It was a unique grounding in the entertainment business. He left William Morris in 1966 to join ABC, where he invented the television miniseries and made-for-TV movies. In 1975 he became chairman and chief executive of Paramount. By 1983 he was earning $2.12 million a year. When Murdoch bought Fox, he gave Diller stock in News Corp worth some $60 million.

Like Murdoch, he was a gambler. He played poker with Warren Beatty, Johnny Carson and other friends; losses might reach over $1,000 an evening, but that was nothing to the men who gathered in Diller's Coldwater Canyon home. At Caesars Palace in Las Vegas, Diller once refused to sit at one table. "This table is pathetic," he said. "This table stinks. This table has no heat." He went to another table more to his liking and piled a whole stack of chips on it. "There! Heat!"

Diller had long wanted to start a fourth network, and in 1984 Murdoch's purchase of Fox and then Metromedia gave him his chance. The three networks, ABC, NBC and CBS, had never had it so bad, and Diller saw that the stranglehold they had exerted over American television since the 1950s was finally weakening. In 1977, on an average TV viewing night, 93 percent of America's ninety million television viewers were watching an NBC, ABC or CBS program. By the end of the 1980s, this figure was less than 70 percent and falling. Competition from independent stations, cable and satellite TV was taking away audiences.

This was the context in which Diller and Murdoch launched Fox as a fledgling fourth network on March 1, 1987. Many thought they were walking the plank. With a string of weak independent stations, it was hard to imagine how they could reach the markets that were necessary to lure rich advertisers. But, by the beginning of the 1990s, Fox had helped transform the landscape of American television. There were those who thought it a worse place. It was certainly different.

Fox did more than spot where the networks were failing. Its success at the end of the 1980s reflected the enormous changes that had been taking place in American life. One needed to loop back to the 1970s to see this. That was when Americans' conviction that they would always enjoy economic success—better housing, more cars, more education—began to falter.

In retrospect, the OPEC embargo of 1973 can be taken as the pivotal moment at which mass upward economic mobility in American society ended. Average weekly earnings peaked in 1973. Productivity abruptly stopped growing. The Midwest industrial belt went into further decline; inflation soared. Until then, there had been the assumption that children do better than their parents. As Nicholas Lemann wrote in *American Heritage* magazine, "Upward mobility wasn't just a characteristic of the national culture; it was the defining characteristic. As it slowly began to sink in that everybody wasn't going to move forward together anymore, the country became more fragmented, more internally rivalrous and less sure of its mythology." Above all, perhaps, the middle class lost confidence, and the nuclear family came under pressure.

In 1980 Ronald Reagan's certainties seemed reassuring. And yet, as the decade proceeded, the gap between the wealthiest and the poorest Americans continued to grow. So-called yuppies seized the imagination of American media and advertisers and made them big money, but the backbone of America was bending. After taking into account inflation, the average hourly pay for U.S. workers went from $8.55 an hour to $7.45.

Something strange, painful and unprecedented began to happen to the country that had sparked the world's imagination with its energy, vitality and bravado. By 1989, 70 percent of American families had no disposable income.

The decade ended with retrenchment. Debt restructuring replaced leveraged buyouts. People might still be mobile, but no longer only upwardly. The Simpsons reflected these truths, but they were not the only reality which Fox purveyed. There were many others.

Fox went for the young. This was exactly the same strategy as Murdoch's friend Leonard Goldenson had adopted for ABC in the early 1950s. In 1955 he had given young families "Cheyenne" (one of the first western series), "Kings Row" and other series. "We selected in every case young, virile men and young, attractive women in order to try and attract the younger families of America," he said later. By the 1990s tastes had become more jaded. But it was still just such families that were chased. By targeting kids and those who had quite recently been kids, Fox did better than anyone thought possible.

Diller's first move, however, was a mistake. He had hired Joan Rivers away from NBC and "The Tonight Show" to host her own "Late Show Starring Joan Rivers." At NBC she had been an occasional and welcome alternative to the steady cool of Johnny Carson, the late-night talk-show king. At Fox her show was all brash, noisy Joan, and it bombed.

"Buy her contract out," Murdoch was reported to have snapped, barely looking up, as the show's numbers were read off to him by a Fox employee. "If we're going down, let's cut our losses and try something else." Rivers' settlement figure was reportedly $5 million.

Murdoch and Diller had hoped that Rivers would bring instant credibility, but their losses in 1987 totaled $96 million. A traditional series, "Mr. President," starring George C. Scott, also failed. In the first two years, 1987–88, over $125 million was invested in Fox Broadcasting, with few signs of a return. "We were grafting an alien thing and it just didn't take," said Diller. They were forced to retrench. They had learned a lesson. If Fox couldn't make it according to the networks' formula, it would take a rashly different turn.

"I tend to have things get worse before they get better," said Diller later. From now on, Murdoch and Diller tried consciously to make Fox's shows distinctive—racier and more provocative. Fox would be an "alternative" network. They went for lower costs and higher ratings, replacing failing programs with inexpensive, news-oriented shows, some of which were developed by the stations that Fox owned.

The 1988 Hollywood screenwriters' strike was a godsend to Fox. It cut the other networks' stream of new shows; they had to air reruns. Fox was different. One of its first successes with younger viewers was "The Tracey Ullman Show," a sophisticated, offbeat comedy skit show, which attracted a loyal group of viewers who kept it on the air from April 1987 to May 1990. There was nothing that Ullman would not try. Her show, filmed before a live audience, was smart, clever and hip, even politically savvy, walking the line between irreverence and condescension. Fox pulled in advertisers by offering cut rates. But still the viewers did not come fast enough. By summer 1989, Diller feared the fledgling network had only months to live.

The film company, however, began to make money. "We cratered the old company," said Diller. "It was *so* bad. We got rid of every senior executive except one and then really juiced it up and got it back into profits." In 1988 the film *Big* grossed more than $100 million; *Working Girl, Die Hard* and *Young Guns* helped studio earnings grow 35 percent in the second half of 1988, over the previous year, to $35.8 million. It was quite a comeback from the nearly $300 million loss that the Fox studio had incurred between 1982 and 1985.

Fox's style was to shout. "We had to do shows that demanded your attention, that yanked you by the throat to get you to change the channel," Diller said. And they did. Diller and Murdoch continually tried to push the boundaries of what was acceptable TV.

"Married . . . with Children" was an early sign of the new times. No one was quite ready for the domestic reality the show ushered in. It was the tale of Al and Peg Bundy, their kids, Kelly and Bud, and a dog called Buck. The Bundys sniped at each other, bickered, belched. According to her husband, Peg was the worst wife/cook/mother ever to call herself a housewife, and she, it was clear, considered Al a woefully inadequate provider/lover/father.

"Married . . ." was first carried by 109 stations in the spring of 1987. It was a modern version of "All in the Family," which had first appeared on CBS in 1971 to similar horror. (In an early episode Al, the henpecked husband, suggested that the initials PMS stood for "pummeling men's scrotums.") "Married . . ." led one mother from Michigan, Terry Rakolta, to launch a letter-writing crusade against Fox. She accused the companies that advertised on the program of "helping feed our kids a steady diet of gratuitous sex and violence."

Fox decided that some of the skits had gone a bit too far, and decided to tone down the show. Still, Coca-Cola demanded the right to decide only on a program-by-program basis whether to advertise. Other advertisers asked for tighter screening procedures. The New York *Times* ran an editorial saying that Rakolta had every right to launch her one-woman campaign, and Fox had the right to run the show, but it urged that the show's time slot be switched back an hour so that children were less likely to see it. "Married . . ." gained two to three points in the ratings after the *Times* made its case. It was a great success. It did not matter what time it aired. Early or late, it was a hit. Advertisers' resistance soon dissipated as its ratings soared.

As Fox grew, it garnered the reputation of being a risk-taking network which allowed people their head and was receptive to new ideas. The industry was ready for a new act to shake the town. Between them, Murdoch and Diller pulled it off. Murdoch liked to call Fox's ideas "subversive," though of just what was not quite clear. Staff turnover was ruthless. Whereas the established networks each employed thousands, the crew of Fox numbered only about two hundred. Within three years, Fox turned a profit. It was doing what no American network had done since the American Broadcasting Company was founded. "We're the little skiff slicing through the water, as the big ocean liners are throwing off furniture and bodies to stay afloat," boasted Diller.

Reality was the watchword by the end of the 1980s, and reality rescued Fox from its early losses. "Truth," of a kind, replaced fiction. No one understood it better than Barry Diller. To Diller, the realities at the end of the 1980s were appalling. He thought the Republican years had depressed all that was good in America: "This country is no longer about anything but memories and myths." Politics was the fundamental difference between him and Murdoch. "He is able to make more fun of it than I am," said Diller. "I can't make fun of conservatives—I just get crazy, tied up."

In the summer of 1986, Murdoch summoned Maury Povich, the talk-show host of Fox's Washington station, to New York. Povich had been told horror stories about Murdoch by Harold Evans and others. The real Murdoch came as a surprise. "He wore a serious and dangerous brow, and spoke softly, politely, minimally, like a Mandarin demigod," Povich later wrote.

Murdoch told him that Fox was starting a new show, first in New York and then perhaps nationally. Povich would be host. Its name would be "A Current Affair," and it would begin to air in a month or so. Povich, used to slow-moving television bureaucracies, was astounded by "the sheer audacity of it all. Nobody mentioned focus groups, or consultants or marketing research. These guys were so casual, as if nothing could be easier. They were fearless: Murdoch's daredevil squadron, heading into the unknown without parachutes."

At first "A Current Affair" ran late in the evening on New York's Channel 5. It was to CBS' "60 Minutes" as the *Post* was to the New York *Times*, or the *Sun* to the *Financial Times*. "We did stories about freeing dogs from pounds in Connecticut and putting them in witness protection programs in Massachusetts, wet T-shirt contests and so on," said Povich. When he complained that they should be doing some serious stories as well, he was told he could make it clear on the air that he thought particular stories frivolous.

Povich thought that what made "A Current Affair" different was that it never tried to be fair—and its bias could be absolutely obvious, as in the sentimental coverage it gave to Mary Beth Whitehead, a working-class woman who had borne a surrogate child which she then wished to keep. She lost to the couple who had hired her. Next, the program staged a grisly re-creation of the Central Park murder of Jennifer Levin and then broadcast a tape, which it had bought, of her alleged murderer, Robert Chambers, pretending to strangle a doll. Good taste was never a problem to what Povich called "Rupert's outlaw gang of scoundrels." But they all needed Murdoch's approval. "There was always the threat of that raised eyebrow, which loomed like an open ICBM silo over our future," said Povich.

In September 1987, after a favorable review in the New York *Times*, Murdoch immediately decided to move the show up to prime time, 7:30 P.M. Stories became more national. Boston, then Houston, picked up the show. It took off and became more aggressive. "It had been a nice, populist, sweet little tabloid," said Diller, "not mean-spirited but fun. Then it went right over the line. Rupert kept pulling it back." By the end of 1989 it was making $25 million a year and its appeal to a nationwide audience propelled the network onward.

The next offering was even more "realistic." Like "A Current Affair," "America's Most Wanted" was born from the sensibility that informed tabloid newspapers. While Fox was not the first station to use the genre, it developed the concept beyond anything that TV had so far done. "Real" criminals became prime-time stars.

The program was hosted by John Walsh, a successful builder who had turned crusader after his six-year-old son had been kidnapped and murdered. He was not only an attractive TV host, but also an outraged American parent who was out to see justice done—a cross between Charles Bronson and the Peter Finch character in *Network*. The premise of the program was painfully simple: you, the viewer, wanted to see the scum caught. The show offered reenactments of gruesome crimes. Questions of invasion of privacy abounded, and some people wondered how long it would be before the TV audience would see a criminal executed. But, instead of feeling threatened by the show, American law enforcers welcomed it with open arms. FBI director William S. Sessions made an appearance, announcing the FBI's three most wanted people. The calls poured in.

As a result, scores of criminals were captured and prosecuted (over two hundred by mid-1992). Fugitives as far away as American Samoa were apprehended. Crimes committed as far back as 1971 were solved. In 1989, "America's Most Wanted" became the second-most-watched program on Fox, right behind "Married . . . with Children." It thrived on America's obsession with violent crime and with voyeuristic crime-solving. As the program became more successful, its grislier aspects were diluted—a little. Advertisers started to call the show "prosocial"—that was Diller's term. "America's Most Wanted," he said, was the show which turned the corner for Fox Broadcasting. In 1989 Fox nearly tripled its 1988 advertising revenue, and pulled in about $325 million in upfront sales to advertisers. By 1990 sales were up to $550 million.

Diller and Murdoch realized that they had hit a gold mine, a string of raunchy, "realistic" programs that the image-conscious networks, with their phalanx of censors and tastemakers, had never dared attempt. As well as finding new, younger viewers, and the advertisers who pursued them, Fox was constantly pushing back the frontiers of what was acceptable to a living-room audience. In a sense Murdoch was doing for Americans with Fox what he had done for the British with the *Sun*.

"Cops," which hit the airwaves in 1989, was a program unlike any other in prime time. Carrying police genre TV as far as anyone could imagine, the program starred real cops going after real criminals committing real crimes—hookers, hit-and-run drivers, thieves, Peeping Toms, wife beaters and child abusers. Each week a Minicam crew dogged several members from a local sheriff's department. "No actors, no scripts, no bull," Fox boasted. Week by week the locale shifted to a different American town. The police loved it—they were its stars. Law enforcement departments across the country offered their own teams of crimebusters. Civil libertarians were outraged. They pointed out that the rights of the "alleged perpetrators" were being seriously violated by the program, which vividly identified them as criminals. Even though it carried the disclaimer "innocent until proven guilty," the implication was quite the opposite.

The show reached a peak of sorts when it traveled to the Soviet Union in May 1989 for an hour-long special that aired in the United States and the U.S.S.R. later in the year. The Soviets placed virtually no limitations on the American crew wandering through Moscow and Leningrad seeking the darker side of *glasnost:* drunks being arrested and suffering cruel punishment, fragile families suffering in the strained Soviet society, a woman confessing to killing her husband with the outburst "I'm tired of life," a little boy turning in his father for possession of drugs.

"Cops" was reviewed by New York *Newsday* as "The Best New Crime Series of the Year," and it soon spawned similar shows on other networks. Whatever criticisms were made of it, it was not as offensive as such confrontational live-audience shows as that hosted by the abusive Morton Downey, Jr., who was then taken off the air. In the next tabloid TV stable were Phil Donahue's exploration of the sexual fantasies of housewives and Geraldo Rivera's screen adventures with Satanism and prostitution.

In all this cavalcade there was no greater star than the tireless Steve Dunleavy, whom Murdoch had moved from the *Post* to Fox. As "The Simpsons" replaced "Dallas," Dunleavy was the man who silver-plated the realism in "reality TV," and who crossed all the *t*'s in "tabloid television." He was still the Mad Dog to Murdoch's Mogul, but he had turned fifty and was now almost an elder statesman in the Murdoch organization. At the Boss' request, he had transformed himself from a hot-metal, cold-typewriter legend in Murdoch's most important newsrooms into a charming caricature of a serious network newsman. He wore well-cut suits and he had polished his prose till the purple really sparkled. He carried a spare tooth to stick in the gap between his front teeth when filming.

Like the veteran reporter he was, Dunleavy talked to people, listened, called them back. He was unstoppable, and was known as "Street Dog." Policemen loved him; he was a hero in all the precincts which he visited and where he praised the man on the beat. But it was not only street-smart police officers who loved him. Street-smart journalists felt a little tenderness too. Jimmy Breslin, no slouch when it came to criticizing the way in which Murdoch shoved journalistic standards downhill, acknowledged, "At least Dunleavy's no goddamn TV clone. I can't watch one more Asian woman who talks like she's from Nebraska. He's got that 'fuck you' attitude and I love it." In the newsroom at Channel 5, most of the staff were kids who would die for Dunleavy's smile. He was the hero as well as the legend.

It was Steve they sent after Jessica Hahn when she revealed her affair with the Reverend Jim Bakker, the television evangelist. Despite serenading her from the street at 4:00 A.M., he failed to get an interview. But when ABC announced that she would be appearing in an exclusive that evening on "Nightline," Dunleavy rushed to her apartment on Long Island and screamed through the locked door, "How can you do this to me, Jessica?" When ABC's limousine pulled up,

Dunleavy told the driver she was sick and had to go to the hospital. The car drove away. Dunleavy called an ambulance and spirited her off. He got the interview.

His hair was a little more gray and rather more coiffed, but the Steve Dunleavy who appeared on the screen for Fox was the same Dunleavy who had followed Murdoch around the globe scripting their shared tabloid vision. Like Murdoch, he still loved to stick in the craw of high-minded journalists and professors of journalism. When he was invited to attend a high-flown seminar in Princeton on the ethics of journalism, he showed up late and with a blonde on each arm. "It was a setup and I loved it," he told Marc Fisher, who profiled him in *GQ*. "The seminar reeked of wall-to-wall journalistic evangelists, who absolutely send me nuts. That's kind of arrogance. . . . The only bosses are the public. That's who runs my life, next to Rupert Murdoch. Those overindulged students left there firmly convinced they had stared into the eye of a journalistic Satan."

Tom Shales, the TV critic of the Washington *Post*, wrote: "Dunleavy makes Geraldo look like Eric Sevareid. . . . This guy is a sleaze, and unfortunately that's no longer a problem on TV." Similarly, the New York *Times* said "A Current Affair" was "Nothing short of vile. What kind of people do we want to be?"

That was a question that the Mad Dog and the Mogul provoked in all the societies through which they ran. The answers were not easy to find. Bart Simpson's famous cry "Eat my shorts" was one.

AUSTRALIA

Rupert and Anna Murdoch saw in the New Year of 1989 at their home in Cavan, New South Wales. They were in Australia for his mother's eightieth birthday party and to sort out some of the problems in News Corp, in particular with the Melbourne *Herald,* which had been a commercial disappointment since he had acquired it in 1987.

At 4:00 A.M. on January 3, he was awakened by a call from Europe, where it was still the afternoon of January 2. It was from Presses de la Cité, the French publisher that had been brought in by Ian Chapman of Collins to help him resist a full takeover by Murdoch. Murdoch already owned a large part of Collins and he had been angered by Chapman's reaction. He told the French that he would never give in.

Murdoch and Chapman had cooperated well since Murdoch's purchase of 42 percent of the voting shares of Collins in 1981, and over their joint acquisition of Harper & Row in 1987. But by 1988, international conglomerates were taking over more and more of the publishing industry. Most significantly, Robert Maxwell bought the American publisher Macmillan for $2.5 billion. (The exaggerated price of this deal was what finally began to sink Maxwell.)

After his purchase of *TV Guide*, Murdoch told Ian Chapman that the financial pressures on him were now such that he would have to make a bid for the whole of Collins. Chapman resisted and told Murdoch that the Collins board considered this a hostile bid, which Murdoch had assured him he would never make. Lord Goodman, Murdoch's lawyer, said later that he understood Chapman's feelings—Murdoch's bid was clearly a breach of his 1981 commitment. On the other hand, said Goodman in an interview for this book, that commitment had been made seven years before and business circumstances had changed. Goodman added, "Having known Murdoch for over thirty years, I cannot remember any other occasion on which he broke his word."

In November 1988, News International launched a cash bid for the 58 percent of William Collins that it did not already own. In the City, opinion held that the bid was puzzlingly low, valuing Collins at £293 million. In its offer document News claimed that staff morale was low and that the performance of the company's core businesses was poor.

According to News, it was only after a contribution from Harper & Row had been included that 1988's figures showed any improvement over 1987's. Ian Chapman told the *FT* that he was astonished by such claims. He began to mobilize Collins' authors against Murdoch and looked for a "white knight." He found the French publisher Presses de la Cité. On December 29, it offered £403 million for Collins.

Murdoch wasted no time in raising his offer. When called by an executive of the French firm, he insisted he would never back down; honor was at stake. He would top any bid the French publisher made. Presses de la Cité believed him to be implacable and, on the strength of one conversation, withdrew. Days later Collins began talks with News International. The board had left itself with few options. To encourage Presses de la Cité's interest, it had put a low value on the company, and the French withdrawal effectively forced it to accept the News International bid. Business opinion held that, even now, News had got itself a bargain, in publishing terms. The purchase price reflected a price/earnings multiple of 17.8, compared, for instance, to the multiple of 29.8 in Pearson's 1988 purchase of the U.S. educational publisher Addison-Wesley.

Many of Collins' authors expressed their horror. Over two hundred of them contributed "letters of support" to the company's management.

Murdoch stated that he was "very much more interested in the ninety-five percent of the authors who did not come out against the bid," adding succinctly that if writers did leave "we will find that other authors will come to us because we will sell more books." Only a handful left.

Murdoch gave Collins signed guarantees regarding the company's future editorial and management autonomy, and the board finally recommended the News bid. "I am sad that we have not managed to keep our independence," Ian Chapman was quoted as saying in the New York *Times.* He left the company.

Murdoch himself took over as Collins' chairman. George Craig, who had moved from Collins to be chief executive of Harper & Row, was now given that position at Collins as well. He began to integrate the two companies, which Chapman felt was a breach of some of the guarantees Murdoch had given.

For all the emotional language it produced, the Collins takeover was ultimately about the business logic of the 1980s. It was part of a worldwide corporate strategy in which newspapers, printing plants, film libraries, databases, books, satellite TV and magazines were converging on one another, in the expectation of global economies of scale for the parent company.

On January 4, Murdoch flew to Melbourne. Australia had not yet digested his takeover of the Herald group and there was still concern about the way in which he had disposed of newspapers to satisfy the Trade Practices Commission. Both the Brisbane *Sun* and the Adelaide *News* (Murdoch's first paper) had been bought by their News Corp editors. Murdoch had helped arrange the financing of the deals, and the papers remained in News buildings and were printed on News presses. He insisted this was the only way to ensure they remained alive. That may well have been true, but many people argued that he could still influence them.

An even greater upheaval was taking place at Fairfax. The twenty-six-year-old Warwick Fairfax had launched a takeover bid against the rest of his family for their company, John Fairfax Limited.

Early in 1988 Warwick Fairfax shut down the two loss-making papers of his new empire—the *Times on Sunday* and the tabloid Sydney *Sun*. The closure of the *Sun* was a major victory for Murdoch. Fairfax had handed the *Sun*'s market and its potential profits to him. Murdoch was delighted. He also tried to buy Fairfax's shares in both Australian Newsprint Mills and the Australian Associated Press. He would have controlled almost 80 percent of the country's largest supplier of newsprint, and more than 70 percent of AAP. On this occasion the Trade Practices Commission intervened to stop him.

In January 1988 it emerged that News was planning to build a A$120 million printing plant and warehouse in Melbourne's docklands area. It bought thirty-nine printing presses from Germany in a deal worth A$800 million, reported to be the world's biggest press order. They were designed to handle high-speed, high-quality color production. Murdoch had been persuaded against his better judgment, and largely by the example of Robert Maxwell, that he had to have color. This massive outlay helped almost to ruin him in 1990.

His father's old paper, the Melbourne *Herald*, was also causing problems. Circulation was not responding adequately to the new ownership, and the paper was losing A$15 million a year. Murdoch had become impatient with both managerial and editorial decisions on the paper. In November 1988 he summoned John D'Arcy, the *Herald*'s managing director, to London, and summarily fired him. D'Arcy, who had worked almost two years for Murdoch, was devastated, and his wife never forgave Murdoch. D'Arcy said later: "I was astonished by the culture of News. It was run like a corner store. No one makes a decision except Rupert. He doesn't care about conventions or customs. He prefers executives who never question him. When you answer back, Rupert says, 'I don't want to hear that.' He wants to own the world. Everything he sees for sale, he wants to buy. Look at *TV Guide*. Madness."

Relations between Murdoch and Eric Beecher, the editor of the *Herald*, were also souring, as Beecher failed to make the paper more profitable. In early 1989, Beecher resigned. He later said that like those of some other editors, his early relationship with Murdoch was like a love affair but when it soured, life became impossible: "Rupert is a great manipulator. He lets you grab his coattails and jump on the magic carpet. But the flight path may change in order to accommodate Rupert's needs for greater profits." (In a similar vein, Anna once told a New York *Times* reporter, "If Rupert was a pilot, I would not board the plane—he cuts too many corners.")

"The basic problem," said Beecher, "is that Rupert has contempt for those who work for him, and total contempt for those whom he can bend. I used to get up and say, 'He's changed.' But he had not." Murdoch's subsequent explanation was quite different. Beecher's sedate editorial approach, he claimed, "*shooed* away the readers. Evening papers are in terminal decline everywhere. Beecher simply sped the process."

On January 6, the family all went to Cruden Farm to attend Dame Elisabeth's eightieth birthday party. Tributes were certainly due, for Dame Elisabeth, sprightly and opinionated as ever, remained a prominent figure in many areas of Australian life—art, charities and, not least, gardening. As a family, the Murdochs had been substantial public benefactors since Sir Keith had taken a leading part in strengthening the National Gallery of Victoria, where a wing was named after him. Rupert Murdoch had assisted many Australian artists by buying their work, sponsoring exhibitions, financing shows overseas.

News had helped finance an oral history program at the museum of the National War Memorial in Canberra, and the company was underwriting the retrieval and cataloging of early Australian films. News marked the twenty-fifth anniversary of the *Australian* by funding Rupert Murdoch scholarships at the graduate school of management at Melbourne University. Murdoch and his mother and sisters had joined in financing the Institute of Birth Defects at the Melbourne Royal Children's Hospital. And in Oxford Murdoch had refurbished the library of his old college, Worcester. In Melbourne and elsewhere, friends attested to other examples of Murdoch family generosity to institutions and individuals.

The party was a great occasion. It could almost have been a set piece in Anna Murdoch's second novel, *Family Business,* the saga of a newspaper dynasty. All Dame Elisabeth's children, their spouses and most of her many grandchildren were there, as well as the cream

of Melbourne's political, commercial, academic and social Establishment—the governor of Victoria, the chairmen of the banks, directors of industry, vice-chancellors of universities. Also present was
Murdoch's old Geelong Grammar headmaster, Sir James Darling.
"Well, you got your way, Rupert," said Darling, as they shook hands.
In his speech Murdoch paid teasing tribute to his mother's strong
character and recalled his childhood.

The next day, Murdoch jetted off. This is how he himself listed his
major engagements in the next few weeks.

SATURDAY JAN 7. Melbourne–Sydney–Los Angeles. Arrive Los
   Angeles 10.30 same day. Lunch with Barry Diller. Fox-TV affiliates dinner on Fox lot.

SUNDAY JAN 8. Black tie affair—TV Academy Hall of Fame.

MONDAY JAN 9—TUES JAN 10. Fox, Sky/Disney, Motion Picture
   Corp meetings.

THURSDAY JAN 12. L A—Washington DC on our plane, a
   Gulfstream 111. Black tie dinner at White House. President and
   Mrs. Reagan. Late return to New York.

FRIDAY JAN 13. Meetings e.g. on Mirabella launch: lunch with
   John Sharp, leading Australian politician; drink with Bibi Netan-
   yahu, leading Israeli politician.

SATURDAY JAN 14. Concorde New York–London.

SUNDAY JAN 15. Meetings on Collins Publishers, Sky-TV, Times.

MONDAY JAN 16. Meetings on Collins, Sky. Concorde to New York,
   arrive 5.50 P.M.

TUESDAY JAN 17. Breakfast with George Ball at Prudential-Bache.
   Meetings at News Corporation.

WEDNESDAY JAN 18. NY–WASHINGTON–NY. I gave testimony in
   the Newhouse IRS case. Dinner: at the William Paleys for Sid
   Bass and Mercedes Kellogg.

THURSDAY JAN 19. Meetings, then major customers' conference on
   "free-standing inserts"—a subtlety of the media business.

FRIDAY JAN 20. (Inauguration Day). Meetings, bull sessions on Mirabella, TV Guide, Collins, Fox.

JAN 22 (SUNDAY). Concorde to London, dinner at Connaught.

JAN 23 (MONDAY). Meetings at Collins all day.

JAN 24 (TUESDAY). At Collins in Glasgow all day.

JAN 25 (WED)–JAN 27 (FRIDAY). Various meetings e.g. with Conrad Black in Wapping. Concorde to New York.

JAN 28 (SAT) New York–Washington D C Black tie dinner at Alfalfa Club, guest of Harry Byrd Jr.

JAN 29 (SUN) D C–Los Angeles.

JAN 30 (MON)—(WED) FEB 1 Los Angeles. Turf Racing Assoc dinner dance on Fox lot (a goodwill function for Daily Racing Form).

FEB 1 (WED). LA to NY.

FEB 4 (SAT). Concorde to London.

FEB 5 (SUNDAY). Launch of Sky-TV.

10

The Clarke Ring

Emboldened by the adventure at Fox, Murdoch felt the need once more to take on his enemies in "the British Establishment." In February 1989, he launched a new four-channel satellite service, Sky. It was the start of a war which cost both sides almost as much as the Channel tunnel, and almost destroyed News Corp.

Like other countries, Britain had five direct broadcast satellite (DBS) channels allocated to it in 1977 by the World Administrative Radio Conference.

Early in 1986, the Independent Broadcasting Authority invited applications to provide a commercial service on three of the DBS channels allocated to Britain.

One of the seven applications received by August that year was from Murdoch for his Sky channel service. He was already broadcasting through European cable systems. The competing groups shared a strong desire to keep Rupert Murdoch out of British television. There was much talk about the danger of his putting the *Sun* on satellite and doing a Wapping of the air. Murdoch looked like a risk to both morals and established television practices.

In the end, the franchise was won by British Satellite Broadcasting (BSB), a consortium made up of Granada, Pearson, Anglia television, Virgin Records and Amstrad. BSB's impressive presentation emphasized program-making. The overall watchword was quality. To

Murdoch, it was uncompromisingly "Establishment oriented," in that it fitted easily into the mainstream of British television.

The technology was expected to be high quality also. Under the terms of its franchise, BSB was compelled to use a new, untried and very expensive transmission system, D-MAC, which was expected to produce a better picture than the old PAL system.

BSB became one of the biggest risk-capital ventures the British markets had ever seen. The original estimates were that it would need over £500 million. By April 1987 the projected costs had risen to around £650 million.

In spring 1987 *Astra,* a private pan-European satellite operated from Luxembourg, was given a confirmed position on the Clarke Ring. Its plan to broadcast sixteen channels in different languages throughout Europe was an obvious challenge to established broadcasters and governments alike. The *Astra* satellite carried sixteen fifty-watt medium-power transponders.

During the 1980s the map of the European sky had changed radically. At the start of the decade the talk had been only of national, high-powered direct broadcast satellite systems. Now the future of the industry seemed to be assured by something quite different: low-powered commercial telecommunications satellites.

By 1987, Murdoch had spent over £40 million on his European Sky Channel in four years. It transmitted eighteen hours a day, and reached by cable into almost twelve million homes in twenty countries. After he decided to challenge BSB in Britain, he withdrew Sky from Continental Europe and planned how to move it onto *Astra* to be beamed to Britain. "*Astra* was not the only possibility. There were other things we could have done. Most importantly, we could have done nothing," said his adviser, Jim Cruthers. But that would not have been Murdoch's style at all. Having had the front door closed against him by the British Establishment, or so he claimed, he decided to use *Astra* to kick down the back door.

❖　❖　❖

When Murdoch announced the relaunch of Sky on Astra in June 1988, his refrain was familiar: British television should be burst right open. "Broadcasting in this country has for too long been the preserve of the old Establishment that has been elitist in its thinking and in its approach to programming," he declared. So-called quality television merely reflected the prejudices of the narrow elite which controlled British broadcasting. He was now going to war not only with the terrestrial stations of the BBC and Independent Television (ITV), but also with the new satellite service of British Satellite Broadcasting. For the first time, and after many frustrations, he was about to become a broadcaster in Britain. Hitherto, this had always been denied him because of the government's restrictions on newspaper and television cross-ownership. Those restrictions still applied, but Murdoch was sidestepping them by broadcasting from a satellite outside British jurisdiction.

His announcement was an unequivocal threat to BSB. Richard Branson, the founder of Virgin Records and one of BSB's investors, immediately understood the scale of it. BSB cost estimates had been based upon the premise that it would have no satellite competitors. Now it was clear that Murdoch was trying to beat them off the Clarke Ring with cheaper existing technology. BSB might be able to promise better reception from its new-fangled D-MAC system, but customers would buy only one system—probably the first to fly.

Branson knew how resolute a competitor Murdoch was and he realized that Sky would be enormously boosted by support from all the News International papers. That plugging began at once. In the months to come, Murdoch's papers, in particular the *Sun*, the *News of the World* and *Today*, all became shameless cheerleaders for Sky.

Branson tried secretly to interest Murdoch in a merger. But Murdoch was too confident for that. And so Branson arranged to sell Virgin's shares in BSB to an existing BSB shareholder, the Australian Alan Bond. Branson offered him his £30 million stake for just £31 million, in order to cover all Virgin's costs. Bond was delighted. The night the deal was done, Branson drank champagne.

BSB and Sky each reckoned that the success of its system depended on the lure of its movie channel. So, in the autumn of 1988, both of them sent teams of buyers to Hollywood to collar the gems of Dreamland.

In a town where excess is the daily fare, this bidding war seemed to the studios like an unbelievable Christmas. The British rivals were offering prices that were out of this world. The BSB team would sign up one studio, Sky the next, and then they would fight over the third. Each later blamed the other for pushing the prices into the heavens. BSB people said that Murdoch promised far too much money up front and insisted that, given his newspaper strength in Britain, it was certain he would eventually win the war.

In the end Sky signed up Fox, of course, and Orion, Touch-stone and Warner Bros. BSB came away with Paramount, Universal, MGM/United Artists and Columbia. Sky was said to have spent £60 million and BSB £85 million.

The studios were concerned about how the films would be encrypted. Murdoch had originally intended to show films on an "all-advertising-funded" free film channel. The studios were unenthusiastic. They were not eager to allow Murdoch to come in ahead of terrestrial TV with a free service to the British, especially if he was spilling it all over the continent of Europe at the same time, as the *Astra* footprint would do. They insisted that the films had to be broadcast in scrambled form, so that only subscribers with decoders could unscramble them. This meant another level of technology, and expense. Murdoch found and acquired such a system from Israel.

The expenditure in Hollywood horrified Murdoch. He also began to worry that development of the studio was going too slowly. He summoned Andrew Neil, the editor of the *Sunday Times* and an enthusiast for the television revolution, to be executive chairman of Sky.

By February, four channels were ready to start sending their signals thousands of miles up to the Clarke Ring above the equator.

The only problem was that there was almost no one watching when the signals came down again as broadcasts. There were virtually no satellite dishes to be had in the shops. This was partly because the unexpected demands by the studios for encryption meant that the receivers had to be altered at the last minute. The fact that so much was being broadcast for so few gave rise to much merriment, if not scorn, among Murdoch's critics.

Sky News was a far more substantial undertaking than most of those who loathed Murdoch had predicted or could now believe. It had cost over £40 million to create, its budget for 1989 was £30 million and it attempted to provide news on a twenty-four-hour basis, as CNN was doing in America and, increasingly, around the world. It broadcast fourteen and a half hours of live news each weekday, and, like Fox, it was lean. It had a staff of 260—Independent Television News, by comparison, broadcast six hours each day with a staff of 930 and a budget of £64 million. The money, effort and time put into Sky News reflected its importance in deflecting the criticism that the more populist output of Sky's other channels attracted.

By the summer of 1989 Sky's dishes were in the shops, but hot weather and continually rising interest rates discouraged consumers. There would have been similar problems for BSB, had it been on the air and had its dishes, known as "squarials," been for sale. But none of BSB's equipment was ready—not the dishes, nor the chips, nor the decoders—and its satellite was still on the ground. The D-MAC technology might eventually prove superior to the old-fashioned PAL systems that Sky was peddling, but that was little comfort when it was not available. BSB tried to shrug it off. What did a few months matter in a fifteen-year project? The answer was: everything.

By the second half of 1989, it was clear that BSB was going to need much more cash to get on the air, and a new round of financing got under way.

With far too few dishes selling, Murdoch decided to "relaunch" Sky. Thousands of dishes were given away to readers whose homes were strategically selected for the copycat effect they might provoke. Then Sky launched a rental package at the loss-leader price of £4.49 a week. Armies of unemployed salesmen were hired, dressed up in white coats and sent in fancy vans to housing developments all over the country. The combination of saturation promotion through Murdoch's popular papers and aggressive young men on the doorstep was irresistible for many, and rentals began to increase.

The sale of advertising time to companies was a disappointment. No real sales research had been done prior to the launch — Murdoch never believed in it. No one would say how much advertising Sky attracted in its first year. Estimates varied from £10 million down to mere thousands. Sky tried to introduce a scheme that had worked well at Fox—that of charter advertisers. It failed. Sky was a mess. But so were its competitors, terrestrial as well as satellite, as Murdoch himself was only too keen to point out.

On the last weekend of August 1989, Murdoch and Anna drove to the Edinburgh Television Festival, where he had agreed to deliver a keynote lecture on "New Television."

A few days before Murdoch arrived in Edinburgh, News Corp announced its results for the year ending June 30, 1989, which showed that Sky was losing the company £2 million a week and had so far cost £75 million since the launch. These daunting figures were not included in that year's accounts; the losses were to be spread over several years. Nonetheless, News International's pretax profits had dropped from £88 million to £20.1 million. Interest payments had more than doubled during the year, from £61.7 million to £138.6 million.

The stock market still had faith in Murdoch. News shares rose when the results were published. But there were other problems. Murdoch was concerned that his growing share of the British media was about to

come under scrutiny. The Office of Fair Trading had been conducting
a preliminary investigation into media ownership of papers and television to see if the issue of media monopoly should be referred to the
Monopolies and Mergers Commission. (His enemies said over half
of all papers sold in the U.K. were owned by him. Murdoch himself
produced figures to show that he owned about a third.)

In Edinburgh the British television Establishment was gathered to
hear Murdoch. Outside the ornate Victorian MacEwan Hall, the evening air bristled with the first chills of autumn. Young people were
darting around handing out flyers for a performance of David Hare
and Howard Brenton's play *Pravda*, which satirized the cynical control
of British newspapers and manipulation of politicians by a Murdoch
figure. (When the play was first performed at London's National Thea-
tre, Anna Murdoch went with a friend, and decided not to take her
husband to see it.)

Murdoch came to the rostrum looking mild and nervous—as he
does on such occasions. After praising Adam Smith, who two hundred
years before had written *The Wealth of Nations* just a few miles away,
Murdoch quietly delivered a forty-minute attack on British television
and the elitism of his listeners: "Much of what is claimed to be quality television here is no more than the parading of the prejudices and
interests of like-minded people who currently control it."

Murdoch argued that the BBC's television had had seriously debili-
tating effects on British society. Its programs "are often obsessed with
class, dominated by anticommercial attitudes and with a tendency to
hark back to the past." Most television drama, he declared, was "run by
the costume department." (This raised an anxious laugh.) "The socially
mobile are portrayed as uncaring; businessmen as crooks; money-
making is to be despised." British television was an "integral part of
the British disease, hostile to the sort of culture needed to cure that
disease."

There was still a place for "public service television" in Britain, but
it should be the subservient, not the dominant, factor. This would lib-

erate broadcasters: "Public service broadcasters here have paid a price for their state-sponsored privileges. That price has been their freedom. . . . I cannot imagine a British Watergate or a British Irangate being pursued by the BBC or ITV with the vigor of the U.S. networks."

This was an odd argument in itself. The print media in America had traditionally broken new ground in almost all the major U.S. scandals from Watergate on. Moreover, Murdoch's papers had never been conspicuous in taking on governments, nor had they given much support to such investigative reporting on television as he was suggesting.

Perhaps his most extraordinary remark was in comparing the British cultural Establishment to an authoritarian dictatorship. If the market, rather than public service, dominated television, freedom, he argued, would be safer. "The multiplicity of channels means that the government thought police, in whatever form, whether the great and good in Britain, or the jackboot-in-the-night elsewhere, will find it hard to control more and more channels."

He had expected tough questions. There were almost none. He must have walked out convinced that the British broadcasting Establishment was even weaker than he had suggested.

There was, of course, a defense against Murdoch's assault, though no one in the audience had the wit to make it. The BBC and Independent Television could not rely on the popularity of their programs for their integrity. They had been established on the basis that the market was an inadequate guardian of the viewer's best interests. The BBC in particular had values and traditions that were part of national identity. It has for decades been a national resource, the heartland of politics, culture, literature, news and entertainment. Murdoch spoke at a time when British broadcasting was under pressure, forced by the convictions of Thatcher, abetted by Murdoch and his papers, toward the open market.

Murdoch's attack was fundamental. He was declaring the values of British broadcasters futile, snobbish, paternalistic. Yet no one really challenged him. This was perhaps because his audience was loath to

see itself as an Establishment of any kind and was frightened to agree
with the BBC's founder, Lord Reith, that there could be a value in
institutions which could be described as Murdoch described them.
The dilemma in which Murdoch placed his audience was perhaps
displayed most charmingly by William Rees-Mogg, the *Times* editor
whom Murdoch had replaced with Harry Evans. Rees-Mogg said he
was not in the minority who had disagreed with the lecture. Yet he
was worried about whether national cultures would be preserved in
the new enveloping world of communications: "International market forces tend to break down national culture, and indeed Rupert
Murdoch can be seen as a powerful agent of that change. Some aspects of these national cultures may be obsolete, some may even be
bad, but people have a loyalty to them."

Rees-Mogg identified the clash between the market and quality.
The market was better than monopoly, "but I do not want the result to
be a McDonald's culture in which television provides the international
fast food of the mind."

The scene in Edinburgh demonstrated nothing so much as the power
of one man's will. Murdoch knew what he believed in. He believed
that "the McDonald's culture" was an elitist phrase which the English
used scathingly to describe the world's freest political and economic
system, and that the more of it that could be beamed down from the
Clarke Ring the better. "The freeing of broadcasting in this country,"
he said, "is very much part of [the] democratic revolution, and an
essential step forward into the Information Age."

ASPEN

Nineteen eighty-nine was a frustrating year for Murdoch. "I'm tapped
out," he kept saying. Revolutionary changes were taking place, from
which he felt excluded, his hands tied by debt.

News claimed that its ratio of debt to equity was 0.98:1, uncomfortably close to the ceiling of 1.1:1 which the banks had imposed. At the same time, it stated that its interest coverage (ratio of income to interest expense) was down to 1.6. (In 1985 it had been 2.9.) Standard & Poor's had warned at the end of 1988 that this left "little margin for error in the company's ability to meet its debt-servicing obligations." In fact, News' figures were optimistic, and depended on Australian accounting rules. Under American rules, the debt-to-equity ratio would have been far worse.

In early March 1989 Murdoch announced the formation of a new company, Media Partners International. It was immediately dubbed "Son of News." The plan was for Media Partners to raise between $1 and $2 billion in a worldwide private placement, with minimum investments of $25 million. News Corp would then transfer its book publishers into the new company. These included Harper & Row, William Collins (it was now clear why he had wanted to buy the whole company) and Bay Books and Angus and Robertson in Australia. The sale price would be set by outside appraisal, but was expected to be at least $1 billion. With the infusion of $200 million of News Corp money, this would reduce News Corp's debt by $800 million. Murdoch would retain control of the new company through a ten-year management contract and News Corp's initial 20 percent stake might go higher. Murdoch would be selling his own assets to himself, using other people's money. Few people would dare even to try such a scheme.

"Son of News" was not an inappropriate nickname. Murdoch himself said that his intention was to "start a second News Corporation" and that "the main purpose is not to be stopped from expanding." If the plan worked, "it means we aren't tapped out. . . . we can go on with everything."

At first, Media Partners was hailed as a brilliant new trick by the great master. The *Financial Times* commented: "The whole venture is a typical piece of Murdoch adroitness: if your own company is too loaded with debt to move, start again with someone else's money."

However, potential investors saw more problems. Murdoch put a great deal of time into Media Partners, traveling in Japan, Australia and Europe, explaining the proposal, answering questions. He found that he was constantly having to reassure institutions that he was not a raider but interested rather in building company values. He found most difficulty in Japan, where banks and institutions seemed to consider the *Sun*'s strictures about the evils of Emperor Hirohito a disincentive to investment.

Other investors also seemed unwilling to make a blind bet on the company. MPI was seen as highly leveraged—and by 1989 debt was beginning to be considered a worry, not a blessing. Moreover, there was a paradox: if News Corp's debt was reduced, then it would seem more attractive than MPI. After all, that was where Murdoch and most of the action would be. By the summer of 1989, he was forced to acknowledge that the idea would not work.

The brief rise and fall of Media Partners coincided with the announcement of the controversial and expensive merger between Time Inc. and Warner Communications. The deal, announced in March 1989, was a proposal to create the dominant media company of the twenty-first century. The new company would be the biggest entertainment group in the world—$15 billion worth of films, TV programs, pre-recorded videos, recorded music, magazine and book publishing and cable and pay-per-view television networks.

Murdoch was irritated at not being able to play an active role. He really would like to own Time, he told John Evans, the president of Murdoch Magazines. He wanted the gravitas that ownership of such an American institution as Time Inc. would confer: "I want to be at the table and a player when they move the pieces around in America."

Talks had been under way between Time and Warner since 1987. Time Inc. was particularly vulnerable. The fabulous creation of Henry Luce and Briton Hadden in 1923, it had become bureaucratic and timid. One of its own internal reports warned in 1988 that it was perceived as "uncreative, overly cautious, investor-driven and risk-averse." The breakup value of its assets was thought to be considerably greater than the value that Wall Street placed on the company through its share price.

The fashionable doctrine of "synergy" was given as one reason for the merger. This was a medical term used to describe a group of muscles working together to produce movement. At the end of the 1980s it was proposed that linking books, video, film, television and other media would create some sort of chain reaction which would reach critical mass and be enormously productive (profitable) for all of them. The vertical integration proposed by the Time-Warner merger was said to represent a whole new level of industry concentration, combining a rich pool of creative talent with just about every possible outlet for distribution and marketing it. Time was the second-biggest cable operator in the States, and Warner already produced programming for its new partner. The synergy argument was that the combined Time Warner would make fabulous profits around the world—for example, from the current deregulation of European TV and also from the vast growing markets in Asia.

In fact, synergy turned out to be elusive. And this deal was, in any case, motivated less by the hope of synergistic lift-off than by concerns over corporate survival. It reflected the paranoia caused by the foreign invasion of the U.S. media and entertainment industry. Richard Munro of Time acknowledged, "We see Robert Maxwell and Rupert Murdoch and Bertelsmann and Sony coming into our market and raising hell. We see [the merger] as an opportunity for an American company to get competitive."

In 1980, ten of the twelve biggest media companies in the world had been American owned. By 1989, after several years of a weak dollar, which had encouraged foreign takeovers, three of the top five were non-American. Nick Nicholas, Time's president, said, "There will emerge on a worldwide basis six, seven, eight vertically integrated media and entertainment conglomerates. At least one will be Japanese, probably two. We think two will be European. There will be a couple of American-led enterprises and we think Time is going to be one of them."

This view was echoed by Steve Ross, the head of Warner. He thought there was only one solution: "Unless American companies join together, there aren't going to be any American media companies. They are all going to be owned by foreign enterprises."

By the end of the decade, there were indeed around half a dozen major media and entertainment companies dominating different parts of the global village and competing with one another as well. The most prominent were News, Walt Disney, Berlusconi, Bertelsmann and Sony.

Each of them reflected its own specific history. Murdoch's jigsaw illustrated more the sense of his own frantic odyssey than anything else. Walt Disney had always been an international company with a clearly defined product; it saw the advent of a single market in Europe and other changes as offering huge new opportunities, particularly for its theme parks.

Until the Time-Warner deal, Bertelsmann was the world's largest media company. In addition to its U.S. interests, it had magazines and newspapers in Europe and a West German TV channel, RTL Plus, the first privately owned TV channel in the country. Bertelsmann's turnover was more than $6 billion. Its invasion of the U.S.A. was followed by that of Hachette, which paid $1.2 billion for Grolier, the encyclopedia publisher, and Diamandis, the magazine giant. Hachette then displaced Time Inc. to become the world's largest magazine publisher.

But although the invasion of the Europeans (and the former Australian) seemed threatening, it was the arrival of the Japanese that caused most angst and heart-searching in the United States.

In 1987, the Japanese media hardware manufacturer Sony had bought CBS Records for $2 billion; this had left Warner as almost the last big American record producer, although, as Steve Ross put it, "this was an industry that America created." Through the first part of 1989 Sony was known to be seeking a film studio—RCA and Columbia were seen as likely targets. Nevertheless, when Sony did buy Columbia, the news was greeted with near hysteria in the United States. Hollywood was at the heart of the American Dream, and the notion that it could be owned by the Japanese seemed to many Americans to be insufferable. As fear of communism receded, with its failure and collapse around the world, it was being replaced by fear or envy of the extraordinary successes of Japan.

Then there was Maxwell. He was still trying to create an international communications company to rival News; in 1988, reacting to Murdoch's purchase of Harper & Row and frustrated in his attempt to buy Harcourt Brace Jovanovich, he finally managed to buy the American publisher Macmillan, after a bruising fight with some of America's deepest-pocketed investors. Maxwell paid $2.5 billion, which, even by the overheated standards of the time, was thought to be hugely expensive. He also paid $750 million for the *Official Airlines Guide*. It was these new debts which his ramshackle and dishonest business was unable in the long run to sustain.

But while most buyout activity was taking place in the American market at the end of the 1980s, one of the most lavish prizes for the new conglomerates would be in Europe, where the new generation of satellites and deregulation would, it was thought, accompany the creation of a single market in 1992. The prospect of this new gold mine was one important reason why so many foreign companies wanted to buy up American studios—they needed the programming.

The move to television was crucial. Bertelsmann was already well placed in Germany. The flamboyant Silvio Berlusconi owned three commercial television channels in Italy, half a cable network in Germany, and a share of La Cinq, a new commercial channel in France. He was also expanding into Spain. Maxwell was increasing his reach through European cable. Murdoch was pinning his hopes on Sky. The

Time-Warner merger showed that American media companies felt the pressure. More and more, media companies were beginning to see that television, not newspapers, would probably be their main source of income in the future.

Ben Bagdikian, a writer on media studies and former dean of the journalism school at Berkeley, warned,

> The lords of the global village have their own political agenda. . . .
> Together, they exert a homogenizing power over ideas, culture
> and commerce that affects populations larger than any in history.
> Neither Caesar nor Hitler, Franklin Roosevelt nor any Pope, has
> commanded as much power to shape the information on which
> so many people depend to make decisions about everything from
> whom to vote for to what to eat.

The enormous power of the new barons to disseminate the news of the village was being more and more dramatically demonstrated by the speed of political changes. In the spring of 1989, communist dictatorships were being swept away in both Poland and Hungary and Mikhail Gorbachev's bold reforms were allowing unprecedented freedoms in the Soviet Union. The most dramatic of these upheavals was taking place in China, where students staged massive peaceful demonstrations in Tiananmen Square around a copy of the Statue of Liberty—their own Goddess of Democracy.

The ensuing massacre, on the night of June 3–4, happened in what television officials call "real time"—and was the first such event to have been broadcast live. Ted Turner's Cable News Network gave a constant commentary. At once the slaughter of Tiananmen Square became a part and product of what is called the information revolution—the linking, but perhaps not the binding, of the world by satellite and by other technologies such as the PC and the fax. After the massacre, people evaded Peking's censorship by faxing information into and out of the West.

Murdoch, along with Ronald Reagan, believed that this information revolution would be absolutely liberating. Certainly in this case, the impact of the technology was on the side of the oppressed. Murdoch thought that "watching the events in China on CNN was the most amazing experience; it was an extraordinary moment in history, to know that what was happening in China was happening in part because we were all watching it." He hoped that in the next ten years Fox and Sky would become a major force like CNN.

The same week as Tiananmen, Paramount Communications tried to disrupt the merger between Time and Warner by launching a $10.7 billion takeover bid for Time Inc. Murdoch was not prepared to be left out and, despite the failure of Media Partners, he announced that he too was now looking at ways to intervene. Eventually, neither he nor Paramount succeeded and the Time-Warner merger took place, though at much greater cost to the two companies than they had originally envisaged.

Shortly afterward, the News Corp colonels assembled in Aspen to discuss global and parochial issues. The weekend was extremely well prepared, with expensively printed booklets and brochures describing people, times and events, and even the weather patterns for the same weekend in the past two years. Participants were given clothes bearing the News Corp logo, and were informed before arrival that "Aspen is a city that requires casual dress. For men, a jacket at dinner is appropriate, but not a tie. For women, slacks will be appropriate at all times during the conference weekend."

The conference was divided into three principal groups. They discussed the synergy to be derived from a multimedia international empire, the impact of new technology and the image of News together with journalistic ethics. As they talked, it became clear that the company worked very differently in each continent where it was based.

Although Murdoch was preoccupied with debt, he was still talking growth rather than consolidation. He emphasized to the gathering of his officers that if they all added another 5 percent to the bottom line, he could borrow another $2 billion and continue the expansion of his empire.

There was also considerable talk about Sky Television. Dish sales were still slow and the service still losing some £2 million a week. John Evans argued the virtues of cable television over television delivered by satellite, largely on the grounds that cable is much more interactive. Evans believed that the culture of television couch potatoes was a thing of the past, and that once fiber-optic links were brought into homes, television would no longer be a mere shadow in the cave. On the other hand, he had to acknowledge that satellites were global in a way that cable never could be.

Grace Mirabella was there as testimony to the speed with which Murdoch moved. In 1988 she had been abruptly fired by Condé Nast after years of success as editor of *Vogue*. Murdoch had immediately asked her if she would like to start a new fashion magazine with her own name, Mirabella, as the title. She had agreed, and so, with a minimum of fuss, it had been accomplished. In more bureaucratic organizations, starting a new magazine would take years of memos, planning and agony. Murdoch authorized it in moments, and it happened in months.

The editor of *Premiere,* Susan Lyne, had a similar story. She had been on the *Village Voice* when John Evans invited her to create a movie magazine. When she had shown him an early dummy, he had said that she did not need to consult him or Murdoch—they had hired her and trusted her. If her concept did not fly, that would be too bad.

Lyne's husband, George Crile, who worked for CBS, was astonished by the creative freedom which News employees could enjoy—at least on Murdoch Magazines. He saw the weekend as a gathering of local chieftains from around the world, summoned to hear the instructions of their controller. It reminded him of the James Bond novel

Goldfinger. Crile thought the company was superbly flexible and responsive. One of the debates at Aspen was on how to preserve that sense of spontaneity as News grew even larger.

But the issues which dominated the weekend were the image of News Corp and the ethics of journalism. The debates centered on the quality broadsheets versus the tabloids in Britain and, in America, Fox Film against the *Star* and Channel 5's investigative programs "A Current Affair" and "The Reporters," where the inimitable Steve Dunleavy reigned.

The Hollywood people, led by Barry Diller, were particularly enraged by the tabloid mentality of much of News, and complained that movie stars were not prepared to work for one part of the News empire while being abused by another. Later there was a report on page six of the New York *Post,* the gossip column which had been a byword for intrusive inquiries when Murdoch owned the paper, that the two sides almost came to blows at Aspen on this issue. That was an exaggeration.

A typical problem had apparently arisen with Arnold Schwarzenegger. At a time when Diller was trying to persuade the superstar to sign a large contract, the *News of the World* published a story alleging that Schwarzenegger's father had had Nazi connections. Another of those who felt themselves damaged by the tabloids was the actor William Hurt, who had been involved in a disagreeable child support suit. Still another was the comedian Danny DeVito, who had objected to the way in which he had been portrayed on the cover of *Premiere.*

Tabloid journalists in the empire resisted any call for a company-wide standard of ethics, while many of the broadsheet editors demanded that something of the sort was essential. Andrew Neil said he felt that the *Sunday Times* was tarred by association with the *Sun* and the *News of the World.* He complained in particular about the *Sun's* celebrated libel of Elton John.

After venting his spleen, Barry Diller roared into the mountains on a motorbike. He fell, breaking his ankle, and when he hobbled back, Murdoch said, "I hope none of you did this."

In the closing plenary session Irwin Stelzer, a wealthy consultant who wrote a column for the *Sunday Times* and was an increasingly important adviser to Murdoch, summed up the proceedings. He put his finger on an important part of the News Corp culture: "Almost everyone in it views himself as a buccaneer; an outrider; an accident waiting to happen to his competitors; and as being involved with a highly unstructured, highly entrepreneurial organization."

On the downside, those same buccaneers were reluctant to criticize. People were afraid to question Murdoch's judgment on matters such as the vast investment in color presses in Britain and Australia.

The ethics of the company were tied to its image, which was different on each of the continents. It was worst in Britain, where it was seen as too powerful and monolithic, controlled by Murdoch, voicing a strident pro-Thatcher, anti-BBC line. In the States since the sale of the New York *Post,* News Corp and Murdoch had had no serious image problems—except for an emergent concern with "tabloid TV." Without the *Post,* News had no visible political power in the States, unlike in Britain or Australia. (In fact, Fox Broadcasting programs often did display a political agenda, as in their vendetta against Edward Kennedy.)

But the papers which caused the most problems also provided the most money. As Stelzer pointed out, "If there were no *Sun* and no *News of the World,* there would almost certainly be no *Times.* . . ."

He suggested ways to alleviate the difficulty without "neutering" the tabloids—an idea which would have been anathema to Murdoch. A 5 percent improvement in their accuracy could lead to a 95 percent improvement in their image. There should be more U.K. citizens in top positions in News Corp, and more constructive answering of criticisms. This proposal was directed especially against Kelvin MacKenzie, who was famous for his bunker mentality.

There was disagreement as to how "the Murdoch image problem" should be addressed. Stelzer recounted that officers at Aspen felt that if their leader would appear more often in public, the problem would disappear—he was so transparently decent and modest that he would win friends everywhere. However, the more cynical among them felt that "the liberals" in the press and television around the world were so irredeemably hostile that this would be a waste of Murdoch's time.

In his reply, Murdoch took the side of the tabloids, where both his heart and his pocketbook resided. "This is a media corporation. We are into news," he said. "There are two kinds of newspaper. There are broadsheets and there are tabloids. Or, as some people say, there are the unpopular and the popular newspapers."

That had always been his view. He still insisted that "downmarket" was the snob's word for "popular" and that elitist intellectuals spent altogether too much time denigrating the appeal of popular papers. But Aspen '89 demonstrated that News was no longer overwhelmingly a newspaper company. The British papers, the *Sunday Times,* the *Sun* and the *News of the World,* still sustained the rest of the empire, but Murdoch's focus was on electronic means of communication—especially film and television. Once more, Rupert Murdoch was reinventing himself, and as a result of Aspen '89 he started to try to present to the world a more responsive and responsible face.

ADELAIDE

Late in the evening of October 9, 1989, after an early dinner with his editors and associates in Melbourne, Rupert Murdoch flew back to where it all began, to Adelaide. Next day was the annual general meeting of News Corporation, which was still registered in the capital of South Australia.

As Murdoch arrived, the editor of the Adelaide *Review,* a tiny free newspaper which was the Murdoch press' only competition in the city, and which attempted a spiky confrontation with News Corp's might, asked a visitor, "Do you smell a certain effulgence in the air? Rupert is here," he said. "Lucifer has come trailing smoke and sulfur."

The meeting was to take place in the tall, almost brand-new, pink tower of the Hyatt Regency, close by the fine railroad station. It stood exactly opposite the little white building of the Adelaide *News,* in which Rupert Murdoch had assumed his inheritance on the death of his father, and whence he had begun to build his empire, some thirty-five years before. Now the *News* building, dwarfed by modern commercial blocks along North Terrace, was locked up and defunct. Murdoch had had to sell the *News* when he bought the Melbourne *Herald,* which owned the other Adelaide paper, the *Advertiser.* The *News* was now owned by Northern Star, though it was still published on the *Advertiser*'s presses.

By 11:25 there were around one hundred people in the conference room, many of them brokers or members of the press. There were probably only about sixty shareholders. Some were elderly retainers of the Murdoch empire who had worked for many years for Rupert and for his father before him, and had done well from their shares. An original shareholder who had bought one hundred of the original News shares at A$2 each in 1922, and had taken up every share issue since then, would have had 92,880 News Corp shares worth almost A$1 million by the end of 1988 in return for a total outlay of merely A$3,000—which would itself have been covered many times by dividends.

News Corp's figures were virtually impossible for a layman to understand. They skated and slipped among U.S. and British and Australian accounting rules, with the same items described and evaluated differently in each place. There were about four hundred different business units within the News Corp empire. Some were shell companies, but all had some purpose. Richard Sarazen was now the man who shuffled them like cards and who pulled rabbits out of hats.

An Italian American from Brooklyn, he had sometimes been described as "the invisible man" behind Rupert Murdoch. He was one of the handful of men who subsumed their own egos to that of the boss, and on whom Murdoch had relied completely throughout the recent years of hectic, helter-skelter growth. Sarazen was the man who provided the technical backup to a dream, the know-how for a scheme. Thus, in the summer of 1988 Murdoch had called Sarazen one morning at his Upper East Side apartment and, according to Sarazen, said, "I'm going to spend three billion dollars for *TV Guide*. Where do you think you can get it?"

Sarazen replied, "Give me an hour." In fact, he had needed a day. By the end of it he had lined up verbal promises of $2 billion in Europe and $1 billion in the U.S. These were formalized into written agreements within the week.

Sarazen had joined News America as chief financial officer in 1974. "Murdoch," Sarazen would say simply, "is a genius." He thought "the beautiful thing about working for Murdoch is that when mistakes are made, he never kicks the dog and says you recommended it." He had the same radical conservative philosophy as Murdoch: "If we criticize the rest of the world for inefficient bureaucratic government that may destroy the Western world, you can put the same criticism on bureaucratic U.S. businessmen who are worried about jobs, position and doing poison-pill deals. They don't give a stuff about U.S. shareholders. They're selfish and inefficient."

Throughout the 1980s Sarazen had retained his wizard's touch. Some of his methods were made possible by the fact that, despite the growth of a global economy, there were still no internationally accepted rules of accounting. Few countries offered such lax or tolerant rules as did Australia—and the differences between Australian and American practices enabled News Corp to steal marches on its competitors.

Unlike the United States, Australia and Britain allowed a firm to revalue its intangible assets periodically. As a result, News Corp could add its intangibles, like newspaper titles, to its balance sheet as assets, instead of gradually writing them off.

Australia also did not require a company to amortize the goodwill of any company it acquired. American firms had to do so, which meant that their earnings were hit when they made a purchase.

Australia allowed a company to add preferred shares to stock-holders' equity. American rules did not—in the United States such shares were classified as debt.

Australian rules allowed companies to capitalize interest payments on loans for investments. Under American rules such interest would be deducted from current earnings. This of course produced quite the opposite effect on earnings. By American rules, the Australian procedure overstated profits, assets and therefore equity.

In America, net operating losses were listed as extraordinary items. In Australia, they were viewed as a reduction of income tax expenses, and so the company viewed them as earnings. This tended to inflate reported profits, because the interest was not being charged to the operators.

In Australia noncurrent equity shares were stock held for long-term investment. News Corp did not recognize any paper losses in such stock. Thus, for example, it ignored fluctuations in the price of its shares in Pearson and Reuters. Under U.S. rules, such falls would be treated as a reduction in shareholders' equity.

In 1989 Allan Sloan of *Newsday* wrote in *Corporate Finance*, "Sarazen's secret is that he treats financial reporting as a game to be won, rather than an obligation to be met. Instead of reacting to what regulators want, as most CFOs are wont to do, Sarazen forces them to react to him." This was exactly how Murdoch had always behaved.

In Australia, as the law allowed, Sarazen treated preferred stock as equity for the sake of the balance sheet. In the States, he was entitled to call it debt, and was therefore able to deduct the dividends from income tax. In the fabulous 1980s it became common practice for Australian companies to overstate the value of their media properties in order to improve the balance sheet as if by magic.

News Corp was a South Australian corporation. It had American depository receipts (ADRs) traded on the New York Stock Exchange, which meant that U.S. investors could buy News Corp just like any other stock. American shareholders were sent the glossy annual report of the Australian company. With it came a leaflet which was supposed to translate the Australian figures into officially accepted American terms. Naturally, this package met American reporting standards, but much significant information for American stockholders was contained in rather more obscure documents, such as financial reports filed by Fox Television or Twentieth Century Fox with the Securities and Exchange Commission.

For example, in several years in the 1980s, News generated substantial profits from currency speculation. This was acknowledged in one line in the annual report and in the footnotes of the 10-K form News America filed with the SEC. It was not mentioned in the ADR leaflet at all. In other years, News Corp lost money on the foreign exchange markets because of the decline in the Australian dollar. These trades were shown as extraordinary losses, which made it hard to understand why the 1986 profits were treated as ordinary income. Sarazen's answer was that currency spot trading was a profit center.

Sarazen liked to use only banks that understood News Corp well: "If a bank wants to lend us fifty million dollars tomorrow, we won't take it unless we're satisfied it knows we're a very complicated company with a lot of cross-ownerships and complicated flows of money." The bank also had to accept Sarazen's clever global accounting practices, and the fact that News Corp would not secure loans with its own holdings and would brook very few restrictive covenants. In the end it often seemed as if News Corp were doing the bank a favor by agreeing to borrow money. At the end of 1989, News Corp still had an unused credit line of $1.8 billion to draw upon if it wished.

Sarazen explained that the banks remained loyal because "regardless of where we borrow, ultimately the parent company guarantees virtually all the debt of all subsidiaries." (Behind the parent companies stood Murdoch's own family holdings.) In 1989 there were about 110 banks associated with and supportive of News Corp. They could expect good treatment from Murdoch, but he demanded quick responses from them.

News used its international structure to minimize its tax liabilities. This was done by establishing what were technically legitimate paper companies in tax-haven countries and washing profits through them, and by arranging affairs in Australia, the U.S. and the U.K. to suit best the tax situation in each one of them.

Of the three, Australia had the highest corporate tax rate and had tended to do so over the years. The rate for the 1987–88 fiscal year was 49 percent, well above the rates in the U.S., U.K. and Hong Kong at the time. It was reduced to 39 percent starting on July 1, 1988.

Australia's accounting standards meant that Murdoch was not forced to reveal a great deal about his financing. Sarazen could charge a lot of the loans for News operations outside Australia to his Australian operations. This reduced the profits from his Australian operations—and even actually produced losses—so that his tax bill was reduced in the country where taxes were higher than in any other nation where News had significant operations.

News' annual reports showed a breakdown of operating profits in each of the three major areas before allocation of interest. Interest was shown as one figure for all the international operations. However, the losses reported by News Ltd. in the fiscal year to June 1988 (a year in which the Australian operations did very well) suggested that something like the allocation of overseas loans to offset his Australian profits had occurred.

This was where tax-shelter companies like News Corp Cayman Islands, created in spring 1989, came in. The Cayman Islands subsidiaries could make loans to other News Corp subsidiaries in high-tax countries, such as Australia. News Corp Cayman made large profits but paid very little tax—because tax was not what the Caymans were for.

In 1989, News Corp Cayman issued $600 million guaranteed preferred shares in three denominations, convertible into shares in Reuters or Pearson. The reason, according to News Corp's deputy finance director, Dave DeVoe, was that it was tax-efficient. There were no corporate taxes in the Cayman Islands and the preferred shares could be treated as equity under Australian accounting procedures. Moreover, the rates were better than in the U.S. And finally, Sarazen had worked in a repeat of his scheme with the 1986 Fox preferred shares: if these funds were lent to an American subsidiary they would be regarded as debt, but by lending them to News International, the British company, News Corp could include the issue as shareholders' equity and reap a tax deduction.

By 1989, News Corp's technique of revaluing its "intangible assets" under the Australian generally accepted accounting practices was causing more concern to some American analysts. A report from Prudential Bache Securities showed that in 1988 News Corp revalued its intangibles upward by A$1.3 billion. This, the report claimed, resulted in shareholders' equity being overstated by 22.8 percent as of June 1988. Moreover, under Australian rules, News Corp's profit increased in 1988; under American rules, it decreased.

The way in which the company exploited all possible tax breaks was well demonstrated in the case of the *South China Morning Post*. Murdoch had bought it for $230 million in March 1987. Through a Hong Kong vehicle named Asher Holdings, the *Post* immediately became a subsidiary of News Publishers Bermuda, which was in turn wholly owned by News Corp of Adelaide. In June 1987, News Publishers sold "the entire publishing business"—that is, the titles of the *Post* and *Sunday Post*—to a new Hong Kong–registered company called SCMP Publishers. SCMP Publishers bought the fixed assets of the old South China Morning Post Ltd. for almost HK$46 million.

Then it bought the titles of the daily and Sunday papers for HK$1.82 billion. According to the *Far Eastern Economic Review,* SCMP Publishers borrowed the cash from a shell company called South China Morning Post Finance which was a direct subsidiary of Murdoch's Bermudan vehicle, News Publishers. South China Morning Post Finance then borrowed HK$2 billion from the banks and SCMP Publishers guaranteed these loans.

The beauty of this scheme was first that the "transfer" went straight to the bottom line of SCMP Publishers in Hong Kong. Registering a loss for tax purposes of HK$1.82 billion enabled Murdoch to make substantial claims against his Hong Kong taxes. Then SCMP Publishers had to pay interest to SCMP Finance. The interest payments were also claimed against tax. As a result of all this, the *Post* paid no tax in the three years after Murdoch took control of it, except for relatively small amounts still owed by the previous management.

Murdoch's tax situation was highlighted in Australia in a May 1989 report by the House of Representatives Standing Committee on Finance and Public Administration. The report, entitled "Tax Payers or Tax Players?," found that News Corporation was the second-biggest Australian avoider of tax as defined by the percentage of profits which were washed through tax havens. (The biggest was a building products/concrete company called Pioneer International.) To be fair to News Corp, the percentage also included profits earned from its operations in Hong Kong, which was classed as a tax haven in the study.

The report found that all of News Corporation's profits of A$387.9 million for 1987–88 were earned through tax havens. The 1988 annual report showed that four subsidiaries of News Corporation in the Netherlands Antilles recorded profits of A$149 million while another three in Bermuda recorded A$165 million.

These tax-haven profits were in stark contrast to the losses made by three of Murdoch's most important operating companies in high-tax countries. News Ltd., incorporated in South Australia, made a loss of over A$202 million; News International, London, made a loss of

A$322 million in the U.K.; and Fox Inc., incorporated in the U.S.A., made a loss of A$213 million.

The 1988 figures show that the gross income from News Corporation's operations and the profits from its associated companies (i.e., those in which News had less than 51 percent, the major one being Ansett) were A$575.6 million in the year to June 1988. Tax paid on this by News Corp and its subsidiaries was A$52.9 million. Income tax paid by associated companies was A$49.9 million. Thus the total tax paid was A$103 million. This represented a rate of 17.8 percent, compared to the Australian corporate tax rate at the time of 49 percent and the U.K. rate of 35 percent.

News Corp declined the committee's request to comment on such findings and merely suggested to the committee that there were "a number of complex issues which would need to be examined to ensure that there is a balance between immediate changes in tax regimes and longer-term benefits accruing to the Australian economy from companies with significant global operations."

Just before half past eleven, Murdoch arrived at the Adelaide Hyatt for the annual general meeting. He came into the conference room carrying a tan leather briefcase and looking slightly harassed, diffident, stooping. Wearing his customary dark blue suit, he walked up from the back, greeting old employees, shaking hands, remembering every name. He sat down to take notes while the chairman of News, Richard Searby, opened the meeting.

Searby might well have been chief justice of Australia had he not agreed to his old friend Rupert's request that he become chairman of the group. Now he warned shareholders of the high level of interest rates, which had had a severe impact on advertising revenues in both the U.S. and the U.K., and told them of the losses incurred by Sky Television. So far it had cost about A$150 million and was now losing some A$4 million a week.

Murdoch, whose family company, Cruden Investments, still owned just under 50 percent of News Corp's ordinary shares, himself spoke hesitantly. He said that the media were becoming more and more central to the functioning of the world—and that meant more valuable. However, under pressure to be realistic, his short-term message was not cheerful. The magazines were doing well, but Twentieth Century Fox was "quite frankly . . . having a bad year." Not enough films, poor management. But next year would be better. Fox Television, on the other hand, was already going well, thanks to an increase in advertising revenues.

Sky Television, he said, "was our largest risk undertaking, perhaps ever."

He ended by thanking Richard Searby for his wise counsel, "and for keeping me out of trouble from time to time." As he sat down, he looked and sounded exhausted.

Searby asked the meeting if there were any questions. There was a short silence. No one stood. No one raised a hand. There were no questions.

That evening Richard Searby rounded off the day as guest of honor at a dinner at the Hilton. He made a rather cryptic speech in which he discussed the problems of citizenship and international businesses such as News. He ended by referring to Athens in the fifth century B.C.: "Alcibiades, a real mover and shaker, was ostracized and Socrates was sentenced to death." This classical reference was unclear. Could it be that these were Rupert Murdoch's role models? Searby did not say.

Meanwhile, Lucifer, or Alcibiades or Socrates—or Rupert—had soared away again, to Sydney, to London, to New York, to Los Angeles, his visit to the financial heart of the empire completed in twenty-four hours.

Part IV

THE VILLAGE

11

THE EVIL EMPIRE

On the evening of January 21, 1990, a Gulfstream executive jet circled in the dark over Bucharest. The passengers could see no lights, no sign of an airport, let alone of a town. Less than a month had elapsed since the execution of the Ceauşescus, still less since the end of the bloody resistance by Ceauşescu's secret police.

As the plane taxied to a halt, the passengers and crew stared into the darkness. At first there was nothing. "It was like landing on the moon," said one of them later. And then they saw dozens of headlights stabbing toward them through the dark. It felt a bit like a roundup and, remembering the brutal fighting in the streets of Bucharest only a few weeks earlier, some of those on board wondered whether they should not take off again at once.

When the door was opened and the steps lowered, the plane was surrounded by men in thick coats and fur hats. Above the head-lights, TV arc lights were switched on. As the passengers descended they were smothered in unexpected embraces. Nothing like that had happened in Warsaw, in Prague or in Budapest, from which they had just flown. But this was Latin Romania. And the man stepping out of the plane was Rupert Murdoch, entering into yet another battlefield in his lifelong war to become communications czar of the world.

*   *   *

The collapse of communism in Eastern Europe in the closing months of 1989 was one of the most startling upheavals in recent history. Murdoch believed it was a triumph for the communications revolution. "Eastern Europe," he had declared in a speech in Washington in 1988, "will be opened up by television, which in turn will certainly change the lives of tens of millions of people. Global communications will prove to be the biggest catalyst for peaceful coexistence. Perhaps that is already happening."

He thought that as an immigrant to America he could more easily recognize a great truth: "Modernization is Americanization. It is the American way of organizing society that is prevailing in the world." What Murdoch perhaps failed to recognize was the fear and alarm that this undoubted truth could provoke in many societies. The only fear he had was of an "atavistic, authoritarian response. This is the real danger in the present revolution. We might be panicked by future shock into one of the inappropriate and regressive schemes of regulation that are always lurking about."

His tour of the battlefields had begun in Warsaw. The party was not large. First there was Anna, who on this trip through the debris behind the Iron Curtain was said to be collecting material for a new novel. She had recently become a member of the board of News Corp.

After the Murdochs, the most senior member of the News organization on the flight was John Evans, whom Murdoch had now made vice-president for corporate development. Evans was the man who decided which dark caves of the future Murdoch should try to explore. He liked to see the new world just over the horizon as a communications heaven, one in which all old orders would change forever. Among the others aboard was Kelvin MacKenzie, the editor of the *Sun,* whose sense of comedy had his fellow travelers rolling in the narrow aisle of the plane. He did constant impersonations of Andy Capp, the working-class cartoon hero, and would frequently knock ash off the end of an imaginary cigarette cupped in his hand as he delivered a homily on the way of the world.

This expeditionary force flew out of London to Warsaw, to Prague and to Budapest before Bucharest, looking at the newly liberated newspapers and television stations, bearing gifts of fax machines and coffee.

In Prague Murdoch gave an interview in which he said that events in Eastern Europe "are the last chapter in the history of the evil empire. It is one of the most hopeful moments in history."

Reminded that he used to be a liberal and even sported a bust of Lenin at Oxford, Murdoch replied, "I was young and even had other harebrained ideas." He agreed with the maxim that a man who is not a socialist at twenty has no heart, while one who is still a socialist at forty has no head, adding:

> But I have always been of the opinion that it is extremely important that everyone should have the same chance, the same opportunity. . . . A really first-rate society must not close the door to anyone.
>
> When I was young I was of the opinion that everything that we want to achieve must be absolutely perfect. Nowadays I know that nothing in this world is perfect, that we only have to aim for the best possible. Real democracy must have both economic and political substance; one cannot exist without the other.

Murdoch was one of several Western publishers seeking investment opportunities in Eastern Europe. Wherever he went, Robert Maxwell had gone before. Indeed, throughout the years of communist dictatorship, Maxwell had fawned upon the area's straps. He had praised General Jaruzelski and condemned Solidarity in Poland. He had serenaded the Czechoslovak President Gustav Husák, who had crushed the Prague Spring of 1968 and imprisoned Václav Havel, as "this impressive man" who "had brought stability and economic progress to his country."

The title of the book he had published on the Bulgarian despot was *Todor Zhivkov: Statesman and Builder of Modern Bulgaria*. In its foreword he wrote that the book was intended to show the Bulgarian people's "heroic struggle . . . to build a prosperous and happy nation under the leadership of the Bulgarian Communist Party and its General Secretary Todor Zhivkov."

"What has, in your opinion, made you so popular with the Romanian people?" he had asked Nicolae Ceaușescu in an interview included in *Ceaucescu: Builder of Modern Romania and International Statesman,* published in Pergamon's "World Leaders" series (general editor Robert Maxwell).

By 1990, with the Soviet empire in collapse, other men might have been abashed by such a record of servility to dictators now dead or deposed. But shame was alien to Maxwell. He was now trawling the new democratic Eastern Europe for investment opportunities as energetically as he had when his former friends had been in power. Somewhat to Murdoch's chagrin, he was being welcomed back.

From Prague, Murdoch's plane made the short flight to Hungary. At the airport in Budapest, they were met by the Hungarian representative of News Corp, Peter Toke, the editor of the weekly newspaper *Reform* and the daily *Mai Nap*. On an earlier visit in 1989, Murdoch had already agreed to buy these two newspapers and had thus become the first Westerner to acquire a significant investment in the new free press of Eastern Europe. Indeed, the signing of the final documents was the original reason for this whole trip.

Reform had the sort of popular pizzazz that Murdoch liked. This splashy color tabloid featured an endless parade of nudes along with stories on political corruption and reform. Soft-porn stars, the Princess of Wales, the legacy of the Hungarian Revolution, and Soviet responsibility for the Katyn massacre were all topics in one issue. Toke described himself as "the Magyar Murdoch," and had persuaded the American one to invest in his paper.

Now, when they went into the newspaper's office, said Anna Murdoch, "there was something very familiar" there. "It was an old dress boutique turned into an office. They'd hung a wonderful Hungarian flag, and they're very lively, very interested in things, being journalists. That was really very exciting. You felt: this is really going to work."

Murdoch flicked through some of the recent back numbers. According to Peter Smith, an engineer from Adelaide who had known Murdoch since the 1950s and had worked for him for about six years, Murdoch actually criticized some of the naked women, whose poses were more explicit than those on page three of the *Sun*. Murdoch said he liked to distinguish between pretty girls and sex.

Anna Murdoch later said that the landing in Bucharest was "surreal." Describing the darkness and the snow, she said, "It was just like a le Carré novel. These cars just came across the ice towards the plane, with TV lights, et cetera, most of the Romanian men with heavy fur hats on and beards. It was marvelous."

The next morning they were taken to Ceauşescu's home, a suburban villa where the bathrobes were still in closets, the toothpaste tubes still in the bathroom and papers still in his office. They went also to an orphanage. This was largely Anna's idea and she found it moving: "Little children were running up to any woman saying, 'Mama, mama,' putting their hands around your legs. Very sad. I asked them about the selling of babies to the West. The doctor in charge said: we are not selling children; all the money given went to pay lawyers' fees."

Anna found the whole city extraordinary. "It was amazing to see young soldiers the age of my son with AK-47s, clicking the bolts and listening to rock music," she said. "Only one little incident need take place and they'd blow up. It was very nerve-racking. And very sad."

They went to the television station, where the revolution had been fomented. The station was seized by the revolutionaries, and from tiny Studio Four, extraordinary exhortations and events were broadcast continuously to the nation after the dictator's fall. Often a helmeted soldier stood with his rifle behind the announcer. Over and over, the people of Bucharest were asked to come and protect the television station from Ceauşescu's armed supporters. All in all, it was the classic type of television-led revolution that Murdoch might have dreamed.

But in its wake came the threat of another kind of mayhem. After Murdoch picked his way around the smashed building, he offered the broadcasters access to Sky News and sports. A senior broadcasting official told him that that was not enough—what they really wanted was a powerful transmitter to beam their programming to ethnic Romanians in Soviet Moldavia. "We must get them back," the official said. "The last ounce of blood into our country."

As the world is homogenized by just such organizations as News, nationalism may well become one of the overwhelming, killing forces of the twenty-first century.

On the evening of January 22 Murdoch and his party boarded the Gulfstream again to fly back to the West. They were suffering from culture shock. It seemed clear to them all, particularly to Murdoch, that working in the new Eastern Europe would be commercially difficult.

Murdoch believed that, in the war against communism, Western businessmen deserved much more praise than intellectuals and journalists who had too often given the communists the benefit of the doubt. "There is now no social model anywhere on earth," he said, "to compete with that developed in the English-speaking world. . . . [It] is composed of popular elections, limited government, a rule of law, private property and free markets." For three generations it had been derided as mere "bourgeois democracy" by journalists, politicians and "chatterers" who also insisted that socialism worked and its people had better values. "At least, that was what I learned and believed at Oxford and at Geelong Grammar. But it was all lies. Many people were clear-sighted enough to know, but only a few people were courageous enough to say so and suffer the exclusion and derision of the chattering classes."

From Bucharest they flew to Milan, where they were to meet Silvio Berlusconi, another lord of the global information village. Berlusconi was a man whom Murdoch admired and must to an extent have envied. He owned the fourth-largest private television network in the world after CBS, NBC and ABC; one of the largest of Italian stores, Standa, which had 400 outlets; 305 movie theaters; the rights to a huge library of Hollywood classics; and a soccer team, A. C. Milan. His company, Fininvest, had an annual turnover of $11 billion.

Much of the programming on his network was similar, sometimes identical, to that which Murdoch used on Sky Television: American game shows and minor soaps, plus "Dallas," "Dynasty" and various Latin American *telenovelas*. His most famous show was called "Calpo Grosso," a game in which Italian housewives took off their clothes.

Berlusconi was ahead of Murdoch in the East European market. He had reached agreement with the Soviet Union in 1988 to have the exclusive right to package West European advertising material for Soviet television. Fininvest had an office in Prague and Berlusconi was negotiating with both Poland and Hungary to set up a new television station in each.

The meeting had been arranged in order for Murdoch and Berlusconi to be able to get to know each other better. There were no joint ventures as yet. But they had a lot in common.

After lunch, members of the Murdoch entourage flew in different directions to Spain, Luxembourg and elsewhere. Murdoch and Anna flew to Britain. As they approached Heathrow, Anna said, "I never thought I'd be so glad to see London again."

The next day, January 24, the *Sun* ran a passionate editorial saying that Britain should become much more deeply involved in Eastern Europe. Otherwise the Germans would take it all. That same day Murdoch went around to Downing Street to see Mrs. Thatcher. He told her the same.

LONDON

The new decade began with serious constraints upon News' vast and astonishing expansion. Australian Ratings downgraded News Corp's debt, for the second time, and Morgan Stanley International downgraded profit forecasts for News and put a sell recommendation on the stock; only a few months before, the bank had been touting Murdoch as a man to back.

News' earnings per share had fallen by 78 percent in the quarter ending September 30. The share price was diving—in New York it fell from $27 to $17 in just six months. News Corp's 1990 profits were expected to be even lower than in 1989. Ansett Airlines had been badly damaged by an Australian pilots' strike. Newspaper sales in Australia and the U.K. were sagging. Debt-service costs were astronomical. And Sky was a tremendous drain. News Corp's leverage—the ratio of debt to equity—was now a high 1.85, and net interest coverage was around 1.6. Banks begin to get nervous when net interest cover falls below 2. Financial analysts argued whether the debt was even higher than those figures the company acknowledged; it should have included the A$1.5 billion attached to Murdoch's book publishing vehicle, HarperCollins, which he had split off after the failure of Media Partners International.

At the beginning of 1990, News Corp declared its assets to be worth A$19 billion. But of these, almost half were made up of intangibles such as publishing rights, newspaper mastheads and television franchises. Their actual market values were much harder to assess accurately than pieces of property—witness the helter-skelter changes in the prices of Australian television stations in the past few years.

Moreover, the Australian government was threatening to tighten up its accountancy rules, in particular on the valuation of intangible assets. This could certainly cramp Murdoch's regular practice of revaluing his assets to enable him to borrow more. The last revaluation in 1987 had added A$600 million to the value of News Corp assets. At the start of 1990, a new revaluation was expected to add at least another A$2 billion to the declared value of the company.

It looked as if Murdoch's magic was beginning, for the first time, to wear very slightly thin on the fund managers and analysts whom he had dazzled for so long.

In Australia, the Hawke government was showing signs of strain as the economy went into recession. The airline pilots' strike had seriously harmed the underlying economy and tourism, as well as leaving Ansett and Australian Airlines with serious losses. In Sydney, Frank Devine became the latest editor of the *Australian* to be removed. Among his errors, he had supported the pilots' strike and had also shown antipathy toward the management of News in Australia. But Devine did not rail against Murdoch; he stayed on the paper as a columnist.

In America, Fox Broadcasting continued to gather audiences and planned to extend its nine hours of programming to fifteen hours a week, the level set by the Federal Communications Commission as the threshold of a "network." Although Fox was expanding, and wished to be seen as the fourth network, Murdoch and Barry Diller were anxious to avoid its being defined as such, for then it would fall under one of the few remaining pieces of communications regulation, the so-called fin-syn rules. These limited the freedom of a network to produce its own shows and benefit from their subsequent syndication. Such rules were fatal to the synergies Murdoch was striving to create. As so often, he was seeking waivers.

The greatest problems were in London. The press, both "populars" and "unpopulars," was alarmed by the growing criticisms of tabloid intrusions and abuses of power. There was a real fear that the process of sanitizing the "populars" could devastate press freedom in Britain.

Both Murdoch and MacKenzie gave evidence to the committee set up by the government to review press conduct. MacKenzie presented thirty recent issues of the *Sun*—each, he said, fit for his maiden aunt. He and Murdoch both argued that any new statutory machinery was unnecessary now that the tabloids had reformed themselves.

Twenty editors signed a new Editors' Code, in which they pledged themselves to show respect for privacy, made a commitment to pursue stories "by straightforward means" and expressed a readiness to grant a right of reply, where reasonable. Legislation was avoided for the moment.

By now the *Sun's* circulation had fallen from 4.3 million a day to 3.87 million. The *Mirror* combined its own sales with those of its Scottish sister paper, the *Daily Record,* and claimed to be ahead.

The *Mirror* had already installed color. Murdoch had never believed that color sold papers, but now he had reluctantly agreed to play catch-up-to-Maxwell for the first time in his life; Wapping was being reequipped with new color MAN presses from Germany. Some of his executives felt that this £500 million investment was a mistake and that News should instead contract printing out, as the *Independent* did. To John Evans, with his vision of an electronic digital world, investing £500 million to run crushed trees through a vast plant of iron bars was to spit in the face of the future.

To supervise all of the Wapping operations, Murdoch appointed a new chairman of News International, Andrew Knight. This caused some astonishment, since Knight seemed to many the antithesis of everything for which Murdoch stood. Murdoch had made a career out of contempt for "the British Establishment"; Knight had spent his life as part of it. A good-looking and impeccably dressed man, Knight was not without distinction. Most of his journalistic career had been spent on the *Economist,* where as editor for eleven years, he had tripled the circulation. He rode the Concorde back and forth to the United States and saw himself as the European interpreter of leading American politicians; he considered Henry Kissinger a close friend. He and his wife, Sabiha, gave important dinner parties.

He came to Murdoch from helping the Canadian entrepreneur Conrad Black buy and rescue Telegraph Newspapers. Knight's languid style was not much appreciated at the *Telegraph* and Black had been enraged by what he saw as Knight's inappropriate courtship of Murdoch. Knight left with £14 million of Telegraph stock.

One of Knight's principal tasks was to ensure that Sky was exempted from the Broadcasting Bill, which was now passing through Parliament. He was to assure the House of Lords and others that Murdoch was not a ravening beast but a delightful human being who wanted nothing more than to be able to work in a market economy. He also had the difficult task of both controlling the behavior of the tabloids and trying to halt their fall in circulation.

In an interview with the *Financial Times,* Knight praised Murdoch as "the greatest newspaper publisher in the world." News, he said, was "superbly run," but Murdoch had "so many balls in the air that he wants—and I think it's a very healthy thing—someone to catch some of them for him." Knight also argued that the quest for quality was essential; with more and more papers in competition, only the best would survive. Newspapers, he said, were like oil wells—they had depleting reserves but could generate a lot of cash if well run.

Like the *Sun* and the *News of the World,* the *Sunday Times* was a money-maker. Murdoch and its editor, Andrew Neil, had their differences, but Murdoch had no interest in changing its formula. The *Times* was another matter. It had been made more "popular" under the editorship of Charles Wilson, but this had not halted its losses. On March 12, Murdoch told Wilson that he wanted a new editor. Wilson was shocked; in his farewell to the journalists, he said he felt he was being sent to the gulag. Murdoch put him in charge of new projects in Eastern Europe. Wilson left to work for Robert Maxwell.

In his place, Murdoch appointed Simon Jenkins, the thoughtful and somewhat iconoclastic star columnist of the *Sunday Times*. An author as well as a journalist, he had previously been editor of the *Evening Standard*, was highly regarded by his peers and had received many awards. Although married to a Texan film actress, Gayle Hunnicutt, he was perhaps the most English editor Murdoch had ever appointed.

Jenkins thought the *Times* should be quieter, should no longer try to appeal to the fundamentalist right wing and needed fewer huge headlines and less blatant Thatcherite propaganda. However, Jenkins did not want Murdoch to feel uncertain with him as he had with Harry Evans, and so he assured him that while he would freely criticize the Conservative government, he would never propose that readers vote Labour or Social Democrat. He fired some of the more predictable columnists, ordered longer stories and smaller headlines and began to improve the quality of the writing. He felt that for the first time Murdoch was seeking a degree of respectability in Britain.

In early 1990, Murdoch decided that he would take personal charge of Sky, which was still losing £2 million a week. "It's my big gamble and I'd better see it through," he said. He gave Sky a five-year commitment.

BSB (Sky's competing network) was finally about to take to the air. At last the "Star Wars" predicted by the popular papers were about to begin. BSB had been beset by both technical and financial troubles. For a time at the end of 1989 it had seemed that Murdoch's attempt to undermine confidence in it might have succeeded. But in January 1990, the four main shareholders pledged a new £900 million funding package to add to the £423 million already committed. The amount of money was extraordinary and, as the *Financial Times* pointed out, it was being committed with very little security.

Sky, said BSB's chief executive, Anthony Simmonds Gooding, was now looking down the barrel of "a well-funded gun." But Murdoch had had more lives than most cats and he was by now seen, as the *Guardian* put it, so much as "the master of mass communications" that his swoop back to London to take personal control of Sky was daunting for BSB.

The Sky team was lean, young and dedicated. By contrast, BSB was burdened with a big, highly paid management. They behaved like established fat cats, spending huge amounts of money on office furniture, cars, lunches and the other accoutrements of the good life. Two granite desks in the hall cost over £70,000. They insisted that they were also going to spend much more on programs than Sky—some £200 million in the first year—and they claimed that they had a far superior movie channel. To most people, there would probably be very little to choose between the two lists of movies; each offered both talent and trash. Sky also had Eurosport; Sky One, its least taxing channel; and Sky News, which was earning grudging approval from those who disapproved of Murdoch.

In April 1990, fifteen months after Sky had launched, BSB started its direct broadcasts. The launch was a fiasco. BSB could not even supply the stores with demonstration receivers. BSB needed to sell around 700,000 receivers in the weeks before Christmas. Sky already had about 750,000 dishes installed.

BSB executives and shareholders could be forgiven for feeling chagrined. When the company had been awarded the national franchise for direct satellite broadcasts to Britain in 1986, no satellite competition was expected. As it staggered onto the air, BSB campaigned hard to pressure the government to bring Sky under the regulations of the pending Broadcasting Bill.

Under the existing Broadcasting Act (1981), no national newspaper proprietor or non-EC shareholder could control more than 20 percent of a British television company. The 1990 Broadcasting Bill was to include new terrestrial franchises and also satellite broadcasts, but legislation did not include broadcasts from medium-power satellites such as *Astra*.

As part of its campaign to have this loophole closed, BSB began to circulate British "opinion formers" with glossy personal attacks upon Murdoch. "Who do you think will be the most influential person in Britain in the 1990s?" was one question posed under portraits of leading British politicians—and Murdoch. At least politicians were elected, BSB declared. "They don't buy their way to power."

Complaining that Sky had escaped regulation by a piece of "technological wizardry," BSB's advertising also condemned the blatant promotion of Sky in News International's papers. One thirty-one-page document was called *Raising Kane;* it carried a picture of Orson Welles as Citizen Kane on its cover. BSB sought to convince people that the real Murdoch was as terrifying as the fictional Kane.

BSB argued—and in this it was correct—that Sky was now no longer a pan-European channel but an attempt to smash British broadcasting. It was driven by Murdoch's personal obsession with the idea that the British system was unforgivably "elitist" and that the British people were all desperate for American or Australian programming. Despite the lobbying, the Thatcher government exempted Sky from the controls of the new act.

In an attempt to improve his British image, Murdoch announced that News was giving £3 million to fund the Murdoch Chair in Language and Communications at Oxford. This news, coming on the day the *Sun* was once again censured by the Press Council—this time for calling homosexuals "poofters"—aroused some mirth among his critics.

Meanwhile, the world's economy was beginning to slide downhill. United States banks started calling in loans. Then the American advertising market began to slump into the worst recession in decades.

During the summer of 1990, the Sky-BSB battle to sell dishes increased in ferocity. BSB was thought to be losing £8 million a week, Sky still £2 million. The banks warned BSB that unless it had signed up a significant number of customers by Christmas, the next installment of operating capital, due in the new year, would be withdrawn.

At this point John Veronis, who had brokered the deal between Murdoch and Annenberg over *TV Guide*, entered the fray. He had been shocked to discover how confused ordinary people were about the two systems. He arranged a meeting between Peter Davis of Reed International and Murdoch. They discussed a merger, but Murdoch showed no eagerness to make terms with his enemy.

In July 1990, Max Newton, the first editor of the *Australian,* onetime brothel keeper and pornographer, more recently Murdoch's economics pundit on the New York *Post,* and prolific writer, died of a stroke in Florida. He was sixty-one.

In his tribute, Murdoch said that Max was "one of the most colourful, prolific and brilliant journalists Australia has produced. Max was a man of extremes. He had both more friends and more enemies than any other living person. . . ."

Any account written by Max about his own life would have been dominated by sex, drink—and his relationship with Murdoch. These three demons together had virtually destroyed him in the past. But, thanks to Murdoch, his last decade in America was his most productive and stable ever, and right up to his death he was obsessed with trying to prove his value to his employer. Max Newton was obviously an extreme case, but many others in News Corp all over the world were bound to Murdoch by similar ties of gratitude, admiration, fear and a kind of longing that was never quite satisfied.

When his third wife saw Max for the last time, lying in his casket, she took many photographs, "and, as I kissed him goodbye, I slipped his platinum American Express card into his pocket, just in case."

But it was Rupert Murdoch, not Max Newton, who really needed credit at this time.

NEW YORK

When he was later trying to explain how he felt when News was nearly destroyed at the end of 1990, Murdoch quoted a verse from Rudyard Kipling. Kipling, he said, was the poet laureate of the British empire, and "nowadays I have a lot more sympathy for embattled empires!"

> The toad beneath the harrow knows
> Exactly where each tooth-point goes;
> The butterfly upon the road
> Preaches contentment to that toad.

Murdoch said that the near destruction of News and his desperate attempts to restructure it at the end of 1990 and in early 1991, made him feel just like that toad, expecting at every moment to be crushed.

The crisis stemmed from his refusal ever to finance expansion by share issues. He had always been determined never to relinquish control and to preserve his family's 45 percent shareholding. Until 1990 he had seemed invincible—in both his own eyes and those of his lenders. Since his victory over the British print unions in 1986–87, News Corporation's revenues and profits before interest had doubled, and its assets had quadrupled—but his new debt had also increased fourfold. Until the end of the 1980s, bankers had been on their knees to Murdoch, begging him to take their cash. By mid-1990 the climate had cooled.

The crisis began to loom early in 1990 as the euphoria of the political revolutions of 1989 was followed by an international recession of unexpected severity. One of the earliest warnings of a liquidity crisis came in the first half of 1990, when the Japanese suddenly withdrew from the short-term money market in Australia. News Corporation had a line of credit of up to A$200 million in this market, where it was in the habit of borrowing overnight, seven-day or thirty-day money. Suddenly this credit line was gone.

By the middle of 1990, the orderly retreat of the banks had turned into a rout. The lending markets had never seemed so dry. The banks themselves were under great pressure as a result of their earlier sprees. "We were dealing with a very fragile banking system," Murdoch said.

Through the previous decade he had devoted himself to acquisitions, and left debt management to his chief financial officer of more than a decade, Richard Sarazen. "We thought we had the year covered," Murdoch later recalled, "though we knew we were tight." But in June 1990 the problems became acute.

The company tried to refinance a short-term bank loan of $750 million which it had raised in December 1989 and which was due for repayment on June 30. News had expected to pay back the loan, as it usually did, out of asset sales. But it was becoming increasingly difficult to sell assets at a reasonable price. And so, at the end of June, News Corp tried to secure a three-year loan to refinance it, but found that impossible to arrange. The company paid back $250 million and asked its bankers to roll over the other $500 million for another three months. With various degrees of reluctance, they agreed.

Richard Sarazen was replaced by Dave DeVoe, only the third chief financial officer since the 1960s. The new man inherited an unenviable task, one which devoured the next eighteen months of his life. In the summer of 1990, News Corp began to enter its slide toward what seemed to many like oblivion. In its annual report for the year ending June 30, 1990, News showed massive losses and equally massive short-term debts. The drain of Sky seemed unending. The accounts also showed that News Corp had just revalued its own assets upward by A$3 billion. The largest salary was shown to be A$12.74 million. Many people assumed this was Murdoch's; in fact, it was Barry Diller's. Murdoch's salary was under A$3 million.

In London, the company had trouble paying its bills for the retooling of Wapping. All over the world, shareholders and institutions began to sell News Corp shares. The banks started to panic. They had lent recklessly; now they wanted to lower their exposure. Standard Chartered Bank suddenly called in money from News — "Bang," said Murdoch, "we were given ten minutes. I went to see the chairman, et cetera, but they were apologetic and said they didn't have the freedom to lend the money. They had their own problems."

Subsequently Murdoch tried to explain to a group of bank presidents just what it had felt like to be a toad. "From my humble reptilian perspective," he had had to watch, aghast, as the shafts of the harrow had come plunging down, one after another, through the autumn and winter of 1990–91.

He had been carried away by his own enthusiasms. He admitted that he had been so busy with acquisitions that he had not paid enough attention to what was going on around him or around the world. Between 1985 and 1991 News had grown from total assets of A$3.5 billion to A$24 billion.

However, he had recently made some good sales too. News' travel magazines had gone for 140 percent more than he had paid for them just three and a half years earlier. News' 50 percent of American *Elle* had fetched $160 million, only two years after a start-up costing $5 million, and the supermarket tabloid the *Star*, into which he said he had only ever invested $9 million, had netted over $400 million.

In mid-1990 Murdoch believed that these and other sales were enough to stabilize News' capital structure. He thought that real interest rates were historically high and that short-term financing was therefore preferable. He believed that he could continue to expand printing capacity with lease finance. He did not expect that there was going to be one of the severest advertising recessions in recent history, a banking crisis in America, liquidity squeezes in the U.K. and Australia and a war in the Persian Gulf — all on top of the appallingly costly competition with BSB.

Murdoch said also that News Corp had always lived on "the risk frontier" — after all, that was how the company had grown from a small afternoon paper in Australia's fourth city to a worldwide empire in less than forty years. News Corp had "hopped" a great deal in that period, and for most of the way the banks had hopped happily along beside it. The experience of 1990–91 taught Murdoch "that the fates of all of us—toads, butterflies and banks—are inextricably interlocked. We need the banks. And banks, if they are to make their way in a changing financial environment, need strong relationships with toads who know which way to hop."

When News Corporation's annual results were published in August 1990, "they showed us with a lot of short-term debt, which shocked the market," Murdoch said—$2.3 billion, to be precise, six times that of the previous year. Murdoch had made a serious mistake. He had expected short-term rates to go down and had therefore kept a lot of borrowings in short-term loans ready to be changed into long-term debt when it became cheaper. Instead, all rates had risen sharply.

Many Australian corporations were in trouble. In September, Bond Corporation announced Australia's biggest ever corporate loss of £1 billion and Alan Bond at last resigned. That month News shares fell by 25 percent and it seemed that the market's love affair with Murdoch was over. The cruelest cut was that some analysts remarked that the shares in Maxwell Communications were holding up better than those of News—not knowing then that Maxwell was illegally supporting them.

At the end of September, the company faced unprecedented difficulties in either repaying or rescheduling a $500 million short-term loan. This was the first time that Murdoch had found himself in such a position. He had always prided himself on—and the banks had always toasted him for—the fact that he had met every single payment on schedule for almost forty years. Worse still, some $2.9 billion of debt was due to mature between September 1990 and the middle of 1991. One banker described News Corporation's situation to the *Financial Times* as "somewhat terminal."

The banks very unhappily granted the September 30 roll, for one more month, but only on condition that News Corp agree to rearrange its jungle of debt and adopt a sensible business plan. Citibank, as News' largest creditor, was charged with unraveling the mess and restructuring the company. The project, code-named "Dolphin," was put in the hands of a thirty-four-year-old vice-president of the bank, Ann Lane. In the next few months Murdoch came to depend on Lane as he had on no one else in his life.

Lane was a slim, well-dressed young woman with a firm handshake, short dark hair and blue eyes that looked straight at you. Born and brought up in New Jersey, the oldest child in a "crazy family," she attended Berkeley and then spent several years in finance before joining Citibank in 1982.

She had spent the first part of 1990 restructuring Donald Trump's company. She found Murdoch a welcome change. As she began to understand News, Lane came to admire Murdoch and to like him. She realized also that she faced a restructuring unparalleled in size and scope. In Murdoch's frantic dash, News had borrowed from all over the world—Australia, the U.K., Japan, the Netherlands, the United States, Singapore, Hong Kong, India and many other places besides. There were hundreds of different News Corp companies; each one had different guarantees and different types of loans.

With the help of Dave DeVoe, whose role on News Corp's side was critical, Lane found that the main banks had sold loans on and on, and that News Corp now owed money to 146 financial institutions. The money was in ten different currencies. Lane and her team were continually asking themselves and News Corp people, "Where are we? Where are the companies? Where are the lenders? What do we have? What's everyone's relative position? Where are they negotiating from?" News Corp's financial and organizational charts looked like nightmare wiring circuits assembled by a Frankenstein.

As Lane began to compile the information, News Corp's share price went into free-fall. The Australian Stock Exchange demanded an explanation. "What's happened to our share price?" Murdoch asked. "The history of the world over the last three months has happened to our share price." The more complicated it all appeared, the simpler Lane knew the solution had to be. She could not afford to allow alternatives or choices—there were so many layers that the participants would talk the whole thing into oblivion. What she had to do was to deliver the company and reduce its debt. Every bank and financial institution, *every one,* had to roll over loans to give Murdoch time. And she had also to tie down News and Murdoch himself. That would not be easy. She realized that until now, Murdoch had always run the company like an Australian Red Baron, by the seat of his pants.

In early October, Murdoch flew to Australia for the annual general meeting of News. While there, he merged his morning and afternoon papers in Sydney and Melbourne. This meant the death of the Melbourne *Herald,* which he had watched his father build. When, predictably, he was asked if this hurt, he insisted, equally predictably, that it did not.

In Australia, the extent of Murdoch's political reach and power once more came under scrutiny. At a packed meeting in the Sydney Opera House, the novelist Thomas Keneally was enthusiastically applauded when he said, "We don't want an unofficial minister of information." Keneally thought Murdoch could not help his acquisitive nature; he was like a killer who pleads, "Stop me before I kill again." He needed help in the form of government regulation. Amongst the other speakers, Eric Beecher said that in his job as editor of the Melbourne *Herald,* "I found my sense of journalistic morality being questioned and tested very regularly." Asked to comment, Piers Akerman, the editor of Murdoch's newly merged Melbourne *Sun-Herald,* said he thought Murdoch was "without doubt the most preeminent newspaper man in the world."

❖   ❖   ❖

By the second half of October, Lane and her team had divided the banks into three tiers. Tier I consisted of nine banks that were major lenders and had made it clear that they would not provide new loans on their own. They wanted any new monies necessary to keep the company functioning to come from a broader group of banks.

In Tier II there were about thirty banks, which were to join the Tier I banks as new moneylenders. Tier III banks were in for no new money and, because they were the smallest investors, many of them thought that their participation was not vital. Lane would not agree.

As she was trying to corral the banks, Lane had to whip News Corporation into order. She insisted the company come up with a sound business plan based on what it thought its various companies could earn.

To hear members of her team tell it, people at News started to panic. News Corp was a company that had never known serious financial covenants. The whole company's ethos was to wing it. Ann Lane wanted to put a stake through the company's heart.

Almost twenty-four hours a day Lane stormed around her office in an Armani suit and old sneakers, shouting people into line. She demanded a fully developed and defensible business plan that would allow the loans to be extended and would provide enough cash flow to cover both the increased interest rate paid by News and a $600 million one-year bridge loan—and also the $1.4 billion debt amortization over three years. She warned them they would be held to the plan, so they had better understand its assumptions.

In the end, the summary of the plan was the size of a phone book. As it was written, Lane and her team were still struggling to understand the debt situation. It was all so complex that she decided the only possible solution was a simple override agreement.

This had just two principles:

1. We are where we are.
2. Nobody gets out.

"We are where we are" was hard for the banks to swallow. It meant some people would remain better off than others. "Nobody gets out" was equally tough, particularly for some of the smaller banks, who had little idea of what they were in. But Lane knew there was no other way. If just one bank got out, the other 145 institutions would swamp the exits.

When Lane and her team went to News with her plan, the first thing News executives asked was "What is Plan B?" She looked her questioners in the eye and said, "There is no Plan B." She told the banks the same. She knew that if anyone thought there was the remotest chance of a fallback position, everyone would want to fall back. Lane was playing hardball. If they failed, it would be a catastrophe. Lane and her team would lose for Citibank, which had a large investment in the company. Murdoch would lose the empire.

Ann Lane took her plan to the Tier I banks in a series of meetings on October 31 and November 1. The fantastic losses of Sky were still the greatest problem. Citibank was able to tell the bankers that Murdoch had agreed that Sky should merge with BSB. This news was crucial in getting the banks to accept the plan.

The merger had not been easily negotiated, even though BSB losses were even greater than those of Sky. By the end of September, BSB had sold at most 120,000 squarials, far below its target. At the *Financial Times,* Frank Barlow, the chief executive, had always been skeptical about BSB and he now believed that merger was essential.

John Veronis intervened again. Each side denied inviting him in, but he shuttled constantly between them and eventually collected a fee of $1 million from each, considerably less than he asked. He talked to Peter Davis at Reed, who said BSB was still interested in discussing a deal, and he called Murdoch in Australia. Murdoch said he could not get back for a fortnight, so Davis' deputy, Ian Irvine, flew there and met in secret with Murdoch. On October 15 and 16, a basic deal was worked out. It was to be a fifty-fifty merger designed to unify the company, stem losses and maximize profits.

At BSB, Simmonds Gooding was told almost nothing. At Sky's headquarters, many people feared that the company was about to be shut down.

After Murdoch and Irvine had come to a tentative agreement, further secret talks were held. Andrew Knight led for News until Murdoch could join them.

The discussions were not easy—many BSB people saw Sky as an example of Murdoch philistinism; Sky considered BSB to be filled with effete British fat cats. BSB thought Murdoch had destroyed it, and that without Sky it would have succeeded.

The Sky men pointed out that BSB's *Marco Polo* satellite had only four channels, whereas *Astra's* were almost unlimited. The Disney Channel was coming onto *Astra,* as was CNN. Had it not been Murdoch, it would have been someone else. Sky thought that BSB deserved to die.

Murdoch and the four chairmen of the BSB consortium had dinner in London, but negotiations subsequently broke down. Murdoch was still reluctant to compromise. Although it was he who had created this competition, he had a visceral dislike of BSB, and wanted to win the battle outright. Without the pressure from his banks, he would have fought on. The blackout on the talks was still total. On October 29 Murdoch went secretly to Downing Street to meet Margaret Thatcher. He said later that they talked about international affairs and that he mentioned the impending merger only in an offhand comment at the end of their chat. He knew that the merger would throw British broadcasting into turmoil, and that it needed the government's acquiescence. BSB did not have the right to give its franchise away to Sky.

On November 2, final details of the deal were negotiated. Murdoch brought his nineteen-year-old son, Lachlan, to the signing. "His son is learning the ropes and he witnessed a deal that probably has saved the empire," ran a New York *Times* article.

Simmonds Gooding was summarily dismissed. Ian Irvine was

named as chairman of the new venture. Sam Chisholm, Sky's tough Australian chief executive, became chief executive officer. An executive committee was made up of Murdoch, Ian Irvine, Frank Barlow of Pearson and Andrew Knight. News now controlled almost 50 percent of the new company, Granada 11 percent, Chargeurs 10.5 percent, Pearson 11 percent, Reed International 10.5 percent, Bond Corporation 3.5 percent and others 3.5 percent.

At first the merged channels would be broadcast on both systems, but eventually *Astra,* Sky's satellite, would prevail. The deal was designed to compensate for the market position Sky had reached; BSB was required to furnish at once an extra £70 million and News International a further £30 million. In substance it was a Murdoch victory.

Both relief and outrage greeted the news of the deal. The relief was felt by Murdoch's bankers and all others seeking to preserve News International. The outrage was more publicly expressed by his enemies. The merger was announced only days after the new Broadcasting Act was approved. The government had refused to include News within the terms of the act, on the grounds that *Astra* operated from Luxembourg. Yet again, Murdoch seemed to have thumbed his nose at government regulations. Sky would still be a pirate ship.

In effect Murdoch—admittedly under financial duress—had at last seized control of a British television station, BSB, and was now daring the authorities to deny it to him. Lord Thompson, the former IBA chairman, described the merger as a characteristically "brutal Wapping in outer space." The home secretary acknowledged that the deal was not technically legal; the Labour Party could therefore claim that the merger made a mockery of the new Broadcasting Act. Murdoch replied, "Well, they would, wouldn't they? The fact is, they hate the idea of a competitive society, and it is only companies like ours that have the guts and strength to risk everything in building a competitor to the existing monopoly. That's what we are still about." Subsequently, he said that his defeat of BSB was "my outstanding achievement as a journalist."

The merger of Sky and BSB coincided with a fierce debate in Britain over the nature of sovereignty within the Common Market, and the consequent fall of Thatcher.

The *Sun* behaved characteristically. True both to its loyalty to Thatcher and to Kelvin MacKenzie's loathing of the French, the paper published a long series of anti-French jokes and campaigned against one of Mrs. Thatcher's *bêtes noires,* the French European commissioner, Jacques Delors. "UP YOURS, DELORS," shouted one of its most memorable front-page headlines.

By coincidence, Murdoch's *Sun* was twenty-one years old in the week of Mrs. Thatcher's leadership crisis. "YER CURRANT BUN IS 21," announced a box on the front page, using the cockney rhyming slang for "sun." Inside were tributes from some of those show-business and other personalities who had not suffered its abuse. Mrs. Thatcher wrote, "Your twenty-first anniversary offers tremendous encouragement to a Prime Minister eleven-and-a-half years into office. The *Sun* has become a great British institution. If it can come up fresh and bubbling for twenty-one years, then so can I, and I shall do so."

She did not. She had to resign, and was replaced by John Major.

With the agreement of the Tier I banks in their pockets, Lane, DeVoe and Murdoch began a swift series of global "road shows" for the banks of Tiers II and III. They intended to get the agreement of them all by Thanksgiving. It was a whistle-stop world tour—Sydney, London, New York—in five days. To start it off, Lane flew with DeVoe from New York to Sydney to join Murdoch in the second week of November.

On all three continents Lane's authority helped swing the bankers.

Murdoch also spoke with quiet persuasiveness about the businesses he had spent so long building. He admitted his mistakes. He promised that he would have a stronger management team around him and that he would consult with them. He would not fly solo anymore. He was very impressive.

The road shows also included briefings from other major pro-consuls in the Murdoch empire, talking about books, films and the newspapers around the world. It was all a matter of presentation and spin. Lane provided the spin. She rehearsed them all, including Murdoch, telling them what the banks would or would not buy.

After the road shows, Lane concentrated on negotiating term sheets with News Corp; the banks needed to know the details of the deal. They turned out a draft of the override agreement by November 30. Lane flew to London to negotiate terms with the company line by line. She wanted to get the first drafts of the override on the banks' desks by mid-December. To negotiate an agreement of such complexity and length in five or six business days and nights is unheard of, but they did it. They were driven by the clock and by loan maturities. This would be the only draft that the banks would see.

All the lenders had a thousand questions. Those from Tier II banks were particularly awkward because those banks were being asked to provide new money to a company which already had fantastic debts. But, of all the institutions, those in Tier III were the most aggrieved and most difficult to please. Night after night they tried to get News Corp to buy them out. Lane's problem, and Murdoch's, was that if one were bought out, everyone would demand the same privilege. She refused them all.

By the end of 1990, there was a roll every two weeks, great waves that Murdoch had to ride. Almost all were difficult; some were almost impossible to stay atop. "We were in some pretty tough conversations at five minutes to midnight," Murdoch told the *Financial Times*. "Real heart-stoppers."

❖   ❖   ❖

In the same week as Mrs. Thatcher's fall, while Murdoch awaited with trepidation the impact of his worldwide road shows upon the banks, another symbol of the 1980s fell further than before: Michael Milken was sentenced to a decade in prison.

His impact on the decade had been huge, particularly in the world of communications and information. Without Milken's assistance, MCI Communications, now the second-largest long-distance telephone company in the United States, and Turner Broadcasting would never have grown so fast. But many other companies were damaged by the methods he pioneered and pursued, and overall he left corporate America with a crippling debt burden. By the beginning of the 1990s, interest payments were devouring more than a quarter of the cash flow of the average American company, an all-time record which was sure to mount higher still as the recession continued to depress revenues. There were predictions that the high debt burden would lead to a chain of bankruptcies which themselves would deepen and prolong the recession.

Murdoch's refinancing problems coincided with a slowdown in the growth of Fox. It retained its air of cocky originality, but as it became established it found progress more elusive. Murdoch himself had decided to move "The Simpsons" to challenge the most popular program in the land, "The Cosby Show," head-on every Thursday night, but Bart Simpson had so far failed to catch Bill Cosby. The network had planned to expand from three to five nights a week in the summer of 1990, but its failure to attract adequate advertising prevented that.

Throughout November and December 1990, Murdoch was on the move, conducting his road shows. Day after day he begged, cajoled and flattered bankers. He was virtually bankrupt—and would have been totally so if not for the Sky-BSB deal. Every week the company was battered by the rolls that came thundering along. All the time Lane was figuring out how to push the banks into line.

The pressure on Lane's team and on Dave DeVoe was fantastic. The images they used constantly were symptomatic: rolls, launching, cliff-hanging, the death spiral. They had only one another to take it out on. They all screamed, but Lane screamed loudest.

The only person Lane did not scream at was Rupert Murdoch. She was his guide away from the precipice. Or, to use Murdoch's own toad idiom, she hopped along beside him, pushing him away from the tooth-points of the harrow as they came crashing down, again and again and again.

Secretly she feared that she could scarcely see further than he could, but she knew too that he needed to have confidence in her. She gritted her teeth and lied. It was going to work, she insisted.

She was not quick to laugh, but she understood the value of humor, bantering wit and smart, sarcastic comments which relieved the tension. While she screamed at DeVoe, she mocked Murdoch. She also urged him to make her a movie star, stressing that "the world needs more than Julia Roberts, maybe a middle-aged yup."

Against this extraordinary background, Murdoch continued his public life. He produced a synopsis for his autobiography; the U.S. and Canadian rights were bought by Random House for $1 million. Then Random House announced it had a new publisher—Murdoch's old enemy Harold Evans. Evans told the New York *Times* that he had written to Murdoch, saying, "The wheel of fortune makes me your publisher as you used to be mine. I think it will be a happier experience for you than it was for me. But please don't pull any punches." Murdoch was not amused.

By the beginning of December, financial news from around the world was worse than ever. In Australia Alan Bond had been arrested and charged with financial offenses, and his Bond Corporation had reported a A$2.2 billion loss. The Bell Group, bought by Bond from the late Robert Holmes à Court, brought in a loss of almost A$1 billion. Consumer confidence had collapsed and shops on the main streets of Australian cities were having going-out-of-business sales.

❖   ❖   ❖

On the morning of December 6, 1990, Murdoch was in Zurich, attempting to charm and cajole officials at Crédit Suisse. That afternoon he flew to London. With him was Dave DeVoe.

The plane was late—"Everything was delayed," Murdoch recalled afterward in his clipped, staccato, but soft tone. As soon as the plane touched down, he was on the phone. Murdoch ran his company by phone.

Today's crisis looked ominous. An obscure bank, the Pittsburgh National, was refusing at the eleventh hour to roll over a minute loan—a $10 million share of a larger line of credit. "We didn't really know them well," said Murdoch. "They had come in through some Australian syndication." The Pittsburgh National Bank knew almost nothing about News Corporation.

DeVoe placed a call to Pittsburgh.

"The guy there just said, 'Give us the money,' " Murdoch recalled later.

"We said, 'We can't. You know what that means. We'd go out of business.'

"He said, 'That's right.'

"We said, 'You're telling us to liquidate our company?' And he said, 'Yes.' "

DeVoe explained, as he had done a hundred times to a hundred bankers, that News only had a liquidity problem. It was consulting with its principal banks. It had a well-structured plan. It had terrific assets. It was going to get out of this hole.

The man in Pittsburgh was skeptical, DeVoe recalled. "He said, 'I'm sorry. I hear what you are saying. We don't think you have the ability to repay us. Let's put it into receivership.' "

It was horrific, Murdoch said later. "*Horrific!* The chief loan officer said, 'Liquidate your company.' All for ten million dollars!"

If this bank refused to roll, News would be on an unstoppable slide. The company would go into worldwide default, and that would accelerate all of its public debt. It would probably be impossible to refinance. Default would utterly destroy the company's relations with its creditors, to whom it owed $3 billion worldwide.

Murdoch called Ann Lane at the London offices of the lawyers who were representing Citibank. She knew that he would never say, "I can't do it anymore." But on this particular afternoon, she also realized that he could not see how to make it happen.

Murdoch told her, "I think it's over. I don't think I'm going to get there with this bank. I'm coming over. I can't deal with it on the phone."

She understood. This roll on December 7, the next day, was for a total of A$1 billion. Pittsburgh could turn it into a dive. Lane felt as if they were falling over a cliff in slow motion.

While Murdoch was on his way over, Lane called Citibank's headquarters in New York. She wanted John Reed, the chairman, to know what was happening.

In any restructuring there are always creditors who do not want to help. They often have good reasons to get out. Sometimes they are just playing chicken. There comes a time, Lane knew, when you had to put on the pressure. More poetically, as Lane and her team constantly put it in her office, you had to "launch" on them.

"Launching" on a lender can take many forms. A multitude of vice-chairmen can call the bank that is holding out. If that is not enough, the chairman himself can call. Any federal regulator can "launch." If a huge warhead is needed, the chairman of the Federal Reserve can do it, and indeed Murdoch tried to reach him that day. Japanese regulators can be "launched" on Japanese banks. The Bank of England can "launch" on British banks. So, as a last resort, can the prime minister. But Murdoch's great ally and friend Margaret Thatcher had just been compelled to resign.

"Launching" is a delicate process. Lane knew that until the last minute, minimum pressure was better. She did not launch lightly. But now she was convinced it was necessary. She asked that John Reed call Pittsburgh to launch on the chairman and explain the ramifications of forcing News under. News would have to be sold off bit by bit in a fire sale. There would be repercussion for the whole Western financial system. Murdoch had made News Corporation more than a company—it controlled over 70 percent of the press in Australia, between 30 and 40 percent in Britain, and a major television network in America. News was one of the most important media firms in the world. Its destruction would reverberate through the world economy, accelerating the recession.

Lane called New York again to make certain that John Reed had "launched" on Pittsburgh before Murdoch called the bank himself. She told one of the partners at the law office to throw out whoever was in their best conference room to make way for Murdoch. She had two objectives: to make sure that Citibank had done all it could to avert disaster, and to calm Murdoch so that he could be effective.

When Murdoch arrived, Lane told him of everything that was being done. Calls to her teams in London and New York, and to banks in America, London and Australia, where it was the middle of the night, were constant. Everyone was tense. Indeed, said Lane, everyone was sweating bullets.

Murdoch asked to be led quietly through the process. What was happening and what needed to be done? Lane could see the pressure he was under. He knew that he might lose his ship in a matter of hours, and he was sobered by the prospect. He did not lose control. But she knew that he was aware that this might be the end.

Lane also felt that Murdoch himself had to talk to the chairman of the Pittsburgh bank. Lane's people in New York talked Murdoch through the psychology of the man. This call could be the most important he had ever made. It could decide whether or not the company he had inherited from his father and built into an empire went down. This call was the only lifeboat, and Murdoch himself must pilot it.

"It's not a pretty sight to see a great man like that," said Lane. "He was so vulnerable. One phone call could mean the end of his whole life's work. And it had been built from real skills, and not just by shifting piles of paper around."

Lane herself was terrified. "But my job was not to show panic. My job was to keep Rupert calm and focused." She was professional, and so, she said, was he. "He didn't wig out. He was visibly shaking, but he didn't go crazy. He wasn't hyperventilating."

"If we can't get them to roll, it's all over," Murdoch said to her. Lane believed that too, but she did not say so. "Nothing is over till it's over," she said. "Keep the artillery moving forward."

After about half an hour, Murdoch was ready to place the call. It was a terrifying moment for everyone there.

The chairman would not take Murdoch's call.

Here was a man who had for decades called presidents and prime ministers almost at whim, and the chairman of a small bank in Pittsburgh would not speak to him.

Instead, Murdoch was put through to the chief loan officer, the man who had chewed up DeVoe a short time before. Before this official in Pittsburgh, "I had to beg," Murdoch recalled. Then, suddenly, and to Murdoch's astonishment, it was all over. The chief loan officer, who had hours before told them to liquidate the company, now could not have been nicer. There was Murdoch, in London, close to the edge and "he didn't let me speak. He said, 'Oh, Mr. Murdoch, it's very nice of you to call. I don't know whether he's told you, I had a very good call from Dave DeVoe. We had a good talk, and I've thought a lot about what he said to me. We don't want to be that difficult.' "

In London, two hours or so to midnight, Murdoch felt the tension draining out of him. "I couldn't believe it," he said later.

The man in Pittsburgh, Murdoch recalled, said, "Perhaps we could come to New York and meet and we could know a bit more about the company, and find a way, see how we can work this thing through. . . ."

"So I said, 'We'd be happy to see you.' "

He put down the telephone and looked at Lane. "Phew" was all he said.

Pittsburgh had been successfully "launched" upon.

"I went out and had a strong drink," said Murdoch. "I was just exhausted."

What was especially exhausting was the unprecedented feeling that he had had no power, no control. If the bank had refused to roll, there was nothing he could have done. "Once the word was out, all the banks would have run. You just couldn't open any crack."

Later, he said he thought many of the smaller banks were so difficult because it gratified their egos: "Chief credit officers of small banks who were two- to three-million-dollar participants had no qualms about telling us to liquidate the whole twenty billion dollars of assets. In fact, one or two seemed to enjoy it."

In the tense days before Christmas, Murdoch called his London editors—not to tell them what to do, but for news. He had been anxious to know about Mrs. Thatcher; now he was more interested in Gorbachev. On December 9, he attended a cocktail party given by Simon Jenkins and his wife. He had seen Mrs. Thatcher that day. She looked like a tired old housewife, he said; all the energy had gone out of her.

British newspapers then alleged that Thatcher had proposed an honorary knighthood for Murdoch in her resignation honors list, but that the committee which scrutinizes such proposals had turned him down. The story was humiliating and he was stung. Unchar-acteristically, Murdoch made a public statement denying it and said that he would have rejected any honor had it been offered. He asked the *Daily Mail* to apologize for printing the rumor, which it did.

The next problem for Murdoch was a television documentary,

broadcast on Channel 4 in Britain, which criticized News Corp's accounting procedures. Even before it came out, leaks of the allegations it would make caused the share price to fall further. Murdoch had agreed to answer written questions. (Maxwell, by contrast, would have taken the producers straight to court.) The film was entitled "Murdoch—The Empire," and it was presented in the style of *Citizen Kane*. The reporter declaimed that it was "the tale of an empire built on political influence and on avoiding media controls . . . groaning under massive debts and teetering on the brink. . . ."

Although it was debatable whether the program lived up to all its claims, coming when it did, it helped send the shares skidding down by another 20 percent on the Australian exchange. Murdoch was now being compared with Alan Bond and several failed Australian financiers. He looked to many like another tycoon who had been too greedy and was fighting for his life.

Murdoch took no action, but he later complained that the film was made by opponents of Sky, who for weeks before "were boasting to London dinner parties of what they planned. . . . It was the sort of thing that tabloid newspapers are supposed to do but don't dare. Only a government-protected television cartel can get away with it."

The toad continued to hop under the fearsome harrow through Christmas and the New Year, as war in the Gulf approached. John Reed, the chairman of Citibank, called upon the assistance of Bill Rhodes, Citibank's famous troubleshooter, sometimes called the Red Adair of the banking industry. He was the man who had renegotiated Citi's loans to bankrupt South American countries. He was the obvious man—after all, News' debt was as large as Ecuador's. He had dinner with Murdoch and Anna at Côte Basque in New York and was impressed with Murdoch's straightforwardness, and his willingness to listen. Rhodes began calling bank presidents all over the world. He warned that News was so large that its collapse could have a very serious impact on the international economy—particularly with the state of panic induced by war in the Gulf. They must help, he said.

The pressure was building. None of the deadlines for completion of the deal that Murdoch and others had incautiously promised would be met. About 90 percent of the money was pledged, but the last 10 percent was proving the hardest of all. The *Wall Street Journal* and other papers published predictions that the share price might fall to zero. One Indian banker, whose signature was desperately needed, could not be found—he was hunting tigers. Lane was infuriated by her British colleagues, who were taking a week off at Christmas. There was no holiday for the Citibank team.

Lane felt that Murdoch did need a holiday. He worked ceaselessly, getting up at 5:00 every morning. Balance sheets aside, she respected the company he had built and the people who worked for him. And she viewed him as a visionary who had used the industry well. She was also struck by his love for his family, and she admired Anna Murdoch for being both independent and a remarkably supportive woman.

Murdoch and his family went to their home at Aspen for Christmas, and there was good news. Fox's movie *Home Alone,* which had cost $18 million to make, was a runaway hit. Barry Diller was ecstatic; he thought it could bring in $225 million in America and at least $65 million overseas. (By 1992, *Home Alone* had in fact earned Fox $285 million.)

By early in the new year, many of the banks had agreed to roll over. Some had agreed on the condition that everyone else be brought in too. Meanwhile, News Corp's maturing debts were rolling up until the deal was completed. As more became due, even more of the debt was short term, which increased the risk that a lender would call the company into default. International bonds issued by News Corp were yielding up to 47 percent because of investor anxieties. That was the sort of return usually expected only on the debt of such no-hope cases as Peru.

Now, the objective was to close by January 31. It was a crucial date. There was a termination date of January 31 on the document. At that time all $2 billion of debt, which had rolled, would be due. Lane knew they could not keep rolling that $2 billion forever. There was a point at which the deal was either going to happen or it was not, even though four months was a record for closing such a mammoth agreement.

On January 14, just before the allied coalition began its air attack on Baghdad, a new crisis of confidence hit News Corp. The company publicly acknowledged that it might be insolvent by June if it did not secure its $8 billion refinancing package. It could not generate the internal cash to meet its obligations at the end of June. It also became known that some banks were holding out against Ann Lane and her terms. This sent shares falling once more on the Australian stock exchange. On January 15, the price fell by 15 percent, 50 cents. The shares of TNT, the transportation company owned by Murdoch's friend Sir Peter Abeles, also dived. News and TNT together owned Ansett Airlines, which operated domestic air services in Australia and New Zealand.

On January 16, 1991, sixteen members of the editorial staff of the *Australian,* the paper which Murdoch had created in 1964 and which remained the flagship of his fleet, were dismissed. At the same time about twenty others were fired from the tabloid *Telegraph-Mirror* in Sydney. They were required to leave not because they had worked badly or were troublemakers, but because of economies Murdoch was making. Many were people with long service. The *Australian's* letters editor, Philip Pearman, who had been on the paper for twenty-two years, was told to pack his desk and go. So was the senior subeditor, Alastair Diffy, who had been there ten years. The firings were done in the casual, almost brutal way that some people had come to expect of News Corp. The Australian Journalists Association called a twenty-four-hour strike of Murdoch's papers.

❖   ❖   ❖

The first American attack on Iraq on the morning of January 17 was broadcast from Iraq, with great drama, by CNN. CNN's link to the world was a portable, independently powered four-line telephone system which microwaved a feed from the roof of the Al Rashid Hotel to a satellite truck across the border in Jordan. From there the signal was bounced up to the satellite and down to CNN headquarters in Atlanta. All the other satellite feeds, from Washington, the United Nations, Moscow, Saudi Arabia and elsewhere, were being gathered there, bounced back up to the satellites and played instantly around the world.

This first night of the Gulf War was perhaps the most dramatic vindication of Ted Turner's decision back in 1980 to create a twenty-four-hour news service for the global village. He had lost $77 million on it in its first five years. By the time of the Gulf War it was valued at $1.5 billion and was seen in sixty-five million homes in ninety-three countries around the world.

The war established CNN as the most influential network in the world. More than any other network, it had helped to create the reality of the global village, in which the manor house was the United States. By this time there were about 120 satellites available for commercial use worldwide—almost half as many again as a decade before. Intelsat alone had fourteen satellites—seven over the Atlantic, four over the Indian Ocean and three over the Pacific. Throughout the world, diplomats, politicians and statesmen would watch CNN to know what was happening everywhere else. Bush, Saddam and Gorbachev were all known to watch it. In Britain, Murdoch's own twenty-four-hour television news service, Sky News, though not in the same league as CNN, showed itself to be fast, efficient and reliable. At the same time, however, all the television companies allowed themselves to be manipulated and censored by governments. The war appeared on TV as a stunning, bloodless video game.

In the midst of war, Japanese banks nearly pushed News over the cliff. The Citibank team found the Japanese banks hard to deal with; they could not make a decision except at their head offices. They held about 20 percent of the lending altogether, most of it placed outside Japan. Neither Lane nor Murdoch had thought a road show necessary in Japan, but by January they had cause to regret their decision. The Japanese banks could not understand why their loans were not being bought out. If it were a Japanese restructuring, the smaller lenders would be rescued. Why not now, in this case?

The week before the deal was to close, fifteen Japanese banks made a move to pull out. Rhodes and Lane needed someone on the ground in Japan. Neither of them could go. In the last week of January Lane sent Bill Sorenson from her team. Lane told him that he didn't have to "launch" on anyone. If the deal fell apart, it would be her fault.

On his first day in Tokyo, Sorenson made no progress. One of his friends in the office in New York tried to cheer him up — "You're lucky you're not here. She's going crazy. She's going to kill us all." That, said Lane later, was an understatement. "I was completely ape that week." She was storming around the Park Avenue office in her designer suit and sneakers, shouting people into line. They were working toward Thursday. On that Monday forty banks were still out. If they didn't get to closure, they would face $2 billion of debt. They decided to roll for another two weeks.

Finally the signatures began to come in. The last waves were breaking, smaller now.

Watching the Gulf War on several of the nine monitors in his Manhattan office, Murdoch told Peter Bart, the editor of *Variety*, that he had won his own battle. "This has been a chastening experience," he said with a pained smile. "There have been, shall we say, some unpleasant moments."

Murdoch appeared astonished at the volatility of the markets. Some 40 percent of the capitalization of the company had disappeared in one trading week. He was sure that speculators had been feeding negative stories to the papers to drive down the share price. It was a feeding frenzy for short sellers.

Murdoch had begun to indicate, even in public, that he might change his ways, and admitted publicly to having "taken my eye off the financial side." He said he would appoint a chief operating officer, and even suggested that he might issue more full-voting shares, which would dilute his family's control. He promised to travel less and let others do more of the work. The idea that he would relinquish control seemed radical to those who knew him and the company best.

In the end, the banks rallied to News because they believed in Murdoch. For thirty years some journalists and editors had disliked him, but he had built up relationships of trust in the business world. He was known as a man of his word. He had never missed an interest payment. "Our credit record was unblemished," he said truthfully.

In the early hours of Friday, February 1, the final signatures of the 146 banks were appended to all the new agreements. It was one of the largest refinancings ever, covering $7.6 billion of short- and medium-term debts, which were to be rescheduled over three years. By February 1992, the company would have to repay $800 million to the banks, $600 million to redeem the bridge and $400 million in three six-month installments after that. When the agreement expired in February 1994, $5.6 billion would fall due. Citibank sent in a bill for $50 million.

They were where they were. Nobody had got out.

But Murdoch knew full well that all this was a stopgap. The harrow had passed—but it could return. To escape completely, he said, meant "managing ruthlessly and managing for cash. Regardless of how unpleasant this can be, there is no choice but to grit your teeth and get on with it." He had to sell assets even if the price was disappointing, squeeze extra margins wherever possible, sell still more assets, consider the possibility of diluting his family share by issuing new equity, cut back or eliminate developments today in the knowledge that there would be other opportunities tomorrow, do whatever else was needed to attract long-term debt and fight his way out.

❖ ❖ ❖

At the end of January 1991, to reassure the banks, Murdoch appointed a new chief operating officer for News Corp. This was Gus Fischer, a Swiss businessman who was already managing director of News International, the British company.

Morale at Wapping was appalling. The circulation of the *Sun* was down, and Murdoch was berating Kelvin MacKenzie. Other editors were also unhappy. The *Evening Standard* ran a story that the *Times* was to be sold. It was not true, but no one called the editor of the *Times* to reassure him. All the papers were, in effect, on autopilot. Andrew Knight, the chairman, looked like a ghost after recovering from a near-fatal skiing accident at Aspen. The day-to-day management of Wapping was more and more in the hands of John Dux, who had been moved from Murdoch's Hong Kong paper, the *South China Morning Post*, and whose beard had turned from black to gray in the preceding months. He told the editors that as a result of the deal with the bankers there would have to be severe cuts in all editorial budgets—perhaps as high as 16 percent.

Production at Wapping was still in confusion. The new and vastly expensive color presses were not effective. Pictures supposed to be in color turned up every day in black and white. Some people blamed it on the British software which had been tacked onto the German presses to appease the anti-German sentiment of some of those who worked at Wapping. Production problems were costing thousands of lost copies every night. A German team was there trying, and so far failing, to put the problems right.

There was another problem. The empire had depended so much on Murdoch's personal touch that many officers felt not only bereft but also betrayed when he did not have time for them. He was like a lighthouse; people needed his beam to warn them from time to time. While some praised the calm and realistic way he had dealt with the crisis, others began to talk ill of him. One of his lieutenants complained, "We are all driven by our character defects. Rupert is too greedy and too mean. He is only interested in control and power, not in building or improving things. He doesn't take enough care of our people. He is on the edge. His magic was vast ambition and energy. *TV Guide* marked the beginning of the end. Now reality has arrived." People noted that almost all those who had helped him expand his empire had been discarded or had fallen away. Bruce Matthews, whose work at Wapping had been crucial, was gone. And now Murdoch's oldest friend, Richard Searby, was falling out of favor. Searby was known to have told Murdoch that Andrew Knight's appointment and extravagant emoluments were a terrible mistake, if only for the effect on loyal, long-serving employees. Murdoch could not accept criticisms like that. Nor could he share power.

Before News' financial crisis, Anna had planned to take the whole family—the beneficiaries of the Cruden Trust—down the Nile to celebrate Rupert's sixtieth birthday. This was made impossible by both the Gulf War and the refinancing crisis. Instead, after refinancing was completed, Anna insisted that Rupert go to the Canyon Ranch health spa in Arizona for a complete rest.

Even there, this was impossible. Frank Barlow, the chief executive of Pearson, had to fly out to discuss a new crisis at BSkyB, as the newly merged company was called. Murdoch's principal fellow shareholders—Pearson, Reed, Granada and Chargeurs, the former owners of BSB—now demanded that he make a further investment of £100 million in a £200 million refinancing package. They knew that he had no cash.

After furious rows, a deal was reached. Murdoch met most of his obligations by bartering film rights from Fox. Reed pulled out of any further funding and its stake dropped from 10.5 percent to 4 percent; its shares were taken up by Pearson and Chargeurs. By now, over £1.6 billion had been spent on the British satellite revolution.

The next and much more painful part of the News restructuring was looming. Murdoch had to sell some of the assets that he had been so pleased to acquire. The bridge that Citibank had put together was just a bridge to that next step. "He knew he had to start selling at once.

Now, not in two and a half years' time," Lane said. "He knew he was selling into a market that was a disaster, but he knew he had to do it."

Among the first assets to go on the block was Murdoch Magazines, which included *New York, Premiere, New Woman, Seventeen, European Travel and Life* and *Soap Opera Weekly*. Talks began with K-III, a subsidiary of Kohlberg Kravis Roberts, the buyout firm whose $25 billion takeover of RJR Nabisco had probably been the most astonishing corporate excess in the 1980s. K-III demanded that Murdoch include the *Racing Form* in the deal, since it was a good daily provider of cash. He agreed and the deal was closed at $650 million, a good price.

He also sold the other 50 percent of the *Star,* which had been his first American paper. Thus, by the middle of the summer of 1991, News was in a position to repay the bridge and had a little breathing room to focus on corporate finance problems. Murdoch knew that even if he met the almost $2 billion payments under the override, he still had $5.6 billion coming due in February 1994. This meant more refinancing. There was no way that sort of debt could come due in one day.

While Rupert Murdoch was selling, Robert Maxwell was still buying, trying to appear to rise as fast as Murdoch was descending. In particular, he was after the New York *Daily News,* which had suffered long strikes and which the Tribune Company of Chicago had finally decided to sell. Maxwell was still obsessed with Murdoch and found it sweet to own a New York paper when Murdoch was not allowed to do so. He flaunted himself as the savior of the *News* and was hailed and embraced by the mayor and other functionaries of the city.

Tribune paid Maxwell $60 million to take the *News* off its hands—but the paper's obligations may have been as high as $100 million. And, although Maxwell's own debt problems were more completely shrouded than Murdoch's, it was clear that they were horrendous. Maxwell Communications and the private companies through which he juggled his finances owed at least $4.5 billion. Ever since his purchase of Macmillan Publishing Company for $2.6 billion in 1988, he had been scrambling to raise cash. *Business Week* reported in March 1991 that at least a third of Maxwell's stake in Maxwell Communications had been pledged as collateral for loans. There was another element, sometimes called "the Max factor": whereas Murdoch's business associates trusted him implicitly, most of Maxwell's associates suspected that there was something unreliable about him, even if they tried to ignore it. He smelled bad. But because of fear, sycophancy and the libel laws, not many people dared say so.

At the beginning of April, Murdoch closed the *Sunday Herald* in Melbourne. He had launched it as an upmarket broadsheet to compete with the *Sunday Age* in August 1989, but its circulation had fallen to under 100,000, well below that of its rival. News said that it had been losing A$15 million a year. Seventy jobs were lost and the journalists in the Herald group went on strike.

Murdoch's sister Janet, the chairman of the Herald and Weekly Times group, sent a photocopied handwritten note around the building to "all you wonderful people working through the strike." Thanking them for their loyalty, she said, "My brother, Rupert, telephoned this morning, asking me to thank you all on his behalf, and to say 'KEEP UP THE GOOD WORK—WE MUST WIN IN THE END.' You are all very much in my thoughts." The company was intransigent and, muttering abuse, the journalists were back at work after almost three days out.

In early May 1991, Murdoch flew out of London to launch his latest newspaper—in what used to be East Berlin. The wall was now in fragments, and Eastern Europe was the new jousting ground for the great information robber barons of our time. Murdoch had already bought a newspaper in Hungary, as had Robert Maxwell. Robert Hersant, owner of *Le Figaro* in France, the Italian Silvio Berlusconi and the German groups Bertelsmann and Springer were all represented there too.

East Germans had had little recent experience of Western sex-and-scandal sheets. Now they had an abundance. Murdoch's offering was a tabloid called *Super!*, which played on the same emotions as the *Sun* in Britain, and was pitted against another new Berlin tabloid—*Berliner Kurier*, launched by Maxwell.

Like the *Sun*, *Super!* encouraged chauvinism. It stressed the accomplishments of East Germany and attacked West Germans, who were known as "Wessies." *Super!* had screaming headlines on the sins of the Wessies, rather as the *Sun* did on the alleged misdeeds of the Frogs. "WESSIE BUYS VILLAGE: 256 CITIZENS IN PANIC"; "WESTERN OFFICIAL SEIZES FARMERS' LAND IN MECKLENBURG." Stories about the influx of pornographic videos blamed West German decadence for destroying East German marriages. But this formula did not attract enough readers, and in 1992 *Super!* was closed.

From Berlin, Murdoch, Anna, Andrew Knight and other members of his staff flew on to Moscow. This was Murdoch's first trip to the capital of "the evil empire." Recently, his own successes had been invoked in the Soviet press. "Why not learn from Murdoch?" one long analysis in *Pravda* had been headlined.

Information is a great force today. Society's actions and people's actions are in many respects determined by the amount of information they receive. . . . Instead of going to Murdoch for money, we must ponder how to learn the ability to manage the information business from people like Murdoch, Maxwell, Hersant and Springer. It is not at all compulsory to copy their gutter-press style.

Murdoch had been invited to visit Mikhail Gorbachev, whose fear of fundamental reform he had been privately decrying. Murdoch was all for Yeltsin; so, passionately, was the *Sun*. Now Murdoch found

Gorbachev "full of energy, and making speeches at you all the time. He was still a communist. He would not grasp what it is all about." He seemed a tragic figure, commanding nothing real.

It became clear that one of the principal reasons Murdoch had been asked to Moscow was to make an offer for Raisa Gorbachev's memoirs. Murdoch and Anna found her a stunning performer. "She was coquettish, sweet, sexy, then brutal," said Murdoch. "Her attitude was one of anger against the world which has turned against her." She told them that she would not change a word of what she had written. She wanted $400,000. Murdoch agreed. This was what Harper & Row had paid for Gorbachev's own book, *Perestroika*, which had sold well.

In July 1990, "Dallas" was broadcast to Soviet television viewers for the first time, and the Soviet Union became the 121st member of Intelsat, the International Telecommunications Satellite Consortium. This event was described by the president of the official American organization Comsat as "the last nail in the Cold War's coffin."

The coup against Gorbachev one month later showed that there were still those in the U.S.S.R. who wished to open the coffin again. The failure of the coup demonstrated once more the power of communications. The U.S. government had first realized that something was amiss when its spy satellites revealed that all telephone traffic from Mikhail Gorbachev's Black Sea villa had ceased—the lines had been cut by the plotters. But the attempt to isolate him failed: his guards, who remained loyal, found a radio in the basement and were able to listen to the BBC's and Radio Liberty's accounts of the resistance mounted in Moscow by Boris Yeltsin, hitherto Gorbachev's chief political rival, and now his savior.

Soviet satellites carried the first pictures of military activity in the streets of Moscow. The image of Yeltsin defiant atop a tank was beamed instantly around the world. Visnews used a Soviet Horizont satellite to carry video from Moscow through London to its European affiliates. At the same time, American users of the Internet sent summaries of the CNN evening headlines to Moscow.

The plotters shut down all the newly independent newspapers and broadcasting stations, but throughout the coup, accurate and uncensored reports from a news agency supporting Boris Yeltsin were distributed around the Soviet Union on private computer networks. Foreign newspapers were able to phone these networks in Moscow and, by modem, pick up messages and reports from the Russian parliament building where resistance to the coup was centered.

As in the Gulf War, the theater of news was global. When John Major called George Bush soon after the coup began, the American president told the British prime minister that he had just seen him on CNN. Yeltsin was in frequent contact with Western political leaders. They helped him rally resistance. Information was everywhere, the most powerful weapon of all. The coup collapsed. Viewers around the world watched the astonishing sight of Muscovites tearing down the statue of the spymaster Feliks Dzerzhinsky in front of the KGB's Lubyanka headquarters, amid cries of "Rossiya, Rossiya." "We were literally watching the fall of the Bastille," said Murdoch. The global village had closed down its principal prison.

12

ON THE ROAD

One morning in December 1991, Rupert Murdoch left his new *pied-à-terre* at the Museum Tower in New York before dawn. The last year had carved the ruts of his face into crevasses, and his hair was a chalky gray. "I'm off to humiliate myself again," he said with a grimace. He was being sent by his bankers to dispose of part of his birthright in the Cruden Trust's share of News Corp, diluting his family's control over the company.

He looked tired, and older than his sixty years. He climbed into the car with the morning's papers, and was driven in the dark through the streets of Manhattan, into the Holland Tunnel and out to Teterboro Airport in New Jersey, where his private plane, a Gulfstream III, was waiting to fly him to Hartford, Connecticut.

There his bankers had arranged a breakfast meeting and then another encounter with a firm of investment brokers to whom he would explain the restructuring of News. En route Murdoch grumbled about the recent fall in the company's share price, which determined how many shares he must sell, how much control he would lose. The share price had been falling for days, from A\$23 to under A\$20. He blamed this on short sellers who had been taken unawares by the stock's rise over recent months, and were now trying to force the price down. He was furious with a report by one New York "shorter," Kynikos Associates, which alleged that the shares "could be worthless." Few others thought that News was "worthless."

By most standards, its transformation over the past year had been extraordinary. At the end of 1990 it had been crushed by a debt of $8.1 billion and constant threats of imminent bankruptcy. By November 1991, the shares had leapt up on the New York Stock Exchange by almost 300 percent above their nadir just eleven months before.

News Corp's annual results had been published in August 1991. In the year ending June 30, revenues had increased 25 percent while profits, before abnormal items but after taxes, rose 14 percent. This was a considerable accomplishment in a time of recession. But News Corp's net loss for the year was A$393 million after abnormal losses of A$714 million.

Then there was tax. News Corp was still paying only 4.5 percent tax on its profits—a far cry from the 30 percent paid by most Australian companies. The Australian Tax Office was investigating its use of offshore tax shelters.

There was also the treatment of losses at BSkyB. Before Sky merged with BSB it had been treated as a subsidiary of News. After the merger, the 49 percent stake News held in BSkyB was treated as a loan. But when the group was refinanced in May, all loan interest was deferred; News Corp started to treat BSkyB as an associate company, so it reverted to equity accounting.

The prospects for BSkyB were beginning to look good. Its losses had been cut from the £11 million a week of the year before to about £2 million a week. The annual budget for Sky News had been reduced from £35 million to £20 million. Dish sales had already reached 2.2 million and advertising was coming in. It was now reported to be worth all of £2 billion.

News was well on the way to reducing its debt by $800 million by February 1992, as the bankers had demanded. Analysts were praising Murdoch. He had cut capital expenditures and reduced his work force by 18 percent. In a moment of unusual euphoria, he had told the *Sunday Telegraph* in October 1991, "We are the pinup boys of the banks. Emotive words like 'bridge loans' have gone."

Nonetheless, the harrow could still threaten the toad. Even if News met the $2 billion payments under the override, there were still repayments of $6.4 billion coming due in February 1994. Murdoch wanted to meet the override debt repayment obligations early. In exchange, the banks would be asked to loosen the covenants imposed on News and extend debt maturities from 1994 to 1997.

He and Dave DeVoe chose to combine three methods—the sale of more assets, an equity offering and a public debt offering. The hardest pill for Murdoch to swallow was the equity offering, for this would dilute Cruden's control over News Corp. He had always kept around 45 percent of the shares in the hands of his family's Cruden Trust.

The premise was to get $3.5 billion of debt extended for three years. The company had a realistic chance of both refinancing and paying down the debt. Lane maintained, "That's how we're going to get paid back, guys—by helping the company fix itself." In essence they created an option on the company. They paid a fee for a commitment to extend from 1994 to 1997, but the commitment was enforceable only if the company met certain conditions—by keeping to the business plan and successfully refinancing the other pieces of the debt. If they did not do so, all the repayment would come due in February 1994 and they would be back to square one. By the early autumn of 1991, Lane thought Murdoch was achieving the plan: "He recognized that he was managing for cash and could not take a breather. He got on with it."

At the end of October, Murdoch's banks, Citibank, Morgan Stanley and Allen and Company, took the new deal to market. They asked the top forty-six banks to extend 60 percent of their outstanding credit for an additional three years, from 1994 to 1997, and to loosen the override covenants imposed in the agreement made by Ann Lane.

Murdoch announced the flotation of his Australian printing and magazine interests to raise A$682 million. News Corp would retain 45 percent. News Corp also announced that it was planning to raise about US$450 million by issuing 16.1 million American depository receipts (each representing two shares) for U.S. investors and five million shares elsewhere. It had already raised some US$180 million through the private placement of convertible preferred shares. These were bought by friends — Hong Kong businessman Robert Miller; William Thomson of the venture capital firm Boston Ventures; and TCI, the world's largest cable TV company. TCI's president, John Malone, said that News was an attractive investment for the firm. TCI bought programming from Fox and was now extending its cabling in Britain, where there would be close links with Sky.

These moves, together with the conversion of notes due in 1992, would dilute Cruden's control of News Corp to some 40 percent. Even though the family, and he within it, would still retain overall control, that was a small death for Murdoch.

By Thanksgiving 1991, the schedule was getting tighter. The equity offering was supposed to take place in December. His bankers told Murdoch that he would have to go on another road show. Even the thought of interminable early-morning flights to bad breakfasts and poorly attended meetings with thirty-year-old analysts all over the United States and Europe nearly killed him. He insisted on covering Australia by a teleconference.

That particular December morning, on the short flight to Hartford, Murdoch talked about the death of Robert Maxwell and the revelations of his massive frauds. He was convinced that Maxwell had committed suicide: "He must have been terrified of going to prison — as he would have done."

As Murdoch had seemed to be pulling News out of his own financial abyss, Maxwell had been slithering into a far deeper one. No

one knew how deep. The accounts of his many companies and holding corporations, registered in secrecy in Liechtenstein, Gibraltar and
elsewhere, were infinitely more complicated and more covert than
those of Murdoch. And, unlike Murdoch, Maxwell had always used
the British libel laws to bludgeon critics into silence.

Murdoch had loathed the way in which he had often been twinned
(or, worse, confused) with Maxwell in the public imagination. Having
observed Maxwell at close quarters for twenty years, he was not surprised by what had now been discovered—"I'm only surprised by the
fact that it's possible to steal so much money." He had long believed
that Maxwell was both dishonest and totally unreliable. They had recently competed for Thatcher's memoirs. HarperCollins had offered
£3 million for world rights. The negotiations had been complicated by
the intervention of her son, Mark Thatcher. "He told us that Maxwell
had offered 'ten million.' It was never clear whether it was pounds or
dollars, but I said fine, go ahead. In the end Maxwell produced neither
and they came back to us."

Murdoch also thought that Maxwell was concerned about his trail
in the KGB files. "He was an agent of influence for the Russians. They
had been blackmailing him for years," Murdoch said. After his death,
the astonishing extent of Maxwell's thefts had begun to emerge. He
had robbed the Mirror group's pension fund of at least £500 million.
The British companies were placed in receivership, as was the *Daily
News* in New York. The empire that Maxwell had spent his life building, and with which he had tried to rival Murdoch, collapsed almost
overnight. Murdoch's *Sun* asked exultantly:

> MIRROR, MIRROR ON THE WALL,
> WHO IS THE BIGGEST CROOK OF ALL?

Murdoch's plane landed in Hartford just after 8:00 A.M., at the private airport belonging to United Technologies, the defense contractor
on whose board he had served since 1984.

Only about a dozen young men and a couple of women came to the

Hartford breakfast. Murdoch's aides showed a video extolling News; in it Murdoch looked even more aged, his hair seemed white, not gray, and he spoke haltingly. After the video, he addressed the analysts himself, explaining the unique attraction of the company for investors. Its media assets, he said, were the greatest in the world: there was Fox, with its movie studio and television stations; there were News' coupon supplements for newspapers known as freestanding inserts, which had been acquired for $80 million and were now making News about $100 million a year; and there was *TV Guide,* which was being retuned to the proliferation of cable. Murdoch continued:

> The objective of this company is to make investment grade. We are not going through this again. As far as I am concerned, this company is my life . . . my time and my worth are in it. I'm taking a very big step here reducing [my holding] from forty-four percent to just under forty percent and could have avoided that by selling more assets. But we believe it is right to keep these assets together—they do make sense and do have very great potential.

Then Murdoch repeated an idea that formed the core of his philosophy: "As the world is modernizing, so it is Americanizing." And as America remade the world in its own image, the world demanded more and more American entertainment. Fox would meet that demand. Within the United States, the network share of the audience was falling. "We are still going to be the only game in town for people who want to reach the masses."

As he left for the next appointment, he asked quietly, "Did that go all right? I think that went all right, didn't it? There were a couple of reasonable questions." He seemed exhausted, but willing.

Down the road, at the office of George Weiss Associates, a small investment-fund management firm, there was a shock. After shaking hands, Mr. Weiss said that he would not be able to listen to Murdoch and Barry Diller, who had flown separately to Hartford to join in the effort.

Murdoch thought something terrible must have happened. Had Tokyo collapsed? he asked. He meant, Was his share price even lower than an hour ago? No, Weiss replied, "just the usual press of business."

He had Murdoch and Diller, two of the most powerful men in one of the world's largest industries, in his office and he did not want to hear them.

Murdoch and Dave DeVoe, who, like Diller, had joined Murdoch in Hartford, told their story again to some young analysts.

Asked about the dilution of his stock, he replied, "My entire net worth is here. That's OK! We don't want to sell more assets so we decided to dilute."

Diller sang the song of Fox. In film, he said, Fox had five competitors, the other major Hollywood studios. In television, he insisted, it had none. Fox Broadcasting reached 93 percent of the U.S.A. The other networks each had 5,000 employees. Fox had only 238. The others would lose $200 million this year; Fox would make at least $50 million. "The Simpsons" was now doing well against "The Cosby Show" and would make a fortune when it went into syndication. And so would BSkyB, Murdoch added. Costs were falling and dish sales rising fast. "We have *all* the product of Hollywood for the next ten years."

On the other hand, Fox's new Bette Midler film, *For the Boys,* had just bombed. Fox had hoped the film would repeat last year's success of *Home Alone,* which had boosted the studio's earnings by 182 percent in the year ending June 30, but the Midler film, which had cost $40 million, had been panned. "We have written it off already," said Murdoch.

Then he left for the United Technologies airfield for the short flight to New York.

Barry Diller's plane was more lavishly appointed than Murdoch's. Coffee did not come in foam cups, but was served by a steward in large pottery cups and saucers on tables beside lush tan leather seats.

Diller was furious that he had to be on the road. "On Sunday night I went to Minneapolis. Almost burned down my hotel room overnight, slept four or five hours, went to Chicago, went to a black-tie dinner in New York Monday night, went to the wrong building, did meetings all day yesterday, flew to Washington to make a speech, and then got up at six A.M. today to come to Hartford."

Diller was certain that he and Murdoch could have sold far more shares from teleconferencing. Indeed, one teleconference alone to Australia had sold almost half the equity. "It's absurd to make me and Rupert traipse around like this," Diller said. In his view, the whole process was merely intended to make yuppie bankers and analysts feel important.

Diller's relationship with Murdoch was complex and competitive. Diller bowed to no one in Hollywood; Murdoch tolerated no peers in News. *Playboy* had once asked Diller what it was like "to get your ass kissed all day long." "It's been true for so many years it really doesn't affect me," Diller retorted.

"Do you ever have to kiss Rupert Murdoch's ass?" *Playboy* asked. Diller replied, "The term 'kissing ass' is not sophisticated enough because you're dealing in the sophisticated leagues. The only issue really is, do you use your charm to persuade people to do things? I suspect that anybody in any kind of structure does that." As well as charm, Diller sowed terror.

On the plane ride, Diller praised Murdoch's organizational genius. Politics was the major subject on which he and Murdoch disagreed, and to Diller that was no laughing matter. Diller's voice rose as he spoke furiously about the laissez-faire conservatism that Murdoch revered. He thought that the long years of Republicanism had killed all ideas. "America is no longer about anything except memories and myths," he said.

Diller was equally scathing about Japan's Hollywood adventure.

Neither Sony nor Matsushita was making progress with Columbia or
MCA, he said, because the Japanese had no understanding of the
culture.

He expounded, in typically hyperbolic manner, on the mistake he
thought that Sony's chairman, Akio Morita, had made in choosing the
controversial team of Peter Guber and Jon Peters to run Columbia.
Diller was convinced that American fears of losing its "Dream" to
Japan were absurd. The Japanese would be defeated by Hollywood:
"They're six thousand miles away and it's not like having a little Sony
Walkman plant in Des Moines, where language is irrelevant."

Such views were quietly dismissed by Akio Morita himself. A few
weeks later the chairman of Sony said in an interview for this book that
Columbia was doing quite well enough for Sony, that the investment
was well worthwhile and that Sony would never pull out of it.

Driving from the airfield back to New York City, Murdoch punched
the car phone constantly, calling his bankers, his lawyer and other
advisers. He heard that his share price had fallen further. He would
now have to sell another 1 percent of the company to raise the cash
he needed. He toyed with the idea of closing the deal that night,
twenty-four hours early, before the price fell further.

Stuck in traffic, Murdoch and Diller jumped out at the Plaza Hotel
to walk to their next road show. Scenes for Fox's *Home Alone 2* were
being filmed at the Plaza. The original film had cost only $18 million
to make; the sequel would cost over $40 million. The child star would
get $5 million, as against $200,000 for the first film.

All that day, through the night, and the next day, Murdoch continued to worry about the falling share price. The bankers would decide
only at the very last minute at what price to offer the stock.

By Thursday morning, the day the deal had to be closed, the Australian market had moved up overnight and New York opened strong.
The shares rose to about $20.875, but to Murdoch's fury, his bankers
told him they wanted to make the offering at $19.25. This seemed a

huge difference. The banks said they wanted the stock to be bought by institutions who would hold it; they did not want it flipped out quickly and into the hands of short sellers. This made some sense, but Murdoch was enraged; he thought the banks had been protecting themselves rather than promoting News.

In the event, he was forced to sell 42 million new shares instead of 37.2 million, as he had hoped. The price was $19.30 for the American depository receipts, and with this he raised $404.3 million instead of the planned $450 million. The extra offering would dilute his control of the company to 39.5 percent. At the same time, News would issue $400 million worth of senior notes due in 2001, carrying an interest rate of 12 percent.

Altogether Murdoch had now raised A$1.5 billion since late October—through the equity issue, the preferred shares and the sale of 55 percent of the Australian commercial printing operations.

The proceeds would be used to reduce the bank debt. As of June 30, the company's net interest-bearing debt had stood at A$10.5 billion. By now News had repaid early about US$2 billion of the debt due in 1994 and stretched out repayment of other maturities. The company's debt had now been reduced to about A$9 billion.

At the same time the banks loosened some of the restrictions that had been imposed in the package negotiated by Ann Lane. They allowed News Corp to increase the annual dividend payout and agreed to lift the ceiling on the funds News could commit to certain investments.

In eleven months, Rupert Murdoch had begun to burst the bonds that the banks had imposed on him. It was an extraordinary achievement. But it would not be correct to say that he was free. There was now speculation that he would have to raise as much as A$1 billion more in equity over the next year, which would dilute his controlling interest to well below 30 percent. This was something which he would obviously resist with all the force at his disposal.

❋   ❋   ❋

After the deal was completed, Murdoch flew back to his home in Beverly Hills, where Anna, following the example of Dame Elisabeth, was designing an English garden. Fully grown trees were dropped into holes by helicopter to give it a look of maturity. There were still not many other English things that Murdoch found tolerable.

His assistant, Dot Wyndoe, had also moved to Los Angeles, and taken up a new office on the Fox lot. She had now worked for Murdoch for thirty years, and she still traveled constantly around the world as he did. She knew all the details of the imperial history and the surge of personalities within it. In a company which made the most effective use of personnel, she might long ago have been promoted. But as an assistant she was crucial to Murdoch.

Barry Diller was not. Of all Murdoch's employees, Barry Diller was the most equal to him—his huge personal wealth guaranteed him independence. But Diller had never seized that independence, and, approaching fifty in 1991, he was determined at last to enjoy it. "I wanted to be a principal, not an employee," he said.

During the long-drawn-out refinancing of News it had at times seemed possible that Murdoch would have to sell all of Fox. That would have relieved his debt. But it would have lost him what he now regarded as the core of the company—its principal electronic division. On several occasions Diller made it clear to Murdoch that if Fox were put on the block, he would willingly buy it. Murdoch replied that he would only sell if he had absolutely no alternative. Through the first six months of 1991, Diller became more and more restless.

In some ways it was surprising that the relationship had lasted so long. Murdoch was politically and socially conservative. Diller was fiercely liberal and quite unlike anyone else Murdoch treated with at a senior level. Some of Murdoch's colleagues suggested that when he bought Fox Murdoch had realized that he needed Diller, but that when he had mastered the business himself he would inevitably move him aside.

In any case, by the summer of 1991, the unlikely combination of the two men had been extraordinarily successful. Above all, they had managed to make Fox Broadcasting a substantial force. It was principally Diller's achievement. He had pushed an untidy bunch of low-powered UHF and VHF stations into a real fourth network. In the process he had, as Peter Bart of *Variety* put it, managed to "zap many of the basic programming precepts of the three established networks; obliterate a chunk of the U.S. syndication business; strike fear in the hearts of basic cable networks that they might lose desirable channel positions; reconfigure the economics of station ownership; and alter the way in which advertisers view television itself."

Diller acknowledged the achievement, but looking back, he said that his preoccupation with Fox Broadcasting meant that he had not done enough for the movie studio. "I just Band-Aided it, but never really fixed it. You *have* to build a company from within. I never did it."

In 1989 he and Murdoch had appointed Joe Roth, who had had some success as an independent producer, as head of the studio and given him a good deal of independence. But by 1991 Diller had begun to chafe at that, even as Murdoch was chafing at Diller. He felt that many of the decisions that Roth was making were mistaken—for example, the making of the Bette Midler film *For the Boys*, which opened and crashed at the end of 1991. Diller felt that if he did stay at Fox, he would have to do more at the studio, and Roth would not be able to tolerate it.

By 1991, Diller still liked and admired Murdoch. He thought him absolutely honest and clear-sighted. But he was continually astonished by the way in which Murdoch ran the company through the "pull" of his own personality. "I often had to fight the desire to join the people who were worshiping the Sun God," said Diller later. "It's a hard fight. He knows it and he's quite good at using it."

In summer 1991, after a bad-tempered board meeting at which his suggestions were ignored, Diller said to Anna Murdoch that he felt like "a hired hand." What he wanted to be was "a principal"; he felt that he had done enough to run his own show. He asked Murdoch once again if he could become a real principal in News Corp. Once again, Murdoch considered but refused. "He told me, not coldly or meanly but just realistically, 'There is in this company only one principal,' " Diller recalled.

And so Diller decided to go; he took the next six months psyching himself up to make the leap. Even while he prepared to move, he noticed that Murdoch was losing interest in him; he was thinking beyond Diller and about how he would deal with the future of Fox.

Diller was sanguine. He understood Murdoch's processes better than most. To many employees, the loss of the Sun God's shining warmth was upsetting—and that was why so many editors had retired, bruised, from News. "The problem is that Rupert and his employees always see the relationship differently," Diller said. "Rupert's force of personality, charm and seduction is so great that they convince themselves his attention is given forever. In fact, it's a loan. The point is that it really is *his* company and he runs it as an extension of his fingertips. People need to understand that."

Diller felt that one of Murdoch's weaknesses was his impatience and his urgent desire always to "get on with it": "He does what works. He has defined what works in a shorthand that is less than his capabilities." Inevitably, quality was sacrificed.

In February 1992, Diller issued a long statement which, even though edited by his friend Diane von Furstenberg, was strikingly flowery and personal, to announce his departure from Fox. He praised Murdoch and insisted that he was leaving only because, at fifty, he wanted to control his own company and his own destiny. He said of Murdoch, "I would say that if you're going to work for somebody, work for him. He's the best . . . straight, supportive, honest and clear." In response, Murdoch praised Diller also. Diller received a financial settlement of approximately $34 million from Fox. But Murdoch was delighted that he would now have Fox to himself.

*   *   *

Murdoch was restlessly reinventing himself once again. At almost the same time as he and Diller parted company, he disposed of Richard Searby. After fifty years of friendship and ten years in which Searby had diligently served the company as its chairman, Murdoch asked him to resign. He did not do this face-to-face; it became known in the company that he had sent Searby a curt note through Ken Cowley. Searby was philosophical; he thought Murdoch had finally tired of his relative independence and their differences of style and values. Others thought that Murdoch merely felt he no longer needed Searby.

By now, *Forbes* estimated News to be worth $11 billion and Murdoch's personal fortune $2.7 billion. Murdoch was the only solo owner of a multimedia empire, and was thus in the happy position of being able to take risks that executives tied to quarterly earnings were not. *Variety* commented that Fox had enabled him to extend his influence to a third continent, "and after that, the world."

He settled easily into the physical if not the political surroundings of L.A., which he saw as "the modern melting pot": "My garden is full of gum trees and eucalyptuses and it's an open society in a way that a lot of Australian cities are." On the Pacific once more, he decided to have a sailboat built for him. It was rather larger than *Ilina,* which he had sailed in the sixties in Sydney.

He redecorated Barry Diller's office on the Fox lot in rather more conservative taste and began putting in twelve-hour days. He would start at 6:00 A.M. with calls to London. During the bulk of the day he dealt with Fox business, and then, as the afternoon signaled the dawn of the next day in Australia, he would begin to call Sydney.

He said that he would be running Fox differently and more privately than Diller. He hoped that people would be reading much more about Joe Roth, the head of the studio, Peter Chernin, the president of the Fox Broadcasting entertainment group, and Jamie Kellner, the president and chief operating officer of Fox Broadcasting, than about him.

But at the same time he began to break down some of the walls Diller had built between different divisions of Fox. Diller had believed in highly charged in-house competition. Murdoch wanted more collaboration. He scrambled the operations and centralized them around him. He said he wanted to integrate Fox more completely into News, to see if there really were synergies—"What skills are there lying in this company which can be applied to other parts of the company?"

One of his first acts was to promote Stephen Chao to be head of the Fox News Service, and then of Fox Television Stations. There were those who thought Murdoch had once again sacrificed judgment to infatuation. Chao was a clever Harvard classics graduate of thirty-six who had been a reporter on the *National Enquirer* and was credited with developing "America's Most Wanted" and "Studs." He delighted in being the *enfant terrible* of Fox: he would pretend to doze off in meetings, and he once walked out when Diller criticized him for not wearing a tie. In his office he had as decoration a phony soiled diaper and pile of fake excrement. On his appointment to head the news division, *Daily Variety* commented that perhaps he would invigorate TV journalism, but "then again, those who see it as a sign that the nation is going to hell in a handbasket could be right, too." Murdoch would hear no criticism of him.

In the 1991–92 season, Fox increased its audience by 28 percent. Murdoch could fairly claim that whereas the other three networks were merely alphabet soup to most viewers, Fox had an identity. It was seen as hip and unconventional. In summer 1992, Murdoch announced that in the next season it would expand its programming to seven nights a week. Chevy Chase would have his own late-night show.

He intended first to have the local Fox stations develop their own news programs, and then to press traditional TV news boundaries to make a national news service in which the "dissemination of news and entertainment, for the good of us and our viewers, must be linked almost umbilically." He said that Fox's contract with CNN for national and international news coverage would not be renewed when it expired later in 1992; he wanted to reinvent the wheel of TV news: "The talent must be real journalists and real characters."

Although newspapers still generated most revenue for News, in the future the company's greatest growth would be in electronic media. The important thing was to have the software—meaning new films every year. That "will be one of the greatest assets that can be had by any company in the world," Murdoch said.

He disliked both the finances and the politics of Hollywood. Costs he thought surreal. Why should Steven Spielberg and the stars of *Hook* be guaranteed millions of dollars even though the film failed to be a smash hit? Why should they not take risks as well as the studios?

He said that while it was obvious that the superagents, who had come to dominate the Hollywood studios, did a good job for their clients, he wanted to do the same for his clients—his stockholders. In summer 1992, Joe Roth, Jeffrey Katzenberg of Disney and Brandon Tartikoff of Paramount were reported as attempting to contain costs associated with "agency packages." This was announced, in effect, in the New York *Times*, which quoted Tartikoff as saying, "We are not spraying the town for the hottest flavors or the biggest-salaried stars that money can buy."

At the same time, Fox revealed that it had turned down a demand from Bruce Willis for $16 million to star in *Die Hard 3;* he had been paid $1.5 million in 1988 to make the original *Die Hard,* which had grossed $94 million. Roth said that Fox was reducing the price of movies. In 1991 Fox's average cost for a film negative—before the expenses of promotion and distribution—had been $23 million. In 1992 it was down to $21 million, compared with an industry average of $26–$28 million.

Murdoch had equally strong views on the content of movies. He thought *Basic Instinct,* though obviously commercial, was a horrible film, with not one redeeming character. Oliver Stone's film *JFK* he thought was "almost anti-American." He thought that Hollywood was "quite monolithically liberal" and out of tune with middle America, whereas his own tastes reflected American concerns much more closely.

Murdoch said that moviemaking was basically an editorial job, much like any other: "There are decisions, there are judgments to be made about the sort of programs you make, how you schedule them, the sort of movies you make, and I think they're the lessons you learn when you've been in newspapers thirty years."

Barry Diller agreed that Murdoch was a good editor, but felt that his conservatism would be a hindrance to his making successful creative decisions. Indeed, it would make that process almost impossible. Diller himself had been almost the only liberal at a senior level in the company. Diller felt it was unhealthy that Murdoch surrounded himself only with people who thought as he did. He thought that what happened at Aspen in summer 1992 was a warning of the perils ahead for Murdoch.

In June 1992 Murdoch summoned his lieutenants once more to Aspen in order "to tear down the walls of this company." He was determined to remake News to exploit more fully the opportunities of the 1990s. Many of the employees gathered there thought that News had changed enormously since the last Aspen meeting in 1989. Fox and its concerns now dominated Murdoch's attention. Some of the British participants felt that they were there merely to service the American broadcasting and movie machine.

Addressing the meeting on global issues were the U.S. secretary of defense, Dick Cheney; Charles Powell, the former foreign affairs adviser to Mrs. Thatcher; and William Rees-Mogg, the former editor of the *Times*. Dave DeVoe, the chief financial officer, explained how News had been brought back from the brink and was now the third-largest media company in the world. But the conference was punctuated by an incident which some saw as an extraordinary reflection of the contradictions at the heart of Murdoch's empire.

One of the stars of the conference was Stephen Chao, Murdoch's new protégé at Fox. That week, his brainchild, "Studs," the program in which young men and women make sexually suggestive conversation in front of a studio audience and a leering host, achieved its highest ratings ever. The show would gross $20 million in 1992 and was expected to make $60 million in 1993. Basking in Murdoch's obvious approval, Chao behaved at Aspen with an insouciance bordering on arrogance—he even threw Murdoch's dog into the swimming pool. As president of Fox Television Stations and Fox News, he took part in a panel discussion of "the threat to democratic capitalism posed by modern culture."

The panelists were Lynne Cheney, the chairwoman of the National Endowment for the Humanities and Dick Cheney's wife; John O'Sullivan, editor of the *National Review;* Irving Kristol, a conservative intellectual; and Michael Medved, a film critic. All these panelists were conservative, and they were critical of the way in which social and moral values were being corrupted by film and television. They warned that censorship might be on its way.

Chao had a different agenda. To illustrate his theme of the effects of sensationalism on news, Chao had secretly arranged that, while he spoke, a young male model would come onto the platform and take off all his clothes. The audience was astonished, and embarrassed. As the man undressed, Chao asked them not to look at the stripper but to listen to him. He even singled out Anna Murdoch: "Anna, don't look at him. Listen to me." The man was close to Lynne Cheney, who turned her back. It is said that Chao had also arranged that another man would burst into the room and shoot the naked man with a fake gun—to provoke Chao's comparison between sex and violence on the screen. That did not happen, it is said, because the "gunman" was warned that Cheney's Secret Service men would have shot him dead.

Nothing about the incident amused Murdoch. He sacked Chao that same day and told the conference, "It's a terrible thing to see a brilliant young career self-destruct. And it's a bitter loss. But the point is that there are limits."

The question of limits was at the heart of the matter. What are the limits at News Corp? Many would argue that topless women on page three of the *Sun* overstepped the proper limit. Others would say that the tabloid shows of Fox are often gratuitously sleazy and violent. Fox traded on being the network most likely to transcend good taste. Yet at Aspen Murdoch would not tolerate a tasteless act in front of his wife and distinguished guests. Inevitably the charge of hypocrisy was raised. A columnist on the New York *Times* asked whether Chao would have been fired if he had shown a clip from "Studs" in which contestants asked of each other, "Which is the guy who has bounce in his butt?" or "Which one is the more likely to find the G-spot?"

To Barry Diller in Los Angeles, the incident raised other issues. He thought that the conservative loading of the panel was a clear and disturbing warning to the News Corp troops that there was no tolerance of other ideas within the company. He felt that if he had been there Chao probably would not have behaved as he did, or at least the incident could have been contained. Diller was not impressed by Murdoch's choice of Van Gordon Sauter to replace Chao. In fact, Van Gordon Sauter did not last long at News.

At the same time, the concerns expressed by Kristol and others about the effects of modern culture on society are real. And News Corp's own role and responsibility are at best ambiguous. The company—and Murdoch's own ambitions—have always been financed by pushing the edge of the envelope of decency. Murdoch's tendency to dismiss such criticisms as "elitist" is an evasion. As the power of News Corp and similar companies grows throughout the world, so will questions about their impact become more urgent.

AFTERWORD

By early 1997 Murdoch was more successful and more powerful than ever. Within the United States, he had therefore become more controversial than ever before. His personal ambition—to create a universal television system—was closer than ever to realization. And so his enemies were even more firmly marshaling against him. Ted Turner, Murdoch's most intemperate critic, said he was hoping for Murdoch's demise.

One of the grand old men of the global media business, Sumner M. Redstone, chairman of Viacom, has said, "Rupert wants to rule the world, and he seems to be doing it."

By early 1997 that was more obvious than ever. News Corp seemed in far finer form than its rivals. TCI and Time Warner were deep in debt and other obligations. Murdoch had $3 billion in cash. He had cut the company's debt from $12 billion to $5.2 billion and converted short-term into long-term obligations. (Some of this debt was one-hundred-year debt.) Cash flow met interest payments with ease.

Nineteen ninety-six had been, even by Murdoch's standards, an astonishing year. "It was a year of big challenges—a lot of progress and a lot of problems," he told the *Financial Times,* which named him its Man of the Year. News Corp now had $10 billion in revenue. In the last ten years the company's operating earnings had increased from $370 million to $1.5 billion. But relative to the opportunities in the worldwide market for media, Murdoch said that News was still "tiny." Because of technological change, economic growth and rising incomes, he thought the worldwide market for media was growing "at a breathtaking speed."

In 1996 he became the largest owner of television stations in the United States; he launched Fox News, the television news channel of which he had long dreamt, and with which he intended to encircle the world; and he decided to invest at least $2 billion in digital satellite television in the U.S., the U.K., Japan, India—and anywhere else he could manage. There is every reason to suppose that within a few years his own programming, together with that of other companies which he distributes, will cover the world.

In the year ending June 1996, News Corp had cash flows of more than $1 billion. It was not yet as large as Time Warner or Disney/Capital Cities, or Germany's Bertelsmann. But, as the *Economist* put it, what was breathtaking about News Corp was "its global reach, its sweeping ambition, and the extent to which it is the creature of one man."

Murdoch was able to do more or less what he wanted because of the crucial fact that he still controlled some 30 percent of News Corp's stock through his family company Cruden. (And, he said, he hoped to rebuild the family holding close to 40 percent by converting nonvoting debentures into voting stock.)

As a result of the family's control, he could still move far faster than any other global media business, making decisions on the basis of his own instincts rather than with a weather eye to the concerns of institutional investors. He was much more interested in how deals would extend the global reach of News Corp than in their short-term effect on the market. His attitude toward the share price often seemed to be that if he, the major shareholder, was willing to wait, then others should be also. As a result, the share price hovered around $22 for much of 1996. Institutional analysts made it clear in newspaper interviews that they thought the company was underperforming. Murdoch did not care.

News, he said in 1996, "for better or worse, is a reflection of my thinking, my character, my values. I am proudly responsible for the best of it and guilty of the worst of it."

He claimed that throughout his life he had been forced by nature, character and circumstances to be a catalyst for change. "Sometimes you're treated like the skunk at a tea party. But that's the fate of anyone who challenges the status quo."

On another occasion he pointed out that News was the first vertically integrated entertainment-and-communications company of truly global reach. It produced programs in the U.S. at Fox, in the U.K. at BSkyB, in India at Zee TV and elsewhere around the globe. It also had such television platforms as the Fox stations, the Fox broadcast network, Fox News and the f X cable channel in the U.S.; Sky and its five million subscribers in the U.K.; Vox in Germany; Star in Asia; and Foxtel in Australia.

The company's liquidity had been helped enormously in 1995 when the telecommunications company MCI announced that it was buying 13 percent of News' equity for $2 billion. It was a good marriage; News had control of software and MCI was adept at moving large amounts of information and at telemarketing, a resource in which News was poorer. As part of the deal, MCI agreed to vote its share with Murdoch—an extraordinary vote of confidence in his vision. (By 1997 this deal had to be modified because British Telecom had made a takeover bid for MCI.) The deal meant that News now had $5 billion to spend on acquisitions. Asked what he might buy, Murdoch replied, "I don't know. I made a joke about CNN just to annoy Ted [Turner]. He gets a bit excited at times." But he did go on an aggressive buying spree; in the next twelve months he spent more than $1.8 billion on acquisitions. Orson Welles once said that a movie studio was the biggest train set a boy could ever have. The tracks of Murdoch's train set were becoming ever more dense as they reached up into the sky and around the world.

His overarching ambition was to create a worldwide information company in which software and distribution systems were forged together in every market—everywhere. That was what he had been doing all his life—the scale of it had just got grander and grander. He told the New York *Times,* "We want to put our programming everywhere and distribute everyone's product around the world."

Murdoch saw distribution as the key to victory. Fox TV had taken a long time to build. "If I were to start again, we would have bought one of the existing networks," he told the *Economist.*

He was once again reshaping the company he had grown out of the tiny Adelaide *News.* He was expanding it beyond its core publishing businesses in order to own rights to every major form of programming—news, sports, films and children's shows—and beam them via satellite or terrestrial TV stations to homes in the U.S., Europe, Asia and South America. In Brazil, News set up a joint venture with Globo, Brazil's largest media group, and Grupo Televisa, Mexico's biggest broadcaster, to provide satellite TV in Latin America.

But his focus remained on the United States, which he called the "biggest center of software creation in the world." News and MCI invested $682 million in slots for direct broadcast satellites in the U.S.A., under the name of ASkyB—American Sky Broadcasting. Murdoch acknowledged that he had come late to this game in the States and that this was the worst mistake he had ever made. But if ASkyB, however belated, worked, it would help spread the programming costs over the American market as well as Asia, Europe and South America. (Though one lesson which had been learned hard was that except in sports, locally produced programs were almost always more popular than American imports in every market. This worked against the principle of economies of scale in program making.)

In July 1996 he crowned his recent American purchases by paying $3.4 billion to buy New World Communications, which owned ten television stations around the U.S. As so often, he was criticized for paying too high a price. But the deal meant that Murdoch was now the biggest owner of U.S. television stations, in terms of viewership—his stations reached 40 percent of the United States. Fox now had twenty-two stations, including nine in the top ten markets. It could now compete on equal terms with the big three networks. When it began in 1987, it had been dismissed by a senior NBC executive as "the coathanger network." By 1997 NBC had to admit that Fox posed it much more serious competition than either CBS or ABC.

Although Murdoch now spent most of his time at his home in Beverly Hills, he still did not really like Hollywood. He hated paying any star $20 million for a film, and loathed the liberal culture of the town. As his friend and adviser, the economist Irwin Stelzer, pointed out, "He still sees New York City as the fountain of creative energy; he remains first and foremost a newspaperman, and L.A. is at the end of the information chain." Perhaps as a result of this emotional distance, the Twentieth Century Fox studio had done less well in the decade since he had owned it than Disney, Paramount or Warner.

But one thing which Murdoch had done was transform Twentieth Century Fox from a domestic U.S. studio which used to sell off the foreign rights of its films to one which increasingly targeted the international market. Since international markets now bring in up to 60 percent of a film's return, this was a shrewd change.

Newspapers still provided about half the profits of News, but the share of television and films was rising all the time. By 1995 it was almost twice what it had been four years earlier.

Murdoch's U.K. base still gives the company power. He has strong newspaper assets in every corner of the British market. In 1995 he slashed the price of the *Times* in an attempt to gain more of the market and to end its perpetual status as a loss maker. This led to what his competitors saw as a vicious price war, which Murdoch could fund from News Corp's much greater resources. The end result was an increase in total newspaper sales, as well as a massive rise in the circulation of the *Times,* which returned it to profit for the first time in living memory.

But the real strength of News in Britain lay in the astonishing success of BSkyB. The fight to get the service going before it bankrupted him "aged me twenty years," Murdoch said. But in 1995 News Corp's

40 percent share of BSkyB generated $285 million profit. BSkyB was now worth $17 billion.

BSkyB succeeded because it clearly met a demand for entertainment—particularly films and sports—that the established British broadcasters had been unable to meet. Its commercial triumph stemmed from the fact that it not only made programs but also rented satellite transponders and ran its own subscription service. Other program makers such as Disney and even the BBC needed BSkyB to deliver their products. By 1996, BSkyB's grip on pay TV in Britain had become unshakable. It was Britain's third-largest media business, bigger than many film studios, and Murdoch, never one to rest on his laurels, was determined to make it bigger still. The achievement, from beginnings that were so derided by Murdoch's critics at the beginning of the decade, was extraordinary. Now those same critics began to warn that Murdoch was threatening to become the all-powerful gatekeeper to British television.

Asia was more complicated. Early in 1993 Murdoch had made another visit to China to talk to senior officials about expanding Fox television interests there. As he had always expected, the Chinese market was now expanding hugely. Fox, he said, had already established a niche. The "Fox Movie of the Week," by now a popular event, had given Shirley Temple a new lease on life. In southern China Fox was showing "Dynasty" to great acclaim.

Murdoch also noticed that Star TV, owned by the Li family and satellited out of Hong Kong, was already becoming a force, particularly in southern China. There was a rumor that Deng Xiaoping had said that he liked the sports on Star, but could they please have a bridge channel?

From China, Murdoch had flown to Hanoi at the invitation of the Vietnamese government. Government officials wished to ask his advice on how to restructure Vietnamese television.

It was an extraordinary visit. One of the most assiduous salesmen of the American Dream, a man who saw himself as an agent of influence for the American Way, was being asked, in effect, how to make communist-controlled television more popular.

Murdoch was impressed by Hanoi, particularly by the lack of security. He was taken to see General Vo Nguyen Giap, commander-in-chief of the North Vietnamese forces during the Vietnam War, whom he found sprightly and gung ho.

"They have nothing," he said in 1993 of Vietnamese television. "If you left them a cassette, the next day it would be broadcast on national television. They are desperate for films. You could probably buy the national TV station for five million dollars."

There could hardly be a more telling symbol of the end of the Vietnam War—and of the identity of its ultimate victor. Here was the one of the greatest capitalists of communications, the Prince of Darkness to thousands of people on the Left in the west, arriving as the guest of the government which those same people had honored for its defeat of the United States.

Asia was now the most aggressively capitalist of areas, and presented almost boundless opportunities for television expansion. And so, in his ambition to create, on the basis of Fox Broadcasting and BSkyB, an international television system, Murdoch paid $525 million to buy 64 percent of Star TV from the Lis.

It was hard to exaggerate the importance of this acquisition. The footprint of Star's satellites covered all Asia and the Middle East. Altogether about three billion people, two thirds of the world's population, live under it. Star's potential power and influence were immense—a fact not lost on authoritarian leaders from Djakarta to Beijing. Governments which restrict the activities of their own press realized that they would find it much harder to control satellite broadcasts. Leading Asian officials began to call for the protection of Asian values and traditions against the onslaught of Western infotainment.

Government suspicions and restrictions were one problem. Defining, creating and satisfying the market was another; this has proved far more difficult than Murdoch anticipated when he bought Star TV. As a result, its growth has been much slower than that of BSkyB. In 1996, Star lost $100 million.

Murdoch had come to realize that there is no such thing as a pan-Asian market. Local programming is what matters. Broadcasting cricket matches might sell hundreds of thousands of satellite dishes in India, but not one in Japan. So he was attempting to develop regional markets.

In China by mid-1996 at least 950 million people watched television and 30 million people were watching cable; many of these watched Star TV. But almost none of them paid for the pleasure. Three years after Murdoch bought Star, News was selling almost no advertising for its China broadcasting and collecting no subscription fees. He had deliberately courted the Chinese leadership. Most notoriously, he had removed the BBC from Star's northern beam, partly because he had never liked the BBC and also (he acknowledged) because he knew the Chinese regime hated it. But the gerontocracy in Beijing apparently remembered more his assertion in 1993 that satellite broadcasting and other technologies were "an unambiguous threat to totalitarian regimes everywhere."

Chris Patten, the governor of Hong Kong, denounced Murdoch's decision to throw the BBC off Star as "the most seedy of betrayals"—of the right to free speech, if nothing else. Sumner Redstone, by contrast, said Murdoch was right—"He's doing what he has to do to solve his problems with the Chinese government. He's smart to do that."

As the media critic Ken Auletta pointed out, Murdoch worked hard in other ways to make Star more attractive to both the Chinese government and the Chinese people. He broadcast more Chinese-language programs; he bought the rights to broadcast badminton and other sports that the Chinese enjoyed; he set up a music channel for Chinese talent; and he started a pay-TV service in Mandarin. He even invested more than $4 million in helping create an on-line version of the *People's Daily*, the propaganda arm of the Chinese regime, the sort of publication which would previously have been anathema to him.

In winter 1994–95, Basic Books, a division of HarperCollins, published a hagiography of Deng Xiaoping by his youngest daughter, Deng Rong. Murdoch may not have paid her a huge advance, but he pushed out the promotional boat, attended the book party thrown by HarperCollins at the Waldorf-Astoria, invited her to his ranch at Carmel and gave a private dinner for her at Le Cirque—other guests included Cyrus Vance and the Chinese ambassadors to Washington and the United Nations.

With all this effort, Murdoch said he thought that in a few years' time Star would start making small profits and that "in ten, maybe fifteen years I hope it will be a bonanza." No one in the Politburo had yet "stood up and said, 'This is true,'" Murdoch said to this author. "The moment that happens, the advertisers will start pouring in."

China was not the only object of his interest. Japan was, for different reasons, almost as hard to crack. Star TV began to broadcast directly to Japan in Japanese in 1996. That was not all. In partnership with Sony and the Japanese software wholesaler Softbank, he set up Japan Sky Broadcast, a 150-channel digital television service, to start broadcasting in April 1998.

JSkyB was to have three pillars—the huge stockpiles of movies owned by Twentieth Century Fox, the TV programs aired by Star and dramas and animated films which JSkyB expected Japanese broadcasters to provide. "We're running it at the moment," said Murdoch. "But we want to hand it over to Japanese management as soon as possible. We'll end up with about twenty-five percent."

By the mid-1990s, Murdoch was certain that sports would drive his television empire. Sports were, quite simply, by far the best way, perhaps the only way, of persuading millions of men to watch television. Unlike films, sports are immediate—miss a game and all you can see

is a replay. Murdoch said at News Corp's annual general meeting in
Adelaide in October 1996 that he intended to use sports as a "battering
ram" to enter pay-television markets around the world.

And so he spent billions of dollars on sports—buying up rights
to as many games, matches, tournaments and races as possible—all
over the world. In 1992 Fox Sports did not exist; by 1997 it was an
increasingly powerful force in broadcasting. His purchases of the exclusive rights to sports fixtures horrified many terrestrial broadcasters
and millions of viewers who were accustomed to watching these
events without having to pay a subscription fee. But Murdoch's dollars
transformed the fortunes of many sports, particularly football, around
the world.

"We will be investing and acquiring long-term rights and becoming part of the sports establishment," said Murdoch. "Football, of all
sports, is number one."

When Murdoch paid $1.6 billion in 1993 to take the rights to
broadcast National Football Conference games from CBS, he was
widely thought to have paid much too much. That judgment had been
made of his purchases many times in the past. Almost always—except, arguably, in the case of *TV Guide*—he had proved his nay-
sayers wrong. On this occasion once again he showed acumen. Fox
immediately gained in ratings and advertising revenue. A whole slew
of stations defected to Fox, most of them CBS affiliates.

With all these successful acquisitions, Murdoch did have setbacks.
He failed to win the television rights for the Atlanta or Sydney Olym-
pics. And the British government decided that pay TV should not be
allowed the exclusive rights to the most popular sporting events in the
U.K., such as the Wimbledon lawn tennis tournament.

In early 1996 an Australian court ruled that News Corp, in an
apparent effort to hurt the ratings of rival channels, had improperly
persuaded rugby players to break their contracts to join its new Super
League rugby competition. The league was banned. But in October
1996 the Australian Federal Court overturned the previous ruling.

"Its going to be a wonderful asset now that we are free to get that competition under way," said Murdoch.

In the global media business, cross-partnerships and deals were now as intricate as highway exchanges. Time Warner spent $7.6 billion to buy Turner Broadcasting; Walt Disney paid $19 billion for Capital Cities/ABC; and News Corp paid $2.8 billion to win total control of New World Communications. Their goal was the same: to manage both programming and distribution. But no one company or combination of companies controlled enough of either to be able to ignore or shut out its rivals. Deals abounded.

Thus, News Corp and Time Warner might be at each other's throats in New York—but in Asia, Star needed film libraries from Time Warner's Warner Bros. and others, and they in turn needed Star's satellites. Nothing showed this more explicitly than the tortured relations between News Corp and NBC.

At the end of 1993 the NAACP filed a petition claiming that Murdoch had misled the FCC when he created the Fox network in 1985. That was when he had become an American citizen in order to own American television stations. But the NAACP argued that its research showed that the majority of the Fox stations' equity was in fact owned by News Corp, a foreign-registered company, and that the network was therefore illegal. Toward the end of 1994, NBC joined with the NAACP in its suit—after the seven affiliates of New World Communications switched from NBC to Fox.

At about that time Murdoch started to make large contributions—$200,000 in all—to the Republican Party. Soon after the Republican landslide in the November 1994 congressional elections he descended on Washington to lobby for Fox and to deny the NAACP/NBC claims. NBC, he said, just hated the competition that Fox provided. He met with almost all relevant public officials, amongst them the new Speaker of the House, Newt Gingrich, who talked to him in the hall outside his office. Murdoch did not mention his troubles with NBC, but according to the *New Yorker*, his aide did so.

A few weeks later came the news that HarperCollins had given Gingrich a two-book contract worth $4.5 million. This was the third-largest advance ever received by a public figure. Murdoch insisted that he had known nothing of the deal. "I was telephoned in Beijing on Christmas Eve and told that it had happened," he said to Ken Auletta. "I went crazy. I knew critics would explode."

They did. Even though other publishers had also been bidding fiercely for the book, the advance seemed clearly to be improper. Here was one of Murdoch's companies offering a huge sum of money to a senior elected official while another of his companies had important business before Congress. The disquiet, among both Democrats and editorial writers as well as (more quietly) among many Republicans, was such that Gingrich was compelled to announce that he would take no advance and would accept only the royalties that the book actually earned. But he and Murdoch had been badly damaged by the deal. The head of HarperCollins, George Craig, subsequently resigned, and Murdoch moved in new management.

The NAACP/NBC suit continued. If they had won the day Murdoch could have lost Fox, the core of his American TV operations. In his own deposition to the FCC, Murdoch said he had been mistreated by "the Establishment" and maintained that the FCC would be playing semantics if it decided that News Corp's equity constituted foreign ownership and did not accept that Murdoch's control of voting stock spelled American ownership. Senior Republican members of Congress agreed and began to put pressure on the FCC, which some right-wingers wanted to see totally abolished.

Before this bitter battle began, NBC had been negotiating to have two of its channels carried on Star in Asia. When NBC joined the NAACP lawsuit, these talks were suspended; NBC made plans to have its channels carried on another Asian satellite, *Apstar 2*, which was about to be launched by China. But in January 1995 *Apstar 2* blew up a few moments after it left the ground. NBC no longer had any alternative vehicle to Star. News Corp refused to make any deal with NBC so long as its challenge at the FCC continued. So NBC backed down in Washington in order to go aloft over Asia—with Murdoch.

But the NAACP continued its suit. Eventually, in May 1995, the FCC ruled that Fox was in fact in violation of the law because of the extent of News Corp's Australian ownership, but said that if Fox could demonstrate that it had served the public interest, it could get a waiver to the law. It did.

In New York in 1996 Murdoch entered his most bitter battle yet with his old rival Ted Turner, whose liberalism he detested. He was able to use one of his favorite papers, the New York *Post,* as part of his campaign.

In 1988 he had been forced, with great reluctance, to sell the *Post* because the FCC would not give a waiver to the rule that prevents one company from owning a newspaper and a television station in one catchment area—and News now owned Channel 5 in New York. Under a succession of new owners, the paper had failed to prosper, and by March 1993 it was about to close. Such stalwart liberals as Governor Mario Cuomo and even Senator Edward Kennedy begged Murdoch to save it. Murdoch savored such requests and agreed to do so—but only if the unions made concessions and if the Federal Communications Commission agreed to allow him to keep Channel 5 as well. Both accepted his conditions. The paper welcomed him back with the headline "MURDOCH TAKES CONTROL OF THE POST—AGAIN. 'IT'S GOOD TO BE HOME.' " Since then, with Murdoch inscribed on the masthead as publisher, the paper had regained some of its sassy style and had championed the free-market, anti-Clinton and usually Republican causes that he believed in.

In January 1996, Murdoch decided at last to challenge the pre-eminence of CNN and to launch Fox News. He had been hoping to do this for years. He hired Roger Ailes, who had long experience of both Republican politics and cable television.

Murdoch entered the news market at a time when all-news channels were suffering. Audiences generally were falling. CNN's prime-time viewing numbers within the U.S. rarely exceeded 1 million. It was being squeezed by newcomers such as Lifetime, a women's channel, and Discovery.

Turner was well aware that CNN was unsafe and that Murdoch was the likely predator. "Who do you think would outbid everyone else for our company?" he asked in fall 1994. "Rupert Murdoch would. Rupert Murdoch is the only one who can do it. The rest of them are astute businessmen. You can't match a madman. . . . He's kind of like a mad genius."

For a time Murdoch had wooed Ted Turner himself, but Turner eventually decided to sell CNN to Time Warner and become a vice-chairman of that company. It was a measure of Murdoch's power, and his recovery from the crash of 1991, that he considered buying Time Warner for some $40 billion. But eventually he decided instead to launch his own news channel.

News—local as well as national and international—will be vital to the construction of any information superhighway. Murdoch knows that. So does Ted Turner. So does John Malone of TCI. So do Bill Gates, Michael Eisner, Sumner Redstone and all the other titans of the information age. "We are a news organization," Murdoch told Geraldine Fabrikant of the New York *Times* in July 1996. "To be a meaningful broadcaster you have to have news. We will do one [a news channel], and it will be much better than CNN." He went on to say that he had a love-hate relationship with CNN. "I watch it when I get on my exercise machine in the morning. There are long commercial breaks and it's quite repetitive."

That was a mild expression of his views on CNN. In a speech to the National Press Club in Washington in February 1996, Murdoch recalled that Ted Turner had recently called him " 'the schlockmeister.' To this, I guess, I must plead guilty . . . if your idea of 'schlock' is 'The X-Files,' the *Times* of London, NFL football, 'The Simpsons,' Sky or Star broadcasting, our Fox educational children's programs, NHL hockey, feature films like *Waiting to Exhale* . . . and perhaps it is. That's what we do.

"We do, however, draw the line at professional wrestling and brown-nosing foreign dictators. You'll have to turn to one of Ted's channels to see that."

He had long made it clear that he thought the opportunity to challenge CNN lay in offering more conservative content. He believed that audiences were falling because of the "growing disconnect" between news broadcasters and their viewers. He thought that a more conservative news channel would attract more viewers. He said that while 45 percent of the American public described itself as conservative, only 5 percent of journalists did. To compete with CNN, he had once said, "We may have to develop another expert source on Cuba other than CNN's bureau chief, Fidel Castro."

To get Fox News launched as widely as possible, Murdoch decided to offer large cash incentives. Usually, cable operators pay a small fee per subscriber to specific channels—though John Malone often demanded a share in the equity of channels he agreed to distribute on TCI. Murdoch, by contrast, elected to pay the cable operators large fees for every subscriber they brought to Fox News. This was a phenomenal change to the economics of the whole industry. Indeed, it caused ABC/Disney to abandon its own proposed news channel.

That meant that only Fox and MSNBC, the new channel formed by an alliance of Microsoft and NBC, were left as competition to CNN. In June 1996 Murdoch leapt ahead with a deal with his sometime rival and sometime partner John Malone, whose cable system, TCI, boasted fourteen million subscribers. Malone agreed to provide Murdoch with an initial ten million subscribers, at a price of $20 each together with an option to buy a 20 percent equity interest in the channel. News also paid $10 a head to get its service on Continental Cablevision and Comcast, the third- and fourth-ranking cable groups, which had around eight million subscribers between them.

Through the summer of 1996 Murdoch and Roger Ailes attempted to persuade Gerald Levin, the CEO of Time Warner, to take Fox News on Time Warner's own cable system. This was the second-largest after TCI, but Murdoch was particularly interested in getting Fox News onto Time Warner's New York cable outlet. He deemed New York, the country's largest television market, and the one in which myriad advertising agencies are based, vital to the start-up. After long discussions, Murdoch believed he had a handshake agreement with Levin and had all but signed a deal for Time Warner to pipe Fox News to nine million households in New York City. "We had the dockets ready for signing," he said.

There was a regulatory reason for this confidence. Before the Federal Trade Commission had approved Time Warner's acquisition of Turner Broadcasting, it had insisted that the new company's cable systems carry one twenty-four-hour news channel in addition to CNN. Murdoch expected that to be Fox News. But on September 17, only three weeks before the launch of Fox News, Gerry Levin walked across Sixth Avenue to tell Murdoch that Time Warner would not carry Fox—it had decided instead to fulfill its commitment to the FCC by broadcasting MSNBC.

Fox News would still launch with twelve million viewers—a record for a start-up cable channel. But its break-even target was twenty million homes. It was also far behind CNN's sixty-eight million connections and the twenty-three million claimed by MSNBC. And it was invisible in New York. Murdoch was furious. He thought he had been lied to: "I called Gerry Levin and told him my people were outraged and wanted to let loose the heavy artillery." Murdoch went to war, and others did so on his behalf. New York City's mayor, Rudolph Giuliani, urged Time Warner to reverse its decision. The governor of New York

State, George Pataki, intervened with Levin, and the state's attorney general, Dennis Vacco, launched an antitrust probe of Time Warner.

Murdoch's Republican allies claimed that they were helping Murdoch because they thought he was being treated unfairly and because the channel would create fifteen hundred new jobs in New York City. Time Warner executives complained that the politicians were trying to ingratiate themselves with the most powerful media magnate in the city. Giuliani retorted that this was absurd—he had close ties to Time Warner executives also. Nonetheless, the editorial pages of the New York *Post* had for a long time reflected similar priorities and policies to those Giuliani espoused.

The long-simmering row between Murdoch and Turner became ever more heated. Turner compared Murdoch to Adolf Hitler and accused him of using his existing U.S. media holdings as propaganda tools in a war on his rivals.

Murdoch, typically, responded that rather than get angry, he would prefer to get even. He left it to the Anti-Defamation League to protest Turner's analogy as one that cheapened the Holocaust. Turner was compelled to apologize. In a court deposition, Turner called Murdoch "slimy" and a "scumbag." The New York *Post* published a front-page picture of Turner in a straitjacket under a headline asking, "IS TED TURNER NUTS? YOU DECIDE."

Fox News hired a plane to fly over Yankee Stadium, where Fox was broadcasting a World Series game (which Turner was attending) between the New York Yankees and Turner's Atlanta Braves. It flashed a message to Turner: "Hey Ted. Be Brave. Don't Censor the Fox News Channel." Murdoch also devoted several pages of the New York *Post* to attacking Turner, Time Warner executives and Turner's wife, Jane Fonda. The *Post* published a picture of Fonda's controversial wartime visit to Hanoi together with a column which referred to her as "just another scatty-brained Hollywood nude-nik."

But as the *Wall Street Journal* pointed out, the irony of the dogfight was that the two companies were in fact closely wedded to each other.

One analyst said that local skirmishes would not stop either of them from engaging in joint ventures to make money. "They rarely stand up for principle. They always stand up for capital." In February 1997 Murdoch himself pointed out to analysts the close and continuing relationship between Fox and Warner Bros.

It was sometimes hard to know whether Turner's anger stemmed from personal hatred of Murdoch or a fear of the business threat posed by Fox News. In a court deposition he said of Fox, "They are the enemy. They plan to keep our employees' children from going to college. Take food off the table of people I work with."

In mid-November 1996, Turner used a forum at the United Nations to defend the secretary-general, Boutros Boutros-Ghali, against the U.S. attempt (later successful) to oust him, and to denounce Murdoch, calling him, according to the New York *Post*, a "no-good bastard" and a "no-good SOB." Murdoch and News Corp, he said, "want to control the world. They want to control the television world. We have got to do everything we can to stop them. Rupert Murdoch, sitting wherever he is—I don't know what country he is supposedly from, he is truly a citizen of the world—he wants to sit here and control Indian television in India, he wants to control Chinese television in China. Bullshit! I don't know how that translates into other languages."

Asked if peace was possible with Murdoch, Turner replied, "This is a battle between good and evil." The New York *Post* reported the speech with the front-page headline

TED TURNER'S MOUTH RUNS AMOK AT U.N.
Time Warner Chief goes Boutros Boutros Bonkers

The war between News and Time Warner continued till year's end. Murdoch filed suit against Time Warner, and in an early court appearance News' lawyers accused the company of being an anticompetitive monopoly. In April 1997 Murdoch told this author that he thought Time Warner would agree to carry Fox News by the end of the year—"I think they realize just what trouble they are in with their license."

Such rows alone made clear that by 1996 Murdoch was not only a far more powerful figure than before, he was also much better known and more controversial within the United States.

His political views were most robustly expressed in the New York *Post,* one of the papers he had always most enjoyed owning. He had also started a new political magazine in Washington, the *Weekly Standard,* which had become a conservative standard-bearer. By 1996 it had 60,000 paid subscriptions and newsstand sales of about 9,000; it needed sales of 100,000 copies a week to break even.

But Fox was where his force in the U.S.A. came from. Its reach was constantly extending. Indeed, many of the huge media mergers in recent years—Disney's acquisition of Capital Cities as well as Time Warner's purchase of Turner Broadcasting System—had been constructed as defenses against the growth of News Corp, and of Fox in particular.

Some American analysts disliked the intricate international accounting procedures used by News Corp. Australian and American accounting procedures are very different. The company shifted its profits around the world in order to minimize tax liabilities. This helped it to escape with an average worldwide tax bill of only about 7 percent. Murdoch took a robust view of the complicated system of tax avoidance he had created: "If you can move assets around like that, isn't that one of the advantages of being global?" But it could also lead to trouble. In fall 1996, the Israel offices of News Datacom, which had developed the smart card used in BSkyB television receivers, was raided. The company was accused of tax fraud; News Corp denied any involvement in wrongdoing. Murdoch told this author that he believes the charges against his company are based on lies and that he is certain they will be dismissed.

In February 1997 Murdoch once again startled his competitors and peers. He announced a plan to combine his satellite operation in the United States, American Sky Broadcasting, with a small but aggressive Colorado satellite company, EchoStar. The new service would be called Sky—it would use a network of seven satellites to cover 75 percent of the country by the end of 1998, and it would beam local stations along with cable networks like MTV and CNN.

Sky was intended to offer up to five hundred channels, including local TV stations, over an eighteen-inch dish. It would finally enable Murdoch to broadcast Fox, and in particular Fox News, right across the United States. If the deal was allowed, it would in effect mean that Murdoch had access to the screens of two thirds of the world's population. He truly would be the preeminent global broadcaster.

Murdoch himself claimed that the service "would take over North America." No surprise, then, that the deal was seen as a threat to the cable television companies. They immediately labeled the venture Death Star and began to lobby Congress and the U.S. regulatory agencies to prevent it from taking off. They argued that this new Sky would give Murdoch far too much control of the U.S. media. He already owned twenty-two TV stations around the country, and Sky would lock up the majority of the satellite slots that reach the entire U.S. market. Murdoch's critics and competitors accused him of building a vast new monopoly.

With cable suppliers, other satellite competitors, city governments which derived revenue from cable, local TV stations and antitrust enforcers at the Federal Trade Commission all opposed to, or at the very least concerned by, the Murdoch advance, it was clear that the new battle would be fierce indeed.

What they feared was what all his competitors had reason to fear—the fact that, unlike most corporations, News could move instantly, and Murdoch was never afraid of absorbing huge losses to win whatever he deemed to be the prize. "Rupert Murdoch is known for spending big and not following economic models," Steve Efftros, head of the Cable Telecommunications Association, told the *Wall*

Street Journal. "I call it ego-nomics." But by the end of April the deal appeared to be off.

Ted Turner allowed his hatred of Murdoch to find even more vivid expression; in the words of *Variety,* he dragged his feud with Murdoch "to a new low" when he said to Larry King (of Turner's CNN) in an onstage interview that Murdoch might soon die. Turner said he was "hoping for it."

Notwithstanding Turner's bad taste, by 1996 questions about the company's future after Murdoch inevitably hung over it. His father, Sir Keith, had died in his sleep at age sixty-five. Murdoch himself turned sixty-five in March 1996; his health and the question of succession were becoming subjects of morbid interest to analysts. He had aged in appearance in the last five years, but he seemed to be in good shape; his wife, Anna, still kept him on a strict regimen of white meats and limited quantities of wine. He had just given up downhill skiing because he only enjoyed it if he could go fast and thought he was bound to break something if he continued. Instead, he had celebrated his sixty-fifth birthday by taking up scuba diving. He had also taken up riding on his ranch in Monterey.

He made it clear that he had no intention of giving up work. Why did he still keep this ceaseless, frenetic pace? "I'm having too good a time to stop. I really love it," he told Ray Snoddy of the *Financial Times.* "I can't see people getting out of bed happy every day and thinking what a wonderful life it is running a commodities company or a gas pipeline or something. . . . This is the greatest fun business in the world." He had no intention of becoming nonexecutive chairman.

But he was thinking of the future. Like the British royal family whose tenure he so despised, Murdoch was intent on using the hereditary principle for his succession. He insisted that shareholders would benefit from a continuation of family control. "I think that media companies need one big strong shareholder."

He had never trained and brought along managers capable of replacing either him or any of his three children. In the unlikely event that he dropped dead tomorrow, many people bet that his wife would take over as regent until some combination of his children could take over.

There was talk of an alleged sibling rivalry between Elisabeth, age twenty-eight, now general manager of broadcasting at BSkyB, and Lachlan, who had just been appointed chairman of News Australia at the age of twenty-five. James, the youngest of Rupert and Anna's three children, was sometimes said to be the brightest. He had dropped out of Harvard to set up his own music business in New York. In late 1996 he was named News Corp's vice-president for music and new media, taking the company into the one branch of the entertainment industry from which Murdoch had previously shied away, in good part because of his dislike of its drug culture.

The relationships and pecking order between the children inevitably intrigued journalists as well as analysts. Murdoch himself denied that he encouraged the "creative tension" between them, but it was clearly there. When Lachlan was promoted, Elisabeth said she realized she had to get a move on. In March 1996 Murdoch told the *Economist* that the betting was now on Lachlan: "It's not me talking, it's the company." Later in 1996 he said, "They are running against each other and I'm too weak to say, 'It's you and not you.' In fact, they are enormously close. They will get together and they will work it out." In February 1997 both Lachlan and Elisabeth addressed News Corp's meeting for investors in Los Angeles. She then took off time in order to have her second baby, but Murdoch said she was determined to get back to work. "They all seem to work very hard."

Whatever combination of the children proved most effective, the fact remained that the empire reflected one man's odyssey. That was its logic, its raison d'être and the source of its success. After Murdoch, an immediate question would be whether it made economic sense for the company to be held together—would the breakup value be greater than the combined value?

The problem for each of his children was that none was likely to have the same instinct as their father for making huge instant decisions which, at least in commercial terms, were nearly always right. By 1997 they seemed to be establishing distinct but complementary areas of interest—Elisabeth in electronic media, Lachlan in print and James in entertainment.

It is not possible to pass judgment on a career before it is ended. Any assessment at this stage of Murdoch's life and empire is bound to be partial. He is a gambler who has seized his opportunities. He has never had a hard-and-fast game plan as such, but he understood how pieces of the information jigsaw puzzle could be fitted together to make an international company of enormous reach and power. By any standards it is an extraordinary achievement. Yet he is still restless. He is still after more. "Because News Corp has some ten billion dollars in revenue, we are thought of as a big company," he said in February 1997. "Well, we don't see ourselves that way. We think of News Corp as tiny—relative to the opportunities in the worldwide market for media. . . . We want to be one of the biggest and, more important, the best software company in the world, providing news and entertainment under great, lasting and profitable brand names."

One could argue endlessly about the precise cocktail of emotions and ambitions that made him. He is a complicated, often ruthless, often charming, usually effective but sometimes uncomfortable mix of Patrick Murdoch and Rupert Greene. He has more than one personality. He can be prim and yet he is a "larrikin," an Australian troublemaker who enjoys confronting established authorities. He sees himself as a radical and likes to provoke. But he has not always been careful of the consequences. He deals in simplicities, and simplicities can be dangerous.

He is an entrepreneur of genius and a dedicated publisher. Throughout his career he has rescued or started newspapers and television stations, but he has not always improved the papers he has saved. He can think faster than most of his competitors and therefore often outsmarts them. His intuitive judgment is usually good—though better of businesses than of people. The power that he has accumulated and deployed on behalf of his allies is awesome to their enemies.

Murdoch has said, "That's the fun of it, isn't it, having a smidgen of power?" He said in an interview for this book that he wanted to leave the world a better place, as he saw it. "There'll be others who'll say it was a worse place . . . I think they'd be wrong. But the worst thing they can say about me is that I have too much power."

He succeeded because he dared—as with Fox, at Wapping and with BSkyB. As a manager he was a constant interferer. Some who fell out with him felt he used people contemptuously and cast them away. Some argued that News was run merely as a treadmill to sustain Murdoch's own ego, with inadequate regard for the responsibilities of a free press in a free society. But within News there were others at every level who testified to his generosity, to the extraordinary enthusiasm he inspired and to his courage. Simon Jenkins, the former editor of the London *Times,* said he could think of no publisher in Britain who would have allowed him such editorial freedom.

In Britain some of his papers were identified with ugly and intrusive attacks upon the royal family. Murdoch's enemies argued that the *Sun* had cheapened British journalism and had debased the values of the class which read the paper. The salacious invasions of privacy that some of his papers have practiced are indeed indefensible. Murdoch himself acknowledged that some of them had had "horrible lapses of taste and done things which shouldn't easily be forgiven." But the *Sun* could also be concise, pertinent and very witty. By 1996 it, like its sibling the *Sunday Times,* had a new, calmer editor—and the circulation of both had increased.

The hatred that Murdoch arouses among a section of people in Britain was displayed in some of the British reviews of this book. One journalist described Murdoch as merely "a pornographer" who sold "excrement." Another wrote that he saw Murdoch once and "never before had I seen evil so clearly expressed in a human face." Such views seem to this author grotesque. Murdoch believes that many British intellectuals have a disdain for business success, and he has a point. In March 1997, Murdoch further confounded his British critics when he had the *Sun* ditch the Conservatives at the very start of the election campaign and support Tony Blair, the new Labour leader. He was accused of jumping onto the winning side. He responded that Britain desperately needed a change of government, and he believed Blair to be sincere in his promise to build on, not destroy, the achievements of Thatcherism.

Even his antagonists have to acknowledge that Murdoch allows them the freedom to speak. That is one reason why he has such a bad press. A book like this could not have been written about Robert Maxwell while he was alive or, indeed, about many other tycoons. It is immensely to Murdoch's credit that, although one of the most successful entrepreneurs in the world, he does not attempt to cow critics.

He inherited from Rupert Greene the need to live on the edge and, like any successful gambler, he was blessed with luck. To some his acquisitiveness seemed a kind of madness. Like Don Giovanni, he could never have enough. Beyond the empire, he had no other real interests apart from his family, to whom he is devoted. In his mid-sixties he is still a man possessed—and lonely. Only a few of those who have helped him build his empire are still close to him.

Murdoch sees himself as "totally internationalist," believing in a free market in ideas as well as goods. What this actually seems to mean is that he thinks the export of American values and products is always a blessing. His views are conservative. He loathes the strictures of feminism and the gay-rights lobby and feels that "political correctness" inhibits needed discussion of the problems of the black ghettos. Far from believing that his New York *Post* inflamed racial tensions, he has said that he did not allow it to be forthright enough about racial problems.

Whatever happens to Murdoch, he has an importance far beyond himself. The information age offers extraordinary opportunities, but there is no guarantee that they will be realized. What will matter are the choices of the barons who control the fantastic new holdings in the global village. Companies such as Murdoch's News, Time Warner, Sony and Bertelsmann are now in a position to set the agenda for the millennium. No one has elected them to such responsibility. Technology, the market and, in Murdoch's case, invincible energy and ambition have given it to them.

The age on which we are now embarked is impossible to map. The agricultural age was driven by the plow and draft animals, the industrial age by engines and their fuel. The information age is formatted by computers, software, television and the satellites and lines that link them.

In the past a nation's transportation infrastructure controlled its wealth. Thus, a small maritime nation like Britain, with excellent deepwater ports, became the principal trading nation of the world, and its richest. Now a powerful new highway system for information is being created.

The new satellite systems and the optical-fiber networks that are currently being laid across the United States and, more slowly, elsewhere are capable of carrying thousands of times more traffic than the traditional copper wire. Four huge industries—computers, consumer electronics, telecommunications and entertainment—are now converging. Digital electronics is marching ever onward, converting everything—information, sound, video, text and images—into a single stream of digits that are encoded for endless transmission around the world. What will happen is almost as hard to predict as it would have been in 1700 to anticipate the car or the plane.

For the makers of consumer software, the march means huge and changing markets. To stave off attacks by newly competitive industries, rather than by old rivals, defensive alliances are being created among the new superpowers. Time Warner, the world's largest media company, and Toshiba, the world's largest computer company, are collaborating to develop the first interactive television system.

In typical Murdoch fashion, News is trying to go it alone and to embrace all at once digital software and hardware, networks and content. If Murdoch's one-man show succeeds, even greater power and influence will lie at his fingertips. How he uses it will affect billions.

Between 1945 and 1991 the world was dominated by the struggle between the West and communism. The victory of the West was both essential and well won, but the struggle was enormously costly, not least to many of the Third World countries in which proxy wars were fought. But the international challenges that the world now faces—such as pollution, global warming, refugees, terrorism, nationalism, AIDS, poverty, crime and racial conflict—make the slaying of the communist dragon seem almost simple in retrospect.

Today three quarters of the world's people earn only 15 percent of its income. The gap is widening.

Information and its processing have less value in poor countries because there are few tangible goods to which they can lead. Exported by Murdoch and a few others, Western consumerist culture is becoming the only global culture.

In India and other parts of Asia, the poorest shacks have televisions and videocassette recorders and, increasingly, satellite dishes. CNN became a worldwide household name during the Gulf War. In the fall of 1991 the hunger for satellite broadcasting was met by Asiasat, which began transmitting MTV rock video, all-day sports, the new BBC World Service Television and much more besides. Star TV's footprint spreads from Turkey through Indonesia and as far north as Korea. In Latin America, Murdoch himself points out, "the appetite for television is so great that many Latin American consumers buy a satellite dish and a television set before they buy a refrigerator."

The world's appetite for American "software" seems insatiable. By the end of this decade, the American film and television industries will probably produce annual revenues of $200 billion—at least half of which will come from abroad. In the year 2000 the joint worth of American film, television and global information businesses (including computers and telecommunications businesses) may reach $3 trillion—or roughly $1 out of every $6 of global GNP. Murdoch is determined to be one of the larger giants of this colossal enterprise, and he is well on the way.

Murdoch believes that the Americanizing of the world is not only profitable for his business, but a great good in itself. But even he asked, in an interview for this book, "Are we going to homogenize the whole world with satellite and cable, with no room for local culture? I think there is a danger. One benefit may be that it is more peaceful. And more prosperous. But there will be fewer differences." In one speech, he told a story (possibly apocryphal) of how the Tuareg tribesmen of North Africa had delayed their annual camel caravan across the Sahara in order to watch an episode of "Dallas."

Americanization is bound to be, at the very least, an uncomfortable and unsettling experience. As people of the South have more and more understanding of the unequal division of resources in the world today, more and more millions of them will try to move to the northern part of the village. Global communications will exacerbate one of the great crises of the nineties—mass migration, to which Western governments have yet found no answer.

Walter Lippmann once said that journalism is a picture of reality that people can act upon. Now society is acting upon reality refracted in a thousand different ways. Where is reality when films such as Oliver Stone's *JFK* purport to tell the truth? Much of what is being transported down fiber-optic cables is either lies or pap. Deregulation lowered the quality of all television channels in France. It threatens the end of serious drama and current-affairs programs in Britain. They are disappearing also in America. In the free market which Murdoch champions, only the number of viewers matters. Yet, as newspapers decline in importance as most people's primary source of news, television needs more than ever to become the vigilant watchdog of a free society. That is not happening. Optimists argue that this is only a transitional stage, from broadcasting to narrowcasting—the digital future is likely to be hundreds of channels, catering to all possible tastes. Murdoch agrees.

Murdoch has argued that "anybody who, within the law of the land, provides a service which the public wants at a price it can afford is providing public service." By contrast, John Reith said at the founding of BBC radio, "He who prides himself on giving what he thinks the people want is creating a fictitious demand for lower standards which he will then satisfy."

Reith was undoubtedly right. But Murdoch can argue that his view is more democratic, and television is a democratic medium. Nonetheless, there is a legitimate concern. It is the democratic right of millions of Americans to enjoy American culture. But by what democratic decision are older cultures in Asia, Central Europe and elsewhere being swamped by it? Can it be controlled? Should it? Are people really being offered more choices than before? The phenomenon is so new that such questions cannot yet be answered. But they need to be asked.

This book has attempted to show how the power of information is growing, and how one man has made himself a uniquely important broker of it. Rupert Murdoch, scion of men and women from the dour beaches of Aberdeenshire, can understand that responsibility. How he meets it will determine how he is remembered.

SOURCE NOTES

PART ONE: THE EARLY YEARS

CHAPTER ONE

Cruden

History of the Free Church and James Murdoch: I am grateful to George Rosie for research in Scotland on many of the facts in this passage; also to Paul Chadwick for research on Patrick Murdoch's ministry in Australia.

Melbourne

Melbourne life: Humphrey McQueen, *Social Sketches of Australia, 1888–1975* (Penguin Books, Ringwood, Victoria, Australia, 1978), pp. 14–15.

Patrick Murdoch's ministry: *Australian Dictionary of National Biography,* vol. 10.

Church life in Melbourne: J. Stanley Martin, *A Tale of Two Churches: From West Melbourne to Box Hill* (Box Hill, St. Andrew's Presbyterian Church, Melbourne, 1967).

Patrick Murdoch's sermons: *Laughter and Tears of God and Other War Sermons* (Arbuckle, Waddell and Fawckner, Melbourne, 1915).

Patrick Murdoch on Camberwell flock: Trinity Presbyterian Church, Camberwell, 1885–1935, jubilee souvenir book (Osboldstone and Co., Melbourne, 1935), p. 17.

"full of Christian fun": *Australian Dictionary of National Biography,* vol. 10.

Recollections of Patrick Murdoch: obituary of the Revd. P. J. Murdoch in Proceedings of the Assembly, Presbyterian Church of Victoria, November 1940 (continuing Presbyterian Church archive, Melbourne).

Keith Murdoch's childhood: Desmond Zwar, *In Search of Keith Murdoch* (Macmillan, Melbourne, 1980), pp. 1–7.

Keith Murdoch's life: *Australian Dictionary of National Biography,* vol. 10.

Keith Murdoch in London: Zwar, *In Search of Keith Murdoch,* pp. 10–16.

Gallipoli

Principal sources include Zwar, *In Search of Keith Murdoch;* John Moorehead, *Gallipoli* (Hamish Hamilton, London, 1956); John Robertson, *Anzac and Empire: The Tragedy and Glory of Gallipoli* (Hamlyn, Melbourne, 1990); C. E. W. Bean, *The Story of Anzac* (Angus and Robertson, Sydney, 1941).

"The Journalist Who Stopped a War": John Avieson, as "The Correspondent Who Stopped a War," *Australian Journalism Review,* January–December 1986.

Sidney Nolan on Gallipoli: *Nolan's Gallipoli* (Australian War Memorial, Canberra, 1978), pamphlet.

Keith Murdoch in the Middle East and London: Zwar, *In Search of Keith Murdoch,* pp. 20–61; Avieson, "The Correspondent Who Stopped a War," passim; Moorehead, *Gallipoli,* pp. 311–312.

Rupert Murdoch interview with Gerard Henderson: *Australian Answers* (Random House, Milsons Point, New South Wales, Australia, 1990), pp. 249–264.

Fleet Street

Northcliffe's career: Piers Brendon, *The Life and Death of the Press Barons* (Secker and Warburg, London, 1982), pp. 108–126; Charles Wintour, *The Rise and Fall of Fleet Street* (Hutchinson, London, 1989), pp. 1–29.

Keith Murdoch on Northcliffe; Zwar, *In Search of Keith Murdoch,* p. 61.

Keith Murdoch's influence on the *Herald:* Michael Cannon, "Shaping the *Herald,*" the *Nation,* June 29, 1963; *Keith Murdoch, Journalist: A Biography* (Herald and Weekly Times, Melbourne, 1952), pamphlet.

Expansion of Herald group: *Keith Murdoch, Journalist,* passim.

Courtship and marriage: Zwar, *In Search of Keith Murdoch,* pp. 76–80; author's interview with Dame Elisabeth Murdoch.

Rupert Greene's career: author's interview with Dame Elisabeth Murdoch, Helen Handbury and Rupert Murdoch; J. Pacini, *A Century Galloped By: The First Hundred Years of the Victoria Racing Club* (Melbourne).

"No gentleman ever spoke about money or age": Melbourne *Age,* December 22, 1986.

Keith Murdoch's enemies: A. A. Calwell, *Be Just and Fear Not* (Lloyd O'Neil, Melbourne, 1972), pp. 88–95.

Rupert Murdoch and his parents: the most negative view is expressed in Thomas Kiernan, *Citizen Murdoch* (Dodd, Mead, New York, 1986), pp. 14–20.

Rupert Murdoch on his parents: author's interview.

Dame Elisabeth on herself and Keith: author's interview; interview with Michael Charlton, BBC Radio 3, February 2, 1989.

Rupert Murdoch on life as a publisher: author's interview; memorial speech at Helsingen Sanomat Centenary Seminar, October 24, 1989.

Rupert Murdoch on Patrick Murdoch: author's interview.

Rupert Murdoch on his father's fear of his being like Rupert Greene: *Financial Times,* February 1, 1988; author's interview.

Rupert Murdoch on Wagga Wagga sheep station: author's interview.

Dame Elisabeth on Rupert Murdoch's liking links with reality: interview with David McNicoll, *Bulletin,* Sydney, January 24, 1984.

Dame Elisabeth on his dislike of dissension and his gentleness: Zwar, *In Search of Keith Murdoch,* p. 96.

Dame Elisabeth on sending Rupert Murdoch to boarding school: author's interview.

Rupert Murdoch on hating Geelong: author's interview.

Rupert Murdoch on rebellion: author's interview.

Oxford

Sir Keith's health: George Munster, *Rupert Murdoch: A Paper Prince* (Penguin Books, Ringwood, Victoria, Australia), pp. 7–9; Zwar, *In Search of Keith Murdoch,* p. 122.

Rupert Murdoch, Pat Gibson and Birmingham *Gazette:* Kiernan, *Citizen Murdoch,* pp. 25–27; author's interviews with Rupert Murdoch and Pat Gibson.

Rupert Murdoch and Rohan Rivett: author's interviews with Nan and Rhyll Rivett. Murdoch-Rivett correspondence courtesy of Nan Rivett.

Rupert Murdoch at Oxford: author's interviews with Rupert Murdoch, Richard Searby, George Masterman, Harry Pitt, Asa Briggs, Nan Rivett and Pat Gibson.

Dame Elisabeth on possibility of withdrawing Rupert Murdoch from Oxford: author's interview.

Rupert Murdoch on farewell from Sir Keith and Crete: author's interview.

Rupert Murdoch on rent reduction: author's interview.

Cherwell on Rupert Murdoch: May 28 and June 11, 1952.

Hugh Cudlipp on Sir Keith Murdoch: Hugh Cudlipp, *Walking on the Water* (Bodley Head, London, 1976), pp. 202–230.

Rupert Murdoch on Keith Murdoch's death: author's interview.

Keith Murdoch's will: Munster, *Rupert Murdoch: A Paper Prince,* p. 8.

Rupert Murdoch's wish to keep Brisbane *Courier-Mail:* author's interview; Murdoch's letters to the Rivetts.

Murdoch on the *Express:* author's interview with Ted Pickering.

Rupert Murdoch's telegram on Kinsey report: Nan Rivett's files.

Adelaide

Dame Elisabeth on Adelaide wilderness: Melbourne *Age,* December 22, 1986; author's interview.

Rupert Murdoch on Brisbane *Courier-Mail:* author's interview.

Lloyd Dumas and Adelaide *News:* Munster, *Rupert Murdoch: A Paper Prince,* pp. 41–55; Michael Leapman, *Barefaced Cheek: The Apotheosis of Rupert Murdoch* (Hodder and Stoughton, London, 1983), p. 22; author's interview with Rupert Murdoch.

Ron Boland on Rupert Murdoch: author's interview.

Frank Shaw on Adelaide *News:* author's interview.

Rupert Murdoch on Robert Menzies: author's interview.

Rupert Murdoch and Commonwealth Bank: Munster, *Rupert Murdoch: A Paper Prince,* p. 41; author's interviews with Merv Rich and Vern Christie.

Rupert Murdoch on Perth *Sunday Times:* author's interview.

Rupert Murdoch on two-up: Simon Regan, quoted in *Time,* January 17, 1977.

America

Rupert Murdoch and Australian television stations: Munster, *Rupert Murdoch: A Paper Prince,* pp. 44–47.

Ron Boland on trip with Rupert Murdoch: author's interview.

Leonard Goldenson on Rupert Murdoch, and Murdoch on Goldenson: Leonard H. Goldenson with Marvin J. Wolf, *Beating the Odds* (Charles Scribner's Sons, New York, 1991), pp. 214–234.

Rupert Murdoch on *TV Guide:* author's interview.

Creation of Southern Television: Munster, *Rupert Murdoch: A Paper Prince,* pp. 44–47; author's interviews with Bill Davies and Graham King.

Sydney

Rupert Murdoch's purchase of Cumberland Newspapers and Sydney *Mirror:* Gavin Souter, *Company of Heralds* (Melbourne University Press, Melbourne, 1981), pp. 344–346; Munster, *Rupert Murdoch: A Paper Prince,* pp. 57–60; Leapman, *Barefaced Cheek,* pp. 26–28; author's interview with Rupert Murdoch.

Rivett sacking: Munster, *Rupert Murdoch: A Paper Prince,* pp. 62, 64; Leapman, *Barefaced Cheek,* p. 26; author's interviews with Rupert Murdoch and Nan Rivett.

Murdoch at Sydney *Mirror:* Munster, *Rupert Murdoch: A Paper Prince,* pp. 60–71; Leapman, *Barefaced Cheek,* pp. 28–30; *Bulletin,* Sydney, October 23, 1990; author's interviews with Rupert Murdoch, Betty Riddell, Graham King, Doug Flaherty and Douglas Brass.

Doug Flaherty: author's interview.

Steve Dunleavy story: Marc Fisher, *GQ,* April 1990.

Schoolboy suicide: author's interview with Richard Neville; Richard Neville, *INK,* May 1, 1971.

Douglas Brass and Rupert Murdoch: author's interview with Douglas Brass.

Betty Riddell and Morris West: *Bulletin,* Sydney, October 23, 1990; author's interview with Betty Riddell.

Graham King on promotion: author's interview.

Murdoch and Sydney television: Munster, *Rupert Murdoch: A Paper Prince,* pp. 65–71.

Murdoch, Goldenson and Plitt: Goldenson, *Beating the Odds,* pp. 214–234; author's interview with Graham King.

Murdoch and Merv Rich: author's interview with Merv Rich.

Canberra

Rupert Murdoch on idea for starting the *Australian:* author's interview.

Rupert Murdoch on Canberra *Times:* author's interview.

Fairfax takeover of Canberra *Times* and early history of the *Australian:* Souter, *Company of Heralds,* pp. 353–359.

Max Newton biography: Clyde Packer, *No Return Ticket* (Angus and Robertson, Sydney, 1984), pp. 100–129; Munster, *Rupert Murdoch: A Paper Prince,* pp. 74–76.

Newton on Murdoch: the *Australian,* July 15, 1989.

The *Australian's* teething troubles: Munster, *Rupert Murdoch: A Paper Prince,* pp. 77–81; Leapman, *Barefaced Cheek,* pp. 31–37.

Newton on being "an impossible bugger": *Times on Sunday,* Melbourne, January 31, 1988.

Murdoch on the *Australian* as "idealistic effort": author's interview.

Cavan

Anna Torv's background: author's interviews with Anna Murdoch and Karin Torv. Also, profiles of and interviews with Anna Murdoch, for example: Sally Bedell Smith, *Time,* January 1976; *Sunday Times,* London, June 16, 1985; *Sunday Express,* London, July 7, 1985; Washington *Post,* October 23, 1985; *Independent* magazine, London, March 9, 1991; *Good Housekeeping,* June 1988; *Times,* London, August 3, 1988; *Telegraph* Sunday magazine, London, August 7, 1988; Boston *Globe,* February 15, 1989; *Sunday Telegraph,* Sydney, June 9, 1991; Sydney *Morning Herald,* December 5, 1986.
Betty Riddell on Rupert Murdoch: *Bulletin,* Sydney, October 23, 1990; author's interview.

PART TWO: BREAKING OUT

CHAPTER TWO

London

The story of Murdoch's purchase of the *News of the World* is told at length in all the biographies of Murdoch and of Robert Maxwell. The author has also interviewed Rupert Murdoch, Lord Catto, Lady Carr, William Carr (son of Sir William and Lady Carr), Sarah Carr and Merv Rich.
Lord Catto on Rupert Murdoch, the *Mirror* and the *News of the World:* author's interview.
Carr family and *News of the World:* Tom Bower, *Maxwell the Outsider* (Mandarin, London, 1991), pp. 170–182; Munster, *Rupert Murdoch: A Paper Prince,* pp. 117–131; Leapman, *Barefaced Cheek,* pp. 41–49.
Carr family reactions to Maxwell and Murdoch: author's interviews with William Carr and Lady Carr.
Shareholders' extraordinary meeting: Munster, *Rupert Murdoch: A Paper Prince,* pp. 123–124; Bower, *Maxwell the Outsider,* pp. 180–182.

Rupert Murdoch on cleaning ladies: Wintour, *The Rise and Fall of Fleet Street*, p. 225.

Sarah Carr's remarks: author's interview.

Murdoch's ownership of *News of the World:* Somerfield, *Banner Headlines*, pp. 183–194; Munster, *Rupert Murdoch: A Paper Prince*, pp. 124–127; Leapman, *Barefaced Cheek*, pp. 48–55; author's interviews with Rupert Murdoch. William Carr and Lady Carr.

David Frost encounter: Leapman, *Barefaced Cheek*, pp. 50–52; author's interviews and correspondence with David Frost.

Fleet Street

Old Spanish customs in Fleet Street: Simon Jenkins, *The Market for Glory* (Faber and Faber, London, 1986), pp. 73–99.

Rupert Murdoch on mess at Bouverie Street: author's interview.

Maxwell and the *Sun:* Leapman, *Barefaced Cheek*, p. 56; author's interviews with Hugh Cudlipp and Frank Rogers.

Larry Lamb's hiring: Larry Lamb, *Sunrise* (Papermac, London, 1989), pp. 6–8.

Early days of the *Sun:* ibid., pp. 9–41; Munster, *Rupert Murdoch: A Paper Prince*, pp. 133–138; Leapman, *Barefaced Cheek*, pp. 58–59; author's interviews with Rupert Murdoch and Graham King.

Sacking of Stafford Somerfield: S. W. Somerfield, *Banner Headlines* (Scan Books, Shoreham-by-Sea, U.K., 1979), pp. 187–194.

Murdoch and London Weekend Television: Munster, *Rupert Murdoch: A Paper Prince*, pp. 140–142; author's interviews with Tom Margerison and David Frost.

Sydney

Murdoch on Deamer: author's interview with Rupert Murdoch; Munster, *Rupert Murdoch: A Paper Prince*, pp. 87–92.

Murdoch and Sydney *Telegraphs:* Munster, *Rupert Murdoch: A Paper Prince*, pp. 95–98.

Whitlam and 1972 election: ibid., pp. 95–103; Kiernan, *Citizen*

Murdoch, p. 141; Henderson, *Australian Answers,* pp. 254–256; author's interview with Rupert Murdoch.

"far too deeply involved": author's interview with Rupert Murdoch.

Texas

San Antonio: Munster, *Rupert Murdoch: A Paper Prince,* pp. 151–153; *Newsweek,* July 14, 1975; David Shaw, Los Angeles *Times,* May 25 and 26, 1983.

Lord Lambton: Munster, *Rupert Murdoch: A Paper Prince,* pp. 144–145.

CHAPTER THREE

America

Glut of information: Neil Postman, *Amusing Ourselves to Death* (Penguin, New York, 1986), p. 68.

Press baron wars: Brendon, *The Life and Death of the Press Barons,* passim; Richard C. Wald, "A Ride on the Truth Machine," *Gannett Center Journal,* Spring 1987, pp. 7–20.

Dorothy Schiff's life story and New York *Post* history: Jeffrey Porter, *Men, Money and Magic: The Story of Dorothy Schiff* (Coward, McCann and Geoghegan, New York, 1976).

New York *Post* takeover: *Time,* January 17, 1977.

Schiff-Murdoch meeting: Leapman, *Barefaced Cheek,* p. 81; Munster, *Rupert Murdoch: A Paper Prince,* p. 158.

Murdoch to Alexander Cockburn: *Village Voice,* November 29, 1976.

Murdoch on the New York *Post:* ibid.; Munster, *Rupert Murdoch: A Paper Prince,* p. 158.

Post staff members on Murdoch takeover: Washington *Post,* November 21, 1986; *Wall Street Journal,* November 22, 1986.

The *Observer* fracas: *Sunday Times,* London, October 24, 1976; *Times,* London, November 15, 1976; *Sunday Times,* London, November 28, 1976; *Cosmopolitan,* July 1986.

Murdoch and Felker: Gail Sheehy wrote in *Rolling Stone,* July 18, 1977, a very full account from Clay Felker's point of view. See also *Time,* January 17, 1977, and *Wall Street Journal,* January 7, 1977.

Peter Tufo's view: author's interview.

Felker on family being broken up by Murdoch: Sheehy, *Rolling Stone*, July 18, 1977.

Denouement: New York *Times*, January 7, 1977; Washington *Post*, January 9, 1977.

Felker on Murdoch's motives: author's interview.

Murdoch's impact on New York *Post: Time*, January 24, 1977; *MORE*, November 1977; *Columbia Journalism Review*, July–August 1982.

Murdoch on elitist journalism: Washington *Post*, May 13, 1977; *Cosmopolitan*, July 1986.

Son of Sam story: Munster, *Rupert Murdoch: A Paper Prince*, pp. 169–170; Leapman, *Barefaced Cheek*, pp. 105–107; *GQ*, April 1990; New York *Times*, August 22, 1977.

Murdoch's apology: *MORE*, November 1977.

Murdoch and Hamill: *MORE*, November 1977; Washington *Post*, November 30, 1977.

Murdoch on support for Ed Koch: *Esquire*, May 22, 1979; Munster, *Rupert Murdoch: A Paper Prince*, pp. 171–174.

New York newspaper strike: Munster, *Rupert Murdoch: A Paper Prince*, pp. 175–183; Leapman, *Barefaced Cheek*, pp. 111–121.

Josef Barletta on Murdoch: Leapman, *Barefaced Cheek*, p. 120; Patrick Brogan, *New Republic*, June 24, 1985.

Abe Rosenthal on Murdoch: quoted in Leapman, ibid., and Brogan, ibid.

Washington Journalism Review: March 1984.

Columbia Journalism Review: January–February 1980, quoted by Rupert Murdoch in the 1990 Chet Huntley Memorial Lecture.

Murdoch's response: *MORE*, November 1977; *Esquire*, May 22, 1979.

The Clarke Ring

Murdoch on Clarke: speech to International Institute of Communications, September 15, 1988.

Clarke's history: *Sunday Times*, London, October 22, 1989.

Satellite history: Ernie Eban, *Listener*, March 11, 1982; author's interviews with Les Brown (editor of *Channels*), Brian Haynes, Jonathan Miller and Jeff Hollister; John Burgess, Washington *Post*, August

27, 1989; Washington *Post*, March 17, 1985, and June 14, 1988.

Clay T. Whitehead's actions: Washington *Post*, November 7, 1971; interview with Marc Champion, on behalf of the author.

WARC 77: author's interviews with Jonathan Miller and Brian Haynes; Marc Champion's interview with Tom Whitehead.

Satellite developments: Rosemary Righter, *Whose News Anyway?* (Burnett Books, London, 1978), pp. 217–228.

Australia

Sun as engine of empire: *Esquire*, May 22, 1979.

Murdoch on children's schooling: McCrann, Melbourne *Age*, November 23, 1979.

Murdoch on Whitlam's socialism: author's interview.

1975 election story: Munster, *Rupert Murdoch: A Paper Prince*, pp. 107–114.

The definitive account of the newspapers and the election is C. J. Lloyd, "The Media and the Elections," in Howard R. Penniman, *Australia at the Polls: The National Elections of 1975* (American Enterprise Institute for Public Policy Research, Washington, D.C., 1977), pp. 171–209.

Gambling background and Robert Sangster on Rupert Murdoch: quoted in Thomas J. O'Hanlon, unpublished biography of Murdoch; O'Hanlon, *Fortune*, November 6, 1978, and May 7, 1979; James Cooke, *Forbes*, March 6, 1989.

Murdoch and television applications: Papers from the Australian Broadcasting Tribunal, 1979–80; Munster, *Rupert Murdoch: A Paper Prince*, pp. 184–199; author's interviews with Rupert Murdoch, Deirdre O'Connor and Jim Cruthers.

Herald share price story: Munster, *Rupert Murdoch: A Paper Prince*, pp. 152–194.

London

The *Sun* and the 1979 election: Larry Lamb, *Sunrise*, pp. 154–168; author's interview with Rupert Murdoch and correspondence with Gordon Reece.

Lamb on Murdoch: Lamb, *Sunrise*, pp. 219–235.

Washington

Max Newton's life: Packer, *No Return Ticket*, pp. 121–129; *Times on Sunday*, Melbourne, January 31, 1988; Sunday *Observer*, Melbourne, August 18, 1990; author's interview with Olivia Newton.

Ansett-Boeing purchase: United States Senate, Ansett Loan and Export-Import Aircraft Financing Policies, *Hearings before the Committee on Banking, Housing and Urban Affairs*, May 12–13, 1980, passim.

CHAPTER FOUR

London

Anna on home: author's interview.

Harry Evans' background: see Harold Evans, *Good Times, Bad Times* (Coronet Books, London, 1984); profile, *Observer*, February 22, 1981.

Times history: Leapman, *Barefaced Cheek*, p. 150.

Brunton's views of Murdoch and others: author's interview.

Evans on Murdoch as favorite: Evans, *Good Times, Bad Times*, p. 153.

Murdoch's call to Evans: ibid., p. 161.

Evans on Murdoch as prime source: ibid., p. 162.

Evans-Murdoch lunch: ibid., pp. 162–163.

Tina Brown on Murdoch's charm: ibid., pp. 164–165.

Evans urged to lead Stop Murdoch campaign: ibid., p. 167.

Hamilton, Evans, Rees-Mogg lunch: ibid., p. 168.

Committee to vet Murdoch, and final *Times* sale negotiations: Evans, *Good Times, Bad Times*, pp. 172–180; author's interviews with Gordon Brunton and William Rees-Mogg; correspondence with Hugh Trevor-Roper.

Murdoch on how well he had done: *Editor and Publisher*, April 11, 1981.

Brunton on referral: author's interview.

Referral considered at cabinet level: Evans, *Good Times, Bad Times*, p. 186; author's correspondence with John Biffen.

Evans on Mrs. Thatcher's determination to reward Murdoch: Evans, *Good Times, Bad Times,* p. 186.

Biffen's concession: in an off-the-record lobby briefing to journalists after the publication of *Good Times, Bad Times*.

Evans' frustration in Press Gallery: Evans, *Good Times, Bad Times,* p. 186.

Linklater's criticism of Evans: *Journalist,* November–December 1983.

Sunday Times journalists' action: Evans, *Good Times, Bad Times,* pp. 196–199; author's interviews with Magnus Linklater, Geoffrey Robertston, Tony Geraghty, Hugo Young and Don Berry.

Murdoch on reasons for appointing Evans: author's interview with Rupert Murdoch.

Evans on his own ambition: "Inside Story," Public Broadcasting System, April 27, 1984.

Frank Giles on accepting appointment: Frank Giles, *Sundry Times* (John Murray, London, 1986), p. 199.

The Village

Murdoch on Reuters: author's interview.

The Reuters story is told in John Lawrenson and Lionel Barber, *The Price of Truth* (Mainstream Publishing, Edinburgh, 1985); also author's interviews with Gerald Long and Glen Renfrew.

Glen Renfrew on Murdoch's fascination: author's interview.

Receiving countries' consent: Righter, *Whose News Anyway?,* pp. 220–221.

Australia

Profits crash: Munster, *Rupert Murdoch: A Paper Prince,* p. 246.

Cowley on Murdoch and the *Australian:* author's interview.

London

Evans' meeting with *Times* journalists: Evans, *Good Times, Bad Times,* p. 266.

Gerald Long on Bernard Donoughue: author's interview.

Evans' vigorous if chaotic methods: author's interviews and correspondence with Richard Williams, Edward Mortimer, Richard Davy, Gerald Long, Richard Searby, Jessica Douglas-Home and Adrian Hamilton.

Evans on *Times*' Bermuda Triangle and other problems: Evans, *Good Times, Bad Times,* pp. 309–349.

Gerald Long on Evans' lack of stamina: letter to the author.

Edward Mortimer and Hugh Trevor-Roper: author's interview with Mortimer and correspondence with Trevor-Roper.

Gerald Long on Evans' budgetary ideas: letter to the author.

Evans on Murdoch and politics: Evans, *Good Times, Bad Times,* p. 296.

Murdoch on Evans: author's interview.

Murdoch to Australian journalist: Terry McCrann, Sydney *Morning Herald,* November 19, 1983.

Gerald Long on working for News: author's interview.

Richard Searby on Gerald Long: author's interview.

Edward Pickering on Gerald Long: author's interview.

Murdoch on Giles' alleged communism: Evans, *Good Times, Bad Times,* p. 358.

Giles on Murdoch's "bitter animus": Giles, *Sundry Times,* pp. 202–203.

Giles on Murdoch's kindness to chauffeur: author's interview.

Affair of the titles: Evans, *Good Times, Bad Times,* pp. 432–449; author's interviews with Richard Searby, Edward Pickering and Gerald Long, and correspondence with Harold Evans.

Evans on Douglas-Home accepting the editorship: Evans, *Good Times, Bad Times,* p. 456.

Murdoch on death of Evans' father: ibid., p. 451.

Searby on Evans' departure: author's interview.

Evans on his resignation dilemma: Evans, *Good Times, Bad Times,* pp. 450–487.

Union demand for Evans to resign: Leapman, *Barefaced Cheek,* pp. 234–235.

Edward Mortimer on Evans: author's interview.

Gerald Long on Evans and Murdoch: author's interview.

The Falklands

A full account of the British press and the Falklands war is in Robert Harris, *Gotcha! The Media, the Government and the Falklands Crisis* (Faber and Faber, London, 1983).

Murdoch as "Communications Man of the Year," and on parallel between Falklands and Israel: New York *Post*, April 22, 1982.

Kelvin MacKenzie's life and times: A full and hilarious account is Peter Chippindale and Chris Horrie, *Stick It Up Your Punter* (Heinemann, London, 1990).

Frank Giles' departure: Giles, *Sundry Times*, pp. 247–251.

Magnus Linklater on *Good Times, Bad Times: Journalist*, November–December 1983.

Harold Evans' letter to Magnus Linklater: January 6, 1984.

Harold Evans' letter to Patrick Brogan: November 29, 1984.

Rupert Murdoch on Evans: Sydney *Morning Herald*, November 19, 1983.

Philip Howard on Charles Douglas-Home: in introduction to Philip Howard, *We Thundered Out: A Bicentenary History of the* Times (Times Books, London, 1985).

Charles Douglas-Home's relations with Murdoch: author's interviews with Edward Mortimer, Richard Davy, Alan Franks and Jessica Douglas-Home.

CHAPTER FIVE

Boston

Murdoch on welfare state: *Fortune*, January 15, 1979.

Murdoch at lunch with Reagan: author's interview with News America executive.

Murdoch criticisms of investigatory journalism: David Shaw, Los Angeles *Times*, May 25 and 26, 1983.

Donald Kummerfeld's role: author's interview.

Paul Rigby's departure from New York *Post:* author's interview.

Murdoch on *Post'*s support for Reagan: *Editor and Publisher,* April 11, 1981.

Murdoch and Koch: Michael Davie, the *Spectator,* February 27, 1982; Patrick Brogan, *New Republic,* June 24, 1985.

Columbia Journalism Review on Steve Dunleavy: July–August 1982.

Mario Cuomo on *Post: Columbia Journalism Review,* July–August 1982.

Bloomingdale's man to *Wall Street Journal:* quoted by Patrick Brogan, *New Republic,* June 24, 1985.

Murdoch's interest in *Courier Express* and *Daily News:* Leapman, *Barefaced Cheek,* pp. 245–250.

"TRIB TO RUPERT: DROP DEAD": *Daily News,* New York, May 1, 1982.

Murdoch and the *Herald:* Lea Kevivali, "The Murdoch Influence on the Boston *Herald,*" thesis submitted to the Royal Melbourne Institute of Technology, November 1988.

Donald Forst and Murdoch: *Boston* magazine, May 1983; Leapman, *Barefaced Cheek,* pp. 250–253.

David Greenway on Boston *Herald:* author's interview.

Murdoch on Boston's passion: *Boston* magazine, May 1983.

The Clarke Ring

Murdoch's move onto Clarke Ring: Washington *Post,* May 6, 1983; *Newsweek,* June 6, 1983; *Business Week,* July 11, 1983; author's interview with Jim Cruthers.

Murdoch signing with SBS: Washington *Post,* May 6, 1983.

SBS background: *Broadcasting,* March 13, 1983; *USA Today,* November 15, 1983; New York *Times,* November 15, 1983; author's interview with Les Brown.

Murdoch on missing cable: interview with Raymond Snoddy, *New Media Markets,* February 17, 1988; Sydney *Morning Herald,* November 13, 1989.

Jim Cruthers on problems with Skyband: author's interview; Murdoch in *Fortune,* February 20, 1984.

Sky television beginnings: author's interview with Jim Haynes.

Development of satellite broadcasting: *Financial Times* survey on broadcasting, September 16, 1985, and *Financial Times* survey on satellites, May 29, 1990.

Tom Whitehead in Luxembourg: Whitehead interview with Marc Champion on behalf of the author.

Chicago

Charles Wilson's account of the *Sun-Times:* author's interview.

Field family and growth and sale of *Sun-Times:* Chicago *Tribune,* January 22, 1984; Garry Wills, *Vanity Fair,* May 1984.

Jim Hoge's role: author's correspondence with Jim Hoge; Wills, *Vanity Fair,* May 1984.

Sale of *Sun-Times* to Murdoch: New York *Times,* November 2, 1983; *Newsweek,* November 14, 1983; *Wall Street Journal,* December 21, 1983.

Royko's departure: interview with Carole Kismaric; Washington *Post,* January 11, 1984; New York *Times,* January 14, 1984; *Chicago Lawyer,* February 1984; *Washington Journalism Review,* March 1984.

Roger Ebert on Murdoch and Field: *Vanity Fair,* May 1984.

Wilson on Brogan: author's interview.

Wilson on changes: author's interview.

Medill School study: "The *Sun-Times:* Before and After Murdoch," Spring 1984.

Frank Devine: author's interview.

PART THREE: THE NEW WORLD

CHAPTER SIX

1984

Forbes on Murdoch: January 30, 1984.

Orwell and Huxley: Postman, *Amusing Ourselves to Death,* pp. 110–112.

Huxleyan future: ibid., p. 156.

Computer history: Gene Smarte and Andrew Reinhardt in *Byte,* September 1990, pp. 369–400.

Computer as "leviathan instrument of Big Brother" and growth of small computer companies: George Gilder, *Microcosm* (Simon and Schuster, New York, 1989), passim.

Walter Wriston on Rupert Murdoch: author's interview.

Walter Wriston on communications revolution: *Foreign Affairs*, Winter 1988/9.

Soviet leaders and telephones: Wilson P. Dizard, Jr., and S. Blake Swensrud, *Gorbachev's Information Revolution: Controlling Glasnost in a New Electronic Era* (The Center for Strategic and International Studies, Westview Press, Boulder, Colorado, 1987).

News Corp's position in 1984: *Australian Business*, November 30, 1983; *Forbes*, January 30, 1984; *Economist*, February 25 and March 2, 1984; *Fortune*, February 20, 1984.

Murdoch on direction of electronic age: *Fortune*, February 20, 1984.

Kiernan-Murdoch agreement: signed March 21, 1984.

News Corp revenues: *Fortune*, February 20, 1984.

Murdoch on "screwing up": *Economist*, February 25, 1984.

Sarazen to *Economist:* ibid.

Changes at the *Australian:* author's interviews with Ken Cowley, Richard Searby and News Ltd. journalists.

New York *Post* figures, etc.: *Economist*, February 25, 1984.

Murdoch acknowledging that Times Newspapers was different: interview with Terry McCrann, Melbourne *Age*, November 21, 1983.

"Let someone else *own* the satellites": *Forbes*, January 30, 1984.

Murdoch on failed editors: *Forbes*, June 30, 1984; *U.S. News & World Report*, May 27, 1985.

Murdoch to Barbara Walters: "20/20," ABC TV, June 28, 1984.

Hollywood

Economist on American entertainment industry: *Economist* survey, December 23, 1989.

Warner Communications story: *Financial Times*, December 29, 1983; *Wall Street Journal*, January 4, 1984; *Financial Times*, January 7, 1984; New York *Times*, January 8, 1984; *Business Week*, January 16,

1984; *Wall Street Journal,* January 18, 1984; author's interview with Rupert Murdoch.

Shuman-Ross-Murdoch meeting: Richard Sarazen deposition, Court of Chancery, Wilmington, Delaware, January 9, 1984.

Warner's decline: *Fortune,* January 13, 1983; *New York* magazine, January 24, 1983.

Murdoch on "investment": *Wall Street Journal,* January 18, 1984.

Murdoch launches campaign for Warner: New York *Times,* January 4, 1984; Washington *Post,* January 6, 1984.

Murdoch-Ross meeting: Boston *Globe,* December 18, 1983.

Warner and Chris-Craft: Jerome Tuccille, *Rupert Murdoch* (Donald I. Fine, New York, 1989), p. 114.

Murdoch files suit to block Warner–Chris-Craft deal: Washington *Post,* January 7, 1984.

Murdoch in court: Washington *Post,* January 12, 1984.

Murdoch on "pattern of racketeering" at Warner: New York *Times,* January 25, 1984; *Daily Telegraph,* London, January 26, 1984; Tuccille, *Rupert Murdoch,* p. 118.

Warner attack on Murdoch: Washington *Post,* January 11, 1984.

Murdoch in Switzerland: Michael Leapman, *Arrogant Aussie* (Lyle Stuart, Secaucus, New Jersey, 1985), p. 266.

Steve Dunleavy and Ross: New York *Times,* January 28, 1984.

Murdoch on not being run down: New York *Times,* February 6, 1984.

Murdoch's $40 million profit: *Newsweek,* March 26, 1984; *Broadcasting,* March 26, 1984.

Murdoch to *Economist:* February 25, 1984.

Twentieth Century Fox history: John Gregory Dunne, *The Studio* (Farrar, Straus & Giroux, New York, 1969), passim; Stephen M. Silverman, *The Fox That Got Away* (Lyle Stuart, Secaucus, New Jersey, 1988), passim.

Davis and Marc Rich: Alex Ben Block, *Outfoxed* (St. Martin's Press, New York, 1990), pp. 15–16, 72–73.

Marvin Davis and Fox: ibid., pp. 14–29, 59–83.

Marc Rich charged with tax evasion: ibid., p. 82.

Barry Diller–Marvin Davis relationship: ibid., pp. 59–83.

Milken and Drexel Burnham Lambert impact on industry: *Wall Street Journal*, September 18, 1989; *Financial Times*, September 20, 1989; *Sunday Telegraph*, London, May 6, 1990; *Business Week*, December 31, 1990.

Milken's fall: Allan Sloan, *Newsday*, April 22, 1990.

Murdoch agrees to buy 50 percent of Fox: Washington *Post*, March 21, 1985; New York *Times*, March 21, 1985; Block, *Outfoxed*, p. 82.

Diller's "exit rights": Block, *Outfoxed*, p. 82.

Murdoch buys half of Fox: *Variety*, September 25, 1985.

Murdoch on entertainment and news reporting: Block, *Outfoxed*, p. 86.

Murdoch in China: statement by Howard Rubenstein, May 1985; *Business Review Weekly*, Sydney, December 5, 1986.

Murdoch taking only minutes to decide to buy Metromedia: interview with Trevor Kennedy in Trevor Kennedy, *Top Guns* (Sun Books, Melbourne, 1988), pp. 280–300.

Kluge story: New York *Herald Tribune*, September 6, 1964; *Fortune*, April 5, 1982.

Kluge's development of Metromedia: Allan Sloan, *Forbes*, April 23, 1984, December 17, 1984, and June 3, 1985, and *Wall Street Journal*, May 8, 1985.

Murdoch's financing of Metromedia: *Business Week*, May 20, 1985; Allan Sloan, *Forbes*, June 3, 1985; *Business Review Weekly*, Sydney, August 23, 1985; *Wall Street Journal*, January 23, 1986.

Sarazen on Murdoch: *Business Review Weekly*, Sydney, August 23, 1985.

Murdoch's anger with Drexel: Block, *Outfoxed*, pp. 106–107.

Davis withdrawal from Fox and Murdoch's reaction: ibid., pp. 108–109.

Alexander Cockburn on selling the *Post: Wall Street Journal*, May 23, 1985.

"Ellis Island"

Citizenship ceremony: New York *Times*, September 5, 1985; *Financial Review*, Sydney, September 6, 1985; additional background supplied by Glenda Korporaal.

Breslin on Murdoch's citizenship: *Daily News,* New York, September 6, 1985.

William Safire on Murdoch's citizenship: quoted in *Media Week,* May 24, 1985.

Mike Royko on Murdoch's citizenship: *Daily News,* New York, May 15, 1985.

Mark Fowler's background and views: *Broadcasting,* February 18, 1985; *Christian Science Monitor,* May 20, 1985; *Business Week,* August 5, 1985.

Murdoch on Mark Fowler: "Implications of the Communications Revolution," United States Information Agency, International Council Conference III, May 1990, p. 16 of transcript.

Quello on "fast-buck artists": *Business Week,* August 5, 1985.

Quello on Murdoch: interview with Glenda Korporaal, 1985; *Business Week,* May 20, 1985.

Murdoch to Sydney *Morning Herald:* May 6, 1985.

Anna Murdoch on Murdoch's ambition: William H. Meyers, New York *Times, Business World* magazine, June 12, 1988; author's interview.

Anna's sharp tongue: Murdoch told *Cosmopolitan,* "She can cut me off at the knees better than anybody else" (July 1986).

Anna Murdoch on not wanting to be a partygoer: Washington *Post,* October 23, 1985.

"We *are* [good people]": ibid.

Anna Murdoch to *Time:* January 6, 1976, interview by Sally Bedell Smith, cover story on Murdoch published January 17, 1977.

Anna Murdoch on Murdoch's "deafness": *Sunday Express,* London, July 7, 1985.

Anna Murdoch on traditional household and marriage: Washington *Post,* October 23, 1985.

Murdoch's "devastating" criticisms: Washington *Post,* October 23, 1985.

Anna Murdoch to *Sunday Times:* June 16, 1985.

Melbourne *Age*'s fun: August 9, 1985.

CHAPTER SEVEN

Wapping

The best account of the Wapping story is Linda Melvern, *The End of the Street* (Methuen, London, 1986). Also essential reading are Simon Jenkins, *The Market for Glory* (Faber and Faber, London, 1986); David Goodhart and Patrick Wintour, *Eddie Shah and the Newspaper Revolution* (Coronet, London, 1986); Brian MacArthur, *Eddie Shah*, Today *and the Newspaper Revolution* (David and Charles, Newton Abbot, U.K., 1988); also Wintour, *The Rise and Fall of Fleet Street*.

State of Fleet Street: Jenkins, *The Market for Glory*, pp. 73–96.

Start of Wapping: *Financial Times*, January 27, 1986. Also author's interviews with Rupert Murdoch, Lewis Chester and Bruce Matthews.

Fleet Street

Kelvin MacKenzie and the *Sun's* newsroom: Melvern, *The End of the Street*, pp. 56–70.

Charlie Wilson and the *Times* newsroom: ibid., pp. 80–84; author's interview with Charles Wilson.

Andrew Neil and the *Sunday Times* newsroom: Melvern, *The End of the Street*, pp. 97–118; author's interviews and correspondence with Don Berry, Lewis Chester, Claire Tomalin and Hugo Young.

Wapping

First days of Wapping: Melvern, *The End of the Street*, pp. 119–188; Wintour, *The Rise and Fall of Fleet Street*, pp. 215–223.

Murdoch on the *Independent's* gains from Wapping: Henderson, *Australian Answers*, pp. 249–264.

CHAPTER EIGHT

Melbourne

Glenda Korporaal provided a long, very useful research memorandum on the story of Murdoch's capture of the Melbourne *Herald*. The story is well told in Paul Chadwick, *Media Mates* (Macmillan, Melbourne, 1989). I have also consulted David Bowman, *The Captive Press* (Penguin, Ringwood, Victoria, Australia, 1988), pp. 85–106. See also *Time,* Australian edition, February 2, 1987. Among those whom the author has interviewed or consulted for this section are Rupert Murdoch, John D'Arcy, Ken Cowley, Keith McDonald and Eric Beecher.

Murdoch "like Father Christmas": Sydney *Morning Herald,* December 4, 1986.

Dame Elisabeth on Murdoch being like his father, and his motives: Sydney *Morning Herald,* December 5, 1986.

Murdoch like Citizen Kane: Melbourne *Age,* December 4, 1986.

Deirdre O'Connor on Australian cross-ownership rules: author's interview.

Hawke on friendship with Packer: Chadwick, *Media Mates,* pp. 31–32.

Murdoch-Keating dinner: ibid., p. 19; author's interview with Rupert Murdoch.

Murdoch's approach to the board: author's interviews with Rupert Murdoch, John D'Arcy and Ken Cowley.

Murdoch's public announcement: Chadwick, *Media Mates,* pp. 45–46.

Chronology of Murdoch's victory: ibid., pp. 41–87; Sydney *Morning Herald,* January 17, 1987.

Financial Review complaint: Chadwick, *Media Mates,* p. 45.

Hawke on Herald management: ibid., p. 36.

Murdoch's deal with Robert Holmes à Court: ibid., pp. 67–69; Sydney *Morning Herald,* January 17, 1987.

Murdoch and Queensland Press: *Financial Review,* Sydney, March 3, 1987; author's interview with Keith McDonald.

Murdoch and Northern Star: Sydney *Morning Herald,* July 30, 1988.

Murdoch's appointment of Eric Beecher: author's interviews with Murdoch, Beecher and Peter Smark.

The Village

News turnover and profits: Paul Johnson, *Spectator,* March 28, 1987.
CBS debts: *Broadcasting,* February 26, 1987.
Sarazen sanguine: ibid.
Murdoch's plans for New York *Post:* author's interview with Frank Devine; the *Nation,* February 13, 1988.
Murdoch's purchase of *South China Morning Post: Business Review Weekly,* Sydney, December 5, 1986; Tuccille, *Rupert Murdoch,* p. 162.
Performance of Fox television: *Broadcasting,* February 12, 1987.
Diller on "counterprogramming": *Broadcasting,* February 26, 1987.
Collins history: author's interviews with Ian Chapman, George Craig and Sonia Land.
Harper & Row history: New York *Times,* April 5, 1987.
Murdoch and Chapman takeover bid for Harper & Row: author's interview with Ian Chapman.
Brookes Thomas on Murdoch's bid: New York *Times,* April 5, 1987.
Murdoch's plan in linking Harper & Row and Collins: Tuccille, *Rupert Murdoch,* p. 175.
Roger Straus on things not pinned to the wall: New York *Times,* April 5, 1987.
Publishing mergers in 1980s: ibid.

London

Murdoch's takeover of *Today:* MacArthur, *Eddie Shah,* Today *and the Newspaper Revolution,* pp. 184–193; also Sydney *Morning Herald,* July 2 and 3, 1987; *Sunday Times,* London, July 5, 1987; author's interviews with Brian MacArthur and Richard Searby, and correspondence with Lord Young.
Murdoch buys Pearson stake: *Times,* London, and *Financial Times,* September 23, 1987; New York *Times,* September 28, 1987; *Financial Weekly,* March 3, 1988.
Anthony Lewis in New York *Times:* November 5, 1987.
Pearson's tactics: author's interview with Frank Barlow; *Financial*

Times, January 12 and September 15, 1988, February 3, 1990; *Financial Weekly,* February 18, 1988.

New York

Murdoch's grief on selling New York *Post:* Tuccille, *Rupert Murdoch,* pp. 187–197; author's interviews with Rupert Murdoch, Frank Devine and Richard Searby.

Max Newton on Kennedy's favor: Tuccille, *Rupert Murdoch,* p. 190.

Steve Dunleavy's style: author's interviews with staff of the *Post;* Fisher, *GQ,* April 1990.

Murdoch on his mistakes with the *Post:* Tuccille, *Rupert Murdoch,* pp. 192–197; interview in *Gannett Center Journal,* Winter 1989, pp. 33–41.

Murdoch's use to administration: *Wall Street Journal,* November 2, 1984.

Frank Devine on *Post's* problems: author's interview.

FCC and cross-ownership rule: New York *Times,* January 11, 1988; Marc Champion interviews with staff of Senate Commerce Committee.

FCC and waivers: Boston *Globe,* May 3 and November 9 and 15, 1985, January 10, 1988.

Fowler on his best action at FCC: Boston *Globe,* January 10, 1988; *Times on Sunday,* Sydney, June 3, 1988; quoted by senior staff member of Senate Commerce Committee in interview with Marc Champion.

Murdoch on delaying the sale of the *Post:* Tuccille, *Rupert Murdoch,* pp. 195–196; the *Nation,* February 13, 1988; author's interviews with Rupert Murdoch and Frank Devine.

Wall Street Journal report: quoted in the *Nation,* February 13, 1988.

Post promotion budgets cut: Roger Franklin, *Bulletin,* Sydney, March 29, 1988.

Freedom of Expression Foundation suit: the *Nation,* February 13, 1988.

William H. Meyers in New York *Times, Business World* magazine: June 12, 1988.

Murdoch papers on Kennedy: *Bulletin,* Sydney, March 29, 1988.

Howie Carr on Kennedy: quoted in *Time,* January 18, 1988.

Time chortling: January 18, 1988.

Marlin Fitzwater on amendment: New York *Times,* January 5, 1988.

Koch on Kennedy's "character flaw" and "in the dead of night": *Time,* January 18, 1988.

Kennedy on "signals," etc.: the *Nation,* February 13, 1988.

Lowell Weicker on Murdoch as "number-one dirtbag": *Congressional Record,* January 25, 1988.

Hollings on "unholy alliance": New York *Times,* February 2, 1988.

Murdoch's attack on Hollings: New York *Times,* February 12, 1988.

Frank Devine on Murdoch's depression: author's interview.

Murdoch's reluctance to sell the *Post,* and subsequent depression: Tuccille, *Rupert Murdoch,* p. 194; author's interviews with Rupert Murdoch and Frank Devine.

Kalikow negotiations: Associated Press, February 5, 1988; Washington *Post,* February 5, 1988.

Washington, D.C., Court of Appeals ruling: New York *Times,* March 30, 1988; quoted by Tuccille, *Rupert Murdoch,* p. 190; *Independent,* London, March 30, 1988.

Murdoch on "nightmare": Tuccille, *Rupert Murdoch,* p. 194.

Aspen

This account of the Aspen conference is derived principally from interviews with those present, including John Evans, Eric Beecher, Philip Crawley, Simon Jenkins, Stephen Milligan, Paul Kelly and Terry McCrann.

Carolyn Wall to New York *Times:* August 14, 1988.

John Evans' history: New York *Press,* November 24, 1989; author's interview.

John Evans on Murdoch: author's interview.

Annenberg's view of Murdoch: author's interview.

Triangle history: *Financial Times,* August 9, 1988; New York *Times,* August 11, 1988.

Annenberg on Murdoch being after "whole ball game" and being "an immense gambler": author's interview.

John Veronis' intervention: New York *Times,* August 9, 1988; *Economist,* August 13, 1988; *Advertising Age,* August 15, 1988.

Murdoch on being "too keen": author's interview.

Warren Buffett's advice to Annenberg: *Wall Street Journal,* November 8, 1991.

John Veronis on "natural conversation": New York *Times,* August 8, 1988.

Howard J. Rubenstein on "circle of friendship": ibid.

Los Angeles *Times* on science fiction fantasy: August 9, 1988.

Norman Lear's comment: interview with *Time,* August 12, 1988.

David Wagenhauser's comment: *Christian Science Monitor,* August 10, 1988.

Andrew Jay Schwartzman comment: New York *Times,* August 8, 1988.

Murdoch on finances of *TV Guide: Newsweek,* August 22, 1988.

John Evans' doubts: author's interview.

TV Guide and News' debt: *Wall Street Journal,* August 9, 1988; *Sunday Times,* London, August 14, 1988.

Colin Reader on financing purchase of *TV Guide:* author's interview.

Evans proposal to sell *TV Guide:* author's interview.

CHAPTER NINE

Sun Country

I am grateful to Peter Chippindale and Chris Horrie for permission to quote from their book, *Stick It Up Your Punter,* a comprehensive and amusing account of the history of the *Sun.* I am also grateful to Alan Rusbridger for providing me with all the research notes that he assembled for a book on the *Sun;* to Madeleine Bunting and to Nick LeQuesne for research into different aspects of the *Sun;* and to Lewis Chester for invaluable help in organizing the material.

Other sources include Roslyn Grose's semiofficial *The Sun-sation* (Angus and Robertson, London, 1989), and interviews by the author and others with *Sun* journalists, most of whom prefer to remain anonymous.

MacKenzie's praise for Murdoch: Chippindale and Horrie, *Stick It Up Your Punter*, p. 8.

Sun and Press Council: Peter Kellner, *Independent*, London, February 1, 1988.

MacKenzie on understanding the readers: Chippindale and Horrie, *Stick It Up Your Punter*, p. 110.

MacKenzie and *Sun* on homosexuals: *Sun*, December 13, 1990; Chippindale and Horrie, *Stick It Up Your Punter*, pp. 181–182.

MacKenzie's relations with Murdoch: ibid., pp. 328–329.

Murdoch on British "decadence": *Gannett Center Journal*, Winter 1989, p. 37.

David Mellor on "Last Chance Saloon": Chippindale and Horrie, *Stick It Up Your Punter*, p. 306.

Springfield, U.S.A.

The Simpsons and the audience: *Rolling Stone*, June 29, 1990; "Television Business," *Adweek*, September 10, 1990.

Barry Diller's background: Huntington Williams, *Beyond Control—ABC and the Fate of the Networks* (Atheneum, New York, 1989); *Playboy* interview, June 1989; *Buzz*, May–June 1992; Ben Block, *Outfoxed*, pp. 75–78.

Murdoch on Diller: *Business Week*, May 20, 1985.

Diller on going bananas: *Manhattan, inc.*, February 1988.

Diller on barbed wire: ibid.

Diller on William Morris background: *Playboy*, June 1989; *Buzz*, May–June 1992.

Diller at Caesars Palace: *Playboy*, June 1989.

Decline of networks after 1977: *Broadcasting*, April 17, 1989; Ken Auletta, "Why ABC Survived Best," *New York Times Magazine*, July 28, 1991.

Fox reflecting American changes: Nicholas Lemann, "How the Seventies Changed America," *American Heritage*, July–August 1991.

Goldenson's strategy: Block, *Outfoxed*, pp. 122–123.

Joan Rivers story: ibid., pp. 140–157.

Murdoch saying "Buy her contract out": *Business Week,* June 1, 1987.

Rivers' settlement: *Broadcasting,* June 8, 1987.

Fox's losses: Los Angeles *Times* calendar, March 12, 1989; *Forbes,* August 1, 1990.

Diller on grafting an alien thing, and things getting worse before better: author's interview.

Impact of screenwriters' strike: J. Max Robbins, *Channels Field Guide,* 1990.

Tracey Ullman success: Jerry Lazar, *New York Times Magazine,* October 15, 1989.

Diller on "cratering" the old company, and grabbing by the throat: author's interview.

"PMS": *Guardian,* April 7, 1989.

Terry Rakolta: New York *Times,* March 2, 1989.

Fox toning down the show: *Wall Street Journal,* May 25, 1989.

New York *Times* editorial: March 11, 1989.

Murdoch on "subversive" Fox: author's interview.

Diller on Republican myths and difference between him and Murdoch: author's interview.

Povich on Murdoch and his "daredevil squadron": Maury Povich, *Current Affairs: A Life on the Edge* (Putnam, New York, 1991), pp. 51–52 and throughout.

John Walsh and "America's Most Wanted": Monica Collins, " 'Wanted' Captures Its Audience," *USA Today,* March 2, 1989, cover story.

Diller on "Most Wanted" success: author's interview.

"Cops" success: Harry F. Waters, "TV's Crime Wave Gets Real," *Newsweek,* May 15, 1989.

"Cops" in Soviet Union: Monica Collins, *USA Today,* July 14, 1989.

Steve Dunleavy story: Fisher, *GQ,* April 1990; Povich, *Current Affairs,* pp. 59–61, 182–187.

Tom Shales in Washington *Post:* Fisher, *GQ,* April 1990.

New York *Times* on "A Current Affair": ibid.

Australia

The story of the Collins takeover is based on contemporary reports and interviews with the contemporaries, including Rupert Murdoch, Ian Chapman, Sonia Land and George Craig.

Murdoch and phone call from France: Murdoch's synopsis for his autobiography.

Murdoch and Chapman's relations: author's interviews with Ian Chapman and George Craig.

News International bid for Collins: *Financial Times*, November 18, 1988; *Independent*, London, November 19, 1988; author's interview with Lord Goodman.

Murdoch's matching bid: *Times*, London, December 31, 1988.

Chapman's reiteration: ibid.

Presses de la Cité call to Murdoch: Murdoch's synopsis for his autobiography.

Collins with few options: *Financial Times*, January 6, 1989.

Michael Frayn on Murdoch: *Guardian*, January 6, 1989.

Ken Follett on Murdoch: *Independent*, London, January 6, 1989.

Murdoch's response to authors' criticisms: *Daily Telegraph*, London, January 7, 1989.

Chapman's departure: author's interview.

Brisbane *Sun* and Adelaide *News* arrangements: Sydney *Morning Herald*, July 30 and August 1, 1988.

Trade Practices Commission report: "Investigation of Disposal by News International of the *Sun* and *Sunday Sun* in Brisbane and the *News* in Adelaide," August 1989.

Fairfax's demise: There are several authoritative books. The author has used V. J. Carroll, *The Man Who Couldn't Wait* (Heinemann, Melbourne, 1990), and Gavin Souter, *Heralds and Angels* (Melbourne University Press, Melbourne, 1991).

Trade Practices Commission Stops Murdoch: Carroll, *The Man Who Couldn't Wait*, p. 282.

Murdoch's new presses: see, for example, Glenda Korporaal, *Bulletin*, Sydney, February 14, 1989.

Problems at the Melbourne *Herald:* author's interviews with Rupert
   Murdoch, Eric Beecher, John D'Arcy and Ken Cowley.
Beecher on Murdoch: author's interview.
Anna Murdoch to New York *Times:* author's interview with William
   H. Myers, who profiled Murdoch in the New York *Times Business
   World* magazine, June 12, 1988.
Murdoch on Beecher's editorial approach: author's interview.
Dame Elisabeth's birthday party: author's interviews with Dame Elisa-
   beth Murdoch, Douglas Brass and Sir James Darling.
Murdoch's diary: from the synopsis for his autobiography.

CHAPTER TEN

The Clarke Ring

Background to BSB franchise: *Independent on Sunday,* March 25,
   1990; *Financial Times,* August 12, 1989; *Times,* London, April 25,
   1990; interview by Nick LeQuesne with Brian Champness, *Marketing Week,* June 17, 1988.
Background to Sky's development 1983–87; author's interviews with
   Jim Cruthers, Peter Smith, Brian Haynes and John O'Loan; inter-
   view by Nick LeQuesne with Richard Platt.
Sky relaunch: *Times, Daily Telegraph, Guardian,* June 9, 1988.
Branson's withdrawal from BSB: Michael Maconochie, *Sunday Times*
   magazine, London, June 23, 1991.
Hollywood expenditure and encryption problems: author's interviews
   with Peter Smith, Jim Cruthers, Jonathan Miller and others.
Andrew Neil at Sky: author's interview with Jonathan Miller.
Lack of dishes: *Observer,* February 5, 1989.
Mockery of Sky: *Daily Telegraph,* London, February 4, 1989; *Inde-
   pendent,* London, February 9, 1989.
BSB's delays: "Money Programme," BBC 2, February 4, 1990; *Inde-
   pendent,* London, April 23, 1990.
Sky's relaunch: *Television Business International,* February 1990.
Sky's advertising sales problems and Sky's charter advertisers: author's
   interview with Pat Mastandrea of Sky.

Murdoch in Edinburgh: *Times* and *Independent,* London, August 26, 1989.

William Rees-Mogg's response: *Independent,* London, August 29, 1989.

Aspen

Murdoch saying he was "tapped out": author's interview with News personnel.

Story of (and Murdoch on failure of) Media Partners: *Wall Street Journal,* June 6, 1989, April 12, 1990.

Murdoch interest in Time Inc.: *Financial Times,* June 15, 1989; author's interview with John Evans.

Richard Munro on threat of Murdoch: *Wall Street Journal,* March 6, 1989; *Business Week,* March 20, 1989.

Nick Nicholas on global companies: *Wall Street Journal,* March 7, 1989.

Steve Ross on American combinations: New York *Times,* March 5, 1989.

Different characters of the media conglomerates: Smith, *The Age of Behemoths,* pp. 21–39.

Ben Bagdikian, "lords of the global village": the *Nation,* June 12, 1989.

The account of the Aspen meeting is based on author's interviews with John Evans, George Crile, Irwin Stelzer, Eric Beecher and others.

Schwarzenegger and DeVito: New York *Post,* July 31, 1989.

Irwin Stelzer's speech was provided to the author by Rupert Murdoch.

Adelaide

Editor of the Adelaide *Review*'s remarks: author's interview.

Original shareholders' bonanza: calculations by Frank Shaw of News Ltd.

News Corp's accountancy methods: the author is grateful to Richard Macdonald, Allan Sloan, Glenda Korporaal and Dominic Prince for advice on interpreting these figures. He is also grateful to Colin Reader, the treasurer of News International.

"Give me an hour" for *TV Guide* money: Sarazen interview with Ida Picker, *Institutional Investor,* November 1989.

Sarazen's background: *Corporate Finance,* April 1989.

Accounting systems: Allan Sloan, *Forbes,* March 10, 1986; also author's interviews with Colin Reader, Allan Sloan and others; Sydney *Morning Herald,* August 12, 1990.

South China Morning Post deal: *Far Eastern Economic Review,* June 21 and 28, 1990.

"Tax Payers or Tax Players?": House of Representatives Standing Committee on Finance and Public Administration, Commonwealth Parliament, May 1989.

Annual general meeting: author's notes.

Searby at the Hilton: author's notes.

Part Four: The Village

CHAPTER ELEVEN

The Evil Empire

The story of this journey is based on author's interviews with Rupert and Anna Murdoch, Peter Smith, John Evans and Rafael Pastore, and Carole Kismaric's interview with Pio Cabinillas.

Murdoch's Washington speech: the International Institute of Communications, 1988 annual conference, September 15, 1988. An abridged version was published in *Intermedia,* London, Autumn 1988; Adelaide *Advertiser,* October 3, 1988.

Murdoch on modernization and Americanization: the Wriston lecture, the Manhattan Institute, New York City, November 9, 1989.

Murdoch interview in Prague: *Lidove Noviny,* January 31, 1990.

Robert Maxwell and Eastern Europe: Francis Wheen, "Late Show," BBC, January 17, 1990.

Peter Toke and Murdoch: *Spectator,* January 13, 1990.

Murdoch on English-speaking social model: speech at the opening of the Foster's Building, University of Melbourne, Graduate School of Management, October 1, 1991.

Berlusconi's background: Anthony Smith, *The Age of Behemoths: The Globalisation of Mass Media Firms* (Twentieth Century Fund, New York, 1991), pp. 30–34; *Listener,* July 19, 1990.

London

Australian Ratings on News: *Guardian,* January 5, 1990.

Morgan Stanley on News: research memo by Glenda Korporaal.

News Corp's debt: Glenda Korporaal, *Bulletin,* Sydney, January 5, 1990; *Wall Street Journal,* April 12, 1990; *Economist,* August 18, 1990.

Fox and "fin-syn" rules: *Broadcasting,* February 5, 1990: *Independent,* London, February 19, 1990.

John Evans on digital world: author's interview.

Andrew Knight's appointment: *Financial Times,* January 3, 1990; *Observer,* January 7, 1990; *Daily Telegraph,* London, January 8, 1990; *Marketing Week,* January 12, 1990; *Spectator,* January 13 and 20, 1990.

Charles Wilson removal: author's interviews; *Independent,* London, March 14, 1990; *Guardian,* March 19, 1990.

Simon Jenkins and the *Times:* author's interviews.

Murdoch and his gamble with Sky: *Financial Times,* October 16, 1989.

Guardian on News International's promotion of Sky: January 6, 1990.

BSB's problems and launch: *Daily Telegraph,* London, February 23, 1990; *Independent on Sunday,* London, March 25, 1990; *Daily Telegraph,* London, April 17, 1990; *Independent,* London, April 23, 1990; *Wall Street Journal,* April 27, 1990; *Broadcast,* May 4, 1990.

Sky-BSB rivalry: *Interspace,* issue 323; *Financial Times,* August 12, 1990; *Independent,* London, September 23, 1990; *Financial Times* Survey of British Broadcasting, October 16, 1990.

Banks' warning to BSB: *Sunday Times* magazine, London, June 23, 1991.

Preliminary talks arranged through John Veronis: ibid.; author's interview with Frank Barlow, chief executive of Pearson.

Max Newton's death: author's interview with Olivia Newton.

New York

The account of News Corp's financial crisis is based on contemporary news accounts and interviews with Rupert Murdoch, Ann Lane, Andrew Knight, Dave DeVoe, Colin Reader, William Rhodes and others. Carole Kismaric also conducted extensive interviews with Ann Lane and others.

Excellent published accounts of the crisis on which the author has drawn are "What Murdoch Does Not Want to See," *Business Review Weekly*, Sydney, November 2, 1990; Stephen Fidler, "Operation Dolphin Rescues Murdoch," *Financial Times*, April 4, 1991; and Ida Picker, "Inside the Murdoch Workout," *Institutional Investor*, May 1991.

Murdoch on Kipling: private speech to bank presidents at the International Monetary Conference, Osaka, Japan, June 4, 1991, provided to the author by Rupert Murdoch.

Murdoch on having the year covered: author's interview.

Beginning of News' problems: *Wall Street Journal*, April 12, 1990; *Economist*, August 18, 1990.

Murdoch on Standard Chartered Bank: author's interview.

Murdoch on toads and "humble reptilian perspective" and "hopping" on "the risk frontier": speech to bank presidents.

Story of September roll: author's interviews and published accounts.

Ann Lane's story: author's interview and interview with Carole Kismaric.

Sky-BSB deal: author's interviews with Rupert Murdoch, Andrew Knight and Frank Barlow, and published accounts, including *Financial Times*, November 5, 1990; *Independent*, London, November 7, 1990; *Sunday Times* magazine, London, June 23, 1991.

Lord Thompson's reaction: *Guardian*, November 5, 1990.

"UP YOURS, DELORS": *Sun*, November 1, 1990.

Fox's problems: *Business Review Weekly*, Sydney, November 2, 1990; New York *Times*, May 20, 1991.

Lane's methods: interviews with Carole Kismaric and author.

Murdoch on the problems with Pittsburgh: author's interview.

DeVoe on the problems with Pittsburgh: author's interview.

"Launching" story: author's interviews, and Carole Kismaric's interview with Ann Lane.

Murdoch's "knighthood": *Observer,* December 23 and 30, 1990.

"Empire" film: *Variety,* December 24, 1990.

Murdoch criticism of TV film: speech to bankers.

Bill Rhodes interventions: author's interview.

Indian banker hunting: Stephen Fidler, *Financial Times,* April 4, 1991.

End-of-year crisis: New York *Times,* December 20, 1990.

January rolls: Stephen Fidler, *Financial Times,* February 4 and April 4, 1991; author's interviews with Rupert Murdoch, Dave DeVoe and Andrew Knight; Carole Kismaric interview with Ann Lane.

Firings at the *Australian:* author's interview with Alastair Diffy.

Sorenson trip to Japan: Carole Kismaric interviews.

Morale at Wapping: author's interviews with News Ltd. personnel.

Frank Barlow visit to Arizona: author's interviews with Barlow and Murdoch.

Murdoch on being realistic and selling properties: *Forbes,* September 2, 1991.

Sale of Murdoch magazines to K-III: New York *Times,* March 18 and April 26 and 27, 1991.

Maxwell and *Daily News:* Allan Sloan and Glen Kessler, *Newsday,* November 8, 1991.

Super!'s behavior: *International Herald Tribune,* May 21, 1991; *Newsweek,* June 10, 1991; *Independent,* London, November 6, 1991; *Wall Street Journal,* November 12, 1991.

Soviet praise for Murdoch: Professor Ya Zassowsky, Dean of Moscow State University, Faculty of Journalism, *Pravda,* May 28, 1990.

Murdoch on Mikhail and Raisa Gorbachev: author's interview; Andrew Knight, *Sunday Times,* London, May 12, 1991.

Soviet Union joins Intelsat, and "last nail": *Broadcasting Abroad,* October 1991.

Information revolution and Soviet coup: *Independent,* London, August 24, 1991.

Murdoch on fall of Soviet Bastille: speech to Melbourne University, October 1, 1991.

CHAPTER TWELVE

On the Road

News Corp's annual report: *Guardian*, August 23, 1991.

Praise from analysts: *Financial Times*, October 5, 6 and 21, 1991.

Murdoch on News as pinup boys of banks: *Sunday Telegraph*, London, October 27, 1991.

New refinancing deal: author's interviews with Rupert Murdoch, Ann Lane, Dave DeVoe and Bill Sorenson; *Wall Street Journal*, October 22, 1991.

Murdoch's comments on trip to Hartford: author's interview.

Diller's comments on plane: author's interview.

December offerings: *Wall Street Journal*, December 9, 1991; author's interview with Dave DeVoe.

Diller's resignation: author's interview; *Wall Street Journal*, February 25, 1992.

Aspen story: author's interview with attendees at Aspen; Los Angeles *Times*, June 23, 1992.

AFTERWORD

Sumner Redstone on Murdoch: quoted by Geraldine Fabrikant, New York *Times*, July 29, 1996.

Murdoch to *Financial Times: Financial Times*, December 24, 1996.

Murdoch on the character of News: speech to National Press Club, February 26, 1996.

Murdoch on skunk at tea party: ibid.

Murdoch on News as first vertically integrated company: speech to Schroeder Wertheim/*Variety* "Big Picture" Entertainment Conference, April 2, 1996.

MCI deal: *Wall Street Journal*, May 12, 1995.

Murdoch to New York *Times:* New York *Times*, July 29, 1996.

Irwin Stelzer on Murdoch: author's interview.

Murdoch in Vietnam: author's interview.

Ken Auletta on Murdoch and China: *New Yorker,* November 13, 1995.

Murdoch on JSkyB: Reuters, March 10, 1997, and author's interview with Murdoch.

Murdoch on "battering ram": Reuters, October 15, 1996.

Murdoch on Gingrich deal: *New Yorker,* November 13, 1995.

NBC and NAACP versus Murdoch: ibid.

Murdoch to National Press Club: February 26, 1996.

Murdoch and Time Warner deal: many published accounts, including *Vanity Fair,* January 1997, and author's interview.

Turner on Murdoch as Hitler: Associated Press, October 2, 1996.

Turner's deposition: in Southern District Court of New York, October 18, 1996.

Murdoch on his children: *Economist,* March 9, 1996.

Future of the information age: Wilson P. Dizard, Jr., *The Coming Information Age* (Longmans, London, 1989), pp. 219–234.

Murdoch on providing a service: Craig Whitney, New York *Times,* October 24, 1989.

John Reith on public broadcasting: James B. Twitchell, *Carnival Culture* (Columbia University Press, New York, 1992), p. 217.

BIBLIOGRAPHY

Ashmead-Bartlett, E., *The Uncensored Dardanelles* (Hutchinson, London, 1928)

Australian Dictionary of National Biography

Baistow, Tom, *Fourth-Rate Estate* (Comedia, London, 1985)

Barber, Lionel, and John Lawrenson, *The Price of Truth: The Story of the Reuters Millions* (Sphere Books, London, 1986)

Bean, C. E. W., *The Story of Anzac* (Angus and Robertson, Sydney, 1941)

Block, Alex Ben, *Outfoxed* (St. Martin's Press, New York, 1990)

Bower, Tom, *Maxwell the Outsider* (Mandarin, London, 1991)

Bowman, David, *The Captive Press* (Penguin, Ringwood, Victoria, Australia, 1988)

Brand, Stewart, *The Media Lab* (Viking, New York, 1988)

Brendon, Piers, *The Life and Death of the Press Barons* (Secker and Warburg, London, 1982)

Calwell, A. A., *Be Just and Fear Not* (Lloyd O'Neil, Melbourne, 1972)

Cannon, Michael, *The Land Boomers* (Melbourne University Press, Melbourne, 1966)

Carey, John, *The Intellectuals and the Masses* (Faber and Faber, London, 1992)

Carroll, V. J., *The Man Who Couldn't Wait* (Heinemann, Melbourne, 1990)

Chadwick, Paul, *Media Mates* (Macmillan, Melbourne, 1989)

Chippindale, Peter, and Chris Horrie, *Stick It Up Your Punter* (Heinemann, London, 1990)

Cockerell, Michael, Peter Hennessy and David Walker, *Sources Close to the Prime Minister* (Macmillan, London, 1984)

Conquest, Robert, *Tyrants and Typewriters* (Hutchinson, London, 1989)

Cooper, William, *Shall We Ever Know? The Trial of the Hosein Brothers for the Murder of Mrs McKay* (Hutchinson, London, 1971)

Coote, Colin R., *Editorial* (Eyre & Spottiswoode, London, 1965)

Cudlipp, Hugh, *Walking on the Water* (Bodley Head, London, 1976)

Curran, James, and Jean Seaton, *Power Without Responsibility: The Press and Broadcasting in Britain* (Routledge, London, 1988)

Dizard, Wilson P., Jr., *The Coming Information Age* (Longmans, London, 1989)

Dizard, Wilson P., Jr., and S. Blake Swensrud, *Gorbachev's Information Revolution: Controlling Glasnost in a New Electronic Era* (The Center for Strategic and International Studies, Westview Press, Boulder, Colorado, 1987)

Dunkley, Christopher, *Television Today and Tomorrow: Wall to Wall Dallas?* (Penguin Books, Harmondsworth, U.K., 1985)

Dunne, John Gregory, *The Studio* (Farrar, Straus & Giroux, New York, 1969)

Edgar, Patricia, *The Politics of the Press* (Sun Books, Melbourne, 1979)

Edwards, Robert, *Goodbye Fleet Street* (Jonathan Cape, London, 1988)

Evans, Harold, *Good Times, Bad Times* (Coronet Books, London, 1984)

Gilder, George, *Microcosm* (Simon and Schuster, New York, 1989)

Giles, Frank, *Sundry Times* (John Murray, London, 1986)

Goldenson, Leonard H., with Marvin J. Wolf, *Beating the Odds* (Charles Scribner's Sons, New York, 1991)

Goodhart, David, and Patrick Wintour, *Eddie Shah and the Newspaper Revolution* (Coronet, London, 1986)

Grose, Roslyn, *The Sun-sation* (Angus and Robertson, London, 1989)

Hall, Richard, *The Secret State: Australia's Spy Industry* (Cassell, Sydney, 1978)

Hamilton, Denis, *Editor-in-Chief* (Hamish Hamilton, London, 1989)

Hammond, Eric, *Maverick* (Weidenfeld and Nicolson, London, 1992)

Harris, Robert, *Gotcha! The Media, the Government and the Falklands Crisis* (Faber and Faber, London, 1983)

——, *Selling Hitler* (Faber and Faber, London, 1986)

Henderson, Gerard, *Australian Answers* (Random House, Milsons Point, New South Wales, Australia, 1990)

Heren, Louis, *Memories of Times Past* (Hamish Hamilton, London, 1988)

Hetherington, John, *Australians: Nine Profiles* (F. W. Cheshire, Melbourne, 1960)

Howard, Philip, *We Thundered Out: A Bicentenary History of the Times* (Times Books, London, 1985)

Inglis, K. S., *The Stuart Case* (Melbourne University Press, Melbourne, 1961)

Jacobs, Eric, *Stop Press: The Inside Story of the* Times *Dispute* (André Deutsch, London, 1980)

Jenkins, Simon, *Newspapers: The Power and the Money* (Faber and Faber, London, 1979)

——, *The Market for Glory* (Faber and Faber, London, 1986)

Keith Murdoch, Journalist: A Biography (Herald and Weekly Times, Melbourne, 1952), pamphlet

Kennedy, Trevor, *Top Guns* (Sun Books, Melbourne, 1988)

Kiernan, Thomas, *Citizen Murdoch* (Dodd, Mead, New York, 1986)

King, Cecil, *The Cecil King Diary, 1965–70* (Jonathan Cape, London, 1972)

Kynaston, David, *The* FT: *A Centenary History* (Viking, London, 1988)

Lamb, Larry, *Sunrise* (Papermac, London, 1989)

Lawrenson, John, and Lionel Barber, *The Price of Truth* (Mainstream Publishing, Edinburgh, 1985)

Leapman, Michael, *Barefaced Cheek: The Apotheosis of Rupert Murdoch* (Hodder and Stoughton, London, 1983); published in the United States as *Arrogant Aussie* (Lyle Stuart, Secaucus, New Jersey, 1985)

——, *The Last Days of the Beeb* (Allen and Unwin, London, 1986)

MacArthur, Brian, *Eddie Shah,* Today *and the Newspaper Revolution* (David and Charles, Newton Abbot, U.K., 1988)

McQueen, Humphrey, *Social Sketches of Australia 1888–1975* (Penguin, Ringwood, Victoria, Australia, 1978)

Martin, J. Stanley, *A Tale of Two Churches: From West Melbourne to Box Hill* (Box Hill, St. Andrew's Presbyterian Church, Melbourne, 1967)

Melvern, Linda, *The End of the Street* (Methuen, London, 1986)

Moorehead, John, *Gallipoli* (Hamish Hamilton, London, 1956)

Munster, George, *Rupert Murdoch: A Paper Prince* (Penguin Books, Ringwood, Victoria, Australia, 1987)

——, *Family Business* (Collins, London, 1988)

Murdoch, Reverend Patrick, *Laughter and Tears of God and Other War Sermons* (Arbuckle, Waddell and Fawckner, Melbourne, 1915)

Nolan, Sydney, *Nolan's Gallipoli* (Australian War Memorial, Canberra, 1978), pamphlet

Pacini, J., *A Century Galloped By: The First Hundred Years of the Victoria Racing Club* (Melbourne)

Packer, Clyde, *No Return Ticket* (Angus and Robertson, Sydney, 1984)

Pearl, Cyril, *Wild Men of Sydney* (W. H. Allen, London, 1958)

Penniman, Howard R., *Australia at the Polls: The National Elections of 1975* (American Enterprise Institute for Public Policy Research, Washington, D.C., 1977)

Pool, Ithiel de Sola, *Technologies of Freedom* (Harvard University Press, Cambridge, Massachusetts, 1983)

Porter, Henry, *Lies, Damned Lies and Some Exclusives* (Chatto and Windus, London, 1984)

Porter, Jeffrey, *Men, Money and Magic: The Story of Dorothy Schiff* (Coward, McCann and Geoghegan, New York, 1976)

Postman, Neil, *Amusing Ourselves to Death* (Penguin, New York, 1986)

Povich, Maury, *Current Affairs: A Life on the Edge* (Putnam, New York, 1991)

Randall, Mike, *The Funny Side of the Street* (Bloomsbury, London, 1988)

Righter, Rosemary, *Whose News Anyway?* (Burnett Books, London, 1978)

Robbins, J. Max, *Channels Field Guide* (1990)

Robertson, John, *Anzac and Empire: The Tragedy and Glory of Gallipoli* (Hamlyn, Melbourne, 1990)

Sampson, Anthony, *The Midas Touch* (Hodder and Stoughton, London, 1989)

Silverman, Stephen M., *The Fox That Got Away* (Lyle Stuart, Secaucus, New Jersey, 1988)

Smith, Anthony, *Shadows in the Cave* (University of Illinois Press, Champaign, 1973)

——, *The British Press Since the War: Sources for Contemporary Issues* (David and Charles, Newton Abbot, U.K., 1974)

——, *The Newspaper* (Thames and Hudson, London, 1979)

——, *The Geopolitics of Information* (Oxford University Press, New York, 1980)

——, *Goodbye Gutenberg* (Oxford University Press, New York, 1980)

——, *The Age of Behemoths: The Globalisation of Mass Media Firms* (Twentieth Century Fund, New York, 1991)

Somerfield, S. W., *Banner Headlines* (Scan Books, Shoreham-by-Sea, U.K., 1979)

Souter, Gavin, *Company of Heralds* (Melbourne University Press, Melbourne, 1981)

——, *Heralds and Angels* (Melbourne University Press, Melbourne, 1991)

Stephens, Mitchell, *A History of News* (Viking, New York, 1988)

Stonier, Tom, *The Wealth of Information* (Methuen, London, 1983)

Swanberg, W. A., *Pulitzer* (Charles Scribner's Sons, New York, 1967)

Thompson, Peter, and Anthony Delano, *Maxwell* (Bantam Press, London, 1988)

Thomson, Lord, *After I Was Sixty* (Hamish Hamilton, London, 1975)

Trinity Presbyterian Church, Camberwell, 1885–1935, jubilee souvenir book (Osboldstone and Co., Melbourne, 1935)

Tuccille, Jerome, *Rupert Murdoch* (Donald I. Fine, New York, 1989)

Twitchell, James B., *Carnival Culture* (Columbia University Press, New York, 1992)

United States Senate, *Hearings Before the Committee on Banking, Housing and Urban Affairs,* May 12–13, 1980

Walker, Mike, *Australia: A History* (Macdonald Optima, London, 1987)

Whitlam, Gough, *The Truth of the Matter* (Penguin Books, Harmondsworth, U.K., 1981)

Williams, Huntington, *Beyond Control: ABC and the Fate of the Networks* (Atheneum, New York, 1989)

Williams, Valentine, *The World of Action* (Hamish Hamilton, London, 1938)

Wintour, Charles, *The Rise and Fall of Fleet Street* (Hutchinson, London, 1989)

Wriston, Walter B., *Risk and Other Four-Letter Words* (Harper & Row, New York, 1986)

Zwar, Desmond, *In Search of Keith Murdoch* (Macmillan, Melbourne, 1980)

ACKNOWLEDGMENTS

The idea for this book came originally from Richard E. Snyder, the then president of Simon & Schuster, and Alice Mayhew, my indomitable and irreplaceable editor; I am very grateful to them both for suggestions and support throughout. Many others at Simon & Schuster were also very helpful. George Hodgman was constant with observations and Julie Strutin-Volkov calmly imposed order. In the copy editing department I am, as before, indebted to Sophie Sorkin and Marcia Peterson, and Steve Messina and Eileen Caughlin did an extraordinary job in checking the text. Other invaluable assistance was given by Wendy Nicholson, Victoria Meyer, Carolyn Reidy, Jennifer Weidman, Jack McKeown, Frank Metz and Eve Metz.

Many people in different countries helped me in the course of the research for this book. Among them were John Wilcock in Los Angeles, who also generously provided me with the preliminary research he had done on Murdoch's life; Carole Kismaric in New York; Nick LeQuesne and Alita Naughton in London; Glenda Korporaal, Robert Milliken and Fiona Matthews in Sydney; Marc Champion in Washington; and Paul Chadwick in Melbourne. Tom O'Hanlon in Connecticut sent me a constant stream of information and gave me his own unpublished manuscript on Murdoch; in London, Michael Leapman gave me access to the documents he had collected for his own book on Murdoch, *Barefaced Cheek*. Anthony Smith was, as ever, most generous with his knowledge and friendship.

Within the News Corp empire, Rupert Murdoch was helpful and

courteous, as I have noted at the beginning of this book. Among his family, so were Anna Murdoch, Dame Elisabeth Murdoch, Helen and Geoff Handbury and Matt Handbury. Almost everyone at News whom I asked to give an interview agreed; some talked on the record, some off. Dorothy Wyndoe, Rupert Murdoch's principal assistant, did everything she could to assist me, and I am grateful to her.

In London I was greatly assisted by Carmen Callil and her associates at Chatto and Windus, especially Alison Samuel, who did an extraordinary job in helping me reduce an unwieldy manuscript to a manageable book. Barry Featherstone was unflappable and allowed none of my delays to upset his production process. In Australia, John Cody of Random House was of great assistance throughout. So were Elaine Greene, Amanda Urban and Lynn Nesbit. As usual, John Meakings of American Express arranged my trips with patience and efficiency, and Ken Boys made Qantas very hospitable. Some order was kept in my titles by Eilean Boniface, and the manuscript was typed and retyped by Coral Pepper.

Among those others who have helped me in various ways, I would like to thank Piers Akerman, Jonathan Alter, Chris Anderson, Ben Bagdikian, Frank Barlow, Peter Bart, Wendy Beckett, Eric Beecher, Jeff Berg, Don Berry, Christiane Besse, Betty Bienen, Michael Binyon, John Birt, Conrad Black, Ron Boland, Mark Bonham Carter, Tom Bower, David Bowman, Rosie Boycott, John Brademas, Ben Bradlee, Frank Brady, Douglas and Joan Brass, Asa Briggs, Patrick Brogan, Les Brown, Gordon Brunton, Ila Massy Burnside, John Button, Roderick Carnegie, Vic Caroll, Jean Carr, Sarah Carr, William Carr, Lord Catto, Alexander Chancellor, Ian and Marjorie Chapman, Lewis Chester, Vern Christie, Andrew Clark, Julie Clarke, Michael Cockerell, Barbara Coonole, David Cornwell, John Cowley, Ken Cowley, George Craig, Philip Crawley, George Crile, Jim Cruthers, Blanche d'Alpuget, George Darby, James d'Arcy, Sir James and Lady Darling, Michael Davie, Bill Davies, Richard Davy, Adrian and Gwen Deamer, Marie de Lepervanche, Fran Devine, Dave DeVoe, Alastair

Diffy, Barry Diller, Wilson Dizard, Bernard Donoughue, Jessica Douglas-Home, Don Dunstan, Ernie Eban, Fred Emery, Claire Enders, Nora Ephron, Faith Evans, Harold Evans, John Evans, Paul Evans, James Fairfax, Stephen Fay, Helen Feger, Liz Fell, Andrew Fisher, Mark Fisher, Tom Fitzgerald, Douglas Flaherty, Rose Foot, Liz Forgan, Bridget Forster, Glen Frankel, Simon Freeman, Greg Geough, Jim Gerrand, George Gilder, Frank Giles, Anthony Gottlieb, Roy Greenslade, David Greenway, Ros Grose, Phil Gurlach, Richard Hall, Ron Hall, Adrian Hamilton, Christine Hanson, Xandra Hardie, Janet Hawley, Brian Haynes, Gerard Henderson, Seymour Hersh, Ian Hicks, Godfrey Hodgson, Jim Hoge, Anthony Holden, Jeff Hollister, Jonathan Holmes, Anthony Howard, John Howkins, Philip Jacobson, Morton Janklow, Margaret Jay, Peter Jay, the late Peter Jenkins, Simon Jenkins, Andrew Jennings, Roland Joffé, Candace Johnson, Paul Johnson, Paul Kelly, Graham King, Philip Knightley, Donald and Beth Kummerfeld, Ann Lane, Heather Laughton, Roger Laughton, Dominic Lawson, Valerie Lawson, Magnus Linklater, Carol Livingston, Patty de Llosa, Gerald Long, Mike Lynskey, Brian MacArthur, Cal MacCrystal, Keith MacDonald, Ranald and Patricia Macdonald, Richard MacDonald, Doyle MacManus, Michael Marray, George Masterman, Melissa Mathis, Terry McCran, Linda Melvern, John Menadue, Nelson and Julie Mews, William Meyers, Jonathan Miller, Stephen Milligan, Alex Mitchell, Edward Mortimer, Richard Neville, Olivia Newton, Bruce Page, Bruce Palling, Jeff Penberthy, Janine Perrett, Ken Phillips, Sir Edward Pickering, Barry Porter, Henry Porter, Maury Povich, Dominic Price, David Prosser, Robert Pullen, David Puttnam, Sally Quinn, Vera Ranki, Colin Reader, Jane Reed, Richard Reeves, Glen Renfrew, Merv Rich, Elizabeth Riddell, Paul and Marlene Rigby, Rosemary Righter, Nan and Rhyll Rivett, Geoffrey Robertson, Sir Frank Rogers, Lord Roll, George Rosie, Sidney Rubin, Alan Rusbridger, Nigel Ryan, Pierre Salinger, Anthony Sampson, Richard Sarazen, John Scailes, Robert Scheer, Andrew Jay Schwartzman, Richard and Caroline Searby, Richard Sennett,

Ross Shackell, David Shaw, Frank Shaw, Brooke Shearer, Stanley Shuman, Victor Shvets, Allan Sloan, Peter and Elisabeth Smark, Peter Smith, Sally Bedell Smith, Raymond Snoddy, Bob Sorby, Gavin Souter, Jim and Alice Spigelman, Irwin Stelzer, Gerald Stone, Robin Stummer, Max Suich, John Sweeney, Strobe Talbott, Tiziano and Angela Terzani, Daniel Thomas, Peter Thomson, Claire Tomalin, Brian Toohey, Dimity Torbett, Karin Torv, Patricia Tot, Malcolm Turnbull, Carmel Travis, Neil Travis, Hugh Trevor-Roper (Lord Dacre), Peter Tufo, Brian Walden, Marjorie Wallace, Max Walsh, Peter Ward, Chris Warren, Matthew Warren, David Webster, Philip Whitehead, Peter Wilenski, Marion Wilkinson, Donald Wise, Karel von Wolferin, Peter Woodward, Walter Wriston, Woodrow Wyatt, Hugo Young and Jules Zanetti.

Above all, I thank Hartley, Conrad and Ellie Shawcross, and Olga Polizzi, for their great patience.

INDEX

PHOTO CREDITS

ABOUT THE AUTHOR

William Shawcross is the author of *Sideshow*, *The Quality of Mercy* and *The Shah's Last Ride*. For *Sideshow*, he was awarded the George Polk Award for reporting and the Sidney Hillman Foundation Prize.